BPP Law School
Core Statute Book

First edition July 2010

Fifth edition July 2015

Published ISBN: 9781 4727 3265 1

Previous ISBN: 9781 4727 2122 8

British Library Cataloguing-in-Publication Data
A catalogue record for this book is available
from the British Library

Published by
BPP Learning Media Ltd
BPP House, Aldine Place
London W12 8AA
www.bpp.com/learningmedia

Printed in the United Kingdom by
Charlesworth Press

Flanshaw Way
Flanshaw Lane
Wakefield
WF2 9LP

Your learning materials, published by BPP
Learning Media Ltd, are printed on paper
obtained from traceable sustainable sources.

Contents

Contents

Part 3: Criminal Law   149

Part 4: Equity & Trusts and Land Law   179

Part 5: The Law of Tort   369

Contents

Part 1

Constitutional and Administrative Law

ACT OF SETTLEMENT 1700

1700 chapter 2 12 and 13 Will 3

An Act for the further Limitation of the Crown and better securing the Rights and Liberties of the Subject

Territorial extent: England and Wales, Northern Ireland; effectively extended to Scotland by the Union with Scotland Act 1706

Recital of Stat. 1 W. & M. Sess. 2. c. 2. §2. and that the late Queen and Duke of Gloucester are dead; and that His Majesty had recommended from the Throne a further Provision for the Succession of the Crown in the Protestant Line. The Princess Sophia, Electress and Duchess Dowager of Hanover, Daughter of the late Queen of Bohemia, Daughter of King James the First, to inherit after the King and the Princess Anne, in Default of Issue of the said Princess and His Majesty, respectively and the Heirs of her Body, being Protestants.

Whereas in the First Year of the Reign of Your Majesty and of our late most gracious Sovereign Lady Queen Mary (of blessed memory) an Act of Parliament was made intituled [An Act for Declaring the Rights and Liberties of the Subject and for setling the Succession of the Crown] wherein it was (amongst other things) enacted established and declared that the Crown and Regall Government of the Kingdoms of England France and Ireland and the Dominions thereunto belonging should be and continue to Your Majestie and the said late Queen during the joynt lives of Your Majesty and the said Queen and to the survivor and that after the Decease of Your Majesty and of the said Queen the said Crown and Regall Government should be and remain to the Heirs of the Body of the said late Queen and for default of such issue to Her Royall Highness the Princess Ann of Denmark and the Heirs of Her Body And for default of such issue to the Heirs of the Body of Your Majesty And it was thereby further enacted that all and every person and persons that then were or afterwards should be reconciled to or shall hold Communion with the See or Church of Rome or should professe the Popish Religion or marry a Papist should be excluded and are by that Act made for ever incapable to inherit possess or enjoy the Crown and Government of this Realm and Ireland and the Dominions thereunto belonging or any part of the same or to have use or exercise any regall Power Authority or Jurisdiction within the same And in all and every such case and cases the People of these Realms shall be and are thereby absolved of their Allegiance And that the said Crown and Government shall from time to time descend to and be enjoyed by such person or persons being Protestants as should have inherited and enjoyed the same in case the said Person or Persons so reconciled holding Communion professing or marrying as aforesaid were naturally dead After the making of which Statute and the Settlement therein contained Your Majesties good Subjects who were restored to the full and free possession and enjoyment of their Religion Rights and Liberties by the Providence of God giving success to Your Majesties just undertakings and unwearied endeavours for that purpose had no greater temporall felicity to hope or wish for then to see a Royall Progeny descending from Your Majesty to whom (under God) they owe their tranquility and whose ancestors have for many years been principall assertors of the reformed Religion and the Liberties of Europe and from our said most gracious Sovereign Lady whose memory will always be precious to the Subjects of these Realms And it having since pleased Almighty God to take away our said Sovereign Lady and also the most hopefull Prince William Duke of Gloucester (the only surviving issue of Her Royall Highness the Princess Ann of Denmark) to the unspeakable grief and sorrow of Your Majesty and your said good Subjects who under such losses being sensibly put in mind that it standeth wholly in the Pleasure of Almighty God to prolong the lives of Your Majesty and of Her Royall Highness and to grant to Your Majesty or to Her Royall Highness such issue as may be inheritable to the Crown and Regall Government aforesaid by the respective Limitations in the said recited Act contained doe constantly implore the Divine Mercy for those blessings And Your Majesties said Subjects having daily experience of your Royall care and concern for the present and future Wellfare of these Kingdoms and particularly recommending from your throne a further provision to be made for the Succession of the Crown in the Protestant Line for the Happiness of the Nation and the Security of our Religion And it being absolutely necessary for the safety peace and quiet of this Realm to obviate all doubts and contentions in the same by reason of any pretended Titles to the Crown and to maintain a certainty in the Succession thereof to which your Subjects may safely have recourse for their protection in case the Limitations in the said recited [Act] should determine Therefore for a further provision of the Succession of the Crown in the Protestant Line we Your Majesties most dutifull and loyall Subjects the Lords Spirituall and Temporall and Commons in this present Parliament assembled do beseech Your Majesty that it may be enacted and declared and be it enacted and declared by the Kings most Excellent Majesty by and with the advice and consent of the Lords Spirituall and Temporall and Comons in this present Parliament assembled and by the Authority of the same that the most Excellent Princess Sophia Electress and Dutchess Dowager of Hannover Daughter of the most Excellent Princess Elizabeth late Queen of Bohemia Daughter of our late Sovereign Lord King James the First of happy Memory be and is hereby declared to be the next in Succession in the Protestant Line to the Imperiall Crown and Dignity of the [said] Realms of England France and Ireland with the Dominions and Territories thereunto belonging after His Majesty and the Princess Ann of Denmark and in default of issue of the said Princess Ann and of His Majesty respectively and that from and after the deceases of His said Majesty our now Sovereign Lord and of Her Royall Highness the Princess Ann of Denmark and for default of issue of the said Princess Ann and of His Majesty respectively the Crown and Regall Government of the said Kingdoms of England France and Ireland and of the Dominions thereunto belonging with the Royall State and Dignity of the said Realms and all Honours Stiles Titles Regalities Prerogatives Powers Jurisdictions and Authorities to the same belonging and appertaining shall be remain and continue to the said most Excellent Princess Sophia and the Heirs of Her Body being Protestants And thereunto the said Lords Spirituall and Temporall and Commons shall and will in the Name of all the People of this Realm most humbly and faithfully submitt themselves their heirs and posterities and do faithfully promise that after the deceases of His Majesty and Her Royall Highness and the failure of the Heirs of their respective Bodies to stand to maintain and defend the said Princess Sophia and the Heirs of Her Body being [Protestants] according to the Limitation and Succession of the Crown in this Act specified and contained to the utmost of their Powers with their lives and estates against all persons whatsoever that shall attempt any thing to the contrary.

II The Persons inheritable by this Act, holding Communion with the Church of Rome, incapacitated as by the former Act; to take the Oath at their Coronation, according to Stat. 1 W. & M. c. 6

Provided always and it is hereby enacted that all and every person and persons who shall or may take or inherit the said Crown by vertue of the Limitation of this present Act and is are or shall be reconciled to or shall hold Communion with the See or Church of Rome or shall profess the Popish Religion or shall marry a Papist shall be subject to such incapacities as in such case or cases are by the said recited Act provided enacted and established And that every King and Queen of this Realm who shall come to and succeed in the Imperiall Crown of this Kingdom by vertue of this Act shall have the Coronation Oath administred to him her or them at their respective Coronations according to the Act of Parliament made in the First Year of the Reign of His Majesty and the said late Queen Mary intituled An Act for Establishing the Coronation Oath and shall make subscribe and repeat the Declaration in the Act first above recited mentioned or referred to in the manner and form thereby prescribed

III Further Provisions for securing the Religion, Laws, and Liberties of these Realms

And whereas it is requisite and necessary that some further provision be made for securing our Religion Laws and Liberties from and after the Death of His Majesty and the Princess Ann of Denmark and in default of Issue of the Body of the said Princess and of His Majesty respectively be it enacted by the Kings most Excellent Majesty by and with the advice and consent of the Lords Spirituall and Temporall and Commons in Parliament assembled and by the Authority of the same

That whosoever shall hereafter come to the Possession of this Crown shall joyn in Communion with the Church of England as by Law established

That in case the Crown and Imperiall Dignity of this Realm shall hereafter come to any Person not being a Native of this Kingdom of England this Nation be not obliged to ingage in any warr for the defence of any Dominions or Territories which do not belong to the Crown of England without the consent of Parliament.

[That after the said Limitation shall take effect as aforesaid no Person born out of the Kingdoms of England Scotland or Ireland or the Dominions thereunto belonging (although he be . . . made a Denizen (except such as are born of English parents) shall be capable to be of the Privy Councill or a Member of either House of Parliament or to enjoy any Office or place of trust either Civill or Military or to have any Grant of Lands Tenements or Hereditaments from the Crown to himself or to any other or others in Trust for him][1]

That no Pardon under the Great Seal of England be pleadable to an impeachment by the Commons in Parliament.

IV The Laws and Statutes of the Realm confirmed

And whereas the Laws of England are the birthright of the People thereof and all the Kings and Queens who shall ascend the Throne of this Realm ought to administer the Government of the same according to the said Laws and all their Officers and Ministers ought to serve them respectively according to the same the said Lords Spirituall and Temporall and Commons do therefore further humbly pray that all the Laws and Statutes of this Realm for securing the established Religion and the Rights and Liberties of the People thereof and all other Laws and Statutes of the same now in force may be ratified and confirmed And the same are by His Majesty by and with the advice and consent of the said Lords Spirituall and Temporall and Commons and by Authority of the same ratified and confirmed accordingly.

---

[1] This has been repealed.

ANTI-TERRORISM, CRIME AND SECURITY ACT 2001

2001 chapter 24

An Act to amend the Terrorism Act 2000; to make further provision about terrorism and security; to provide for the freezing of assets; to make provision about immigration and asylum; to amend or extend the criminal law and powers for preventing crime and enforcing that law; to make provision about the control of pathogens and toxins; to provide for the retention of communications data; to provide for implementation of Title VI of the Treaty on European Union; and for connected purposes.

[14 December 2001]

Part 4 Immigration and Asylum

Suspected international terrorists

23 Detention

(1)   A suspected international terrorist may be detained under a provision specified in subsection

(2)   Despite the fact that his removal or departure from the United Kingdom is prevented (whether temporarily or indefinitely) by a:

    (a)   Point of law which wholly or partly relates to an international agreement

    (b)   Practical consideration.

(3)   The provisions mentioned in subsection (1) are:

    (a)   Paragraph 16 of Schedule 2 to the Immigration Act 1971 (c. 77) (detention of persons liable to examination or removal)

    (b)   Paragraph 2 of Schedule 3 to that Act (detention pending deportation][2]

129 Short title

This Act may be cited as the Anti-terrorism, Crime and Security Act 2001.

BILL OF RIGHTS

1688 chapter 2 1 Will and Mar Sess 2

An Act declareing the Rights and Liberties of the Subject and Setleing the Succession of the Crowne.

Territorial extent: England and Wales, Northern Ireland (for Scotland see the equivalent Act of the Scottish Parliament, the Claim of Right 1689).

Whereas the Lords Spirituall and Temporall and Comons assembled at Westminster lawfully fully and freely representing all the Estates of the People of this Realme did upon the thirteenth day of February in the yeare of our Lord one thousand six hundred eighty eight present unto their Majesties then called and known by the Names and Stile of William and Mary Prince and Princesse of Orange being present in their proper Persons a certaine Declaration in Writeing made by the said Lords and Comons in the Words following viz

---

[2] These provisions have been repealed.

The Heads of Declaration of Lords and Commons, recited.

Whereas the late King James the Second by the Assistance of diverse evill Councellors Judges and Ministers imployed by him did endeavour to subvert and extirpate the Protestant Religion and the Lawes and Liberties of this Kingdome.

Dispensing and Suspending Power.

By Assumeing and Exerciseing a Power of Dispensing with and Suspending of Lawes and the Execution of Lawes without Consent of Parlyament.

Committing Prelates.

By Committing and Prosecuting diverse Worthy Prelates for humbly Petitioning to be excused from Concurring to the said Assumed Power.

Ecclesiastical Commission.

By issueing and causeing to be executed a Commission under the Great Seale for Erecting a Court called The Court of Commissioners for Ecclesiasticall Causes.

Levying Money.

By Levying Money for and to the Use of the Crowne by pretence of Prerogative for other time and in other manner then the same was granted by Parlyament.

Standing Army.

By raising and keeping a Standing Army within this Kingdome in time of Peace without Consent of Parlyament and Quartering Soldiers contrary to Law.

Disarming Protestants, &c.

By causing severall good Subjects being Protestants to be disarmed at the same time when Papists were both Armed and Imployed contrary to Law.

Violating Elections.

By Violating the Freedome of Election of Members to serve in Parlyament.

Illegal Prosecutions.

By Prosecutions in the Court of Kings Bench for Matters and Causes cognizable onely in Parlyament and by diverse other Arbitrary and Illegall Courses.

Juries.

And whereas of late yeares Partiall Corrupt and Unqualifyed Persons have beene returned and served on Juryes in Tryalls and particularly diverse Jurors in Tryalls for High Treason which were not Freeholders,

Excessive Bail.

And excessive Baile hath beene required of Persons committed in Criminall Cases to elude the Benefitt of the Lawes made for the Liberty of the Subjects.

Fines.

And excessive Fines have beene imposed.

Punishments.

And illegall and cruell Punishments inflicted.

Grants of Fines, &c. before Conviction, &c.

And severall Grants and Promises made of Fines and Forfeitures before any Conviction or Judgement against the Persons upon whome the same were to be levyed. All which are utterly directly contrary to the knowne Lawes and Statutes and Freedome of this Realme.

Recital that the late King James II. had abdicated the Government, and that the Throne was vacant, and that the Prince of Orange had written Letters to the Lords and Commons for the choosing Representatives in Parliament.

And whereas the said late King James the Second haveing Abdicated the Government and the Throne being thereby Vacant His Hignesse the Prince of Orange (whome it hath pleased Almighty God to make the glorious Instrument of Delivering this Kingdome from Popery and Arbitrary Power) did (by the Advice of the Lords Spirituall and Temporall and diverse principall Persons of the Commons) cause Letters to be written to the Lords Spirituall and Temporall being Protestants and other Letters to the severall Countyes Cityes Universities Burroughs and Cinque Ports for the Choosing of such Persons to represent them as were of right to be sent to Parlyament to meete and sitt at Westminster upon the two and twentyeth day of January in this Yeare one thousand six hundred eighty and eight in order to such an Establishment as that their Religion Lawes and Liberties might not againe be in danger of being Subverted, Upon which Letters Elections haveing beene accordingly made.

The Subject's Rights.

And thereupon the said Lords Spirituall and Temporall and Commons pursuant to their respective Letters and Elections being now assembled in a full and free Representative of this Nation takeing into their most serious consideration the best meanes for attaining the ends aforesaid doe in the first place (as their auncestors in like case have usually done) for the vindicating and asserting their auntient Rights and Liberties, declare

Dispensing Power.

That the pretended power of suspending of Laws or the execution of Laws by Regall authority without consent of Parlyament is illegall.

Late Dispensing Power.

That the pretended power of dispensing with Laws or the execution of Laws by regall authoritie as it hath beene assumed and exercised of late is illegall.

Ecclesiastical Courts Illegal.

That the Commission for erecting the late Court of Commissioners for Ecclesiasticall Causes and all other Commissions and Courts of like nature are illegall and pernicious.

Levying Money.

That levying money for or to the use of the Crowne by pretence of Prerogative without Grant of Parlyament for longer time or in other manner then the same is or shall be granted is illegall.

Right to Petition.

That it is the Right of the Subjects to petition the King and all commitments and prosecutions for such petitioning are illegall.

Standing Army.

That the raising or keeping a standing Army within the Kingdome in time of peace unlesse it be with consent of Parlyament is against Law.

Subjects' Arms.

That the Subjects which are Protestants may have arms for their defence suitable to their conditions and as allowed by Law.

Freedom of Election.

That election of Members of Parlyament ought to be free.

Freedom of Speech.

That the freedome of speech and debates or proceedings in Parlyament ought not to be impeached or questioned in any Court or place out of Parlyament.

Excessive Bail.

That excessive Baile ought not to be required nor excessive fines imposed nor cruell and unusuall punishments inflicted.

Juries.

That Jurors ought to be duely impannelled and returned . . .

Grants of Forfeitures.

That all grants and promises of fines and forfeitures of particular persons before conviction are illegall and void.

Frequent Parliaments.

And that for Redresse of all grievances and for the amending strengthening and preserveing of the Lawes Parlyaments ought to be held frequently.

The said Rights claimed. Tender of the Crown. Regal power exercised. Limitation of the Crown.

And they doe claime demand and insist upon all and singular the premises as their undoubted Rights and Liberties and that noe declarations judgements doeings or proceedings to the prejudice of the people in any of the said Premisses ought in any wise to be drawne hereafter into consequence or example. To which demand of their Rights they are particularly encouraged by the Declaration of this Highnesse the Prince of Orange as being the onely meanes for obtaining a full redresse and remedy therein. Haveing therefore an intire confidence that his said Highnesse the Prince of Orange will perfect the deliverance soe farr advanced by him and will still preserve them from the Violation of their Rights which they have here asserted and from all other Attempts upon their Religion Rights and Liberties. The said Lords Spirituall and Temporall and Commons assembled at Westminster doe resolve That William and Mary Prince and Princesse of Orange be and be declared King and Queene of England France and Ireland and the Dominions thereunto belonging to· hold the Crowne and Royall Dignity of the said Kingdomes and Dominions to them the said Prince and Princesse dureing their lives and the life of the survivour of them And that the sole and full exercise of the Regall Power be onely in and executed by the said Prince of Orange in the Names of the said Prince and Princesse dureing their joynt Lives And after their deceases the said Crowne and Royall Dignitie of the said Kingdoms and Dominions to be to the Heires of the Body of the said Princesse And for default of such Issue to the Princesse Anne of Denmarke and the Heires of her Body And for default of such Issue to the Heires of the Body of the said Prince of Orange. And the Lords Spirituall and Temporall and Commons doe pray the said Prince and Princesse to accept the same accordingly.

New Oaths of Allegiance, &c.

And that the Oathes hereafter mentioned be taken by all Persons of whome the Oathes of Allegiance and Supremacy might be required by Law instead of them And that the said Oathes of Allegiance and Supremacy be abrogated.

Allegiance

I A B doe sincerely promise and sweare That I will be faithfull and beare true Allegiance to their Majestyes King William and Queene Mary Soe helpe me God[.]

Supremacy

I A B doe sweare that I doe from my heart abhorr, detest and abjure as impious and hereticall this damnable Doctrine and Position that Princes excommunicated or deprived by the Pope or any Authority of the See of Rome may be deposed or murdered by their Subjects or any other whatsoever. And I doe declare that noe forreigne Prince Person Prelate, State or Potentate hath or ought to have any Jurisdiction Power Superiority Preeminence or Authoritie Ecclesiasticall or Spirituall within this Realme[.] Soe helpe me God.

Acceptance of the Crown. The Two Houses to sit. Subjects' Liberties to be allowed, and Ministers hereafter to serve according to the same. William and Mary declared King and Queen. Limitation of the Crown. Papists debarred the Crown. Every King, &c. shall make the Declaration of 30 Car. II. If under 12 Years old, to be done after Attainment thereof. King's and Queen's Assent

Upon which their said Majestyes did accept the Crowne and Royall Dignitie of the Kingdoms of England France and Ireland and the Dominions thereunto belonging according to the Resolution and Desire of the said Lords and Commons contained in the said Declaration. And thereupon their Majestyes were pleased that the said Lords Spirituall and Temporall and Commons being the two Houses of Parlyament should continue to sitt and with their Majesties Royall Concurrence make effectuall Provision for the Setlement of the Religion Lawes and Liberties of this Kingdome soe that the same for the future might not be in danger againe of being subverted, To which the said Lords Spirituall and Temporall and Commons did agree and proceede to act accordingly. Now in pursuance of the Premisses the said Lords Spirituall and Temporall and Commons in Parlyament assembled for the ratifying confirming and establishing the said Declaration and the Articles Clauses Matters and Things therein contained by the Force of a Law made in due forme by Authority of Parlyament doe pray that it may be declared and enacted that all and singular the Rights and Liberties asserted and claimed in the said Declaration are the true auntient and indubitable Rights and Liberties of the People of this Kingdome and soe shall be esteemed allowed adjudged deemed and taken to be and that all and every the particulars aforesaid shall be firmly and strictly holden and observed as they are expressed in the said Declaration And all Officers and Ministers whatsoever shall serve their Majestyes and their Successors according to the same in all times to come. And the said Lords Spirituall and Temporall and Commons seriously considering how it hath pleased Almighty God in his marvellous Providence and mercifull Goodness to this Nation to provide and preserve their said Majestyes Royall Persons most happily to raigne over us upon the Throne of their auncestors for which they render unto him from the bottome of their hearts their humblest thanks and praises doe truely firmely assuredly and in the sincerity of their hearts thinke and doe hereby recognize acknowledge and declare that King James the Second haveing abdicated the Government and their Majestyes haveing accepted the Crowne and Royall Dignity aforesaid their said Majestyes did become were are and of right ought to be by the Lawes of this Realme our Soveraigne Liege Lord and Lady King and Queene of England France and Ireland and the Dominions thereunto belonging in and to whose Princely Persons the Royall State Crowne and Dignity of the said Realmes with all Honours Stiles Titles Regalities Prerogatives Powers Jurisdictions and Authorities to the same belonging and appertaining are most fully rightfully and intirely invested and incorporated united and annexed And for preventing all Questions and Divisions in this Realme by reason of any pretended Titles to the Crowne and for preserveing a certainty in the succession thereof in and upon which the Unity Peace Tranquillity and Safety of this Nation doth under God wholly consist and depend The said Lords Spirituall and Temporall and Commons doe beseech their Majestyes that it may be enacted established and declared that the Crowne and Regall Government of the said Kingdoms and Dominions with all and singular the Premisses thereunto belonging and appertaining shall bee and continue to their said Majestyes and the survivour of them dureing their Lives and the Life of the survivour of them And that the entire perfect and full exercise of the Regall Power and Government be onely in and executed by his Majestie in the Names of both their Majestyes dureing their joynt lives And after their deceases the said Crowne and Premisses shall be and remaine to the Heires of the Body of her Majestie and for default of such Issue to her Royall Highnesse the Princess Anne of Denmarke and the Heires of her Body and for default of such Issue to the Heires of the Body of his said Majestie And thereunto the said Lords Spirituall and Temporall and Commons doe in the Name of all the People aforesaid most humbly and faithfully submitt themselves their Heires and Posterities for ever and doe faithfully promise that they will stand to maintaine and defend their said Majesties and alsoe the Limitation and Succession of the Crowne herein specified and contained to the utmost of their powers with their lives and estates against all Persons whatsoever that shall attempt any thing to the contrary. And whereas it hath beene found by experience that it is inconsistent with the safety and welfare of this Protestant Kingdome to be governed by a Popish Prince or by any King or Queene marrying a Papist the said Lords Spirituall and Temporall and Commons doe further pray that it may be enacted that all and every person and persons that is are or shall be reconciled to or shall hold Communion with the See or Church of Rome or shall professe the Popish Religion or shall marry a Papist shall be excluded and be for ever uncapeable to inherit possesse or enjoy the Crowne and Government of this Realme and Ireland and the Dominions thereunto belonging or any part of the same or to have use or exercise any Regall Power Authoritie or Jurisdiction within the same And in all and every such Case or Cases the People of these Realmes shall be and are hereby absolved of their Allegiance. And the said Crowne and Government shall from time to time descend to and be enjoyed by such person or persons being Protestants as should have inherited and enjoyed the same in case the said person or persons soe reconciled holding Communion or professing or marrying as aforesaid were naturally dead And that every King and Queene of this Realme who at any time hereafter shall come to and succeede in the Imperiall Crowne of this Kingdome shall on the first day of the meeting of the first Parlyament next after his or her comeing to the Crowne sitting in his or her Throne in the House of Peeres in the presence of the Lords and Commons therein assembled or at his or her Coronation before such person or persons who shall administer the Coronation Oath to him or her at the time of his or her takeing the said Oath (which shall first happen) make subscribe and audibly repeate the Declaration mentioned in the Statute made in the thirtyeth yeare of the raigne of King Charles the Second entituled An Act for the More Effectuall Preserveing the Kings Person and Government by disableing Papists from sitting in either House of Parlyament But if it shall happen that such King or Queene upon his or her Succession to the Crowne of this Realme shall be under the age of twelve yeares then every such King or Queene shall make subscribe and audibly repeate the said Declaration at his or her Coronation or the first day of the meeting of the first Parlyament as aforesaid which shall first happen after such King or Queene shall have attained the said age of twelve yeares. All which Their Majestyes are contented and pleased shall be declared enacted and established by authoritie of this present Parliament and shall stand remaine and be the Law of this Realme for ever And the same are by their said Majesties by and with the advice and consent of the Lords Spirituall and Temporall and Commons in Parlyament assembled and by the authoritie of the same declared enacted and established accordingly

II Non obstantes made void

Noe dispensation by Non obstante of or to any Statute or any part thereof shall be allowed but the same shall be held void and of noe effect except a dispensation be allowed of in such Statute.

THE CIVIL PROCEDURE RULES 1998

Statutory Instrument 1998 No. 3132 L.17

54 Judicial Review

54. 1 Scope and interpretation

(1)   This section of this Part contains rules about judicial review.

(2)   In this Section –

    (a)   A 'claim for judicial review' means a claim to review the lawfulness of:

        (i)   An enactment

        (ii)   A decision, action or failure to act in relation to the exercise of a public function

(b) to (d) Revoked

(e)   'The judicial review procedure' means the Part 8 procedure as modified by this Section

(f)   'Interested party' means any person (other than the claimant and defendant) who is directly affected by the claim

(g)   'Court' means the High Court, unless otherwise stated

(Rule 8.1(6)(b) provides that a rule or practice direction may, in relation to a specified type of proceedings, disapply or modify any of the rules set out in Part 8 as they apply to those proceedings.)

54.2 When this [section] must be used

The judicial review procedure must be used in a claim for judicial review where the claimant is seeking:

(a)   A mandatory order

(b)   A prohibiting order

(c)   A quashing order

(d)   An injunction under section 30 of the Supreme Court Act 19811 (restraining a person from acting in any office in which he is not entitled to act)

54.3 When this Section may be used

(1)   The judicial review procedure may be used in a claim for judicial review where the claimant is seeking:

    (a)   A declaration
    (b)   An injunction

    (Section 31(2) of the Supreme Court Act 1981Acts sets out the circumstances in which the court may grant a declaration or injunction in a claim for judicial review.)

    (Where the claimant is seeking a declaration or injunction in addition to one of the remedies listed in rule 54.2, the judicial review procedure must be used.)

(2)   A claim for judicial review may include a claim for damages , restitution or the recovery of a sum due but may not seek such a remedy alone.

    (Section 31(4) of the Supreme Court Act 1981 sets out the circumstances in which the court may award damages , restitution or the recovery of a sum due] on a claim for judicial review.

54.4 Permission required

The court's permission to proceed is required in a claim for judicial review whether started under this Section or transferred to the Administrative Court.

54.5 Time limit for filing claim form

(1)   The claim form must be filed:

    (a)   Promptly

    (b)   In any event not later than 3 months after the grounds to make the claim first arose

(2)   The time limit in this rule may not be extended by agreement between the parties.

(3)   This rule does not apply when any other enactment specifies a shorter time limit for making the claim for judicial review.

54.6 Claim form

(1)   In addition to the matters set out in rule 8.2 (contents of the claim form) the claimant must also state:

(a)   The Name and address of any person he considers to be an interested party

(b)   That he is requesting permission to proceed with a claim for judicial review

(c)   Any remedy (including any interim remedy) he is claiming

(Part 25 sets out how to apply for an interim remedy.)

(2)   The claim form must be accompanied by the documents required by the relevant practice direction.

This Rule is referred to in: PDP 54 (4.1), (5.1), PDP 54a (4.1), (5.1).

54.7 Service of claim form

The claim form must be served on:

(a)   The defendant

(b)   Unless the court otherwise directs, any person the claimant considers to be an interested party within 7 days after the date of issue.

54.8 Acknowledgment of service

(1)   Any person served with the claim form who wishes to take part in the judicial review must file an acknowledgment of service in the relevant practice form in accordance with the following provisions of this rule.

(2)   Any acknowledgment of service must be:

(a)   Filed not more than 21 days after service of the claim form

(b)   Served on:

(i)   The claimant

(ii)   Subject to any direction under rule 54.7(b), any other person Named in the claim form

as soon as practicable and, in any event, not later than 7 days after it is filed.

(3)   The time limits under this rule may not be extended by agreement between the parties.

(4)   The acknowledgment of service:

(a)   Must:

(i)   Where the person filing it intends to contest the claim, set out a summary of his grounds for doing so

(ii)   State the Name and address of any person the person filing it considers to be an interested party

(b)   May include or be accompanied by an application for directions.

(5)   Rule 10.3(2) does not apply.

54.9 Failure to file acknowledgment of service

(1)   Where a person served with the claim form has failed to file an acknowledgment of service in accordance with rule 54.8, he –

    (a)   may not take part in a hearing to decide whether permission should be given unless the court allows him to do so; but

    (b)   provided he complies with rule 54.14 or any other direction of the court regarding the filing and service of –

        (i) detailed grounds for contesting the claim or supporting it on additional grounds; and

        (ii)   any written evidence,

    may take part in the hearing of the judicial review.

(2)   Where that person takes part in the hearing of the judicial review, the court may take his failure to file an acknowledgment of service into account when deciding what order to make about costs.

(3)   Rule 8.4 does not apply.

54.10 Permission given

(1)   Where permission to proceed is given the court may also give directions.

(2)   Directions under paragraph (1) may include a stay of proceedings to which the claim relates.

(Rule 3.7 provides a sanction for the non-payment of the fee payable when permission to proceed has been given)

54.11 Service of order giving or refusing permission

The court will serve –

    (a)   the order giving or refusing permission; and

    (b)   any directions,

on –

        (i) the claimant;

        (ii) the defendant; and

        (iii) any other person who filed an acknowledgment of service.

54.12 Permission decision without a hearing

(1)   This rule applies where the court, without a hearing –

    (a)   refuses permission to proceed; or

    (b)   gives permission to proceed –

        (i) subject to conditions; or

        (ii) on certain grounds only.

(2)   The court will serve its reasons for making the decision when it serves the order giving or refusing permission in accordance with rule 54.11.

(3)   The claimant may not appeal but may request the decision to be reconsidered at a hearing.

(4)   A request under paragraph (3) must be filed within 7 days after service of the reasons under paragraph (2).

(5)   The claimant, defendant and any other person who has filed an acknowledgment of service will be given at least 2 days' notice of the hearing date.

54.13 Defendant etc. may not apply to set aside

Neither the defendant nor any other person served with the claim form may apply to set aside an order giving permission to proceed.

54.14 Response

(1)   A defendant and any other person served with the claim form who wishes to contest the claim or support it on additional grounds must file and serve –

(a)   detailed grounds for contesting the claim or supporting it on additional grounds; and

(b)   any written evidence,

within 35 days after service of the order giving permission.

(2)   The following rules do not apply –

(a)   rule 8.5 (3) and 8.5 (4)(defendant to file and serve written evidence at the same time as acknowledgment of service); and

(b)   rule 8.5 (5) and 8.5(6) (claimant to file and serve any reply within 14 days).

54.15 Where claimant seeks to rely on additional grounds

The court's permission is required if a claimant seeks to rely on grounds other than those for which he has been given permission to proceed.

54.16 Evidence

(1)   Rule 8.6 (1) does not apply.

(2)   No written evidence may be relied on unless –

(a)   it has been served in accordance with any –

(i)   rule under this Section; or

(ii)   direction of the court; or

(b)   the court gives permission.

54.17 Court's powers to hear any person

(1)   Any person may apply for permission:

(a)   To file evidence

(b)   Make representations at the hearing of the judicial review.

(2)   An application under paragraph (1) should be made promptly.

54.18 Judicial review may be decided without a hearing

The court may decide the claim for judicial review without a hearing where all the parties agree.

54.19 Court's powers in respect of quashing orders

(1)   This rule applies where the court makes a quashing order in respect of the decision to which the claim relates.

(2)   The court may:

   (a)   Remit the matter to the decision-maker

   (b)   Direct it to reconsider the matter and reach a decision in accordance with the judgment of the court.

(3)   (Section 31 of the Supreme Court Act 1981 enables the High Court, subject to certain conditions, to substitute its own decision for the decision in question.)

54.20 Transfer

The court may:

(a)   Order a claim to continue as if it had not been started under this Section
(b)   Where it does so, give directions about the future management of the claim.

(Part 30 (transfer) applies to transfers to and from the Administrative Court.)

CONSTITUTIONAL REFORM ACT 2005

2005 chapter 4

An Act to make provision for modifying the office of Lord Chancellor, and to make provision relating to the functions of that office; to establish a Supreme Court of the United Kingdom, and to abolish the appellate jurisdiction of the House of Lords; to make provision about the jurisdiction of the Judicial Committee of the Privy Council and the judicial functions of the President of the Council; to make other provision about the judiciary, their appointment and discipline; and for connected purposes. [24th March 2005]

Part 1 The rule of law

1 The rule of law

This Act does not adversely affect—

(a)   the existing constitutional principle of the rule of law, or

(b)   the Lord Chancellor's existing constitutional role in relation to that principle.

Part 2 Arrangements to modify the office of Lord Chancellor

Continued judicial independence

3 Guarantee of continued judicial independence

(1)   The Lord Chancellor, other Ministers of the Crown and all with responsibility for matters relating to the judiciary or otherwise to the administration of justice must uphold the continued independence of the judiciary.

(2)   Subsection (1) does not impose any duty which it would be within the legislative competence of the Scottish Parliament to impose.

(3)   A person is not subject to the duty imposed by subsection (1) if he is subject to the duty imposed by section 1(1) of the Justice (Northern Ireland) Act 2002 (c. 26).

(4)   The following particular duties are imposed for the purpose of upholding that independence.

(5)   The Lord Chancellor and other Ministers of the Crown must not seek to influence particular judicial decisions through any special access to the judiciary.

(6)   The Lord Chancellor must have regard to—

(a)   the need to defend that independence;

(b)   the need for the judiciary to have the support necessary to enable them to exercise their functions;

(c)   the need for the public interest in regard to matters relating to the judiciary or otherwise to the administration of justice to be properly represented in decisions affecting those matters.

(7)   In this section "the judiciary" includes the judiciary of any of the following—

(a)   the Supreme Court;

(b)   any other court established under the law of any part of the United Kingdom;

(c)   any international court.

(8)   In subsection (7) "international court" means the International Court of Justice or any other court or tribunal which exercises jurisdiction, or performs functions of a judicial nature, in pursuance of—

(a)   an agreement to which the United Kingdom or Her Majesty's Government in the United Kingdom is a party, or

(b)   a resolution of the Security Council or General Assembly of the United Nations.

Judiciary and courts in England and Wales

7 President of the Courts of England and Wales

(1)   The Lord Chief Justice holds the office of President of the Courts of England and Wales and is Head of the Judiciary of England and Wales.

(2)   As President of the Courts of England and Wales he is responsible for:

    (a)   Representing the views of the judiciary of England and Wales to Parliament, to the Lord Chancellor and to Ministers of the Crown generally

    (b)   The maintenance of appropriate arrangements for the welfare, training and guidance of the judiciary of England and Wales within the resources made available by the Lord Chancellor

    (c)   The maintenance of appropriate arrangements for the deployment of the judiciary of England and Wales and the allocation of work within courts

(3)   The President of the Courts of England and Wales is president of the courts listed in subsection (4) and is entitled to sit in any of those courts.

(4)   The courts are the:

    (a)   Court of Appeal
    (b)   High Court
    (c)   Crown Court
    (d)   county courts
    (e)   magistrates' courts.

(5)   In section 1 of the Supreme Court Act 1981 (c. 54), subsection (2) (Lord Chancellor to be president of the Supreme Court of England and Wales) ceases to have effect.

Lord Chancellor's oath

17 Lord Chancellor's oath

(1)   In the Promissory Oaths Act 1868 (c. 72) after section 6 insert—

"6A Lord Chancellor's Oath

    (1)   The oath set out in subsection (2) shall be tendered to and taken by the Lord Chancellor, after and in the same manner as the official oath, as soon as may be after his acceptance of office.

    (2)   The oath is—

        ""I,   , do swear that in the office of Lord High Chancellor of Great Britain I will respect the rule of law, defend the independence of the judiciary and discharge my duty to ensure the provision of resources for the efficient and effective support of the courts for which I am responsible.   So help me God."."

(2)   The section inserted by subsection (1) does not apply in the case of acceptance of office before the coming into force of this section.

Part 3 The Supreme Court

The Supreme Court

23 The Supreme Court

(1)   There is to be a Supreme Court of the United Kingdom.

(2)   The Court consists of 12 judges appointed by Her Majesty by letters patent.

(3)   Her Majesty may from time to time by Order in Council amend subsection (2) so as to increase or further increase the number of judges of the Court.

(4)   No recommendation may be made to Her Majesty in Council to make an Order under subsection (3) unless a draft of the Order has been laid before and approved by resolution of each House of Parliament.

(5)   Her Majesty may by letters patent appoint one of the judges to be President and one to be Deputy President of the Court.

(6)   The judges other than the President and Deputy President are to be styled "Justices of the Supreme Court".

(7)   The Court is to be taken to be duly constituted despite any vacancy among the judges of the Court or in the office of President or Deputy President.

Appointment of judges

25 Qualification for appointment

(1)   A person is not qualified to be appointed a judge of the Supreme Court unless he has (at any time)—

(a)   held high judicial office for a period of at least 2 years, or

(b)   been a qualifying practitioner for a period of at least 15 years.

(2)   A person is a qualifying practitioner for the purposes of this section at any time when—

(a)   he has a Senior Courts qualification, within the meaning of section 71 of the Courts and Legal Services Act 1990 (c. 41),

(b)   he is an advocate in Scotland or a solicitor entitled to appear in the Court of Session and the High Court of Justiciary, or

(c)   he is a member of the Bar of Northern Ireland or a solicitor of the Court of Judicature of Northern Ireland.

Part 4 Judicial appointments and discipline

Chapter 1 Commission and Ombudsman

61 The Judicial Appointments Commission

(1)   There is to be a body corporate called the Judicial Appointments Commission.

(2)   Schedule 12 is about the Commission.

Chapter 2 Appointments

General provisions

63 Merit and good character

(1)   Subsections (2) and (3) apply to any selection under this Part by the Commission or a selection panel ("the selecting body").

(2)   Selection must be solely on merit.

(3)   A person must not be selected unless the selecting body is satisfied that he is of good character.

64 Encouragement of diversity

(1)   The Commission, in performing its functions under this Part, must have regard to the need to encourage diversity in the range of persons available for selection for appointments.

(2)   This section is subject to section 63.

EUROPEAN COMMUNITIES ACT 1972

1972 chapter 68

An Act to make provision in connection with the enlargement of the European Communities to include the United Kingdom, together with (for certain purposes) the Channel Islands, the Isle of Man and Gibraltar.[17th October 1972]

Territorial extent: United Kingdom

Part I General Provisions

1 Short title and interpretation

(1)   This Act may be cited as the European Communities Act 1972.

(2)   In this Act . . .

"The Communities" means the European Economic Community, the European Coal and Steel Community and the European Atomic Energy Community.

"The Treaties" or "the Community Treaties" means, subject to subsection (3) below, the pre-accession treaties, that is to say, those described in Part I of Schedule 1 to this Act, taken with –

(a)   the treaty relating to the accession of the United Kingdom to the European Economic Community and to the European Atomic Energy Community, signed at Brussels on the 22nd January 1972; and

(b)   the decision, of the same date, of the Council of the European Communities relating to the accession of the United Kingdom to the European Coal and Steel Community; and

(c)   the treaty relating to the accession of the Hellenic Republic to the European Economic Community and to the European Atomic Energy Community, signed at Athens on 28th May 1979; and

(d)   the decision, of 24th May 1979, of the Council relating to the accession of the Hellenic Republic to the European Coal and Steel Community; and

(e)   the decisions of the Council of 7th May 1985, 24th June 1988, 31st October 1994, 29th September 2000 and 7th June 2007 on the Communities' system of own resources; and

(g)   the treaty relating to the accession of the Kingdom of Spain and the Portuguese Republic to the European Economic Community and to the European Atomic Energy Community, signed at Lisbon and Madrid on 12th June 1985; and

(h)   the decision, of 11th June 1985, of the Council relating to the accession of the Kingdom of Spain and the Portuguese Republic to the European Coal and Steel Community; and

(j)   the following provisions of the Single European Act signed at Luxembourg and The Hague on 17th and 28th February 1986, namely Title II (amendment of the treaties establishing the Communities) and, so far as they relate to any of the Communities or any Community institution, the preamble and Titles I (common provisions) and IV (general and final provisions); and

(k)   Titles II, III and IV of the Treaty on European Union signed at Maastricht on 7th February 1992, together with the other provisions of the Treaty so far as they relate to those Titles, and the Protocols adopted at Maastricht on that date and annexed to the Treaty establishing the European Community with the exception of the Protocol on Social Policy on page 117 of Cm 1934 and

(l)   the decision, of 1st February 1993, of the Council amending the Act concerning the election of the representatives of the European Parliament by direct universal suffrage annexed to Council Decision 76/787/ECSC, EEC, Euratom of 20th September 1976 and

(m)   the Agreement on the European Economic Area signed at Oporto on 2nd May 1992 together with the Protocol adjusting that Agreement signed at Brussels on 17th March 1993 and

(n)   the treaty concerning the accession of the Kingdom of Norway, the Republic of Austria, the Republic of Finland and the Kingdom of Sweden to the European Union, signed at Corfu on 24th June 1994; and

(o)   the following provisions of the Treaty signed at Amsterdam on 2nd October 1997 amending the Treaty on European Union, the Treaties establishing the European Communities and certain related Acts—

   (i)   Articles 2 to 9,

   (ii)   Article 12, and

   (iii)   the other provisions of the Treaty so far as they relate to those Articles,

   and the Protocols adopted on that occasion other than the Protocol on Article J.7 of the Treaty on European Union; and

(p)   the following provisions of the Treaty signed at Nice on 26th February 2001 amending the Treaty on European Union, the Treaties establishing the European Communities and certain related Acts—

   (i)   Articles 2 to 10, and

   (ii)   the other provisions of the Treaty so far as they relate to those Articles,

   and the Protocols adopted on that occasion; and

(q)   the treaty concerning the accession of the Czech Republic, the Republic of Estonia, the Republic of Cyprus, the Republic of Latvia, the Republic of Lithuania, the Republic of Hungary, the Republic of Malta, the Republic of Poland, the Republic of Slovenia and the Slovak Republic to the European Union, signed at Athens on 16th April 2003; and

(r)   the treaty concerning the accession of the Republic of Bulgaria and Romania to the European Union, signed at Luxembourg on 25th April 2005; and

(s)   the Treaty of Lisbon Amending the Treaty on European Union and the Treaty Establishing the European Community signed at Lisbon on 13th December 2007 (together with its Annex and protocols), excluding any provision that relates to, or in so far as it relates to or could be applied in relation to, the Common Foreign and Security Policy;

and any other treaty entered into by the EU (except in so far as it relates to, or could be applied in relation to, the Common Foreign and Security Policy) , with or without any of the member States, or entered into, as a treaty ancillary to any of the Treaties, by the United Kingdom;

and any expression defined in Schedule 1 to this Act has the meaning there given to it.

(3)   If Her Majesty by Order in Council declares that a treaty specified in the Order is to be regarded as one of the Community Treaties as herein defined, the Order shall be conclusive that it is to be so regarded; but a treaty entered into by the United Kingdom after the 22nd January 1972, other than a pre-accession treaty to which the United Kingdom accedes on terms settled on or before that date, shall not be so regarded unless it is so specified, nor be so specified unless a draft of the Order in Council has been approved by resolution of each House of Parliament.

(4)   For purposes of subsections (2) and (3) above, "treaty" includes any international agreement, and any protocol or annex to a treaty or international agreement.

2 General implementation of Treaties

(1)   All such rights, powers, liabilities, obligations and restrictions from time to time created or arising by or under the Treaties, and all such remedies and procedures from time to time provided for by or under the Treaties, as in accordance with the Treaties are without further enactment to be given legal effect or used in the United Kingdom shall be recognised and available in law, and be enforced, allowed and followed accordingly; and the expression "enforceable Community right" and similar expressions shall be read as referring to one to which this subsection applies.

(2)   Subject to Schedule 2 to this Act, at any time after its passing Her Majesty may by Order in Council, and any designated Minister or department may by regulations, make provision for the purpose of:

(a)   Implementing any Community obligation of the United Kingdom, or enabling any such obligation to be implemented, or of enabling any rights enjoyed or to be enjoyed by the United Kingdom under or by virtue of the Treaties to be exercised

(b)   Dealing with matters arising out of or related to any such obligation or rights or the coming into force, or the operation from time to time, of subsection (1) above,

and in the exercise of any statutory power or duty, including any power to give directions or to legislate by means of orders, rules, regulations or other subordinate instrument, the person entrusted with the power or duty may have regard to the objects of the Communities and to any such obligation or rights as aforesaid.

In this subsection "designated Minister or department" means such Minister of the Crown or government department as may from time to time be designated by Order in Council in relation to any matter or for any purpose, but subject to such restrictions or conditions (if any) as may be specified by the Order in Council.

(3)   There shall be charged on and issued out of the Consolidated Fund or, if so determined by the Treasury, the National Loans Fund the amounts required to meet any Community obligation to make payments to any of the Communities or member States, or any Community obligation in respect of contributions to the capital or reserves of the European Investment Bank or in respect of loans to the Bank, or to redeem any notes or obligations issued or created in respect of any such Community obligation; and, except as otherwise provided by or under any enactment any:

(a)   Other expenses incurred under or by virtue of the Treaties or this Act by any Minister of the Crown or government department may be paid out of moneys provided by Parliament

(b)   Sums received under or by virtue of the Treaties or this Act by any Minister of the Crown or government department, save for such sums as may be required for disbursements permitted by any other enactment, shall be paid into the Consolidated Fund or, if so determined by the Treasury, the National Loans Fund.

(4) The provision that may be made under subsection (2) above includes, subject to Schedule 2 to this Act, any such provision (of any such extent) as might be made by Act of Parliament, and any enactment passed or to be passed, other than one contained in this part of this Act, shall be construed and have effect subject to the foregoing provisions of this section; but, except as may be provided by any Act passed after this Act, Schedule 2 shall have effect in connection with the powers conferred by this and the following sections of this Act to make Orders in Council [or orders, rules, regulations and schemes].

3 Decisions on, and proof of, Treaties and Community instruments etc

(1) For the purposes of all legal proceedings any question as to the meaning or effect of any of the Treaties, or as to the validity, meaning or effect of any Community instrument, shall be treated as a question of law (and, if not referred to the European Court, be for determination as such in accordance with the principles laid down by and any relevant [decision of the European Court or any court attached thereto)].

(2) Judicial notice shall be taken of the Treaties, of the Official Journal of the Communities and of any decision of, or expression of opinion by, the European Court [or any court attached thereto] on any such question as aforesaid; and the Official Journal shall be admissible as evidence of any instrument or other act thereby communicated of any of the Communities or of any Community institution.

(3) Evidence of any instrument issued by a EU institution , including any judgment or order of the European Court, or of any document in the custody of a EU institution , or any entry in or extract from such a document, may be given in any legal proceedings by production of a copy certified as a true copy by an official of that institution; and any document purporting to be such a copy shall be received in evidence without proof of the official position or handwriting of the person signing the certificate.

(4) Evidence of any EU instrument may also be given in any legal proceedings—

   (a) by production of a copy purporting to be printed by the Queen's Printer;

   (b) where the instrument is in the custody of a government department (including a department of the Government of Northern Ireland), by production of a copy certified on behalf of the department to be a true copy by an officer of the department generally or specially authorised so to do;

   and any document purporting to be such a copy as is mentioned in paragraph (b) above of an instrument in the custody of a department shall be received in evidence without proof of the official position or handwriting of the person signing the certificate, or of his authority to do so, or of the document being in the custody of the department.

(5) *****

EUROPEAN CONVENTION FOR THE PROTECTION OF HUMAN RIGHTS AND FUNDAMENTAL FREEDOMS 1950

Rome, 4.XI.1950

[The European Convention on Human Rights]

The Governments signatory hereto, being Members of the Council of Europe,

Considering the Universal Declaration of Human Rights proclaimed by the General Assembly of the United Nations on 10th December 1948; Considering that this Declaration aims at securing the universal and effective recognition and observance of the Rights therein declared; Considering that the aim of the Council of Europe is the achievement of greater unity between its Members and that one of the methods by which that aim is to be pursued is the maintenance and further realization of Human Rights and Fundamental Freedoms; Reaffirming their profound belief in those fundamental freedoms which are the foundation of justice and peace in the world and are best maintained on the one hand by an effective political democracy and on the other by a common understanding and observance of the human rights upon which they depend; Being resolved, as the Governments of European countries which are like-minded and have a common heritage of political traditions, ideals, freedom and the rule of law, to take the first steps for the collective enforcement of certain of the Rights stated in the Universal Declaration, Have agreed as follows:

Article 1 Obligation to respect human rights

The High Contracting Parties shall secure to everyone within their jurisdiction the rights and freedoms defined in Section I of this Convention.

SECTION I – RIGHTS AND FREEDOMS

Article 2 Right to life

(1)   Everyone's right to life shall be protected by law. No one shall be deprived of his life intentionally save in the execution of a sentence of a court following his conviction of a crime for which this penalty is provided by law.

(2)   Deprivation of life shall not be regarded as inflicted in contravention of this article when it results from the use of force which is no more than absolutely necessary in:

(a)   Defence of any person from unlawful violence

(b)   Order to effect a lawful arrest or to prevent the escape of a person lawfully detained

(c)   Action lawfully taken for the purpose of quelling a riot or insurrection.

Article 3 Prohibition of torture

No one shall be subjected to torture or to inhuman or degrading treatment or punishment.

Article 4 Prohibition of slavery and forced labour

(1) No one shall be held in slavery or servitude.

(2) No one shall be required to perform forced or compulsory labour.

(3) For the purpose of this article the term forced or compulsory labour shall not include any:

    (a) Work required to be done in the ordinary course of detention imposed according to the provisions of Article 5 of this Convention or during conditional release from such detention

    (b) Service of a military character or, in case of conscientious objectors in countries where they are recognised, service exacted instead of compulsory military service

    (c) Service exacted in case of an emergency or calamity threatening the life or well-being of the community

    (d) Work or service which forms part of normal civic obligations

Article 5 Right to liberty and security

(1) Everyone has the right to liberty and security of person. No one shall be deprived of his liberty save in the following cases and in accordance with a procedure prescribed by law:

    (a) The lawful detention of a person after conviction by a competent court

    (b) The lawful arrest or detention of a person for non-compliance with the lawful order of a court or in order to secure the fulfilment of any obligation prescribed by law

    (c) The lawful arrest or detention of a person effected for the purpose of bringing him before the competent legal authority on reasonable suspicion of having committed an offence or when it is reasonably considered necessary to prevent his committing an offence or fleeing after having done so

    (d) The detention of a minor by lawful order for the purpose of educational supervision or his lawful detention for the purpose of bringing him before the competent legal authority

    (e) The lawful detention of persons for the prevention of the spreading of infectious diseases, of persons of unsound mind, alcoholics or drug addicts or vagrants

    (f) The lawful arrest or detention of a person to prevent his effecting an unauthorised entry into the country or of a person against whom action is being taken with a view to deportation or extradition.

(2) Everyone who is arrested shall be informed promptly, in a language which he understands, of the reasons for his arrest and of any charge against him.

(3) Everyone arrested or detained in accordance with the provisions of paragraph 1(c) of this article shall be brought promptly before a judge or other officer authorised by law to exercise judicial power and shall be entitled to trial within a reasonable time or to release pending trial. Release may be conditioned by guarantees to appear for trial.

(4)   Everyone who is deprived of his liberty by arrest or detention shall be entitled to take proceedings by which the lawfulness of his detention shall be decided speedily by a court and his release ordered if the detention is not lawful.

(5)   Everyone who has been the victim of arrest or detention in contravention of the provisions of this article shall have an enforceable right to compensation.

Article 6 Right to a fair trial

(1)   In the determination of his civil rights and obligations or of any criminal charge against him, everyone is entitled to a fair and public hearing within a reasonable time by an independent and impartial tribunal established by law. Judgment shall be pronounced publicly but the press and public may be excluded from all or part of the trial in the interests of morals, public order or national security in a democratic society, where the interests of juveniles or the protection of the private life of the parties so require, or to the extent strictly necessary in the opinion of the court in special circumstances where publicity would prejudice the interests of justice.

(2)   Everyone charged with a criminal offence shall be presumed innocent until proved guilty according to law.

(3)   Everyone charged with a criminal offence has the following minimum rights to:

    (a)   Be informed promptly, in a language which he understands and in detail, of the nature and cause of the accusation against him

    (b)   Have adequate time and facilities for the preparation of his defence

    (c)   Defend himself in person or through legal assistance of his own choosing or, if he has not sufficient means to pay for legal assistance, to be given it free when the interests of justice so require

    (d)   Examine or have examined witnesses against him and to obtain the attendance and examination of witnesses on his behalf under the same conditions as witnesses against him

    (e)   Have the free assistance of an interpreter if he cannot understand or speak the language used in court

Article 7 No punishment without law

(1)   No one shall be held guilty of any criminal offence on account of any act or omission which did not constitute a criminal offence under national or international law at the time when it was committed. Nor shall a heavier penalty be imposed than the one that was applicable at the time the criminal offence was committed.

(2)   This article shall not prejudice the trial and punishment of any person for any act or omission which, at the time when it was committed, was criminal according to the general principles of law recognised by civilised nations.

Article 8 Right to respect for private and family life

(1)   Everyone has the right to respect for his private and family life, his home and his correspondence.

(2) There shall be no interference by a public authority with the exercise of this right except such as is in accordance with the law and is necessary in a democratic society in the interests of national security, public safety or the economic well-being of the country, for the prevention of disorder or crime, for the protection of health or morals, or for the protection of the rights and freedoms of others.

Article 9 Freedom of thought, conscience and religion

(1) Everyone has the right to freedom of thought, conscience and religion; this right includes freedom to change his religion or belief and freedom, either alone or in community with others and in public or private, to manifest his religion or belief, in worship, teaching, practice and observance.

(2) Freedom to manifest one's religion or beliefs shall be subject only to such limitations as are prescribed by law and are necessary in a democratic society in the interests of public safety, for the protection of public order, health or morals, or for the protection of the rights and freedoms of others.

Article 10 Freedom of expression

(1) Everyone has the right to freedom of expression. This right shall include freedom to hold opinions and to receive and impart information and ideas without interference by public authority and regardless of frontiers. This article shall not prevent States from requiring the licensing of broadcasting, television or cinema enterprises.

(2) The exercise of these freedoms, since it carries with it duties and responsibilities, may be subject to such formalities, conditions, restrictions or penalties as are prescribed by law and are necessary in a democratic society, in the interests of national security, territorial integrity or public safety, for the prevention of disorder or crime, for the protection of health or morals, for the protection of the reputation or rights of others, for preventing the disclosure of information received in confidence, or for maintaining the authority and impartiality of the judiciary.

Article 11 Freedom of assembly and association

(1) Everyone has the right to freedom of peaceful assembly and to freedom of association with others, including the right to form and to join trade unions for the protection of his interests.

(2) No restrictions shall be placed on the exercise of these rights other than such as are prescribed by law and are necessary in a democratic society in the interests of national security or public safety, for the prevention of disorder or crime, for the protection of health or morals or for the protection of the rights and freedoms of others. This article shall not prevent the imposition of lawful restrictions on the exercise of these rights by members of the armed forces, of the police or of the administration of the State.

Article 12 Right to marry

Men and women of marriageable age have the right to marry and to found a family, according to the national laws governing the exercise of this right.

Article 13 Right to an effective remedy

Everyone whose rights and freedoms as set forth in this Convention are violated shall have an effective remedy before a national authority notwithstanding that the violation has been committed by persons acting in an official capacity.

Article 14 Prohibition of discrimination

The enjoyment of the rights and freedoms set forth in this Convention shall be secured without discrimination on any ground such as sex, race, colour, language, religion, political or other opinion, national or social origin, association with a national minority, property, birth or other status.

Article 15 Derogation in time of emergency

(1)   In time of war or other public emergency threatening the life of the nation any High Contracting Party may take measures derogating from its obligations under this Convention to the extent strictly required by the exigencies of the situation, provided that such measures are not inconsistent with its other obligations under international law.

(2)   No derogation from Article 2, except in respect of deaths resulting from lawful acts of war, or from Articles 3, 4 (paragraph 1) and 7 shall be made under this provision.

(3)   Any High Contracting Party availing itself of this right of derogation shall keep the Secretary General of the Council of Europe fully informed of the measures which it has taken and the reasons therefor. It shall also inform the Secretary General of the Council of Europe when such measures have ceased to operate and the provisions of the Convention are again being fully executed.

SECTION II – EUROPEAN COURT OF HUMAN RIGHTS

Article 33 Inter-State cases

Any High Contracting Party may refer to the Court any alleged breach of the provisions of the Convention and the protocols thereto by another High Contracting Party.

Article 34 Individual applications

The Court may receive applications from any person, non-governmental organisation or group of individuals claiming to be the victim of a violation by one of the High Contracting Parties of the rights set forth in the Convention or the protocols thereto. The High Contracting Parties undertake not to hinder in any way the effective exercise of this right.

Protocol to the Convention for the Protection of Human Rights ad Fundamental Freedoms

The Governments signatory hereto, being Members of the Council of Europe,

Being resolved to take steps to ensure the collective enforcement of certain Rights and Freedoms other than those already included in Section 1 of the Convention for the Protection of Human Rights and Fundamental Freedoms signed at Rome on 4 November 1950 (hereinafter referred to as the Convention),

Have agreed as follows:

Article 1 Protection of property

Every natural or legal person is entitled to the peaceful enjoyment of his possessions. No one shall be deprived of his possessions except in the public interest and subject to the conditions provided for by law and by the general principles of international law.

The preceding provisions shall not, however, in any way impair the rightof a State to enforce such laws as it deems necessary to control the use of property in accordance with the general interest or to secure the payment of taxes or other contributions or penalties.

13 to the Convention for the Protection of Human Rights and Fundamental Freedoms concerning the abolition of the death penalty in all circumstances

The member States of the Council of Europe signatory hereto,

Convinced that everyone's right to life is a basic value in a democratic society and that the abolition of the death penalty is essential for the protection of this right and for the full recognition of the inherent dignity of all human beings;

Wishing to strengthen the protection of the right to life guaranteed by the Convention for the Protection of Human Rights and Fundamental Freedoms signed at Rome on 4 November 1950 (hereinafter referred to as "the Convention");

Noting that Protocol No. 6 to the Convention concerning the abolition of the death penalty, signed at Strasbourg on 28 April 1983, does not exclude the death penalty in respect of acts com-mitted in time of war or of imminent threat of war;

Being resolved to take the final step in order to abolish the death penalty in all circumstances,

Have agreed as follows:

Article 1

Abolition of the death penalty

The death penalty shall be abolished. No one shall be condemned to such penalty or executed.

HEALTH AND SOCIAL CARE ACT 2008

2008 chapter 14

An Act to establish and make provision in connection with a Care Quality Commission; to make provision about health care (including provision about the National Health Service) and about social care; to make provision about reviews and investigations under the Mental Health Act 1983; to establish and make provision in connection with an Office of the Health Professions Adjudicator and make other provision about the regulation of the health care professions; to confer power to modify the regulation of social care workers; to amend the Public Health (Control of Disease) Act 1984; to provide for the payment of a grant to women in connection with pregnancy; to amend the functions of the Health Protection Agency; and for connected purposes.[21st July 2008]

Social care

145 Human Rights Act 1998: provision of certain social care to be public function

(1)   A person ("P") who provides accommodation, together with nursing or personal care, in a care home for an individual under arrangements made with P under the relevant statutory provisions is to be taken for the purposes of subsection (3)(b) of section 6 of the Human Rights Act 1998 (c. 42) (acts of public authorities) to be exercising a function of a public nature in doing so.

(2)   The "relevant statutory provisions" are in relation to:

(a)   England and Wales, sections 21(1)(a) and 26 of the National Assistance Act 1948 (c. 29)

(b)   Scotland, section 12 or 13A of the Social Work (Scotland) Act 1968 (c. 49)

(c)   Northern Ireland, Articles 15 and 36 of the Health and Personal Social Services (Northern Ireland) Order 1972 (S.I. 1972/1265 (N.I. 14))

(3)   In subsection (1) "care home" in relation to:

(a)   England and Wales, has the same meaning as in the Care Standards Act 2000 (c. 14)

(b)   Northern Ireland, means a residential care home as defined by Article 10 of the Health and Personal Social Services (Quality, Improvement and Regulation) (Northern Ireland) Order 2003 (S.I. 2003/431 (N.I. 9)) or a nursing home as defined by Article 11 of that Order

(4)   In relation to Scotland, the reference in subsection (1) to the provision of accommodation, together with nursing or personal care, in a care home is to be read as a reference to the provision of accommodation, together with nursing, personal care or personal support, as a care home service as defined by section 2(3) of the Regulation of Care (Scotland) Act 2001 (asp 8).

(5)   Subsection (1) does not apply to acts (within the meaning of section 6 of the Human Rights Act 1998 (c. 42)) taking place before the coming into force of this section.

HOUSE OF COMMONS DISQUALIFICATION ACT 1975

1975 chapter 24

An Act to consolidate certain enactments relating to disqualification for membership of the House of Commons.[8th May 1975]

1 Disqualification of holders of certain offices and places

(1)   Subject to the provisions of this Act, a person is disqualified for membership of the House of Commons who for the time being:

[(za)is a Lord Spiritual;]

(a)   Holds any of the judicial offices specified in Part I of Schedule 1 to this Act

(b)   Is employed in the civil service of the Crown, whether in an established capacity or not, and whether for the whole or part of his time

(c)   Is a member of any of the regular armed forces of the Crown . . .

(d)   Is a member of any police force maintained by a police authority; . . .

[(da)   . . .]

(e)   Is a member of the legislature of any country or territory outside the Commonwealth [(other than Ireland)]

(f)   Holds any office described in Part II or Part III of Schedule 1

(2) * * * * *

(3)   In this section —

- "civil service of the Crown" includes the civil service of Northern Ireland, the Northern Ireland Court Service, Her Majesty's Diplomatic Service and Her Majesty's Overseas Civil Service;

- "police authority" means any police authority within the meaning of the Police Act 1996] or the Police (Scotland) Act 1967, or the Northern Ireland Policing Board; and "member" in relation to a police force means a person employed as a full-time constable;

- "regular armed forces of the Crown" means the Royal Navy, [the Royal Marines, the regular army (as defined by section 374 of the Armed Forces Act 2006) or the Royal Air Force.

(4)   Except as provided by this Act, a person shall not be disqualified for membership of the House of Commons by reason of his holding an office or place of profit under the Crown or any other office or place; and a person shall not be disqualified for appointment to or for holding any office or place by reason of his being a member of that House.

2 Ministerial offices

(1)   Not more than ninety-five persons being the holders of offices specified in Schedule 2 to this Act (in this section referred to as Ministerial offices) shall be entitled to sit and vote in the House of Commons at any one time.

(2)   If at any time the number of members of the House of Commons who are holders of Ministerial offices exceeds the number entitled to sit and vote in that House under subsection (1) above, none except any who were both members of that House and holders of Ministerial offices before the excess occurred shall sit or vote therein until the number has been reduced, by death, resignation or otherwise, to the number entitled to sit and vote as aforesaid.

(3)   A person holding a Ministerial office is not disqualified by this Act by reason of any office held by him ex officio as the holder of that Ministerial office.

HUMAN RIGHTS ACT 1998

1998 chapter 42

An Act to give further effect to rights and freedoms guaranteed under the European Convention on Human Rights; to make provision with respect to holders of certain judicial offices who become judges of the European Court of Human Rights; and for connected purposes.[9th November 1998]

Introduction

1 The Convention Rights

(1)   In this Act "the Convention rights" means the rights and fundamental freedoms set out in:

(a)   Articles 2 to 12 and 14 of the Convention

(b)   Articles 1 to 3 of the First Protocol

(c)   [Article 1 of the Thirteenth Protocol]

As read with Articles 16 to 18 of the Convention.

(2)   Those Articles are to have effect for the purposes of this Act subject to any designated derogation or reservation (as to which see sections 14 and 15).

(3)   The Articles are set out in Schedule 1.

(4)   The [Secretary of State] may by order make such amendments to this Act as he considers appropriate to reflect the effect, in relation to the United Kingdom, of a protocol.

(5)   In subsection (4) "protocol" means a protocol to the Convention which the United Kingdom has:

(a)   Ratified

(b)   Signed with a view to ratification

(6)   No amendment may be made by an order under subsection (4) so as to come into force before the protocol concerned is in force in relation to the United Kingdom.

2 Interpretation of Convention rights

(1)   A court or tribunal determining a question which has arisen in connection with a Convention right must take into account any:

(a)   Judgment, decision, declaration or advisory opinion of the European Court of Human Rights

(b)   Opinion of the Commission given in a report adopted under Article 31 of the Convention

(c)   Decision of the Commission in connection with Article 26 or 27(2) of the Convention

(d)   Decision of the Committee of Ministers taken under Article 46 of the Convention

Whenever made or given, so far as, in the opinion of the court or tribunal, it is relevant to the proceedings in which that question has arisen.

(2)   Evidence of any judgment, decision, declaration or opinion of which account may have to be taken under this section is to be given in proceedings before any court or tribunal in such manner as may be provided by rules.

(3)   In this section "rules" means rules of court or, in the case of proceedings before a tribunal, rules made for the purposes of this section—

(a)   by the Lord Chancellor or the Secretary of State, in relation to any proceedings outside Scotland;

(b)   by the Secretary of State, in relation to proceedings in Scotland; or

(c)   by a Northern Ireland department, in relation to proceedings before a tribunal in Northern Ireland—

(i)   which deals with transferred matters; and

(ii)   for which no rules made under paragraph (a) are in force.

Legislation

3 Interpretation of legislation

(1)   So far as it is possible to do so, primary legislation and subordinate legislation must be read and given effect in a way which is compatible with the Convention rights.

(2)   This section:

(a)   Applies to primary legislation and subordinate legislation whenever enacted

(b)   Does not affect the validity, continuing operation or enforcement of any incompatible primary legislation

(c)   Does not affect the validity, continuing operation or enforcement of any incompatible subordinate legislation if (disregarding any possibility of revocation) primary legislation prevents removal of the incompatibility

4 Declaration of incompatibility

(1)   Subsection (2) applies in any proceedings in which a court determines whether a provision of primary legislation is compatible with a Convention right.

(2)   If the court is satisfied that the provision is incompatible with a Convention right, it may make a declaration of that incompatibility.

(3)   Subsection (4) applies in any proceedings in which a court determines whether a provision of subordinate legislation, made in the exercise of a power conferred by primary legislation, is compatible with a Convention right.

(4)   If the court is satisfied that:

(a)   The provision is incompatible with a Convention right

(b)   (Disregarding any possibility of revocation) the primary legislation concerned prevents removal of the incompatibility

It may make a declaration of that incompatibility.

(5)   In this section "court" means:

(a)   The House of Lords

(b)   The Judicial Committee of the Privy Council

(c)   The Courts-Martial Appeal Court

(d)   In Scotland, the High Court of Justiciary sitting otherwise than as a trial court or the Court of Session

(e)   In England and Wales or Northern Ireland, the High Court or the Court of Appeal

[(f)   The Court of Protection, in any matter being dealt with by the President of the Family Division, the Vice-Chancellor or a puisne judge of the High Court]

(6)   A declaration under this section ("a declaration of incompatibility"):

(a)   Does not affect the validity, continuing operation or enforcement of the provision in respect of which it is given

(b)   Is not binding on the parties to the proceedings in which it is made

5 Right of Crown to intervene

(1)   Where a court is considering whether to make a declaration of incompatibility, the Crown is entitled to notice in accordance with rules of court.

(2)   In any case to which subsection (1) applies a:

(a)   Minister of the Crown (or a person nominated by him)

(b)   Member of the Scottish Executive

(c)   Northern Ireland Minister

(d)   Northern Ireland department

Is entitled, on giving notice in accordance with rules of court, to be joined as a party to the proceedings.

(3)   Notice under subsection (2) may be given at any time during the proceedings.

(4)   A person who has been made a party to criminal proceedings (other than in Scotland) as the result of a notice under subsection (2) may, with leave, appeal to the House of Lords against any declaration of incompatibility made in the proceedings.

(5)   In subsection (4):

(a)   "Criminal proceedings" includes all proceedings before the Courts-Martial Appeal Court

(b)   "Leave" means leave granted by the court making the declaration of incompatibility or by the House of Lords.

Public authorities

6 Acts of public authorities

(1) It is unlawful for a public authority to act in a way which is incompatible with a Convention right.

(2) Subsection (1) does not apply to an act if:

    (a) As the result of one or more provisions of primary legislation, the authority could not have acted differently

    (b) In the case of one or more provisions of, or made under, primary legislation which cannot be read or given effect in a way which is compatible with the Convention rights, the authority was acting so as to give effect to or enforce those provisions

(3) In this section "public authority" includes:

    (a) A court or tribunal
    (b) Any person certain of whose functions are functions of a public nature

But does not include either House of Parliament or a person exercising functions in connection with proceedings in Parliament.

(4) In subsection (3) "Parliament" does not include the House of Lords in its judicial capacity.

(5) In relation to a particular act, a person is not a public authority by virtue only of subsection (3)(b) if the nature of the act is private.

(6) "An act" includes a failure to act but does not include a failure to:

    (a) Introduce in, or lay before, Parliament a proposal for legislation
    (b) Make any primary legislation or remedial order

7 Proceedings

(1) A person who claims that a public authority has acted (or proposes to act) in a way which is made unlawful by section 6(1) may:

    (a) Bring proceedings against the authority under this Act in the appropriate court or tribunal

    (b) Rely on the Convention right or rights concerned in any legal proceedings

But only if he is (or would be) a victim of the unlawful act.

(2) In subsection (1)(a) "appropriate court or tribunal" means such court or tribunal as may be determined in accordance with rules; and proceedings against an authority include a counterclaim or similar proceeding.

(3) If the proceedings are brought on an application for judicial review, the applicant is to be taken to have a sufficient interest in relation to the unlawful act only if he is, or would be, a victim of that act.

(4) If the proceedings are made by way of a petition for judicial review in Scotland, the applicant shall be taken to have title and interest to sue in relation to the unlawful act only if he is, or would be, a victim of that act.

(5)   Proceedings under subsection (1)(a) must be brought before the end of:

(a)   The period of one year beginning with the date on which the act complained of took place

(b)   Such longer period as the court or tribunal considers equitable having regard to all the circumstances

But that is subject to any rule imposing a stricter time limit in relation to the procedure in question.

(6)   In subsection (1)(b) "legal proceedings" includes:

(a)   Proceedings brought by or at the instigation of a public authority

(b)   An appeal against the decision of a court or tribunal

(7)   For the purposes of this section, a person is a victim of an unlawful act only if he would be a victim for the purposes of Article 34 of the Convention if proceedings were brought in the European Court of Human Rights in respect of that act.

(8)   Nothing in this Act creates a criminal offence.

(9) – (13) *****

8 Judicial remedies

(1)   In relation to any act (or proposed act) of a public authority which the court finds is (or would be) unlawful, it may grant such relief or remedy, or make such order, within its powers as it considers just and appropriate.

(2)   But damages may be awarded only by a court which has power to award damages, or to order the payment of compensation, in civil proceedings.

(3)   No award of damages is to be made unless, taking account of all the circumstances of the case, including:

(a)   Any other relief or remedy granted, or order made, in relation to the act in question (by that or any other court)

(b)   Consequences of any decision (of that or any other court) in respect of that act

The court is satisfied that the award is necessary to afford just satisfaction to the person in whose favour it is made.

(4)   In determining:

(a)   Whether to award damages

(b)   The amount of an award

The court must take into account the principles applied by the European Court of Human Rights in relation to the award of compensation under Article 41 of the Convention.

(5) *****

(6)   In this section—

- "court" includes a tribunal;
- "damages" means damages for an unlawful act of a public authority; and
- "unlawful" means unlawful under section 6(1).

9 Judicial acts

(1)   Proceedings under section 7(1)(a) in respect of a judicial act may be brought only:

(a)   By exercising a right of appeal
(b)   On an application (in Scotland a petition) for judicial review
(c)   In such other forum as may be prescribed by rules

(2)   That does not affect any rule of law which prevents a court from being the subject of judicial review.

(3)   In proceedings under this Act in respect of a judicial act done in good faith, damages may not be awarded otherwise than to compensate a person to the extent required by Article 5(5) of the Convention.

(4)   An award of damages permitted by subsection (3) is to be made against the Crown; but no award may be made unless the appropriate person, if not a party to the proceedings, is joined.

(5)   In this section:

(a)   "Appropriate person" means the Minister responsible for the court concerned, or a person or government department nominated by him

(b)   "Court" includes a tribunal

(c)   "Judge" includes a member of a tribunal, a justice of the peace [(or, in Northern Ireland, a lay magistrate)] and a clerk or other officer entitled to exercise the jurisdiction of a court

(d)   "Judicial act" means a judicial act of a court and includes an act done on the instructions, or on behalf, of a judge

"Rules" has the same meaning as in section 7(9).

Remedial action

10 Power to take remedial action

(1)   This section applies if:

(a)   A provision of legislation has been declared under section 4 to be incompatible with a Convention right and, if an appeal lies:

(I)   All persons who may appeal have stated in writing that they do not intend to do so

(ii)   The time for bringing an appeal has expired and no appeal has been brought within that time

(iii)   An appeal brought within that time has been determined or abandoned (b)　　It appears to a Minister of the Crown or Her Majesty in Council that, having regard to a finding of the European Court of Human Rights made after the coming into force of this section in proceedings against the United Kingdom, a provision of legislation is incompatible with an obligation of the United Kingdom arising from the Convention.

(2)　　If a Minister of the Crown considers that there are compelling reasons for proceeding under this section, he may by order make such amendments to the legislation as he considers necessary to remove the incompatibility.

(3)　　If, in the case of subordinate legislation, a Minister of the Crown considers that:

(a)　　It is necessary to amend the primary legislation under which the subordinate legislation in question was made, in order to enable the incompatibility to be removed

(b)　　There are compelling reasons for proceeding under this section

He may by order make such amendments to the primary legislation as he considers necessary.

(4) – (7) *****

Other rights and proceedings

11 Safeguard for existing human rights

A person's reliance on a Convention right does not restrict:

(a)　　Any other right or freedom conferred on him by or under any law having effect in any part of the United Kingdom

(b)　　His right to make any claim or bring any proceedings which he could make or bring apart from sections 7 to 9

12 Freedom of expression

(1)　　This section applies if a court is considering whether to grant any relief which, if granted, might affect the exercise of the Convention right to freedom of expression.

(2)　　If the person against whom the application for relief is made ("the respondent") is neither present nor represented, no such relief is to be granted unless the court is satisfied that:

(a)　　The applicant has taken all practicable steps to notify the respondent
(b)　　There are compelling reasons why the respondent should not be notified

(3)　　No such relief is to be granted so as to restrain publication before trial unless the court is satisfied that the applicant is likely to establish that publication should not be allowed.

(4)　　The court must have particular regard to the importance of the Convention right to freedom of expression and, where the proceedings relate to material which the respondent claims, or which appears to the court, to be journalistic, literary or artistic material (or to conduct connected with such material), to:

(a)　　the extent to which:

(i)　　The material has, or is about to, become available to the public

(ii)   It is, or would be, in the public interest for the material to be published

(b)   Any relevant privacy code.

(5)   In this section:

(a)   "Court" includes a tribunal

(b)   "Relief" includes any remedy or order (other than in criminal proceedings)

13 Freedom of thought, conscience and religion

(1)   If a court's determination of any question arising under this Act might affect the exercise by a religious organisation (itself or its members collectively) of the Convention right to freedom of thought, conscience and religion, it must have particular regard to the importance of that right.

(2)   In this section "court" includes a tribunal.

Derogations and reservations

14 Derogations

(1)   In this Act "designated derogation" means . . . any derogation by the United Kingdom from an Article of the Convention, or of any protocol to the Convention, which is designated for the purposes of this Act in an order made by the [Secretary of State].

15 Reservations

(1)   In this Act "designated reservation" means:

(a)   The United Kingdom's reservation to Article 2 of the First Protocol to the Convention

(b)   Any other reservation by the United Kingdom to an Article of the Convention, or of any protocol to the Convention, which is designated for the purposes of this Act in an order made by the [Secretary of State]

(2)   The text of the reservation referred to in subsection (1)(a) is set out in Part II of Schedule 3.

(3)   If a designated reservation is withdrawn wholly or in part it ceases to be a designated reservation.

(4)   But subsection (3) does not prevent the [Secretary of State] from exercising his power under subsection (1)(b) to make a fresh designation order in respect of the Article concerned.

(5)   [Secretary of State] must by order make such amendments to this Act as he considers appropriate to reflect:

(a)   Any designation order
(b)   The effect of subsection (3)

16 Period for which designated derogations have effect

(1)   If it has not already been withdrawn by the United Kingdom, a designated derogation ceases to have effect for the purposes of this Act at the end of the period of five years beginning with the date on which the order designating it was made.

(2)   At any time before the period:

   (a)   Fixed by subsection (1). . .,

   (b)   Extended by an order under this subsection

Comes to an end, the [Secretary of State] may by order extend it by a further period of five years.

(3)   An order under section 14(1). . . ceases to have effect at the end of the period for consideration, unless a resolution has been passed by each House approving the order.

(4)   Subsection (3) does not affect:

   (a)   Anything done in reliance on the order
   (b)   The power to make a fresh order under section 14(1). . .

(5)   In subsection (3) "period for consideration" means the period of forty days beginning with the day on which the order was made.

(6)   In calculating the period for consideration, no account is to be taken of any time during which:

   (a)   Parliament is dissolved or prorogued
   (b)   Both Houses are adjourned for more than four days

(7)   If a designated derogation is withdrawn by the United Kingdom, the [Secretary of State] must by order make such amendments to this Act as he considers are required to reflect that withdrawal.

17 Periodic review of designated reservations

(1)   The appropriate Minister must review the designated reservation referred to in section 15(1)(a):

   (a)   Before the end of the period of five years beginning with the date on which section 1(2) came into force

   (b)   If that designation is still in force, before the end of the period of five years beginning with the date on which the last report relating to it was laid under subsection (3)

(2)   The appropriate Minister must review each of the other designated reservations (if any):

   (a)   Before the end of the period of five years beginning with the date on which the order designating the reservation first came into force

   (b)   If the designation is still in force, before the end of the period of five years beginning with the date on which the last report relating to it was laid under subsection (3)

(3)   The Minister conducting a review under this section must prepare a report on the result of the review and lay a copy of it before each House of Parliament.

Parliamentary procedure

19 Statements of compatibility

(1)   A Minister of the Crown in charge of a Bill in either House of Parliament must, before Second Reading of the Bill—

  (a)   make a statement to the effect that in his view the provisions of the Bill are compatible with the Convention rights ("a statement of compatibility"); or

  (b)   make a statement to the effect that although he is unable to make a statement of compatibility the government nevertheless wishes the House to proceed with the Bill.

(2)   The statement must be in writing and be published in such manner as the Minister making it considers appropriate.

22 Short title, commencement, application and extent

(1)   This Act may be cited as the Human Rights Act 1998.

MAGNA CARTA (1297)

1297 chapter 9 25 Edw 1 cc 1 9 29

THE GREAT CHARTER OF THE LIBERTIES OF ENGLAND, AND OF THE LIBERTIES OF THE FOREST; CONFIRMED BY KING EDWARD, IN THE TWENTY-FIFTH YEAR OF HIS REIGN.

EDWARD by the Grace of God King of England, Lord of Ireland, and Duke of Guyan, [to all Archbishops, Bishops, &c.] We have seen the Great Charter of the Lord Henry sometimes King of England, our Father, of the Liberties of England in these words:

HENRY by the Grace of God King of England, Lord of Ireland, Duke of Normandy and Guyan, and Earl of Anjou, to all Archbishops, Bishops, Abbots, Priors, Earls, Barons, Sheriffs, Provosts, Officers, and to all Bailiffs, and other our faithful Subjects, which shall see this present Charter, Greeting: Know Ye, that We, unto the honour of Almighty God, and for the salvation of the souls of our Progenitors and Successors [Kings of England,] to the advancement of Holy Church and amendment of our Realm, of our meer and free will, have given and granted to all Archbishops, Bishops, Abbots, Priors, Earls, Barons, and to all [Freemen] of this our Realm, these Liberties following, to be kept in our Kingdom of England for ever.

I Confirmation of Liberties

FIRST, We have granted to God, and by this our present Charter have confirmed, for Us and our Heirs for ever, that the Church of England shall be free, and shall have all her whole Rights and Liberties inviolable. We have granted also, and given to all the Freemen of our Realm, for Us and our Heirs for ever, these Liberties under-written, to have and to hold to them and their Heirs, of Us and our Heirs for ever.

XXIX Imprisonment, &c. contrary to Law

NO Freeman shall be taken or imprisoned, or be disseised of his Freehold, or Liberties, or free Customs, or be outlawed, or exiled, or any other wise destroyed; nor will We not pass upon him, nor [condemn him,] but by lawful judgment of his Peers, or by the Law of the Land. We will sell to no man, we will not deny or defer to any man either Justice or Right.

PARLIAMENT ACT 1911

1911 chapter 13 1 and 2 Geo 5

An Act to make provision with respect to the powers of the House of Lords in relation to those of the House of Commons, and to limit the duration of Parliament. [18th August 1911]

Whereas it is expedient that provision should be made for regulating the relations between the two Houses of Parliament:

And whereas it is intended to substitute for the House of Lords as it at present exists a Second Chamber constituted on a popular instead of hereditary basis, but such substitution cannot be immediately brought into operation:

And whereas provision will require hereafter to be made by Parliament in a measure effecting such substitution for limiting and defining the powers of the new Second Chamber, but it is expedient to make such provision as in this Act appears for restricting the existing powers of the House of Lords:

1 Powers of House of Lords as to Money Bills

(1) If a Money Bill, having been passed by the House of Commons, and sent up to the House of Lords at least one month before the end of the session, is not passed by the House of Lords without amendment within one month after it is so sent up to that House, the Bill shall, unless the House of Commons direct to the contrary, be presented to His Majesty and become an Act of Parliament on the Royal Assent being signified, notwithstanding that the House of Lords have not consented to the Bill.

(2) A Money Bill means a Public Bill which in the opinion of the Speaker of the House of Commons contains only provisions dealing with all or any of the following subjects, namely, the imposition, repeal, remission, alteration, or regulation of taxation; the imposition for the payment of debt or other financial purposes of charges on the Consolidated Fund, the National Loans Fund or on money provided by Parliament, or the variation or repeal of any such charges; supply; the appropriation, receipt, custody, issue or audit of accounts of public money; the raising or guarantee of any loan or the repayment thereof; or subordinate matters incidental to those subjects or any of them. In this subsection the expressions "taxation," "public money," and "loan" respectively do not include any taxation, money, or loan raised by local authorities or bodies for local purposes.

(3) There shall be endorsed on every Money Bill when it is sent up to the House of Lords and when it is presented to His Majesty for assent the certificate of the Speaker of the House of Commons signed by him that it is a Money Bill. Before giving his certificate the Speaker shall consult, if practicable, two members to be appointed from the Chairmen's Panel at the beginning of each Session by the Committee of Selection.

2 Restriction of the powers of the House of Lords as to Bills other than Money Bills

(1) If any Public Bill (other than a Money Bill or a Bill containing any provision to extend the maximum duration of Parliament beyond five years) is passed by the House of Commons [in two successive sessions] (whether of the same Parliament or not), and, having been sent up to the House of Lords at least one month before the end of the session, is rejected by the House of Lords in each of those sessions, that Bill shall, on its rejection [for the second time] by the House of Lords, unless the House of Commons direct to the contrary, be presented to His Majesty and become an Act of Parliament on the Royal Assent being signified thereto, notwithstanding that the House of Lords have not consented to the Bill: Provided that this provision shall not take effect unless [one year has elapsed] between the date of the second reading in the first of those sessions of the Bill in the House of Commons and the date on which it passes the House of Commons [in the second of these sessions.]

(2) When a Bill is presented to His Majesty for assent in pursuance of the provisions of this section, there shall be endorsed on the Bill the certificate of the Speaker of the House of Commons signed by him that the provisions of this section have been duly complied with.

(3) A Bill shall be deemed to be rejected by the House of Lords if it is not passed by the House of Lords either without amendment or with such amendments only as may be agreed to by both Houses.

(4) A Bill shall be deemed to be the same Bill as a former Bill sent up to the House of Lords in the preceding session if, when it is sent up to the House of Lords, it is identical with the former Bill or contains only such alterations as are certified by the Speaker of the House of Commons to be necessary owing to the time which has elapsed since the date of the former Bill, or to represent any amendments which have been made by the House of Lords in the former Bill in the preceding session, and any amendments which are certified by the Speaker to have been made by the House of Lords [in the second session] and agreed to by the House of Commons shall be inserted in the Bill as presented for Royal Assent in pursuance of this section:

Provided that the House of Commons may, if they think fit, on the passage of such a Bill through the House [in the second session,] suggest any further amendments without inserting the amendments in the Bill, and any such suggested amendments shall be considered by the House of Lords, and, if agreed to by that House, shall be treated as amendments made by the House of Lords and agreed to by the House of Commons; but the exercise of this power by the House of Commons shall not affect the operation of this section in the event of the Bill being rejected by the House of Lords.

3 Certificate of Speaker

Any certificate of the Speaker of the House of Commons given under this Act shall be conclusive for all purposes, and shall not be questioned in any court of law.

4 Enacting words

(1) In every Bill presented to His Majesty under the preceding provisions of this Act, the words of enactment shall be as follows, that is to say:

"Be it enacted by the King's most Excellent Majesty, by and with the advice and consent of the Commons in this present Parliament assembled, in accordance with the provisions of [the Parliament Acts 1911 and 1949] and by authority of the same, as follows."

(2)   Any alteration of a Bill necessary to give effect to this section shall not be deemed to be an amendment of the Bill.

5 Provisional Order Bills excluded

In this Act the expression "Public Bill" does not include any Bill for confirming a Provisional Order.

6 Saving for existing rights and privileges of the House of Commons

Nothing in this Act shall diminish or qualify the existing rights and privileges of the House of Commons.

7 Duration of Parliament

Five years shall be substituted for seven years as the time fixed for the maximum duration of Parliament under the Septennial Act 1715.

8 Short title

This Act may be cited as the Parliament Act 1911.

PARLIAMENT ACT 1949

1949 chapter 103 12 13 and 14 Geo 6

An Act to amend the Parliament Act 1911. [16th December 1949]

1 Substitution of references to two sessions and one year for reference to three sessions and two years respectively

The Parliament Act, 1911, shall have effect, and shall be deemed to have had effect from the beginning of the session in which the Bill for this Act originated (save as regards that Bill itself), as if:

(a)   There had been substituted in subsections (1) and (4) of section two thereof, for the words "in three successive sessions", "for the third time", "in the third of those sessions", "in the third session", and "in the second or third session" respectively, the words " in two successive sessions", "for the second time", "in the second of those sessions", "in the second session", and "in the second session" respectively

(b)   There had been substituted in subsection (1)of the said section two, for the words "two years have elapsed" the words "one year has elapsed":

Provided that, if a Bill has been rejected for the second time by the House of Lords before the signification of the Royal Assent to the Bill for this Act, whether such rejection was in the same session as that in which the Royal Assent to the Bill for this Act was signified or in an earlier session, the requirement of the said section two that a Bill is to be presented to His Majesty on its rejection for the second time by the House of Lords shall have effect in relation to the Bill rejected as a requirement that it is to be presented to His Majesty as soon as the Royal Assent to the Bill for this Act has been signified, and, notwithstanding that such rejection was in an earlier session, the Royal Assent to the Bill rejected may be signified in the session in which the Royal Assent to the Bill for this Act was signified.

2 Short title, construction and citation

(1) This Act may be cited as the Parliament Act 1949.

(2) This Act and the Parliament Act 1911, shall be construed as one and may be cited together as the Parliament Acts 1911 and 1949, . . .

POLICE AND CRIMINAL EVIDENCE ACT 1984

(1984, chapter 60)

An Act to make further provision in relation to the powers and duties of the police, persons in police detention, criminal evidence, police discipline and complaints against the police; to provide for arrangements for obtaining the views of the community on policing and for a rank of deputy chief constable; to amend the law relating to the Police Federations and Police Forces and Police Cadets in Scotland; and for connected purposes. [31st October 1984]

41 Limits on period of detention without charge

(1) Subject to the following provisions of this section and to sections 42 and 43 below, a person shall not be kept in police detention for more than 24 hours without being charged.

(2) The time from which the period of detention of a person is to be calculated (in this Act referred to as "the relevant time") in:

(a) The case of a person to whom this paragraph applies, shall be the time:

(i) At which that person arrives at the relevant police station
(ii) 24 hours after the time of that person's arrest

Whichever is the earlier

(b) The case of a person arrested outside England and Wales, shall be:

(i) the time at which that person arrives at the first police station to which he is taken in the police area in England or Wales in which the offence for which he was arrested is being investigated

(ii) the time 24 hours after the time of that person's entry into England and Wales

Whichever is the earlier

(c) The case of a person who:

(i) attends voluntarily at a police station

(ii) accompanies a constable to a police station without having been arrested

And is arrested at the police station, the time of his arrest;

[(ca)in the case of a person who attends a police station to answer to bail granted under section 30A, the time when he arrives at the police station;]

(d) Any other case, except where subsection (5) below applies, shall be the time at which the person arrested arrives at the first police station to which he is taken after his arrest.

(3) Subsection (2)(a) above applies to a person if—

(a) his arrest is sought in one police area in England and Wales;

(b) he is arrested in another police area; and

(c) he is not questioned in the area in which he is arrested in order to obtain evidence in relation to an offence for which he is arrested;

and in sub-paragraph (i) of that paragraph "the relevant police station" means the first police station to which he is taken in the police area in which his arrest was sought.

(4) Subsection (2) above shall have effect in relation to a person arrested under section 31 above as if every reference in it to his arrest or his being arrested were a reference to his arrest or his being arrested for the offence for which he was originally arrested.

(5) If—

(a) a person is in police detention in a police area in England and Wales ("the first area"); and

(b) his arrest for an offence is sought in some other police area in England and Wales ("the second area"); and

(c) he is taken to the second area for the purposes of investigating that offence, without being questioned in the first area in order to obtain evidence in relation to it,

the relevant time shall be—

(i) the time 24 hours after he leaves the place where he is detained in the first area; or

(ii) the time at which he arrives at the first police station to which he is taken in the second area,

whichever is the earlier.

(6) When a person who is in police detention is removed to hospital because he is in need of medical treatment, any time during which he is being questioned in hospital or on the way there or back by a police officer for the purpose of obtaining evidence relating to an offence shall be included in any period which falls to be calculated for the purposes of this Part of this Act, but any other time while he is in hospital or on his way there or back shall not be so included.

(7) Subject to subsection (8) below, a person who at the expiry of 24 hours after the relevant time is in police detention and has not been charged shall be released at that time either on bail or without bail.

(8) Subsection (7) above does not apply to a person whose detention for more than 24 hours after the relevant time has been authorised or is otherwise permitted in accordance with section 42 or 43 below.

(9) A person released under subsection (7) above shall not be re-arrested without a warrant for the offence for which he was previously arrested unless new evidence justifying a further arrest has come to light since his release...

42 Authorisation of continued detention

(1) Where a police officer of the rank of superintendent or above who is responsible for the police station at which a person is detained has reasonable grounds for believing that:

(a) The detention of that person without charge is necessary to secure or preserve evidence relating to an offence for which he is under arrest or to obtain such evidence by questioning him

[(b) An offence for which he is under arrest is an [indictable] offence]

(c) The investigation is being conducted diligently and expeditiously

He may authorise the keeping of that person in police detention for a period expiring at or before 36 hours after the relevant time.

(2) Where an officer such as is mentioned in subsection (1) above has authorised the keeping of a person in police detention for a period expiring less than 36 hours after the relevant time, such an officer may authorise the keeping of that person in police detention for a further period expiring not more than 36 hours after that time if the conditions specified in subsection (1) above are still satisfied when he gives the authorisation.

(3) If it is proposed to transfer a person in police detention to another police area, the officer determining whether or not to authorise keeping him in detention under subsection (1) above shall have regard to the distance and the time the journey would take.

(4) No authorisation under subsection (1) above shall be given in respect of any person—

(a) more than 24 hours after the relevant time; or

(b) before the second review of his detention under section 40 above has been carried out.

(5) Where an officer authorises the keeping of a person in police detention under subsection (1) above, it shall be his duty—

(a) to inform that person of the grounds for his continued detention; and

(b) to record the grounds in that person's custody record.

(6) Before determining whether to authorise the keeping of a person in detention under subsection (1) or (2) above, an officer shall give:

(a) That person

(b) Any solicitor representing him who is available at the time when it falls to the officer to determine whether to give the authorisation

An opportunity to make representations to him about the detention.

(7) Subject to subsection (8) below, the person in detention or his solicitor may make representations under subsection (6) above either orally or in writing.

(8)   The officer to whom it falls to determine whether to give the authorisation may refuse to hear oral representations from the person in detention if he considers that he is unfit to make such representations by reason of his condition or behaviour.

(9)   Where—

(a)   an officer authorises the keeping of a person in detention under subsection (1) above; and

(b)   at the time of the authorisation he has not yet exercised a right conferred on him by section 56 or 58 below,

the officer—

(i)   shall inform him of that right;

(ii)   shall decide whether he should be permitted to exercise it;

(iii)   shall record the decision in his custody record; and

(iv)   if the decision is to refuse to permit the exercise of the right, shall also record the grounds for the decision in that record.

(10)   Where an officer has authorised the keeping of a person who has not been charged in detention under subsection (1) or (2) above, he shall be released from detention, either on bail or without bail, not later than 36 hours after the relevant time, unless:

(a)   He has been charged with an offence

(b)   His continued detention is authorised or otherwise permitted in accordance with section 43 below

(11)   A person released under subsection (10) above shall not be re-arrested without a warrant for the offence for which he was previously arrested unless new evidence justifying a further arrest has come to light since his release...

43 Warrants of further detention

(1)   Where, on an application on oath made by a constable and supported by an information, a magistrates' court is satisfied that there are reasonable grounds for believing that the further detention of the person to whom the application relates is justified, it may issue a warrant of further detention authorising the keeping of that person in police detention.

(2)   A court may not hear an application for a warrant of further detention unless the person to whom the application relates, has been:

(a)   Furnished with a copy of the information
(b)   Brought before the court for the hearing

(3)   The person to whom the application relates shall be entitled to be legally represented at the hearing and, if he is not so represented but wishes to be so represented:

(a)   The court shall adjourn the hearing to enable him to obtain representation
(b)   He may be kept in police detention during the adjournment

(4)   A person's further detention is only justified for the purposes of this section or section 44 below if:

   (a)   His detention without charge is necessary to secure or preserve evidence relating to an offence for which he is under arrest or to obtain such evidence by questioning him

   (b)   An offence for which he is under arrest is [an indictable offence]

   (c)   The investigation is being conducted diligently and expeditiously

(5)   Subject to subsection (7) below, an application for a warrant of further detention may be made—

   (a)   at any time before the expiry of 36 hours after the relevant time; or

   (b)   in a case where—

      (i)   it is not practicable for the magistrates' court to which the application will be made to sit at the expiry of 36 hours after the relevant time; but

      (ii)   the court will sit during the 6 hours following the end of that period,

   at any time before the expiry of the said 6 hours.

(6)   In a case to which subsection (5)(b) above applies—

   (a)   the person to whom the application relates may be kept in police detention until the application is heard; and

   (b)   the custody officer shall make a note in that person's custody record—

      (i)   of the fact that he was kept in police detention for more than 36 hours after the relevant time; and

      (ii)   of the reason why he was so kept.

(7)   If—

   (a)   an application for a warrant of further detention is made after the expiry of 36 hours after the relevant time; and

   (b)   it appears to the magistrates' court that it would have been reasonable for the police to make it before the expiry of that period,

(8)   Where on an application such as is mentioned in subsection (1) above a magistrates' court is not satisfied that there are reasonable grounds for believing that the further detention of the person to whom the application relates is justified, it shall be its duty to:

   (a)   Refuse the application

   (b)   Adjourn the hearing of it until a time not later than 36 hours after the relevant time

(9)   The person to whom the application relates may be kept in police detention during the adjournment.

(10)   A warrant of further detention shall:

   (a)   State the time at which it is issued

   (b)   Authorise the keeping in police detention of the person to whom it relates for the period stated in it

(11) Subject to subsection (12) below, the period stated in a warrant of further detention shall be such period as the magistrates' court thinks fit, having regard to the evidence before it.

(12) The period shall not be longer than 36 hours.

(13) If it is proposed to transfer a person in police detention to a police area other than that in which he is detained when the application for a warrant of further detention is made, the court hearing the application shall have regard to the distance and the time the journey would take.

(14) Any information submitted in support of an application under this section shall state—

    (a) the nature of the offence for which the person to whom the application relates has been arrested;

    (b) the general nature of the evidence on which that person was arrested;

    (c) what inquiries relating to the offence have been made by the police and what further inquiries are proposed by them;

    (d) the reasons for believing the continued detention of that person to be necessary for the purposes of such further inquiries.

(15) Where an application under this section is refused, the person to whom the application relates shall forthwith be charged or, subject to subsection (16) below, released, either on bail or without bail.

(16) A person need not be released under subsection (15) above, before the expiry of:

    (a) 24 hours after the relevant time

    (b) Any longer period for which his continued detention is or has been authorised under section 42 above

(17) Where an application under this section is refused, no further application shall be made under this section in respect of the person to whom the refusal relates, unless supported by evidence which has come to light since the refusal.

(18) Where a warrant of further detention is issued, the person to whom it relates shall be released from police detention, either on bail or without bail, upon or before the expiry of the warrant unless he is charged.

(19) A person released under subsection (18) above shall not be re-arrested without a warrant for the offence for which he was previously arrested unless new evidence justifying a further arrest has come to light since his release...

44 Extension of warrants of further detention

(1) On an application on oath made by a constable and supported by an information a magistrates' court may extend a warrant of further detention issued under section 43 above if it is satisfied that there are reasonable grounds for believing that the further detention of the person to whom the application relates is justified.

(2) Subject to subsection (3) below, the period for which a warrant of further detention may be extended shall be such period as the court thinks fit, having regard to the evidence before it.

(3) The period shall not:

   (a) Be longer than 36 hours
   (b) End later than 96 hours after the relevant time

(4) Where a warrant of further detention has been extended under subsection (1) above, or further extended under this subsection, for a period ending before 96 hours after the relevant time, on an application such as is mentioned in that subsection a magistrates' court may further extend the warrant if it is satisfied as there mentioned; and subsections (2) and (3) above apply to such further extensions as they apply to extensions under subsection (1) above.

(5) A warrant of further detention shall, if extended or further extended under this section, be endorsed with a note of the period of the extension.

(6) Subsections (2), (3) and (14) of section 43 above shall apply to an application made under this section as they apply to an application made under that section.

(7) Where an application under this section is refused, the person to whom the application relates shall forthwith be charged or, subject to subsection (8) below, released, either on bail or without bail.

(8) A person need not be released under subsection (7) above before the expiry of any period for which a warrant of further detention issued in relation to him has been extended or further extended on an earlier application made under this section.

45 Detention before charge—supplementary

(1) In sections 43 and 44 of this Act "magistrates' court" means a court consisting of two or more justices of the peace sitting otherwise than in open court.

(2) Any reference in this Part of this Act to a period of time or a time of day is to be treated as approximate only.

58 Access to legal advice

(1) A person arrested and held in custody in a police station or other premises shall be entitled, if he so requests, to consult a solicitor privately at any time.

(2) Subject to subsection (3) below, a request under subsection (1) above and the time at which it was made shall be recorded in the custody record.

(3) Such a request need not be recorded in the custody record of a person who makes it at a time while he is at a court after being charged with an offence.

(4) If a person makes such a request, he must be permitted to consult a solicitor as soon as is practicable except to the extent that delay is permitted by this section.

(5) In any case he must be permitted to consult a solicitor within 36 hours from the relevant time, as defined in section 41(2) above.

(6) Delay in compliance with a request is only permitted:

   (a) In the case of a person who is in police detention for [an indictable offence]
   (b) If an officer of at least the rank of superintendent authorises it

(7) *****

(8)   Subject to sub-section (8A) below An officer may only authorise delay where he has reasonable grounds for believing that the exercise of the right conferred by subsection (1) above at the time when the person detained desires to exercise it—

(a)   will lead to interference with or harm to evidence connected with an indictable offence or interference with or physical injury to other persons; or

(b)   will lead to the alerting of other persons suspected of having committed such an offence but not yet arrested for it; or

(c)   will hinder the recovery of any property obtained as a result of such an offence.

(8A)   An officer may also authorise delay where he has reasonable grounds for believing that—

(a)   the person detained for the indictable offence has benefited from his criminal conduct, and

(b)   the recovery of the value of the property constituting the benefit will be hindered by the exercise of the right conferred by subsection (1) above.

(8B)   For the purposes of subsection (8A) above the question whether a person has benefited from his criminal conduct is to be decided in accordance with Part 2 of the Proceeds of Crime Act 2002.]

(9)   If delay is authorised the:

(a)   Detained person shall be told the reasons for it
(b)   Reason shall be noted on his custody record.

(10)   The duties imposed by subsection (9) above shall be performed as soon as is practicable.

(11)   There may be no further delay in permitting the exercise of the right conferred by subsection (1) above once the reason for authorising delay ceases to subsist.

[(12)   Nothing in this section applies to a person arrested or detained under the terrorism provisions.]

Confessions

76 Confessions

(1)   In any proceedings a confession made by an accused person may be given in evidence against him in so far as it is relevant to any matter in issue in the proceedings and is not excluded by the court in pursuance of this section.

(2)   If, in any proceedings where the prosecution proposes to give in evidence a confession made by an accused person, it is represented to the court that the confession was or may have been obtained:

(a)   By oppression of the person who made it

(b)   In consequence of anything said or done which was likely, in the circumstances existing at the time, to render unreliable any confession which might be made by him in consequence thereof

The court shall not allow the confession to be given in evidence against him except in so far as the prosecution proves to the court beyond reasonable doubt that the confession (notwithstanding that it may be true) was not obtained as aforesaid.

(3)   In any proceedings where the prosecution proposes to give in evidence a confession made by an accused person, the court may of its own motion require the prosecution, as a condition of allowing it to do so, to prove that the confession was not obtained as mentioned in subsection (2) above.

(4)   The fact that a confession is wholly or partly excluded in pursuance of this section shall not affect the admissibility in evidence:

(a)   Of any facts discovered as a result of the confession

(b)   Where the confession is relevant as showing that the accused speaks, writes or expresses himself in a particular way, of so much of the confession as is necessary to show that he does so

(5)   Evidence that a fact to which this subsection applies was discovered as a result of a statement made by an accused person shall not be admissible unless evidence of how it was discovered is given by him or on his behalf.

(6)   Subsection (5) above applies to any fact discovered as a result of a confession which is:

(a)   Wholly excluded in pursuance of this section

(b)   Partly so excluded, if the fact is discovered as a result of the excluded part of the confession

(7)   Nothing in Part VII of this Act shall prejudice the admissibility of a confession made by an accused person.

(8)   In this section "oppression" includes torture, inhuman or degrading treatment, and the use or threat of violence (whether or not amounting to torture).

(9)   Where the proceedings mentioned in subsection (1) above are proceedings before a magistrates' court inquiring into an offence as examining justices this section shall have effect with the omission of—

(a)   in subsection (1) the words "and is not excluded by the court in pursuance of this section", and

(b)   subsections (2) to (6) and (8).]

Miscellaneous

78 Exclusion of unfair evidence

(1)   In any proceedings the court may refuse to allow evidence on which the prosecution proposes to rely to be given if it appears to the court that, having regard to all the circumstances, including the circumstances in which the evidence was obtained, the admission of the evidence would have such an adverse effect on the fairness of the proceedings that the court ought not to admit it.

(2) Nothing in this section shall prejudice any rule of law requiring a court to exclude evidence.

(3) This section shall not apply in the case of proceedings before a magistrates' court inquiring into an offence as examining justices.

CODE C CODE OF PRACTICE FOR THE DETENTION, TREATMENT AND QUESTIONING OF PERSONS BY POLICE OFFICERS

6 Right to legal advice

(a) Action

6.1 Unless *Annex B* applies, all detainees must be informed that they may at any time consult and communicate privately with a solicitor, whether in person, in writing or by telephone, and that free independent legal advice is available. See *paragraph 3.1*.

6.2 Not Used

6.3 A poster advertising the right to legal advice must be prominently displayed in the charging area of every police station.

6.4 No police officer should, at any time, do or say anything with the intention of dissuading a detainee from obtaining legal advice.

6.5 The exercise of the right of access to legal advice may be delayed only as in *Annex B*.

Whenever legal advice is requested, and unless *Annex B* applies, the custody officer must act without delay to secure the provision of such advice. If, on being informed or reminded of this right, the detainee declines to speak to a solicitor in person, the officer should point out that the right includes the right to speak with a solicitor on the telephone. If the detainee continues to waive this right the officer should ask them why and any reasons should be recorded on the custody record or the interview record as appropriate. Reminders of the right to legal advice must be given as in *paragraphs 3.5, 11.2, 15.4, 16.4, 2B of Annex A, 3 of Annex K* and *16.5* and Code D, *paragraphs 3.17(ii)* and *6.3*. Once it is clear a detainee does not want to speak to a solicitor in person or by telephone they should cease to be asked their reasons. See *Note 6K*

6.5A In the case of a juvenile, an appropriate adult should consider whether legal advice from a solicitor is required. If the juvenile indicates that they do not want legal advice, the appropriate adult has the right to ask for a solicitor to attend if this would be in the best interests of the person. However, the detained person cannot be forced to see the solicitor if he is adamant that he does not wish to do so.

6.6 A detainee who wants legal advice may not be interviewed or continue to be interviewed until they have received such advice unless:

(a) *Annex B* applies, when the restriction on drawing adverse inferences from silence in *Annex C* will apply because the detainee is not allowed an opportunity to consult a solicitor

(b)   An officer of superintendent rank or above has reasonable grounds for believing that:

   (i)   The consequent delay might:

      –   Lead to interference with, or harm to, evidence connected with an offence

      –   Lead to interference with, or physical harm to, other people

      –   Lead to serious loss of, or damage to, property

      –   Lead to alerting other people suspected of having committed an offence but not yet arrested for it

      –   Hinder the recovery of property obtained in consequence of the commission of an offence

   (ii)   When a solicitor, including a duty solicitor, has been contacted and has agreed to attend, awaiting their arrival would cause unreasonable delay to the process of investigation.

   Note: In these cases the restriction on drawing adverse inferences from silence in *Annex C* will apply because the detainee is not allowed an opportunity to consult a solicitor.

(c)   The solicitor the detainee has nominated or selected from a list:

   (i)   Cannot be contacted

   (ii)   Has previously indicated they do not wish to be contacted

   (iii)   Having been contacted, has declined to attend; and the detainee has been advised of the Duty Solicitor Scheme but has declined to ask for the duty solicitor

   In these circumstances the interview may be started or continued without further delay provided an officer of inspector rank or above has agreed to the interview proceeding.

   Note: The restriction on drawing adverse inferences from silence in Annex C will not apply because the detainee is allowed an opportunity to consult the duty solicitor.

(d)   The detainee changes their mind, about wanting legal advice

   In these circumstances the interview may be started or continued without delay provided that:

   (i)   The detainee agrees to do so, in writing or on the interview record made in accordance with Code E or F

(d)   The detainee changes their mind, about wanting legal advice.

   In these circumstances the interview may be started or continued without delay provided that:

   (i)   The detainee agrees to do so, in writing or on the interview record made in accordance with Code E or F; and

   (ii)   An officer of inspector rank or above has inquired about the detainee's reasons for their change of mind and gives authority for the interview to proceed.

Confirmation of the detainee's agreement, their change of mind, the reasons for it if given and, subject to *paragraph 2.6A*, the name of the authorising officer shall be recorded in the written interview record or the interview record made in accordance with Code E or F. See *Note 6I*.

Confirmation of the detainee's agreement, their change of mind, the reasons for it if given and, subject to paragraph 2.6A, the name of the authorising officer shall be recorded in the written interview record or the interview record made in accordance with Code E or F. Note: In these circumstances the restriction on drawing adverse inferences from silence in *Annex C* will not apply because the detainee is allowed an opportunity to consult a solicitor if they wish.

6.7   If *paragraph 6.6(b)(i)* applies, once sufficient information has been obtained to avert the risk, questioning must cease until the detainee has received legal advice unless *paragraph 6.6(a), (b)(ii), (c) or (d) applies.*

6.8   A detainee who has been permitted to consult a solicitor shall be entitled on request to have the solicitor present when they are interviewed unless one of the exceptions in *paragraph 6.6* applies.

6.9   The solicitor may only be required to leave the interview if their conduct is such that the interviewer is unable properly to put questions to the suspect. See *Notes 6D and 6E*

6.10   If the interviewer considers a solicitor is acting in such a way, they will stop the interview and consult an officer not below superintendent rank, if one is readily available, and otherwise an officer not below inspector rank not connected with the investigation. After speaking to the solicitor, the officer consulted will decide if the interview should continue in the presence of that solicitor. If they decide it should not, the suspect will be given the opportunity to consult another solicitor before the interview continues and that solicitor given an opportunity to be present at the interview. See *Note 6E*

6.11   The removal of a solicitor from an interview is a serious step and, if it occurs, the officer of superintendent rank or above who took the decision will consider if the incident should be reported to the Law Society. If the decision to remove the solicitor has been taken by an officer below superintendent rank, the facts must be reported to an officer of superintendent rank or above who will similarly consider whether a report to the Law Society would be appropriate. When the solicitor concerned is a duty solicitor, the report should be both to the Law Society and to the Legal Services Commission.

6.12   'Solicitor' in this Code means:

- a solicitor who holds a current practising certificate

- an accredited or probationary representative included on the register of representatives maintained by the Legal Services Commission.

6.12A   An accredited or probationary representative sent to provide advice by, and on behalf of, a solicitor shall be admitted to the police station for this purpose unless an officer of inspector rank or above considers such a visit will hinder the investigation and directs otherwise. Hindering the investigation does not include giving proper legal advice to a detainee as in *Note 6D*. Once admitted to the police station, *paragraphs 6.6 to 6.10* apply.

6.13 In exercising their discretion under *paragraph 6.12A*, the officer should take into account in particular:

- whether:
    - the identity and status of an accredited or probationary representative have been satisfactorily established;
    - they are of suitable character to provide legal advice, e.g. a person with a criminal record is unlikely to be suitable unless the conviction was for a minor offence and not recent.
- any other matters in any written letter of authorisation provided by the solicitor on whose behalf the person is attending the police station. See *Note 6F*

6.14 If the inspector refuses access to an accredited or probationary representative or a decision is taken that such a person should not be permitted to remain at an interview, the inspector must notify the solicitor on whose behalf the representative was acting and give them an opportunity to make alternative arrangements. The detainee must be informed and the custody record noted.

6.15 If a solicitor arrives at the station to see a particular person, that person must, unless *Annex B* applies, be so informed whether or not they are being interviewed and asked if they would like to see the solicitor. This applies even if the detainee has declined legal advice or, having requested it, subsequently agreed to be interviewed without receiving advice. The solicitor's attendance and the detainee's decision must be noted in the custody record.

(b) Documentation

6.16 Any request for legal advice and the action taken shall be recorded.

6.17 A record shall be made in the interview record if a detainee asks for legal advice and an interview is begun either in the absence of a solicitor or their representative, or they have been required to leave an interview.

Notes for guidance

6A In considering if paragraph 6.6(b) applies, the officer should, if practicable, ask the solicitor for an estimate of how long it will take to come to the station and relate this to the time detention is permitted, the time of day (i.e. whether the rest period under paragraph 12.2 is imminent) and the requirements of other investigations. If the solicitor is on their way or is to set off immediately, it will not normally be appropriate to begin an interview before they arrive. If it appears necessary to begin an interview before the solicitor's arrival, they should be given an indication of how long the police would be able to wait before 6.6(b) applies so there is an opportunity to make arrangements for someone else to provide legal advice.

6B A detainee who asks for legal advice to be paid for by himself should be given an opportunity to consult a specific solicitor or another solicitor from that solicitor's firm. If this solicitor is unavailable by these means, they may choose up to two alternatives. If these attempts are unsuccessful, the custody officer has discretion to allow further attempts until a solicitor has been contacted and agrees to provide legal advice. Otherwise, publicly funded legal advice shall in the first instance be accessed by telephoning a call centre authorised by the Legal Services Commission (LSC) to deal with calls from the police station. The Defence Solicitor Call Centre will determine whether legal advice should be limited to telephone advice or whether a solicitor should attend. Legal advice will be by telephone if a detainee is:

- Detained for a non-imprisonable offence

- Arrested on a bench warrant for failing to appear and being held for production before the court (except where the solicitor has clear documentary evidence available that would result in the client being released from custody)

- Arrested on suspicion of driving with excess alcohol (failure to provide a specimen, driving whilst unfit/drunk in charge of a motor vehicle)

- Detained in relation to breach of police or court bail conditions

An attendance by a solicitor for an offence suitable for telephone advice will depend on whether limited exceptions apply, such as whether the:

- Police are going to carry out an interview or an identification parade
- Detainee is eligible for assistance from an appropriate adult
- Detainee is unable to communicate over the telephone
- Detainee alleges serious maltreatment by the police

Apart from carrying out these duties, an officer must not advise the suspect about any particular firm of solicitors.

6C   Not Used

6D   A detainee has a right to free legal advice and to be represented by a solicitor. Legal advice by telephone advice may be provided in respect of those offences listed in Note for Guidance 6B1 and 6B2 above. The Defence Solicitor Call Centre will determine whether attendance is required by a solicitor. The solicitor's only role in the police station is to protect and advance the legal rights of their client. On occasions this may require the solicitor to give advice which has the effect of the client avoiding giving evidence which strengthens a prosecution case. The solicitor may intervene in order to seek clarification, challenge an improper question to their client or the manner in which it is put, advise their client not to reply to particular questions, or if they wish to give their client further legal advice. Paragraph 6.9 only applies if the solicitor's approach or conduct prevents or unreasonably obstructs proper questions being put to the suspect or the suspect's response being recorded. Examples of unacceptable conduct include answering questions on a suspect's behalf or providing written replies for the suspect to quote.

6E   An officer who takes the decision to exclude a solicitor must be in a position to satisfy the court the decision was properly made. In order to do this they may need to witness what is happening.

6F   If an officer of at least inspector rank considers a particular solicitor or firm of solicitors is persistently sending probationary representatives who are unsuited to provide legal advice, they should inform an officer of at least superintendent rank, who may wish to take the matter up with the Law Society.

6G   Subject to the constraints of Annex B, a solicitor may advise more than one client in an investigation if they wish. Any question of a conflict of interest is for the solicitor under their professional code of conduct. If, however, waiting for a solicitor to give advice to one client may lead to unreasonable delay to the interview with another, the provisions of paragraph 6.6(b) may apply.

6H   In addition to a poster in English, a poster or posters containing translations into Welsh, the main minority ethnic languages and the principal European languages should be displayed wherever they are likely to be helpful and it is practicable to do so.

6I   Paragraph 6.6(d) requires the authorisation of an officer of inspector rank or above to the continuation of an interview when a detainee who wanted legal advice changes their mind. It is permissible for such authorisation to be given over the telephone, if the authorising officer is able to satisfy themselves about the reason for the detainee's change of mind and is satisfied it is proper to continue the interview in those circumstances.

6J   Whenever a detainee exercises their right to legal advice by consulting or communicating with a solicitor, they must be allowed to do so in private. This right to consult or communicate in private is fundamental. If the requirement for privacy is compromised because what is said or written by the detainee or solicitor for the purpose of giving and receiving legal advice is overheard, listened to, or read by others without the informed consent of the detainee, the right will effectively have been denied. When a detainee chooses to speak to a solicitor on the telephone, they should be allowed to do so in private unless this is impractical because of the design and layout of the custody area or the location of telephones. However, the normal expectation should be that facilities will be available, unless they are being used, at all police stations to enable detainees to speak in private to a solicitor either face to face or over the telephone.

6K   A detainee is not obliged to give reasons for declining legal advice and should not be pressed to do so.

8 Conditions of detention

(a) Action

8.1   So far as it is practicable, not more than one detainee should be detained in each cell.

8.2   Cells in use must be adequately heated, cleaned and ventilated. They must be adequately lit, subject to such dimming as is compatible with safety and security to allow people detained overnight to sleep. No additional restraints shall be used within a locked cell unless absolutely necessary and then only restraint equipment, approved for use in that force by the Chief Officer, which is reasonable and necessary in the circumstances having regard to the detainee's demeanour and with a view to ensuring their safety and the safety of others. If a detainee is deaf, mentally disordered or otherwise mentally vulnerable, particular care must be taken when deciding whether to use any form of approved restraints.

8.3   Blankets, mattresses, pillows and other bedding supplied shall be of a reasonable standard and in a clean and sanitary condition.

8.4   Access to toilet and washing facilities must be provided.

8.5   If it is necessary to remove a detainee's clothes for the purposes of investigation, for hygiene, health reasons or cleaning, replacement clothing of a reasonable standard of comfort and cleanliness shall be provided. A detainee may not be interviewed unless adequate clothing has been offered.

8.6 At least two light meals and one main meal should be offered in any 24 hour period. Drinks should be provided at meal times and upon reasonable request between meals. Whenever necessary, advice shall be sought from the appropriate health care professional. As far as practicable, meals provided shall offer a varied diet and meet any specific dietary needs or religious beliefs the detainee may have. The detainee may, at the custody officer's discretion, have meals supplied by their family or friends at their expense.

8.7 Brief outdoor exercise shall be offered daily if practicable.

8.8 A juvenile shall not be placed in a police cell unless no other secure accommodation is available and the custody officer considers it is not practicable to supervise them if they are not placed in a cell or that a cell provides more comfortable accommodation than other secure accommodation in the station. A juvenile may not be placed in a cell with a detained adult.

(b) Documentation

8.9 A record must be kept of replacement clothing and meals offered.

8.10 If a juvenile is placed in a cell, the reason must be recorded.

8.11 The use of any restraints on a detainee whilst in a cell, the reasons for it and, if appropriate, the arrangements for enhanced supervision

Notes for guidance

8A The provisions in paragraph 8.3 and 8.6 respectively are of particular importance in the case of a person likely to be detained for an extended period. In deciding whether to allow meals to be supplied by family or friends, the custody officer is entitled to take account of the risk of items being concealed in any food or package and the officer's duties and responsibilities under food handling legislation.

8B Meals should, so far as practicable, be offered at recognised meal times, or at other times that take account of when the detainee last had a meal.

9 Care and treatment of detained persons

(a) General

9.1 Nothing in this section prevents the police from calling the police surgeon or, if appropriate, some other health care professional, to examine a detainee for the purposes of obtaining evidence relating to any offence in which the detainee is suspected of being involved. See Note 9A

9.2 If a complaint is made by, or on behalf of, a detainee about their treatment since their arrest, or it comes to notice that a detainee may have been treated improperly, a report must be made as soon as practicable to an officer of inspector rank or above not connected with the investigation. If the matter concerns a possible assault or the possibility of the unnecessary or unreasonable use of force, an appropriate health care professional must also be called as soon as practicable.

9.3 Detainees should be visited at least every hour. If no reasonably foreseeable risk was identified in a risk assessment, see paragraphs 3.6 – 3.10, there is no need to wake a sleeping detainee. Those suspected of being intoxicated through drink or drugs or having swallowed drugs, see

Note 9CA, or whose level of consciousness causes concern must, subject to any clinical directions given by the appropriate health care professional, see paragraph 9.13:

- be visited and roused at least every half hour
- have their condition assessed as in *Annex H*
- and clinical treatment arranged if appropriate

See Notes 9B, 9C and 9H

9.4   When arrangements are made to secure clinical attention for a detainee, the custody officer must make sure all relevant information which might assist in the treatment of the detainee's condition is made available to the responsible health care professional. This applies whether or not the health care professional asks for such information. Any officer or police

(b) Clinical treatment and attention

9.5   The custody officer must make sure a detainee receives appropriate clinical attention as soon as reasonably practicable if the person:

(a)   Appears to be suffering from physical illness
(b)   Is injured
(c)   Appears to be suffering from a mental disorder
(d)   Appears to need clinical attention

9.5A   This applies even if the detainee makes no request for clinical attention and whether or not they have already received clinical attention elsewhere. If the need for attention appears urgent, e.g. when indicated as in *Annex H*, the nearest available health care professional or an ambulance must be called immediately.

9.5B   The custody officer must also consider the need for clinical attention as set out in Note for Guidance 9C in relation to those suffering the effects of alcohol or drugs.

9.6   *Paragraph 9.5* is not meant to prevent or delay the transfer to a hospital if necessary of a person detained under the Mental Health Act 1983, section 136. See *Note 9D*. When an assessment under that Act takes place at a police station, see *paragraph 3.16*, the custody officer must consider whether an appropriate health care professional should be called to conduct an initial clinical check on the detainee. This applies particularly when there is likely to be any significant delay in the arrival of a suitably qualified medical practitioner.

9.7   If it appears to the custody officer, or they are told, that a person brought to a station under arrest may be suffering from an infectious disease or condition, the custody officer must take reasonable steps to safeguard the health of the detainee and others at the station. In deciding what action to take, advice must be sought from an appropriate health care professional. See *Note 9E*. The custody officer has discretion to isolate the person and their property until clinical directions have been obtained.

9.8   If a detainee requests a clinical examination, an appropriate health care professional must be called as soon as practicable to assess the detainee's clinical needs. If a safe and appropriate care plan cannot be provided, the police surgeon's advice must be sought. The detainee may also be examined by a medical practitioner of their choice at their expense.

9.9   If a detainee is required to take or apply any medication in compliance with clinical directions prescribed before their detention, the custody officer must consult the appropriate health care professional before the use of the medication. Subject to the restrictions in *paragraph 9.10*, the custody officer is responsible for the safekeeping of any medication and for making sure the detainee is given the opportunity to take or apply prescribed or approved medication. Any such consultation and its outcome shall be noted in the custody record.

9.10 No police officer may administer or supervise the self-administration of medically prescribed controlled drugs of the types and forms listed in the Misuse of Drugs Regulations 2001, Schedule 2 or 3. A detainee may only self-administer such drugs under the personal supervision of the registered medical practitioner authorising their use. Drugs listed in Schedule 4 or 5 may be distributed by the custody officer for self-administration if they have consulted the registered medical practitioner authorising their use, this may be done by telephone, and both parties are satisfied self-administration will not expose the detainee, police officers or anyone else to the risk of harm or injury.

Codes of practice – Code C Detention, treatment and questioning of persons by police officers 31 C

9.11 When appropriate health care professionals administer drugs or other medications, or supervise their self-administration, it must be within current medicines legislation and the scope of practice as determined by their relevant professional body.

9.12 If a detainee has in their possession, or claims to need, medication relating to a heart condition, diabetes, epilepsy or a condition of comparable potential seriousness then, even though *paragraph 9.5* may not apply, the advice of the appropriate health care professional must be obtained.

9.13 Whenever the appropriate health care professional is called in accordance with this section to examine or treat a detainee, the custody officer shall ask for their opinion about:

- any risks or problems which police need to take into account when making decisions about the detainee's continued detention;

- when to carry out an interview if applicable; and

- the need for safeguards.

9.14 When clinical directions are given by the appropriate health care professional, whether orally or in writing, and the custody officer has any doubts or is in any way uncertain about any aspect of the directions, the custody officer shall ask for clarification. It is particularly important that directions concerning the frequency of visits are clear, precise and capable of being implemented. See *Note 9F*.

(c) Documentation

9.15 A record must be made in the custody record of:

(a)   the arrangements made for an examination by an appropriate health care professional under *paragraph 9.2* and of any complaint reported under that paragraph together with any relevant remarks by the custody officer;

(b)   any arrangements made in accordance with *paragraph 9.5*;

(c)   any request for a clinical examination under *paragraph 9.8* and any arrangements made in response;

(d)   the injury, ailment, condition or other reason which made it necessary to make the arrangements in (a) to (c), *see Note 9G*;

(e)   any clinical directions and advice, including any further clarifications, given to police by a health care professional concerning the care and treatment of the detainee in connection with any of the arrangements made in (a) to (c), *see Note 9F; Codes of practice – Code C Detention, treatment and questioning of persons by police officers* 32 **C**

(f)   if applicable, the responses received when attempting to rouse a person using the procedure in *Annex H, see Note 9H*.

9.16 If a health care professional does not record their clinical findings in the custody record, the record must show where they are recorded. See *Note 9G*. However, information which is necessary to custody staff to ensure the effective ongoing care and well being of the detainee must be recorded openly in the custody record, see *paragraph 3.8* and *Annex G, paragraph 7*.

9.17 Subject to the requirements of *Section 4*, the custody record shall include:

- a record of all medication a detainee has in their possession on arrival at the police station;

- a note of any such medication they claim to need but do not have with them.

Notes for guidance

9A   A 'health care professional' means a clinically qualified person working within the scope of practice as determined by their relevant professional body. Whether a health care professional is 'appropriate' depends on the circumstances of the duties they carry out at the time.

9B   Whenever possible juveniles and mentally vulnerable detainees should be visited more frequently.

9C   A detainee who appears drunk or behaves abnormally may be suffering from illness, the effects of drugs or may have sustained injury, particularly a head injury which is not apparent. A detainee needing or dependent on certain drugs, including alcohol, may experience harmful effects within a short time of being deprived of their supply. In these circumstances, when there is any doubt, police should always act urgently to call an appropriate health care professional or an ambulance. Paragraph 9.5 does not apply to minor ailments or injuries which do not need attention. However, all such ailments or injuries must be recorded in the custody record and any doubt must be resolved in favour of calling the appropriate health care professional.

9CA Paragraph 9.3 would apply to a person in police custody by order of a magistrates' court under the Criminal Justice Act 1988, section 152 (as amended by the Drugs Act 2005, section 8) to facilitate the recovery of evidence after being charged with drug possession or drug trafficking and suspected of having swallowed drugs. In the case of the healthcare needs of a person who has swallowed drugs, the custody officer subject to any clinical directions, should consider the necessity for rousing every half hour. This does not negate the need for regular visiting of the suspect in the cell.

Codes of practice – Code C Detention, treatment and questioning of persons by police officers 33 C

9D   Whenever practicable, arrangements should be made for persons detained for assessment under the Mental Health Act 1983, section 136 to be taken to a hospital. There is no power under that Act to transfer a person detained under section 136 from one place of safety to another place of safety for assessment.

9E   It is important to respect a person's right to privacy and information about their health must be kept confidential and only disclosed with their consent or in accordance with clinical advice when it is necessary to protect the detainee's health or that of others who come into contact with them.

9F   The custody officer should always seek to clarify directions that the detainee requires constant observation or supervision and should ask the appropriate health care professional to explain precisely what action needs to be taken to implement such directions.

9G   Paragraphs 9.15 and 9.16 do not require any information about the cause of any injury, ailment or condition to be recorded on the custody record if it appears capable of providing evidence of an offence.

9H   The purpose of recording a person's responses when attempting to rouse them using the procedure in Annex H is to enable any change in the individual's consciousness level to be noted and clinical treatment arranged if appropriate.

Annex B – DELAY IN NOTIFYING ARREST OR ALLOWING ACCESS TO LEGAL ADVICE

A Persons detained under PACE

1   The exercise of the rights in *Section 5* or *Section 6,* or both, may be delayed if the person is in police detention, as in PACE, section 118(2), in connection with an indictable offence, has not yet been charged with an offence and an officer of superintendent rank or above, or inspector rank or above only for the rights in *Section 5*, has reasonable grounds for believing their exercise will:

    (a)   Lead to:

        (i)   Interference with, or harm to, evidence connected with an indictable offence

        (ii)   Interference with, or physical harm to, other people

    (b)   Lead to alerting other people suspected of having committed an indictable offence but not yet arrested for it

    (c)   Hinder the recovery of property obtained in consequence of the commission of such an offence

2   These rights may also be delayed if the officer has reasonable grounds to believe that the:

    (a)   Person detained for an indictable offence has benefited from their criminal conduct (decided in accordance with Part 2 of the Proceeds of Crime Act 2002)

(b)   Recovery of the value of the property constituting that benefit will be hindered by the exercise of either right

3   Authority to delay a detainee's right to consult privately with a solicitor may be given only if the authorising officer has reasonable grounds to believe the solicitor the detainee wants to consult will, inadvertently or otherwise, pass on a message from the detainee or act in some other way which will have any of the consequences specified under *paragraphs 1 or 2*. In these circumstances the detainee must be allowed to choose another solicitor.

4   If the detainee wishes to see a solicitor, access to that solicitor may not be delayed on the grounds they might advise the detainee not to answer questions or the solicitor was initially asked to attend the police station by someone else. In the latter case the detainee must be told the solicitor has come to the police station at another person's request, and must be asked to sign the custody record to signify whether they want to see the solicitor.

5   The fact the grounds for delaying notification of arrest may be satisfied does not automatically mean the grounds for delaying access to legal advice will also be satisfied.

6   These rights may be delayed only for as long as grounds exist and in no case beyond 36 hours after the relevant time as in PACE, section 41. If the grounds cease to apply within this time, the detainee must, as soon as practicable, be asked if they want to exercise either right, the custody record must be noted accordingly, and action taken in accordance with the relevant section of the Code.

7   A detained person must be permitted to consult a solicitor for a reasonable time before any court hearing.

PREVENTION OF TERRORISM ACT 2005

2005 chapter 2

An Act to provide for the making against individuals involved in terrorism-related activity of orders imposing obligations on them for purposes connected with preventing or restricting their further involvement in such activity; to make provision about appeals and other proceedings relating to such orders; and for connected purposes.[11th March 2005]

Control orders

1 Power to make control orders

(1)   In this Act "control order" means an order against an individual that imposes obligations on him for purposes connected with protecting members of the public from a risk of terrorism.

(2)   The power to make a control order against an individual shall be exercisable:

(a)   Except in the case of an order imposing obligations that are incompatible with the individual's right to liberty under Article 5 of the Human Rights Convention, by the Secretary of State

(b)   In the case of an order imposing obligations that are or include derogating obligations, by the court on an application by the Secretary of State

(3)   The obligations that may be imposed by a control order made against an individual are any obligations that the Secretary of State or (as the case may be) the court considers necessary for purposes connected with preventing or restricting involvement by that individual in terrorism-related activity.

(4)   Those obligations may include, in particular a:

(a)   Prohibition or restriction on his possession or use of specified articles or substances

(b)   Prohibition or restriction on his use of specified services or specified facilities, or on his carrying on specified activities

(c)   Restriction in respect of his work or other occupation, or in respect of his business

(d)   Restriction on his association or communications with specified persons or with other persons generally

(e)   Restriction in respect of his place of residence or on the persons to whom he gives access to his place of residence

(f)   Prohibition on his being at specified places or within a specified area at specified times or on specified days

(g)   Prohibition or restriction on his movements to, from or within the United Kingdom, a specified part of the United Kingdom or a specified place or area within the United Kingdom

(h)   Requirement on him to comply with such other prohibitions or restrictions on his movements as may be imposed, for a period not exceeding 24 hours, by directions given to him in the specified manner, by a specified person and for the purpose of securing compliance with other obligations imposed by or under the order

(i)   Requirement on him to surrender his passport, or anything in his possession to which a prohibition or restriction imposed by the order relates, to a specified person for a period not exceeding the period for which the order remains in force

(j)   Requirement on him to give access to specified persons to his place of residence or to other premises to which he has power to grant access

(k)   Requirement on him to allow specified persons to search that place or any such premises for the purpose of ascertaining whether obligations imposed by or under the order have been, are being or are about to be contravened

(l)   Requirement on him to allow specified persons, either for that purpose or for the purpose of securing that the order is complied with, to remove anything found in that place or on any such premises and to subject it to tests or to retain it for a period not exceeding the period for which the order remains in force

(m)   Requirement on him to allow himself to be photographed

(n)   Requirement on him to co-operate with specified arrangements for enabling his movements, communications or other activities to be monitored by electronic or other means

(o)   Requirement on him to comply with a demand made in the specified manner to provide information to a specified person in accordance with the demand

(p)   Requirement on him to report to a specified person at specified times and places

(5)   Power by or under a control order to prohibit or restrict the controlled person's movements includes, in particular, power to impose a requirement on him to remain at or within a particular place or area (whether for a particular period or at particular times or generally).

(6)   The reference in subsection (4)(n) to co-operating with specified arrangements for monitoring includes a reference to each of the following:

(a)   Submitting to procedures required by the arrangements

(b)   Wearing or otherwise using apparatus approved by or in accordance with the arrangements

(c)   Maintaining such apparatus in the specified manner

(d)   Complying with directions given by persons carrying out functions for the purposes of those arrangements

(7)   The information that the controlled person may be required to provide under a control order includes, in particular, advance information about his proposed movements or other activities.

(8)   A control order may provide for a prohibition, restriction or requirement imposed by or under the order to apply only where a specified person has not given his consent or approval to what would otherwise contravene the prohibition, restriction or requirement.

(9)   For the purposes of this Act involvement in terrorism-related activity is any one or more of the following:

(a)   The commission, preparation or instigation of acts of terrorism

(b)   Conduct which facilitates the commission, preparation or instigation of such acts, or which is intended to do so

(c)   Conduct which gives encouragement to the commission, preparation or instigation of such acts, or which is intended to do so

(d)   Conduct which gives support or assistance to individuals who are known or believed to be involved in terrorism-related activity

And for the purposes of this subsection it is immaterial whether the acts of terrorism in question are specific acts of terrorism or acts of terrorism generally.

(10) In this Act "derogating obligation" means an obligation on an individual which:

(a)   is incompatible with his right to liberty under Article 5 of the Human Rights Convention; but

(b)   Is of a description of obligations which, for the purposes of the designation of a designated derogation, is set out in the designation order

"Designated derogation" has the same meaning as in the Human Rights Act 1998 (c. 42) (see section 14(1) of that Act)

"Designation order", in relation to a designated derogation, means the order under section 14(1) of the Human Rights Act 1998 by which the derogation is designated

2 Making of non-derogating control orders

(1)   The Secretary of State may make a control order against an individual if he:

(a)   Has reasonable grounds for suspecting that the individual is or has been involved in terrorism-related activity

(b)   Considers that it is necessary, for purposes connected with protecting members of the public from a risk of terrorism, to make a control order imposing obligations on that individual

(2)   The Secretary of State may make a control order against an individual who is for the time being bound by a control order made by the court only if he does so:

(a)   After the court has determined that its order should be revoked

(b)   While the effect of the revocation has been postponed for the purpose of giving the Secretary of State an opportunity to decide whether to exercise his own powers to make a control order against the individual

(3)   A control order made by the Secretary of State is called a non-derogating control order.

(4)   A non-derogating control order:

(a)   Has effect for a period of 12 months beginning with the day on which it is made

(b)   May be renewed on one or more occasions in accordance with this section

(5)   A non-derogating control order must specify when the period for which it is to have effect will end.

(6)   The Secretary of State may renew a non-derogating control order (with or without modifications) for a period of 12 months if he considers that:

(a)   It is necessary, for purposes connected with protecting members of the public from a risk of terrorism, for an order imposing obligations on the controlled person to continue in force

(b)   The obligations to be imposed by the renewed order are necessary for purposes connected with preventing or restricting involvement by that person in terrorism-related activity

SCOTLAND ACT 1998

1998 chapter 46

An Act to provide for the establishment of a Scottish Parliament and Administration and other changes in the government of Scotland; to provide for changes in the constitution and functions of certain public authorities; to provide for the variation of the basic rate of income tax in relation to income of Scottish taxpayers in accordance with a resolution of the Scottish Parliament; to amend the law about parliamentary constituencies in Scotland; and for connected purposes. [19th November 1998]

Part I The Scottish Parliament

Legislation

28 Acts of the Scottish Parliament

(1)   Subject to section 29, the Parliament may make laws, to be known as Acts of the Scottish Parliament.

(2)   Proposed Acts of the Scottish Parliament shall be known as Bills; and a Bill shall become an Act of the Scottish Parliament when it has been passed by the Parliament and has received Royal Assent.

(3)   A Bill receives Royal Assent at the beginning of the day on which Letters Patent under the Scottish Seal signed with Her Majesty's own hand signifying Her Assent are recorded in the Register of the Great Seal.

(4)   The date of Royal Assent shall be written on the Act of the Scottish Parliament by the Clerk, and shall form part of the Act.

(5)   The validity of an Act of the Scottish Parliament is not affected by any invalidity in the proceedings of the Parliament leading to its enactment.

(6)   Every Act of the Scottish Parliament shall be judicially noticed.

(7)   This section does not affect the power of the Parliament of the United Kingdom to make laws for Scotland.

STATUTE OF WESTMINSTER 1931

1931 chapter 4 22 and 23 Geo 5

An Act to give effect to certain resolutions passed by Imperial Conferences held in the years 1926 and 1930. [11th December 1931]

Whereas the delegates of His Majesty's Governments in the United Kingdom, the Dominion of Canada, the Commonwealth of Australia, the Dominion of New Zealand, the Union of South Africa, the Irish Free State and Newfoundland, at Imperial Conferences holden at Westminster in the years of our Lord nineteen hundred and twenty-six and nineteen hundred and thirty did concur in making the declarations and resolutions set forth in the Reports of the said Conferences:

And whereas it is meet and proper to set out by way of preamble to this Act that, inasmuch as the Crown is the symbol of the free association of the members of the British Commonwealth of Nations, and as they are united by a common allegiance to the Crown, it would be in accord with the established constitutional position of all the members of the Commonwealth in relation to one another that any alteration in the law touching the Succession to the Throne or the Royal Style and Titles shall hereafter require the assent as well of the Parliaments of all the Dominions as of the Parliament of the United Kingdom:

And whereas it is in accord with the established constitutional position that no law hereafter made by the Parliament of the United Kingdom shall extend to any of the said Dominions as part of the law of that Dominion otherwise than at the request and with the consent of that Dominion:

And whereas it is necessary for the ratifying, confirming and establishing of certain of the said declarations and resolutions of the said Conferences that a law be made and enacted in due form by authority of the Parliament of the United Kingdom:

And whereas the Dominion of Canada, the Commonwealth of Australia, the Dominion of New Zealand, the Union of South Africa, the Irish Free State and Newfoundland have severally requested and consented to the submission of a measure to the Parliament of the United Kingdom for making such provision with regard to the matters aforesaid as is hereafter in this Act contained:

1 Meaning of "Dominion" in this Act

In this Act the expression "Dominion" means any of the following Dominions, that is to say, the Dominion of Canada, the Commonwealth of Australia, the Dominion of New Zealand, . . the Irish Free State and Newfoundland.

4 Parliament of United Kingdom not to legislate for Dominion except by consent

No Act of Parliament of the United Kingdom passed after the commencement of this Act shall extend, or be deemed to extend, to a Dominion as part of the law of that Dominion, unless it is expressly declared in that Act that that Dominion has requested, and consented to, the enactment thereof.

SENIOR COURTS ACT 1981

1981 chapter 54

An Act to consolidate with amendments the Supreme Court of Judicature (Consolidation) Act 1925 and other enactments relating to the Supreme Court in England and Wales and the administration of justice therein; to repeal certain obsolete or unnecessary enactments so relating; to amend Part VIII of the Mental Health Act 1959, the Courts-Martial (Appeals) Act 1968, the Arbitration Act 1979 and the law relating to county courts; and for connected purposes. [28th July 1981]

31 Application for judicial review

(1)   An application to the High Court for one or more of the following forms of relief, namely:

    (a)   A mandatory, prohibiting or quashing order

(b)   A declaration or injunction under subsection (2)

(c)   An injunction under section 30 restraining a person not entitled to do so from acting in an office to which that section applies

Shall be made in accordance with rules of court by a procedure to be known as an application for judicial review.

(2)   A declaration may be made or an injunction granted under this subsection in any case where an application for judicial review, seeking that relief, has been made and the High Court considers that, having regard to:

(a)   The nature of the matters in respect of which relief may be granted by [mandatory, prohibiting or quashing orders]

(b)   The nature of the persons and bodies against whom relief may be granted by such orders

(c)   All the circumstances of the case

It would be just and convenient for the declaration to be made or the injunction to be granted, as the case may be.

(3)   No application for judicial review shall be made unless the leave of the High Court has been obtained in accordance with rules of court; and the court shall not grant leave to make such an application unless it considers that the applicant has a sufficient interest in the matter to which the application relates.

(4)   On an application for judicial review the High Court may award to the applicant damages, restitution or the recovery of a sum if the:

(a)   Application includes a claim for such an award arising from any matter to which the application relates

(b)   Court is satisfied that such an award would have been made if the claim had been made in action begun by the applicant at the time of making the application]

(5)   If, on an application for judicial review seeking [a quashing order], the High Court quashes the decision to which the application relates, the High Court may remit the matter to the court, tribunal or authority concerned, with a direction to reconsider it and reach a decision in accordance with the findings of the High Court.

(6)   Where the High Court considers that there has been undue delay in making an application for judicial review, the court may refuse to grant:

(a)   Leave for the making of the application
(b)   Any relief sought on the application

If it considers that the granting of the relief sought would be likely to cause substantial hardship to, or substantially prejudice the rights of, any person or would be detrimental to good administration.

(7)   Subsection (6) is without prejudice to any enactment or rule of court which has the effect of limiting the time within which an application for judicial review may be made.

37 Powers of High Court with respect to injunctions and receivers

(1) The High Court may by order (whether interlocutory or final) grant an injunction or appoint a receiver in all cases in which it appears to the court to be just and convenient to do so.

(2) Any such order may be made either unconditionally or on such terms and conditions as the court thinks just.

(3) The power of the High Court under subsection (1) to grant an interlocutory injunction restraining a party to any proceedings from removing from the jurisdiction of the High Court, or otherwise dealing with, assets located within that jurisdiction shall be exercisable in cases where that party is, as well as in cases where he is not, domiciled, resident or present within that jurisdiction.

(4) The power of the High Court to appoint a receiver by way of equitable execution shall operate in relation to all legal estates and interests in land; and that power—

    (a) may be exercised in relation to an estate or interest in land whether or not a charge has been imposed on that land under section 1 of the Charging Orders Act 1979 for the purpose of enforcing the judgment, order or award in question; and

    (b) shall be in addition to, and not in derogation of, any power of any court to appoint a receiver in proceedings for enforcing such a charge.

(5) Where an order under the said section 1 imposing a charge for the purpose of enforcing a judgment, order or award has been, or has effect as if, registered under section 6 of the Land Charges Act 1972, subsection (4) of the said section 6 (effect of non-registration of writs and orders registrable under that section) shall not apply to an order appointing a receiver made either—

    (a) in proceedings for enforcing the charge; or

    (b) by way of equitable execution of the judgment, order or award or, as the case may be, of so much of it as requires payment of moneys secured by the charge.

TERRORISM ACT 2000

2000 chapter 11

An Act to make provision about terrorism; and to make temporary provision for Northern Ireland about the prosecution and punishment of certain offences, the preservation of peace and the maintenance of order.[20th July 2000]

Be it enacted by the Queen's most Excellent Majesty, by and with the advice and consent of the Lords Spiritual and Temporal, and Commons, in this present Parliament assembled, and by the authority of the same, as follows:

Part V Counter-terrorist Powers

Suspected terrorists

40 Terrorist: interpretation

(1)   In this Part "terrorist" means a person who:

(a)   Has committed an offence under any of sections 11, 12, 15 to 18, 54 and 56 to 63

(b)   Is or has been concerned in the commission, preparation or instigation of acts of terrorism

(2)   The reference in subsection (1)(b) to a person who has been concerned in the commission, preparation or instigation of acts of terrorism includes a reference to a person who has been, whether before or after the passing of this Act, concerned in the commission, preparation or instigation of acts of terrorism within the meaning given by section 1.

41 Arrest without warrant

(1)   A constable may arrest without a warrant a person whom he reasonably suspects to be a terrorist.

(2)   Where a person is arrested under this section the provisions of Schedule 8 (detention: treatment, review and extension) shall apply.

(3)   Subject to subsections (4) to (7), a person detained under this section shall (unless detained under any other power) be released not later than the end of the period of 48 hours beginning:

(a)   With the time of his arrest under this section

(b)   If he was being detained under Schedule 7 when he was arrested under this section, with the time when his examination under that Schedule began

(4)   If on a review of a person's detention under Part II of Schedule 8 the review officer does not authorise continued detention, the person shall (unless detained in accordance with subsection (5) or (6) or under any other power) be released.

(5)   Where a police officer intends to make an application for a warrant under paragraph 29 of Schedule 8 extending a person's detention, the person may be detained pending the making of the application.

(6)   Where an application has been made under paragraph 29 or 36 of Schedule 8 in respect of a person's detention, he may be detained pending the conclusion of proceedings on the application.

(7)   Where an application under paragraph 29 or 36 of Schedule 8 is granted in respect of a person's detention, he may be detained, subject to paragraph 37 of that Schedule, during the period specified in the warrant.

(8)   The refusal of an application in respect of a person's detention under paragraph 29 or 36 of Schedule 8 shall not prevent his continued detention in accordance with this section.

(9)   A person who has the powers of a constable in one Part of the United Kingdom may exercise the power under subsection (1) in any Part of the United Kingdom.

42 Search of premises

(1)   A justice of the peace may on the application of a constable issue a warrant in relation to specified premises if he is satisfied that there are reasonable grounds for suspecting that a person whom the constable reasonably suspects to be a person falling within section 40(1)(b) is to be found there.

(2)   A warrant under this section shall authorise any constable to enter and search the specified premises for the purpose of arresting the person referred to in subsection (1) under section 41.

(3)   In the application of subsection (1) to Scotland:

(a)   "Justice of the peace" includes the sheriff

(b)   The justice of the peace or sheriff can be satisfied as mentioned in that subsection only by having heard evidence on oath

43 Search of persons

(1)   A constable may stop and search a person whom he reasonably suspects to be a terrorist to discover whether he has in his possession anything which may constitute evidence that he is a terrorist.

(2)   A constable may search a person arrested under section 41 to discover whether he has in his possession anything which may constitute evidence that he is a terrorist.

(3)   A search of a person under this section must be carried out by someone of the same sex.

(4)   A constable may seize and retain anything which he discovers in the course of a search of a person under subsection (1) or (2) and which he reasonably suspects may constitute evidence that the person is a terrorist.

(5)   A person who has the powers of a constable in one Part of the United Kingdom may exercise a power under this section in any Part of the United Kingdom.

Power to stop and search

44 Authorisations

(1)   An authorisation under this subsection authorises any constable in uniform to stop a vehicle in an area or at a place specified in the authorisation and to search:

(a)   The vehicle
(b)   The driver of the vehicle
(c)   A passenger in the vehicle
(d)   Anything in or on the vehicle or carried by the driver or a passenger

(2)   An authorisation under this subsection authorises any constable in uniform to stop a pedestrian in an area or at a place specified in the authorisation and to search:

(a)   The pedestrian
(b)   Anything carried by him

(3)   An authorisation under subsection (1) or (2) may be given only if the person giving it considers it expedient for the prevention of acts of terrorism.

(4)   An authorisation may be given where the specified area or place is the whole or part of:

(a)   A police area outside Northern Ireland other than one mentioned in paragraph (b) or (c), by a police officer for the area who is of at least the rank of assistant chief constable

(b)   The metropolitan police district, by a police officer for the district who is of at least the rank of commander of the metropolitan police

(c)   The City of London, by a police officer for the City who is of at least the rank of commander in the City of London police force

(d)   Northern Ireland, by a member of the Royal Ulster Constabulary who is of at least the rank of assistant chief constable

[(4ZA) The power of a person mentioned in subsection (4) to give an authorisation specifying an area or place so mentioned includes power to give such an authorisation specifying such an area or place together with:
(a)   The internal waters adjacent to that area or place
(b)   Such area of those internal waters as is specified in the authorisation]

[[(4A) In a case (within subsection (4)(a), (b) or (c) in which the specified area or place is in a place described in section 34(1A), an authorisation may also be given by a member of the British Transport Police Force who is of at least the rank of assistant chief constable.]

(4B)   In a case in which the specified area or place is a place to which section 2(2) of the Ministry of Defence Police Act 1987 applies, an authorisation may also be given by a member of the Ministry of Defence Police who is of at least the rank of assistant chief constable.

[(4BA) In a case in which the specified area or place is a place in which members of the Civil Nuclear Constabulary have the powers and privileges of a constable, an authorisation may also be given by a member of that Constabulary who is of at least the rank of assistant chief constable.]

(4C)   But an authorisation may not be given by a member of the:

(a)   British Transport Police Force,. . .

(b)   Ministry of Defence Police

[(c)   Civil Nuclear Constabulary]

In any other case.]

(5)   If an authorisation is given orally, the person giving it shall confirm it in writing as soon as is reasonably practicable.

[(5A)   In this section:

(a)   "Driver", in relation to an aircraft, hovercraft or vessel, means the captain, pilot or other person with control of the aircraft, hovercraft or vessel or any member of its crew and, in relation to a train, includes any member of its crew

(b)   "Internal waters" means waters in the United Kingdom that are not comprised in any police area]

45 Exercise of power

(1)   The power conferred by an authorisation under section 44(1) or (2) may be exercised:

(a)   Only for the purpose of searching for articles of a kind which could be used in connection with terrorism

(b)   Whether or not the constable has grounds for suspecting the presence of articles of that kind

(2)   A constable may seize and retain an article which he discovers in the course of a search by virtue of section 44(1) or (2) and which he reasonably suspects is intended to be used in connection with terrorism.

(3)   A constable exercising the power conferred by an authorisation may not require a person to remove any clothing in public except for headgear, footwear, an outer coat, a jacket or gloves.

(4)   Where a constable proposes to search a person or vehicle by virtue of section 44(1) or (2) he may detain the person or vehicle for such time as is reasonably required to permit the search to be carried out at or near the place where the person or vehicle is stopped.

(5)   Where:

(a)   A vehicle or pedestrian is stopped by virtue of section 44(1) or (2)

(b)   The driver of the vehicle or the pedestrian applies for a written statement that the vehicle was stopped, or that he was stopped, by virtue of section 44(1) or (2)

The written statement shall be provided.

(6)   An application under subsection (5) must be made within the period of 12 months beginning with the date on which the vehicle or pedestrian was stopped.

[(7)   In this section "driver" has the same meaning as in section 44.]

46 Duration of authorisation

(1)   An authorisation under section 44 has effect, subject to subsections (2) to (7), during the period:

(a)   Beginning at the time when the authorisation is given
(b)   Ending with a date or at a time specified in the authorisation

(2)   The date or time specified under subsection (1)(b) must not occur after the end of the period of 28 days beginning with the day on which the authorisation is given.

[(2A) An authorisation under section 44(4BA) does not have effect except in relation to times when the specified area or place is a place where members of the Civil Nuclear Constabulary have the powers and privileges of a constable.]

(3)   The person who gives an authorisation shall inform the Secretary of State as soon as is reasonably practicable.

(4)   If an authorisation is not confirmed by the Secretary of State before the end of the period of 48 hours beginning with the time when it is given:

(a)   It shall cease to have effect at the end of that period

(b)   Its ceasing to have effect shall not affect the lawfulness of anything done in reliance on it before the end of that period

(5)   Where the Secretary of State confirms an authorisation he may substitute an earlier date or time for the date or time specified under subsection (1)(b).

(6)   The Secretary of State may cancel an authorisation with effect from a specified time.

(7)   An authorisation may be renewed in writing by the person who gave it or by a person who could have given it; and subsections (1) to (6) shall apply as if a new authorisation were given on each occasion on which the authorisation is renewed.

47 Offences

(1)   A person commits an offence if he:

(a)   Fails to stop a vehicle when required to do so by a constable in the exercise of the power conferred by an authorisation under section 44(1)

(b)   Fails to stop when required to do so by a constable in the exercise of the power conferred by an authorisation under section 44(2)

(c)   Wilfully obstructs a constable in the exercise of the power conferred by an authorisation under section 44(1) or (2)

(2)   A person guilty of an offence under this section shall be liable on summary conviction to:

(a)   Imprisonment for a term not exceeding six months
(b)   A fine not exceeding level 5 on the standard scale
(c)   Both

TERRORISM ACT 2006

2006 chapter 11

An Act to make provision for and about offences relating to conduct carried out, or capable of being carried out, for purposes connected with terrorism; to amend enactments relating to terrorism; to amend the Intelligence Services Act 1994 and the Regulation of Investigatory Powers Act 2000; and for connected purposes.[30th March 2006]

23 Extension of period of detention of terrorist suspects

(1)   Schedule 8 to the Terrorism Act 2000 (c. 11) (detention of terrorist suspects) is amended as follows.

(2)   In sub-paragraph (1) of each of paragraphs 29 and 36 (applications by a superintendent or above for a warrant extending detention or for the extension of the period of such a warrant), for the words from the beginning to "may" substitute—

"(1)   Each of the following—

(a)   in England and Wales, a Crown Prosecutor,

(b)   in Scotland, the Lord Advocate or a procurator fiscal,

(c)   in Northern Ireland, the Director of Public Prosecutions for Northern Ireland,

(d)   in any part of the United Kingdom, a police officer of at least the rank of superintendent may".

(3)   In sub-paragraph (3) of paragraph 29 (period of extension to end no later than 7 days after arrest) —

     (a)   for "Subject to paragraph 36(3A)" substitute "Subject to sub-paragraph (3A) and paragraph 36"; and

     (b)   for "end not later than the end of" substitute "be".

(4)   After that sub-paragraph insert—

     "(3A) A judicial authority may issue a warrant of further detention in relation to a person which specifies a shorter period as the period for which that person's further detention is authorised if—

          (a)   the application for the warrant is an application for a warrant specifying a shorter period; or

          (b)   the judicial authority is satisfied that there are circumstances that would make it inappropriate for the specified period to be as long as the period of seven days mentioned in sub-paragraph (3)."

(5)   In paragraph 34(1) (persons who can apply for information to be withheld from person to whom application for a warrant relates) for "officer" substitute "person".

(6)   In paragraph 36 (applications for extension or further extension), omit the words "to a judicial authority" in sub-paragraph (1), and after that sub-paragraph insert—

     "(1A) The person to whom an application under sub-paragraph (1) may be made is—

          (a)   in the case of an application falling within sub-paragraph (1B), a judicial authority; and
          (b)   in any other case, a senior judge.

     (1B) An application for the extension or further extension of a period falls within this sub-paragraph if—

          (a)   the grant of the application otherwise than in accordance with sub-paragraph (3AA)(b) would extend that period to a time that is no more than fourteen days after the relevant time; and

          (b)   no application has previously been made to a senior judge in respect of that period."

(7)   For sub-paragraphs (3) and (3A) of that paragraph (period for which warrants may be extended) substitute—

     "(3)   Subject to sub-paragraph (3AA), the period by which the specified period is extended or further extended shall be the period which—

          (a)   begins with the time specified in sub-paragraph (3A); and

          (b)   ends with whichever is the earlier of—

               (i)   the end of the period of seven days beginning with that time; and
               (ii)   the end of the period of 28 days beginning with the relevant time.

(3A) The time referred to in sub-paragraph (3)(a) is—

    (a) in the case of a warrant specifying a period which has not previously been extended under this paragraph, the end of the period specified in the warrant, and

    (b) in any other case, the end of the period for which the period specified in the warrant was last extended under this paragraph.

(3AA) A judicial authority or senior judge may extend or further extend the period specified in a warrant by a shorter period than is required by sub-paragraph (3) if—

    (a) the application for the extension is an application for an extension by a period that is shorter than is so required; or

    (b) the judicial authority or senior judge is satisfied that there are circumstances that would make it inappropriate for the period of the extension to be as long as the period so required."

(8) In sub-paragraph (4) of that paragraph (application of paragraphs 30(3), and 31 to 34), at the end insert "but, in relation to an application made by virtue of sub-paragraph (1A)(b) to a senior judge, as if—

    (a) references to a judicial authority were references to a senior judge; and

    (b) references to the judicial authority in question were references to the senior judge in question."

(9) In sub-paragraph (5) of that paragraph, after "authority" insert "or senior judge".

(10) After sub-paragraph (6) of that paragraph insert—

    "(7) In this paragraph and paragraph 37 'senior judge' means a judge of the High Court or of the High Court of Justiciary."

(11) For paragraph 37 (release of detained person) substitute—

    "37(1) This paragraph applies where—

        (a) a person ('the detained person') is detained by virtue of a warrant issued under this Part of this Schedule; and

        (b) his detention is not authorised by virtue of section 41(5) or (6) or otherwise apart from the warrant.

    (2) If it at any time appears to the police officer or other person in charge of the detained person's case that any of the matters mentioned in paragraph 32(1)(a) and (b) on which the judicial authority or senior judge last authorised his further detention no longer apply, he must—

        (a) if he has custody of the detained person, release him immediately; and

        (b) if he does not, immediately inform the person who does have custody of the detained person that those matters no longer apply in the detained person's case.

    (3) A person with custody of the detained person who is informed in accordance with this paragraph that those matters no longer apply in his case must release that person immediately."

(12) This section does not apply in a case in which—

    (a) the arrest of the person detained under section 41 of the Terrorism Act 2000 (c. 11) took place before the commencement of this section; or

    (b) his examination under Schedule 7 to that Act began before the commencement of this section.

THE CONSTITUTION OF THE UNITED STATES (US CONSTITUTION), 1787

We the people of the United States, in order to form a more perfect Union, establish Justice, ensure domestic Tranquility, provide for the common Defence, promote the general Welfare, and secure the Blessings of Liberty to ourselves and our Posterity, do ordain and establish this CONSTITUTION for the United States of America.

Article I

Section 1. All legislative powers herein granted shall be vested in a Congress of the United States, which shall consist of a Senate and House of Representatives.

Section 2. The House of Representatives shall be composed of members chosen every second year by the people of the several states, and the electors in each state shall have the qualifications requisite for electors of the most numerous branch of the state legislature.

No person shall be a Representative who shall not have attained to the age of twenty five years, and been seven years a citizen of the United States, and who shall not, when elected, be an inhabitant of that state in which he shall be chosen.

Representatives and direct taxes shall be apportioned among the several states which may be included within this union, according to their respective numbers, which shall be determined by adding to the whole number of free persons, including those bound to service for a term of years, and excluding Indians not taxed, three fifths of all other Persons. The actual Enumeration shall be made within three years after the first meeting of the Congress of the United States, and within every subsequent term of ten years, in such manner as they shall by law direct. The number of Representatives shall not exceed one for every thirty thousand, but each state shall have at least one Representative; and until such enumeration shall be made, the state of New Hampshire shall be entitled to chuse three, Massachusetts eight, Rhode Island and Providence Plantations one, Connecticut five, New York six, New Jersey four, Pennsylvania eight, Delaware one, Maryland six, Virginia ten, North Carolina five, South Carolina five, and Georgia three.

When vacancies happen in the Representation from any state, the executive authority thereof shall issue writs of election to fill such vacancies.

The House of Representatives shall choose their speaker and other officers; and shall have the sole power of impeachment.

Section 3. The Senate of the United States shall be composed of two Senators from each state, chosen by the legislature thereof, for six years; and each Senator shall have one vote.

Immediately after they shall be assembled in consequence of the first election, they shall be divided as equally as may be into three classes. The seats of the Senators of the first class shall be vacated at the expiration of the second year, of the second class at the expiration of the fourth year, and the third class at the expiration of the sixth year, so that one third may be chosen every second year; and if vacancies happen by resignation, or otherwise, during the recess of the legislature of any state, the executive thereof may make temporary appointments until the next meeting of the legislature, which shall then fill such vacancies.

No person shall be a Senator who shall not have attained to the age of thirty years, and been nine years a citizen of the United States and who shall not, when elected, be an inhabitant of that state for which he shall be chosen.

The Vice President of the United States shall be President of the Senate, but shall have no vote, unless they be equally divided.

The Senate shall choose their other officers, and also a President pro tempore, in the absence of the Vice President, or when he shall exercise the office of President of the United States.

The Senate shall have the sole power to try all impeachments. When sitting for that purpose, they shall be on oath or affirmation. When the President of the United States is tried, the Chief Justice shall preside: And no person shall be convicted without the concurrence of two thirds of the members present.

Judgment in cases of impeachment shall not extend further than to removal from office, and disqualification to hold and enjoy any office of honor, trust or profit under the United States: but the party convicted shall nevertheless be liable and subject to indictment, trial, judgment and punishment, according to law.

Section 4. The times, places and manner of holding elections for Senators and Representatives, shall be prescribed in each state by the legislature thereof; but the Congress may at any time by law make or alter such regulations, except as to the places of choosing Senators.

The Congress shall assemble at least once in every year, and such meeting shall be on the first Monday in December, unless they shall by law appoint a different day.

Section 5. Each House shall be the judge of the elections, returns and qualifications of its own members, and a majority of each shall constitute a quorum to do business; but a smaller number may adjourn from day to day, and may be authorized to compel the attendance of absent members, in such manner, and under such penalties as each House may provide.

Each House may determine the rules of its proceedings, punish its members for disorderly behavior, and, with the concurrence of two thirds, expel a member.

Each House shall keep a journal of its proceedings, and from time to time publish the same, excepting such parts as may in their judgment require secrecy; and the yeas and nays of the members of either House on any question shall, at the desire of one fifth of those present, be entered on the journal.

Neither House, during the session of Congress, shall, without the consent of the other, adjourn for more than three days, nor to any other place than that in which the two Houses shall be sitting.

Section 6. The Senators and Representatives shall receive a compensation for their services, to be ascertained by law, and paid out of the treasury of the United States. They shall in all cases, except treason, felony and breach of the peace, be privileged from arrest during their attendance at the session of their respective Houses, and in going to and returning from the same; and for any speech or debate in either House, they shall not be questioned in any other place.

No Senator or Representative shall, during the time for which he was elected, be appointed to any civil office under the authority of the United States, which shall have been created, or the emoluments whereof shall have been increased during such time: and no person holding any office under the United States, shall be a member of either House during his continuance in office.

Section 7. All bills for raising revenue shall originate in the House of Representatives; but the Senate may propose or concur with amendments as on other Bills.

Every bill which shall have passed the House of Representatives and the Senate, shall, before it become a law, be presented to the President of the United States; if he approve he shall sign it, but if not he shall return it, with his objections to that House in which it shall have originated, who shall enter the objections at large on their journal, and proceed to reconsider it. If after such reconsideration two thirds of that House shall agree to pass the bill, it shall be sent, together with the objections, to the other House, by which it shall likewise be reconsidered, and if approved by two thirds of that House, it shall become a law. But in all such cases the votes of both Houses shall be determined by yeas and nays, and the names of the persons voting for and against the bill shall be entered on the journal of each House respectively. If any bill shall not be returned by the President within ten days (Sundays excepted) after it shall have been presented to him, the same shall be a law, in like manner as if he had signed it, unless the Congress by their adjournment prevent its return, in which case it shall not be a law.

Every order, resolution, or vote to which the concurrence of the Senate and House of Representatives may be necessary (except on a question of adjournment) shall be presented to the President of the United States; and before the same shall take effect, shall be approved by him, or being disapproved by him, shall be repassed by two thirds of the Senate and House of Representatives, according to the rules and limitations prescribed in the case of a bill.

Section 8. The Congress shall have power to lay and collect taxes, duties, imposts and excises, to pay the debts and provide for the common defense and general welfare of the United States; but all duties, imposts and excises shall be uniform throughout the United States to:

(a)   Borrow money on the credit of the United States

(b)   Regulate commerce with foreign nations, and among the several states, and with the Indian tribes

(c)   Establish a uniform rule of naturalization, and uniform laws on the subject of bankruptcies throughout the United States

(d)   Coin money, regulate the value thereof, and of foreign coin, and fix the standard of weights and measures

(e)   Provide for the punishment of counterfeiting the securities and current coin of the United States

(f)   Establish post offices and post roads

(g)   Promote the progress of science and useful arts, by securing for limited times to authors and inventors the exclusive right to their respective writings and discoveries

(h)   Constitute tribunals inferior to the Supreme Court

(i)   Define and punish piracies and felonies committed on the high seas, and offenses against the law of nations

(j)   Declare war, grant letters of marque and reprisal, and make rules concerning captures on land and water

(k)   Raise and support armies, but no appropriation of money to that use shall be for a longer term than two years

(l)   Provide and maintain a navy

(m)   Make rules for the government and regulation of the land and naval forces

(n)   Provide for calling forth the militia to execute the laws of the union, suppress insurrections and repel invasions

(o)   Provide for organizing, arming, and disciplining, the militia, and for governing such part of them as may be employed in the service of the United States, reserving to the states respectively, the appointment of the officers, and the authority of training the militia according to the discipline prescribed by Congress

(p)   Exercise exclusive legislation in all cases whatsoever, over such District (not exceeding ten miles square) as may, by cession of particular states, and the acceptance of Congress, become the seat of the government of the United States, and to exercise like authority over all places purchased by the consent of the legislature of the state in which the same shall be, for the erection of forts, magazines, arsenals, dockyards, and other needful buildings

(q)   Make all laws which shall be necessary and proper for carrying into execution the foregoing powers, and all other powers vested by this Constitution in the government of the United States, or in any department or officer thereof

Section 9. The migration or importation of such persons as any of the states now existing shall think proper to admit, shall not be prohibited by the Congress prior to the year one thousand eight hundred and eight, but a tax or duty may be imposed on such importation, not exceeding ten dollars for each person.

The privilege of the writ of habeas corpus shall not be suspended, unless when in cases of rebellion or invasion the public safety may require it.

No bill of attainder or ex post facto Law shall be passed.

No capitation, or other direct, tax shall be laid, unless in proportion to the census or enumeration herein before directed to be taken.

No tax or duty shall be laid on articles exported from any state.

No preference shall be given by any regulation of commerce or revenue to the ports of one state over those of another: nor shall vessels bound to, or from, one state, be obliged to enter, clear or pay duties in another.

No money shall be drawn from the treasury, but in consequence of appropriations made by law; and a regular statement and account of receipts and expenditures of all public money shall be published from time to time.

No title of nobility shall be granted by the United States: and no person holding any office of profit or trust under them, shall, without the consent of the Congress, accept of any present, emolument, office, or title, of any kind whatever, from any king, prince, or foreign state.

Section 10. No state shall enter into any treaty, alliance, or confederation; grant letters of marque and reprisal; coin money; emit bills of credit; make anything but gold and silver coin a tender in payment of debts; pass any bill of attainder, ex post facto law, or law impairing the obligation of contracts, or grant any title of nobility.

No state shall, without the consent of the Congress, lay any imposts or duties on imports or exports, except what may be absolutely necessary for executing it's inspection laws: and the net produce of all duties and imposts, laid by any state on imports or exports, shall be for the use of the treasury of the United States; and all such laws shall be subject to the revision and control of the Congress.

No state shall, without the consent of Congress, lay any duty of tonnage, keep troops, or ships of war in time of peace, enter into any agreement or compact with another state, or with a foreign power, or engage in war, unless actually invaded, or in such imminent danger as will not admit of delay.

Article II

Section 1. The executive power shall be vested in a President of the United States of America. He shall hold his office during the term of four years, and, together with the Vice President, chosen for the same term, be elected, as follows:

Each state shall appoint, in such manner as the Legislature thereof may direct, a number of electors, equal to the whole number of Senators and Representatives to which the State may be entitled in the Congress: but no Senator or Representative, or person holding an office of trust or profit under the United States, shall be appointed an elector.

The electors shall meet in their respective states, and vote by ballot for two persons, of whom one at least shall not be an inhabitant of the same state with themselves. And they shall make a list of all the persons voted for, and of the number of votes for each; which list they shall sign and certify, and transmit sealed to the seat of the government of the United States, directed to the President of the Senate. The President of the Senate shall, in the presence of the Senate and House of Representatives, open all the certificates, and the votes shall then be counted. The person having the greatest number of votes shall be the President, if such number be a majority of the whole number of electors appointed; and if there be more than one who have such majority, and have an equal number of votes, then the House of Representatives shall immediately choose by ballot one of them for President; and if no person have a majority, then from the five highest on the list the said House shall in like manner choose the President. But in choosing the President, the votes shall be taken by States, the representation from each state having one vote; A quorum for this purpose shall consist of a member or members from two thirds of the states, and a majority of all the states shall be necessary to a choice. In every case, after the choice of the President, the person having the greatest number of votes of the electors shall be the Vice President. But if there should remain two or more who have equal votes, the Senate shall choose from them by ballot the Vice President.

The Congress may determine the time of choosing the electors, and the day on which they shall give their votes; which day shall be the same throughout the United States.

No person except a natural born citizen, or a citizen of the United States, at the time of the adoption of this Constitution, shall be eligible to the office of President; neither shall any person be eligible to that office who shall not have attained to the age of thirty five years, and been fourteen Years a resident within the United States.

In case of the removal of the President from office, or of his death, resignation, or inability to discharge the powers and duties of the said office, the same shall devolve on the Vice President, and the Congress may by law provide for the case of removal, death, resignation or inability, both of the President and Vice President, declaring what officer shall then act as President, and such officer shall act accordingly, until the disability be removed, or a President shall be elected.

The President shall, at stated times, receive for his services, a compensation, which shall neither be increased nor diminished during the period for which he shall have been elected, and he shall not receive within that period any other emolument from the United States, or any of them.

Before he enter on the execution of his office, he shall take the following oath or affirmation:–"I do solemnly swear (or affirm) that I will faithfully execute the office of President of the United States, and will to the best of my ability, preserve, protect and defend the Constitution of the United States."

Section 2. The President shall be commander in chief of the Army and Navy of the United States, and of the militia of the several states, when called into the actual service of the United States; he may require the opinion, in writing, of the principal officer in each of the executive departments, upon any subject relating to the duties of their respective offices, and he shall have power to grant reprieves and pardons for offenses against the United States, except in cases of impeachment.

He shall have power, by and with the advice and consent of the Senate, to make treaties, provided two thirds of the Senators present concur; and he shall nominate, and by and with the advice and consent of the Senate, shall appoint ambassadors, other public ministers and consuls, judges of the Supreme Court, and all other officers of the United States, whose appointments are not herein otherwise provided for, and which shall be established by law: but the Congress may by law vest the appointment of such inferior officers, as they think proper, in the President alone, in the courts of law, or in the heads of departments.

The President shall have power to fill up all vacancies that may happen during the recess of the Senate, by granting commissions which shall expire at the end of their next session.

Section 3. He shall from time to time give to the Congress information of the state of the union, and recommend to their consideration such measures as he shall judge necessary and expedient; he may, on extraordinary occasions, convene both Houses, or either of them, and in case of disagreement between them, with respect to the time of adjournment, he may adjourn them to such time as he shall think proper; he shall receive ambassadors and other public ministers; he shall take care that the laws be faithfully executed, and shall commission all the officers of the United States.

Section 4. The President, Vice President and all civil officers of the United States, shall be removed from office on impeachment for, and conviction of, treason, bribery, or other high crimes and misdemeanors.

Article III

Section 1. The judicial power of the United States, shall be vested in one Supreme Court, and in such inferior courts as the Congress may from time to time ordain and establish. The judges, both of the supreme and inferior courts, shall hold their offices during good behaviour, and shall, at stated times, receive for their services, a compensation, which shall not be diminished during their continuance in office.

Section 2. The judicial power shall extend to all cases, in law and equity, arising under this Constitution, the laws of the United States, and treaties made, or which shall be made, under their authority; —to all cases affecting ambassadors, other public ministers and consuls; —to all cases of admiralty and maritime jurisdiction; —to controversies to which the United States shall be a party; —to controversies between two or more states; —between a state and citizens of another state; —between citizens of different states; —between citizens of the same state claiming lands under grants of different states, and between a state, or the citizens thereof, and foreign states, citizens or subjects.

In all cases affecting ambassadors, other public ministers and consuls, and those in which a state shall be party, the Supreme Court shall have original jurisdiction. In all the other cases before mentioned, the Supreme Court shall have appellate jurisdiction, both as to law and fact, with such exceptions, and under such regulations as the Congress shall make.

The trial of all crimes, except in cases of impeachment, shall be by jury; and such trial shall be held in the state where the said crimes shall have been committed; but when not committed within any state, the trial shall be at such place or places as the Congress may by law have directed.

Section 3. Treason against the United States, shall consist only in levying war against them, or in adhering to their enemies, giving them aid and comfort. No person shall be convicted of treason unless on the testimony of two witnesses to the same overt act, or on confession in open court.

The Congress shall have power to declare the punishment of treason, but no attainder of treason shall work corruption of blood, or forfeiture except during the life of the person attainted.

Article IV

Section 1. Full faith and credit shall be given in each state to the public acts, records, and judicial proceedings of every other state. And the Congress may by general laws prescribe the manner in which such acts, records, and proceedings shall be proved, and the effect thereof.

Section 2. The citizens of each state shall be entitled to all privileges and immunities of citizens in the several states.

A person charged in any state with treason, felony, or other crime, who shall flee from justice, and be found in another state, shall on demand of the executive authority of the state from which he fled, be delivered up, to be removed to the state having jurisdiction of the crime.

No person held to service or labor in one state, under the laws thereof, escaping into another, shall, in consequence of any law or regulation therein, be discharged from such service or labor, but shall be delivered up on claim of the party to whom such service or labor may be due.

Section 3. New states may be admitted by the Congress into this union; but no new states shall be formed or erected within the jurisdiction of any other state; nor any state be formed by the junction of two or more states, or parts of states, without the consent of the legislatures of the states concerned as well as of the Congress.

The Congress shall have power to dispose of and make all needful rules and regulations respecting the territory or other property belonging to the United States; and nothing in this Constitution shall be so construed as to prejudice any claims of the United States, or of any particular state.

Section 4. The United States shall guarantee to every state in this union a republican form of government, and shall protect each of them against invasion; and on application of the legislature, or of the executive (when the legislature cannot be convened) against domestic violence.

Article V

The Congress, whenever two thirds of both houses shall deem it necessary, shall propose amendments to this Constitution, or, on the application of the legislatures of two thirds of the several states, shall call a convention for proposing amendments, which, in either case, shall be valid to all intents and purposes, as part of this Constitution, when ratified by the legislatures of three fourths of the several states, or by conventions in three fourths thereof, as the one or the other mode of ratification may be proposed by the Congress; provided that no amendment which may be made prior to the year one thousand eight hundred and eight shall in any manner affect the first and fourth clauses in the ninth section of the first article; and that no state, without its consent, shall be deprived of its equal suffrage in the Senate.

Article VI

All debts contracted and engagements entered into, before the adoption of this Constitution, shall be as valid against the United States under this Constitution, as under the Confederation.

This Constitution, and the laws of the United States which shall be made in pursuance thereof; and all treaties made, or which shall be made, under the authority of the United States, shall be the supreme law of the land; and the judges in every state shall be bound thereby, anything in the Constitution or laws of any State to the contrary notwithstanding.

The Senators and Representatives before mentioned, and the members of the several state legislatures, and all executive and judicial officers, both of the United States and of the several states, shall be bound by oath or affirmation, to support this Constitution; but no religious test shall ever be required as a qualification to any office or public trust under the United States.

Amendments to the Constitution

Article I

Congress shall make no law respecting an establishment of religion, or prohibiting the free exercise thereof; or abridging the freedom of speech or of the press; or the right of the people peaceably to assemble, and to petition the government for redress of grievances.

Article II

A well-regulated militia being necessary to the security of a free state, the right of the people to keep and bear arms shall not be infringed.

Article III

No soldier shall, in time of peace, be quartered in any house without the consent of the owner, nor in time of war but in a manner to be prescribed by law.

Article IV

The right of the people to be secure in their persons, houses, paper and effects, against unreasonable searches and seizures, shall not be violated, and no warrants shall issue but upon probable cause, supported by oath or affirmation, and particularly describing the place to be searched, and the persons or things to be seized.

Article V

No person shall be held to answer for a capital or other infamous crime unless on presentment or indictment of a grand jury, except in cases arising in the land or naval forces, or in the militia, when in actual service, in time of war or public danger; nor shall any person be subject for the same offence to be twice put in jeopardy of life or limb; nor shall be compelled in any criminal case to be a witness against himself, nor be deprived of life, liberty, or property, without due process of law; nor shall private property be taken for public use without just compensation.

Article VI

In all criminal prosecutions, the accused shall enjoy the right to a speedy and public trial, by an impartial jury of the state and district wherein the crime shall have been committed, which district shall have been previously ascertained by law, and be informed of the nature and cause of the accusation; to be confronted with the witnesses against him; to have compulsory process for obtaining witnesses in his favor, and to have the assistance and control for his defence.

Article VII

In suits at common law, where the value in controversy shall exceed twenty dollars, the right of trial by jury shall be preserved, and no fact tried by a jury shall be otherwise re-examined in any court of the United States than according to the rules of the common law.

Article VIII

Excessive bail shall not be required, nor excessive fines imposed, nor cruel and unusual punishments inflicted.

Article IX

The enumeration in the Constitution of certain rights shall be construed to deny or disparage others retained by the people.

Article X

The powers not delegated to the United States by the Constitution, nor prohibited by it to the states, are reserved to the states respectively, or to the people.

[The forgoing ten amendments were adopted at the first session of Congress, and were declared to be in force, December 15, 1791.]

YOUTH JUSTICE AND CRIMINAL EVIDENCE ACT 1999

1999 chapter 23

An Act to provide for the referral of offenders under 18 to youth offender panels; to make provision in connection with the giving of evidence or information for the purposes of criminal proceedings; to amend section 51 of the Criminal Justice and Public Order Act 1994; to make pre-consolidation amendments relating to youth justice; and for connected purposes.[27th July 1999]

41 Restriction on evidence or questions about complainant's sexual history

(1)   If at a trial a person is charged with a sexual offence, then, except with the leave of the court—

   (a)   no evidence may be adduced, and

   (b)   no question may be asked in cross-examination,

   by or on behalf of any accused at the trial, about any sexual behaviour of the complainant.

THE FIXED-TERM PARLIAMENTS ACT 2011

1 Polling days for parliamentary general elections

(1)   This section applies for the purposes of the Timetable in rule 1 in Schedule 1 to the Representation of the People Act 1983 and is subject to section 2.

(2)   The polling day for the next parliamentary general election after the passing of this Act is to be 7 May 2015.

(3)   The polling day for each subsequent parliamentary general election is to be the first Thursday in May in the fifth calendar year following that in which the polling day for the previous parliamentary general election fell.

(4) – (7) *****

2 Early parliamentary general elections

(1)   An early parliamentary general election is to take place if—

   (a)   the House of Commons passes a motion in the form set out in subsection (2), and

   (b)   if the motion is passed on a division, the number of members who vote in favour of the motion is a number equal to or greater than two thirds of the number of seats in the House (including vacant seats).

(2)   The form of motion for the purposes of subsection (1)(a) is—

   "That there shall be an early parliamentary general election."

(3)   An early parliamentary general election is also to take place if—

(a)   the House of Commons passes a motion in the form set out in subsection (4), and

(b)   the period of 14 days after the day on which that motion is passed ends without the House passing a motion in the form set out in subsection (5).

(4)   The form of motion for the purposes of subsection (3)(a) is—

"That this House has no confidence in Her Majesty's Government."

(5)   The form of motion for the purposes of subsection (3)(b) is—

"That this House has confidence in Her Majesty's Government."

(6)   Subsection (7) applies for the purposes of the Timetable in rule 1 in Schedule 1 to the Representation of the People Act 1983.

(7)   If a parliamentary general election is to take place as provided for by subsection (1) or (3), the polling day for the election is to be the day appointed by Her Majesty by proclamation on the recommendation of the Prime Minister (and, accordingly, the appointed day replaces the day which would otherwise have been the polling day for the next election determined under section 1).

Part 2

Contract Law

CONSUMER RIGHTS ACT 2015

2015 Chapter 15

An Act to amend the law relating to the rights of consumers and protection of their interests; to make provision about investigatory powers for enforcing the regulation of traders; to make provision about private actions in competition law and the Competition Appeal Tribunal; and for connected purposes.

PART 1 CONSUMER CONTRACTS FOR GOODS, DIGITAL CONTENT AND SERVICES

Chapter 1

Introduction

1 Where Part 1 applies

(1)   This Part applies where there is an agreement between a trader and a consumer for the trader to supply goods, digital content or services, if the agreement is a contract.

(2)   It applies whether the contract is written or oral or implied from the parties' conduct, or more than one of these combined.

(3)   Any of Chapters 2, 3 and 4 may apply to a contract—

(a)   if it is a contract for the trader to supply goods, see Chapter 2;

(b)   if it is a contract for the trader to supply digital content, see Chapter 3 (also, subsection (6));

(c)   if it is a contract for the trader to supply a service, see Chapter 4 (also, subsection (6)).

(4)   In each case the Chapter applies even if the contract also covers something covered by another Chapter (a mixed contract).

(5)   Two or all three of those Chapters may apply to a mixed contract.

(6)   For provisions about particular mixed contracts, see—

(a)   section 15 (goods and installation);

(b)   section 16 (goods and digital content).

(7)   For other provision applying to contracts to which this Part applies, see Part 2 (unfair terms)

2 Key definitions

(1)   These definitions apply in this Part (as well as the definitions in section 59).

(2) "Trader" means a person acting for purposes relating to that person's trade, business, craft or profession, whether acting personally or through another person acting in the trader's name or on the trader's behalf.

(3) "Consumer" means an individual acting for purposes that are wholly or mainly outside that individual's trade, business, craft or profession.

(4) A trader claiming that an individual was not acting for purposes wholly or mainly outside the individual's trade, business, craft or profession must prove it.

(5) For the purposes of Chapter 2, except to the extent mentioned in subsection (6), a person is not a consumer in relation to a sales contract if—

　　(a)　the goods are second hand goods sold at public auction, and
　　(b)　individuals have the opportunity of attending the sale in person.

(6) A person is a consumer in relation to such a contract for the purposes of—

　　(a)　sections 11(4) and (5), 12, 28 and 29, and
　　(b)　the other provisions of Chapter 2 as they apply in relation to those sections.

(7) "Business" includes the activities of any government department or local or public authority.

(8) "Goods" means any tangible moveable items, but that includes water, gas and electricity if and only if they are put up for supply in a limited volume or set quantity.

(9) "Digital content" means data which are produced and supplied in digital form.

Chapter 2

Goods

What Goods Contracts are Covered?

3 Contracts covered by this Chapter

(1) This Chapter applies to a contract for a trader to supply goods to a consumer.

(2) It applies only if the contract is one of these (defined for the purposes of this Part in sections 5 to 8)—

　　(a)　a sales contract;
　　(b)　a contract for the hire of goods;
　　(c)　a hire-purchase agreement;
　　(d)　a contract for transfer of goods.

(3) It does not apply—

　　(a)　to a contract for a trader to supply coins or notes to a consumer for use as currency;

　　(b)　to a contract for goods to be sold by way of execution or otherwise by authority of law;

　　(c)　to a contract intended to operate as a mortgage, pledge, charge or other security;

(d)   in relation to England and Wales or Northern Ireland, to a contract made by deed and for which the only consideration is the presumed consideration imported by the deed;

(e)   in relation to Scotland, to a gratuitous contract.

(4)   A contract to which this Chapter applies is referred to in this Part as a "contract to supply goods".

(5)   Contracts to supply goods include—

(a)   contracts entered into between one part owner and another;
(b)   contracts for the transfer of an undivided share in goods;
(c)   contracts that are absolute and contracts that are conditional.

(6)   Subsection (1) is subject to any provision of this Chapter that applies a section or part of a section to only some of the kinds of contracts listed in subsection (2).

(7)   A mixed contract (see section 1(4)) may be a contract of any of those kinds.

4 Ownership of goods

(1)   In this Chapter ownership of goods means the general property in goods, not merely a special property.

...

5 Sales contracts

(1)   A contract is a sales contract if under it—

(a)   the trader transfers or agrees to transfer ownership of goods to the consumer, and
(b)   the consumer pays or agrees to pay the price.

(2)   A contract is a sales contract (whether or not it would be one under subsection (1)) if under the contract—

(a)   goods are to be manufactured or produced and the trader agrees to supply them to the consumer,

(b)   on being supplied, the goods will be owned by the consumer, and

(c)   the consumer pays or agrees to pay the price.

(3)   A sales contract may be conditional (see section 3(5)), but in this Part "conditional sales contract" means a sales contract under which—

(a)   the price for the goods or part of it is payable by instalments, and

(b)   the trader retains ownership of the goods until the conditions specified in the contract (for the payment of instalments or otherwise) are met;

and it makes no difference whether or not the consumer possesses the goods.

6 Contracts for the hire of goods

...

WHAT STATUTORY RIGHTS ARE THERE UNDER A GOODS CONTRACT?

9 Goods to be of satisfactory quality

(1)   Every contract to supply goods is to be treated as including a term that the quality of the goods is satisfactory.

(2)   The quality of goods is satisfactory if they meet the standard that a reasonable person would consider satisfactory, taking account of—

    (a)   any description of the goods,

    (b)   the price or other consideration for the goods (if relevant), and

    (c)   all the other relevant circumstances (see subsection (5)).

(3)   The quality of goods includes their state and condition; and the following aspects (among others) are in appropriate cases aspects of the quality of goods—

    (a)   fitness for all the purposes for which goods of that kind are usually supplied;

    (b)   appearance and finish;

    (c)   freedom from minor defects;

    (d)   safety;

    (e)   durability.

(4)   The term mentioned in subsection (1) does not cover anything which makes the quality of the goods unsatisfactory—

    (a)   which is specifically drawn to the consumer's attention before the contract is made,

    (b)   where the consumer examines the goods before the contract is made, which that examination ought to reveal, or

    (c)   in the case of a contract to supply goods by sample, which would have been apparent on a reasonable examination of the sample.

(5)   The relevant circumstances mentioned in subsection (2)(c) include any public statement about the specific characteristics of the goods made by the trader, the producer or any representative of the trader or the producer.

(6)   That includes, in particular, any public statement made in advertising or labelling.

(7)   But a public statement is not a relevant circumstance for the purposes of subsection (2)(c) if the trader shows that—

    (a)   when the contract was made, the trader was not, and could not reasonably have been, aware of the statement,

    (b)   before the contract was made, the statement had been publicly withdrawn or, to the extent that it contained anything which was incorrect or misleading, it had been publicly corrected, or

    (c)   the consumer's decision to contract for the goods could not have been influenced by the statement.

(8)   In a contract to supply goods a term about the quality of the goods may be treated as included as a matter of custom.

(9)   See section 19 for a consumer's rights if the trader is in breach of a term that this section requires to be treated as included in a contract.

10   Goods to be fit for particular purpose

(1)   Subsection (3) applies to a contract to supply goods if before the contract is made the consumer makes known to the trader (expressly or by implication) any particular purpose for which the consumer is contracting for the goods.

(2)   Subsection (3) also applies to a contract to supply goods if—

(a)   the goods were previously sold by a credit-broker to the trader,

(b)   in the case of a sales contract or contract for transfer of goods, the consideration or part of it is a sum payable by instalments, and

(c)   before the contract is made, the consumer makes known to the credit-broker (expressly or by implication) any particular purpose for which the consumer is contracting for the goods.

(3)   The contract is to be treated as including a term that the goods are reasonably fit for that purpose, whether or not that is a purpose for which goods of that kind are usually supplied.

(4)   Subsection (3) does not apply if the circumstances show that the consumer does not rely, or it is unreasonable for the consumer to rely, on the skill or judgment of the trader or credit-broker.

(5)   In a contract to supply goods a term about the fitness of the goods for a particular purpose may be treated as included as a matter of custom.

(6)   See section 19 for a consumer's rights if the trader is in breach of a term that this section requires to be treated as included in a contract.

11   Goods to be as described

(1)   Every contract to supply goods by description is to be treated as including a term that the goods will match the description.

(2)   If the supply is by sample as well as by description, it is not sufficient that the bulk of the goods matches the sample if the goods do not also match the description.

(3)   A supply of goods is not prevented from being a supply by description just because—

(a)   the goods are exposed for supply, and
(b)   they are selected by the consumer.

(4)   Any information that is provided by the trader about the goods and is information mentioned in paragraph (a) of Schedule 1 or 2 to the Consumer Contracts (Information, Cancellation and Additional Charges) Regulations 2013 (SI 2013/3134) (main characteristics of goods) is to be treated as included as a term of the contract.

(5)   A change to any of that information, made before entering into the contract or later, is not effective unless expressly agreed between the consumer and the trader.

(6) See section 2(5) and (6) for the application of subsections (4) and (5) where goods are sold at public auction.

(7) See section 19 for a consumer's rights if the trader is in breach of a term that this section requires to be treated as included in a contract.

...

13 Goods to match a sample

(1) This section applies to a contract to supply goods by reference to a sample of the goods that is seen or examined by the consumer before the contract is made.

(2) Every contract to which this section applies is to be treated as including a term that—

(a) the goods will match the sample except to the extent that any differences between the sample and the goods are brought to the consumer's attention before the contract is made, and

(b) the goods will be free from any defect that makes their quality unsatisfactory and that would not be apparent on a reasonable examination of the sample.

(3) See section 19 for a consumer's rights if the trader is in breach of a term that this section requires to be treated as included in a contract.

14 Goods to match a model seen or examined

(1) This section applies to a contract to supply goods by reference to a model of the goods that is seen or examined by the consumer before entering into the contract.

(2) Every contract to which this section applies is to be treated as including a term that the goods will match the model except to the extent that any differences between the model and the goods are brought to the consumer's attention before the consumer enters into the contract.

(3) See section 19 for a consumer's rights if the trader is in breach of a term that this section requires to be treated as included in a contract.

15 Installation as part of conformity of the goods with the contract

(1) Goods do not conform to a contract to supply goods if—

(a) installation of the goods forms part of the contract,
(b) the goods are installed by the trader or under the trader's responsibility, and
(c) the goods are installed incorrectly.

(2) See section 19 for the effect of goods not conforming to the contract.

17 Trader to have right to supply the goods etc

(1) Every contract to supply goods, except one within subsection (4), is to be treated as including a term—

(a) in the case of a contract for the hire of goods, that at the beginning of the period of hire the trader must have the right to transfer possession of the goods by way of hire for that period,

(b)   in any other case, that the trader must have the right to sell or transfer the goods at the time when ownership of the goods is to be transferred.

(2)   Every contract to supply goods, except a contract for the hire of goods or a contract within subsection (4), is to be treated as including a term that—

(a)   the goods are free from any charge or encumbrance not disclosed or known to the consumer before entering into the contract,

(b)   the goods will remain free from any such charge or encumbrance until ownership of them is to be transferred, and

(c)   the consumer will enjoy quiet possession of the goods except so far as it may be disturbed by the owner or other person entitled to the benefit of any charge or encumbrance so disclosed or known.

(3)   Every contract for the hire of goods is to be treated as including a term that the consumer will enjoy quiet possession of the goods for the period of the hire except so far as the possession may be disturbed by the owner or other person entitled to the benefit of any charge or encumbrance disclosed or known to the consumer before entering into the contract.

(4)   This subsection applies to a contract if the contract shows, or the circumstances when they enter into the contract imply, that the trader and the consumer intend the trader to transfer only—

(a)   whatever title the trader has, even if it is limited, or

(b)   whatever title a third person has, even if it is limited.

(5)   Every contract within subsection (4) is to be treated as including a term that all charges or encumbrances known to the trader and not known to the consumer were disclosed to the consumer before entering into the contract.

(6)   Every contract within subsection (4) is to be treated as including a term that the consumer's quiet possession of the goods—

(a)   will not be disturbed by the trader, and

(b)   will not be disturbed by a person claiming through or under the trader, unless that person is claiming under a charge or encumbrance that was disclosed or known to the consumer before entering into the contract.

(7)   If subsection (4)(b) applies (transfer of title that a third person has), the contract is also to be treated as including a term that the consumer's quiet possession of the goods—

(a)   will not be disturbed by the third person, and

(b)   will not be disturbed by a person claiming through or under the third person, unless the claim is under a charge or encumbrance that was disclosed or known to the consumer before entering into the contract.

(8)   In the case of a contract for the hire of goods, this section does not affect the right of the trader to repossess the goods where the contract provides or is to be treated as providing for this.

(9)   See section 19 for a consumer's rights if the trader is in breach of a term that this section requires to be treated as included in a contract.

18 No other requirement to treat term about quality or fitness as included

(1)   Except as provided by sections 9, 10, 13 and 16, a contract to supply goods is not to be treated as including any term about the quality of the goods or their fitness for any particular purpose, unless the term is expressly included in the contract.

(2)   Subsection (1) is subject to provision made by any other enactment (whenever passed or made).

WHAT REMEDIES ARE THERE IF STATUTORY RIGHTS UNDER A GOODS CONTRACT ARE NOT MET?

19 Consumer's rights to enforce terms about goods

(1)   In this section and sections 22 to 24 references to goods conforming to a contract are references to—

    (a)   the goods conforming to the terms described in sections 9, 10, 11, 13 and 14,

    (b)   the goods not failing to conform to the contract under section 15 or 16, and

    (c)   the goods conforming to requirements that are stated in the contract.

(2)   But, for the purposes of this section and sections 22 to 24, a failure to conform as mentioned in subsection (1)(a) to (c) is not a failure to conform to the contract if it has its origin in materials supplied by the consumer.

(3)   If the goods do not conform to the contract because of a breach of any of the terms described in sections 9, 10, 11, 13 and 14, or if they do not conform to the contract under section 16, the consumer's rights (and the provisions about them and when they are available) are—

    (a)   the short-term right to reject (sections 20 and 22);

    (b)   the right to repair or replacement (section 23); and

    (c)   the right to a price reduction or the final right to reject (sections 20 and 24).

(4)   If the goods do not conform to the contract under section 15 or because of a breach of requirements that are stated in the contract, the consumer's rights (and the provisions about them and when they are available) are—

    (a)   the right to repair or replacement (section 23); and

    (b)   the right to a price reduction or the final right to reject (sections 20 and 24).

(5)   If the trader is in breach of a term that section 12 requires to be treated as included in the contract, the consumer has the right to recover from the trader the amount of any costs incurred by the consumer as a result of the breach, up to the amount of the price paid or the value of other consideration given for the goods.

(6)   If the trader is in breach of the term that section 17(1) (right to supply etc) requires to be treated as included in the contract, the consumer has a right to reject (see section 20 for provisions about that right and when it is available).

(7)   Subsections (3) to (6) are subject to section 25 and subsections (3)(a) and (6) are subject to section 26.

(8)   Section 28 makes provision about remedies for breach of a term about the time for delivery of goods.

(9)   This Chapter does not prevent the consumer seeking other remedies—

(a)   for a breach of a term that this Chapter requires to be treated as included in the contract,
(b)   on the grounds that, under section 15 or 16, goods do not conform to the contract, or
(c)   for a breach of a requirement stated in the contract.

(10)   Those other remedies may be ones—

(a)   in addition to a remedy referred to in subsections (3) to (6) (but not so as to recover twice for the same loss), or

(b)   instead of such a remedy, or

(c)   where no such remedy is provided for.

(11)   Those other remedies include any of the following that is open to the consumer in the circumstances—

(a)   claiming damages;
(b)   seeking specific performance;
(c)   seeking an order for specific implement;
(d)   relying on the breach against a claim by the trader for the price;
(e)   for breach of an express term, exercising a right to treat the contract as at an end.

(12)   It is not open to the consumer to treat the contract as at an end for breach of a term that this Chapter requires to be treated as included in the contract, or on the grounds that, under section 15 or 16, goods do not conform to the contract, except as provided by subsections (3), (4) and (6).

(13)   In this Part, treating a contract as at an end means treating it as repudiated.

(14)   For the purposes of subsections (3)(b) and (c) and (4), goods which do not conform to the contract at any time within the period of six months beginning with the day on which the goods were delivered to the consumer must be taken not to have conformed to it on that day.

(15)   Subsection (14) does not apply if—

(a)   it is established that the goods did conform to the contract on that day, or

(b)   its application is incompatible with the nature of the goods or with how they fail to conform to the contract.

20 Right to reject

(1)   The short-term right to reject is subject to section 22.

(2)   The final right to reject is subject to section 24.

(3)   The right to reject under section 19(6) is not limited by those sections.

(4)   Each of these rights entitles the consumer to reject the goods and treat the contract as at an end, subject to subsections (20) and (21).

(5)   The right is exercised if the consumer indicates to the trader that the consumer is rejecting the goods and treating the contract as at an end.

(6)   The indication may be something the consumer says or does, but it must be clear enough to be understood by the trader.

(7)   From the time when the right is exercised—

(a)   the trader has a duty to give the consumer a refund, subject to subsection (18), and

(b)   the consumer has a duty to make the goods available for collection by the trader or (if there is an agreement for the consumer to return rejected goods) to return them as agreed.

(8)   Whether or not the consumer has a duty to return the rejected goods, the trader must bear any reasonable costs of returning them, other than any costs incurred by the consumer in returning the goods in person to the place where the consumer took physical possession of them.

(9)   The consumer's entitlement to receive a refund works as follows.

(10)   To the extent that the consumer paid money under the contract, the consumer is entitled to receive back the same amount of money.

(11)   To the extent that the consumer transferred anything else under the contract, the consumer is entitled to receive back the same amount of what the consumer transferred, unless subsection (12) applies.

(12)   To the extent that the consumer transferred under the contract something for which the same amount of the same thing cannot be substituted, the consumer is entitled to receive back in its original state whatever the consumer transferred.

(13)   If the contract is for the hire of goods, the entitlement to a refund extends only to anything paid or otherwise transferred for a period of hire that the consumer does not get because the contract is treated as at an end.

(14)   If the contract is a hire-purchase agreement or a conditional sales contract and the contract is treated as at an end before the whole of the price has been paid, the entitlement to a refund extends only to the part of the price paid.

(15)   A refund under this section must be given without undue delay, and in any event within 14 days beginning with the day on which the trader agrees that the consumer is entitled to a refund.

(16)   If the consumer paid money under the contract, the trader must give the refund using the same means of payment as the consumer used, unless the consumer expressly agrees otherwise.

(17)   The trader must not impose any fee on the consumer in respect of the refund.

(18)   There is no entitlement to receive a refund—

(a)   if none of subsections (10) to (12) applies,

(b)   to the extent that anything to which subsection (12) applies cannot be given back in its original state, or

(c)   where subsection (13) applies, to the extent that anything the consumer transferred under the contract cannot be divided so as to give back only the amount, or part of the amount, to which the consumer is entitled.

(19)   It may be open to a consumer to claim damages where there is no entitlement to receive a refund, or because of the limits of the entitlement, or instead of a refund.

(20)   Subsection (21) qualifies the application in relation to England and Wales and Northern Ireland of the rights mentioned in subsections (1) to (3) where—

(a)   the contract is a severable contract,

(b)   in relation to the final right to reject, the contract is a contract for the hire of goods, a hire-purchase agreement or a contract for transfer of goods, and

(c)   section 26(3) does not apply.

(21)   The consumer is entitled, depending on the terms of the contract and the circumstances of the case—

(a)   to reject the goods to which a severable obligation relates and treat that obligation as at an end (so that the entitlement to a refund relates only to what the consumer paid or transferred in relation to that obligation), or

(b)   to exercise any of the rights mentioned in subsections (1) to (3) in respect of the whole contract.

21 Partial rejection of goods

(1)   If the consumer has any of the rights mentioned in section 20(1) to (3), but does not reject all of the goods and treat the contract as at an end, the consumer—

(a)   may reject some or all of the goods that do not conform to the contract, but

(b)   may not reject any goods that do conform to the contract.

…

22 Time limit for short-term right to reject

(1)   A consumer who has the short-term right to reject loses it if the time limit for exercising it passes without the consumer exercising it, unless the trader and the consumer agree that it may be exercised later.

(2)   An agreement under which the short-term right to reject would be lost before the time limit passes is not binding on the consumer.

(3)   The time limit for exercising the short-term right to reject (unless subsection (4) applies) is the end of 30 days beginning with the first day after these have all happened—

(a)   ownership or (in the case of a contract for the hire of goods, a hire-purchase agreement or a conditional sales contract) possession of the goods has been transferred to the consumer,

(b)   the goods have been delivered, and

(c)   where the contract requires the trader to install the goods or take other action to enable the consumer to use them, the trader has notified the consumer that the action has been taken.

(4)   If any of the goods are of a kind that can reasonably be expected to perish after a shorter period, the time limit for exercising the short-term right to reject in relation to those goods is the end of that shorter period (but without affecting the time limit in relation to goods that are not of that kind).

(5)   Subsections (3) and (4) do not prevent the consumer exercising the short-term right to reject before something mentioned in subsection (3)(a), (b) or (c) has happened.

(6)   If the consumer requests or agrees to the repair or replacement of goods, the period mentioned in subsection (3) or (4) stops running for the length of the waiting period.

(7)   If goods supplied by the trader in response to that request or agreement do not conform to the contract, the time limit for exercising the short-term right to reject is then either—

(a)   7 days after the waiting period ends, or
(b)   if later, the original time limit for exercising that right, extended by the waiting period.

(8)   The waiting period—

(a)   begins with the day the consumer requests or agrees to the repair or replacement of the goods, and

(b)   ends with the day on which the consumer receives goods supplied by the trader in response to the request or agreement.

23 Right to repair or replacement

(1)   This section applies if the consumer has the right to repair or replacement (see section 19(3) and (4)).

(2)   If the consumer requires the trader to repair or replace the goods, the trader must—

(a)   do so within a reasonable time and without significant inconvenience to the consumer, and

(b)   bear any necessary costs incurred in doing so (including in particular the cost of any labour, materials or postage).

(3)   The consumer cannot require the trader to repair or replace the goods if that remedy (the repair or the replacement)—

(a)   is impossible, or

(b)   is disproportionate compared to the other of those remedies.

(4)   Either of those remedies is disproportionate compared to the other if it imposes costs on the trader which, compared to those imposed by the other, are unreasonable, taking into account—

   (a)   the value which the goods would have if they conformed to the contract,

   (b)   the significance of the lack of conformity, and

   (c)   whether the other remedy could be effected without significant inconvenience to the consumer.

(5)   Any question as to what is a reasonable time or significant inconvenience is to be determined taking account of—

   (a)   the nature of the goods, and

   (b)   the purpose for which the goods were acquired.

(6)   A consumer who requires or agrees to the repair of goods cannot require the trader to replace them, or exercise the short-term right to reject, without giving the trader a reasonable time to repair them (unless giving the trader that time would cause significant inconvenience to the consumer).

(7)   A consumer who requires or agrees to the replacement of goods cannot require the trader to repair them, or exercise the short-term right to reject, without giving the trader a reasonable time to replace them (unless giving the trader that time would cause significant inconvenience to the consumer).

(8)   In this Chapter, "repair" in relation to goods that do not conform to a contract, means making them conform.

24 Right to price reduction or final right to reject

(1)   The right to a price reduction is the right—

   (a)   to require the trader to reduce by an appropriate amount the price the consumer is required to pay under the contract, or anything else the consumer is required to transfer under the contract, and

   (b)   to receive a refund from the trader for anything already paid or otherwise transferred by the consumer above the reduced amount.

(2)   The amount of the reduction may, where appropriate, be the full amount of the price or whatever the consumer is required to transfer.

(3)   Section 20(10) to (17) applies to a consumer's right to receive a refund under subsection (1)(b).

(4)   The right to a price reduction does not apply—

   (a)   if what the consumer is (before the reduction) required to transfer under the contract, whether or not already transferred, cannot be divided up so as to enable the trader to receive or retain only the reduced amount, or

   (b)   if anything to which section 20(12) applies cannot be given back in its original state.

(5) A consumer who has the right to a price reduction and the final right to reject may only exercise one (not both), and may only do so in one of these situations—

(a) after one repair or one replacement, the goods do not conform to the contract;

(b) because of section 23(3) the consumer can require neither repair nor replacement of the goods; or

(c) the consumer has required the trader to repair or replace the goods, but the trader is in breach of the requirement of section 23(2)(a) to do so within a reasonable time and without significant inconvenience to the consumer.

(6) There has been a repair or replacement for the purposes of subsection (5)(a) if—

(a) the consumer has requested or agreed to repair or replacement of the goods (whether in relation to one fault or more than one), and

(b) the trader has delivered goods to the consumer, or made goods available to the consumer, in response to the request or agreement.

(7) For the purposes of subsection (6) goods that the trader arranges to repair at the consumer's premises are made available when the trader indicates that the repairs are finished.

(8) If the consumer exercises the final right to reject, any refund to the consumer may be reduced by a deduction for use, to take account of the use the consumer has had of the goods in the period since they were delivered, but this is subject to subsections (9) and (10).

(9) No deduction may be made to take account of use in any period when the consumer had the goods only because the trader failed to collect them at an agreed time.

(10) No deduction may be made if the final right to reject is exercised in the first 6 months (see subsection (11)), unless—

(a) the goods consist of a motor vehicle, or

(b) the goods are of a description specified by order made by the Secretary of State by statutory instrument.

(11) In subsection (10) the first 6 months means 6 months beginning with the first day after these have all happened—

(a) ownership or (in the case of a contract for the hire of goods, a hire-purchase agreement or a conditional sales contract) possession of the goods has been transferred to the consumer,

(b) the goods have been delivered, and

(c) where the contract requires the trader to install the goods or take other action to enable the consumer to use them, the trader has notified the consumer that the action has been taken.

OTHER RULES ABOUT REMEDIES UNDER GOODS CONTRACTS

25 Delivery of wrong quantity

…

26 Instalment deliveries

…

OTHER RULES ABOUT GOODS CONTRACTS

28 Delivery of goods

(1) This section applies to any sales contract.

(2) Unless the trader and the consumer have agreed otherwise, the contract is to be treated as including a term that the trader must deliver the goods to the consumer.

(3) Unless there is an agreed time or period, the contract is to be treated as including a term that the trader must deliver the goods—

(a) without undue delay, and

(b) in any event, not more than 30 days after the day on which the contract is entered into.

…

CAN A TRADER CONTRACT OUT OF STATUTORY RIGHTS AND REMEDIES UNDER A GOODS CONTRACT?

31 Liability that cannot be excluded or restricted

(1) A term of a contract to supply goods is not binding on the consumer to the extent that it would exclude or restrict the trader's liability arising under any of these provisions—

(a) section 9 (goods to be of satisfactory quality);
(b) section 10 (goods to be fit for particular purpose);
(c) section 11 (goods to be as described);
(d) section 12 (other pre-contract information included in contract);
(e) section 13 (goods to match a sample);
(f) section 14 (goods to match a model seen or examined);
(g) section 15 (installation as part of conformity of the goods with the contract);
(h) section 16 (goods not conforming to contract if digital content does not conform);
(i) section 17 (trader to have right to supply the goods etc);
(j) section 28 (delivery of goods);

      (k)   section 29 (passing of risk).

(2)   That also means that a term of a contract to supply goods is not binding on the consumer to the extent that it would—

      (a)   exclude or restrict a right or remedy in respect of a liability under a provision listed in subsection (1),

      (b)   make such a right or remedy or its enforcement subject to a restrictive or onerous condition,

      (c)   allow a trader to put a person at a disadvantage as a result of pursuing such a right or remedy, or

      (d)   exclude or restrict rules of evidence or procedure.

(3)   The reference in subsection (1) to excluding or restricting a liability also includes preventing an obligation or duty arising or limiting its extent.

(4)   An agreement in writing to submit present or future differences to arbitration is not to be regarded as excluding or restricting any liability for the purposes of this section.

…

Chapter 3

Digital Content

…

Chapter 4

Services

What Services Contracts are Covered?

48 Contracts covered by this Chapter

(1)   This Chapter applies to a contract for a trader to supply a service to a consumer.

(2)   That does not include a contract of employment or apprenticeship.

(3)   In relation to Scotland, this Chapter does not apply to a gratuitous contract.

(4)   A contract to which this Chapter applies is referred to in this Part as a "contract to supply a service".

…

WHAT STATUTORY RIGHTS ARE THERE UNDER A SERVICES CONTRACT?

49 Service to be performed with reasonable care and skill

(1)   Every contract to supply a service is to be treated as including a term that the trader must perform the service with reasonable care and skill.

(2)   See section 54 for a consumer's rights if the trader is in breach of a term that this section requires to be treated as included in a contract.

50 Information about the trader or service to be binding

(1)   Every contract to supply a service is to be treated as including as a term of the contract anything that is said or written to the consumer, by or on behalf of the trader, about the trader or the service, if—

(a)   it is taken into account by the consumer when deciding to enter into the contract, or

(b)   it is taken into account by the consumer when making any decision about the service after entering into the contract.

(2)   Anything taken into account by the consumer as mentioned in subsection (1)(a) or (b) is subject to—

(a)   anything that qualified it and was said or written to the consumer by the trader on the same occasion, and

(b)   any change to it that has been expressly agreed between the consumer and the trader (before entering into the contract or later).

...

(5)   See section 54 for a consumer's rights if the trader is in breach of a term that this section requires to be treated as included in a contract.

51 Reasonable price to be paid for a service

(1)   This section applies to a contract to supply a service if—

(a)   the consumer has not paid a price or other consideration for the service,

(b)   the contract does not expressly fix a price or other consideration, and does not say how it is to be fixed, and

(c)   anything that is to be treated under section 50 as included in the contract does not fix a price or other consideration either.

(2)   In that case the contract is to be treated as including a term that the consumer must pay a reasonable price for the service, and no more.

(3)   What is a reasonable price is a question of fact.

52 Service to be performed within a reasonable time

(1) This section applies to a contract to supply a service, if—

    (a) the contract does not expressly fix the time for the service to be performed, and does not say how it is to be fixed, and

    (b) information that is to be treated under section 50 as included in the contract does not fix the time either.

(2) In that case the contract is to be treated as including a term that the trader must perform the service within a reasonable time.

(3) What is a reasonable time is a question of fact.

(4) See section 54 for a consumer's rights if the trader is in breach of a term that this section requires to be treated as included in a contract.

WHAT REMEDIES ARE THERE IF STATUTORY RIGHTS UNDER A SERVICES CONTRACT ARE NOT MET?

54 Consumer's rights to enforce terms about services

(1) The consumer's rights under this section and sections 55 and 56 do not affect any rights that the contract provides for, if those are not inconsistent.

(2) In this section and section 55 a reference to a service conforming to a contract is a reference to—

    (a) the service being performed in accordance with section 49, or

    (b) the service conforming to a term that section 50 requires to be treated as included in the contract and that relates to the performance of the service.

(3) If the service does not conform to the contract, the consumer's rights (and the provisions about them and when they are available) are—

    (a) the right to require repeat performance (see section 55);

    (b) the right to a price reduction (see section 56).

(4) If the trader is in breach of a term that section 50 requires to be treated as included in the contract but that does not relate to the service, the consumer has the right to a price reduction (see section 56 for provisions about that right and when it is available).

(5) If the trader is in breach of what the contract requires under section 52 (performance within a reasonable time), the consumer has the right to a price reduction (see section 56 for provisions about that right and when it is available).

(6) This section and sections 55 and 56 do not prevent the consumer seeking other remedies for a breach of a term to which any of subsections (3) to (5) applies, instead of or in addition to a remedy referred to there (but not so as to recover twice for the same loss).

(7)   Those other remedies include any of the following that is open to the consumer in the circumstances—

(a)   claiming damages;

(b)   seeking to recover money paid where the consideration for payment of the money has failed;

(c)   seeking specific performance;

(d)   seeking an order for specific implement;

(e)   relying on the breach against a claim by the trader under the contract;

(f)   exercising a right to treat the contract as at an end.

55 Right to repeat performance

(1)   The right to require repeat performance is a right to require the trader to perform the service again, to the extent necessary to complete its performance in conformity with the contract.

(2)   If the consumer requires such repeat performance, the trader—

(a)   must provide it within a reasonable time and without significant inconvenience to the consumer; and

(b)   must bear any necessary costs incurred in doing so (including in particular the cost of any labour or materials).

(3)   The consumer cannot require repeat performance if completing performance of the service in conformity with the contract is impossible.

(4)   Any question as to what is a reasonable time or significant inconvenience is to be determined taking account of—

(a)   the nature of the service, and

(b)   the purpose for which the service was to be performed.

56 Right to price reduction

...

CAN A TRADER CONTRACT OUT OF STATUTORY RIGHTS AND REMEDIES UNDER A SERVICES CONTRACT?

57 Liability that cannot be excluded or restricted

(1) A term of a contract to supply services is not binding on the consumer to the extent that it would exclude the trader's liability arising under section 49 (service to be performed with reasonable care and skill).

(2) Subject to section 50(2), a term of a contract to supply services is not binding on the consumer to the extent that it would exclude the trader's liability arising under section 50 (information about trader or service to be binding).

(3) A term of a contract to supply services is not binding on the consumer to the extent that it would restrict the trader's liability arising under any of sections 49 and 50 and, where they apply, sections 51 and 52 (reasonable price and reasonable time), if it would prevent the consumer in an appropriate case from recovering the price paid or the value of any other consideration. (If it would not prevent the consumer from doing so, Part 2 (unfair terms) may apply.)

(4) That also means that a term of a contract to supply services is not binding on the consumer to the extent that it would —

    (a) exclude or restrict a right or remedy in respect of a liability under any of sections 49 to 52,

    (b) make such a right or remedy or its enforcement subject to a restrictive or onerous condition,

    (c) allow a trader to put a person at a disadvantage as a result of pursuing such a right or remedy, or

    (d) exclude or restrict rules of evidence or procedure.

(5) The references in subsections (1) to (3) to excluding or restricting a liability also include preventing an obligation or duty arising or limiting its extent.

(6) An agreement in writing to submit present or future differences to arbitration is not to be regarded as excluding or restricting any liability for the purposes of this section.

(7) See Schedule 3 for provision about the enforcement of this section

Chapter 5

General and Supplementary Provisions

...

Part 2 Unfair Terms

What Contracts and Notices are Covered by this Part?

61 Contracts and notices covered by this Part

(1)   This Part applies to a contract between a trader and a consumer.

(2)   This does not include a contract of employment or apprenticeship.

(3)   A contract to which this Part applies is referred to in this Part as a "consumer contract".

(4)   This Part applies to a notice to the extent that it—

   (a)   relates to rights or obligations as between a trader and a consumer, or

   (b)   purports to exclude or restrict a trader's liability to a consumer.

(5)   This does not include a notice relating to rights, obligations or liabilities as between an employer and an employee.

(6)   It does not matter for the purposes of subsection (4) whether the notice is expressed to apply to a consumer, as long as it is reasonable to assume it is intended to be seen or heard by a consumer.

(7)   A notice to which this Part applies is referred to in this Part as a "consumer notice".

(8)   In this section "notice" includes an announcement, whether or not in writing, and any other communication or purported communication.

WHAT ARE THE GENERAL RULES ABOUT FAIRNESS OF CONTRACT TERMS AND NOTICES?

62 Requirement for contract terms and notices to be fair

(1)   An unfair term of a consumer contract is not binding on the consumer.

(2)   An unfair consumer notice is not binding on the consumer.

(3)   This does not prevent the consumer from relying on the term or notice if the consumer chooses to do so.

(4)   A term is unfair if, contrary to the requirement of good faith, it causes a significant imbalance in the parties' rights and obligations under the contract to the detriment of the consumer.

(5)   Whether a term is fair is to be determined—

   (a)   taking into account the nature of the subject matter of the contract, and

   (b)   by reference to all the circumstances existing when the term was agreed and to all of the other terms of the contract or of any other contract on which it depends.

(6)   A notice is unfair if, contrary to the requirement of good faith, it causes a significant imbalance in the parties' rights and obligations to the detriment of the consumer.

(7)   Whether a notice is fair is to be determined—

    (a)   taking into account the nature of the subject matter of the notice, and

    (b)   by reference to all the circumstances existing when the rights or obligations to which it relates arose and to the terms of any contract on which it depends.

(8)   This section does not affect the operation of—

    (a)   section 31 (exclusion of liability: goods contracts),

        ...

    (c)   section 57 (exclusion of liability: services contracts), or

    (d)   section 65 (exclusion of negligence liability).

63 Contract terms which may or must be regarded as unfair

(1)   Part 1 of Schedule 2 contains an indicative and non-exhaustive list of terms of consumer contracts that may be regarded as unfair for the purposes of this Part.

(2)   Part 1 of Schedule 2 is subject to Part 2 of that Schedule; but a term listed in Part 2 of that Schedule may nevertheless be assessed for fairness under section 62 unless section 64 or 73 applies to it.

...

64 Exclusion from assessment of fairness

(1)   A term of a consumer contract may not be assessed for fairness under section 62 to the extent that—

    (a)   it specifies the main subject matter of the contract, or

    (b)   the assessment is of the appropriateness of the price payable under the contract by comparison with the goods, digital content or services supplied under it.

(2)   Subsection (1) excludes a term from an assessment under section 62 only if it is transparent and prominent.

(3)   A term is transparent for the purposes of this Part if it is expressed in plain and intelligible language and (in the case of a written term) is legible.

(4)   A term is prominent for the purposes of this section if it is brought to the consumer's attention in such a way that an average consumer would be aware of the term.

(5)   In subsection (4) "average consumer" means a consumer who is reasonably well-informed, observant and circumspect.

(6)   This section does not apply to a term of a contract listed in Part 1 of Schedule 2.

65 Bar on exclusion or restriction of negligence liability

(1)   A trader cannot by a term of a consumer contract or by a consumer notice exclude or restrict liability for death or personal injury resulting from negligence.

(2)   Where a term of a consumer contract, or a consumer notice, purports to exclude or restrict a trader's liability for negligence, a person is not to be taken to have voluntarily accepted any risk merely because the person agreed to or knew about the term or notice.

(3)   In this section "personal injury" includes any disease and any impairment of physical or mental condition.

(4)   In this section "negligence" means the breach of—

(a)   any obligation to take reasonable care or exercise reasonable skill in the performance of a contract where the obligation arises from an express or implied term of the contract,

(b)   a common law duty to take reasonable care or exercise reasonable skill,

(c)   the common duty of care imposed by the Occupiers' Liability Act 1957 or the Occupiers' Liability Act (Northern Ireland) 1957, or

(d)   the duty of reasonable care imposed by section 2(1) of the Occupiers' Liability (Scotland) Act 1960.

(5)   It is immaterial for the purposes of subsection (4)—

(a)   whether a breach of duty or obligation was inadvertent or intentional, or

(b)   whether liability for it arises directly or vicariously.

(6)   This section is subject to section 66 (which makes provision about the scope of this section).

66 Scope of section 65

(1)   Section 65 does not apply to—

(a)   any contract so far as it is a contract of insurance, including a contract to pay an annuity on human life, or

(b)   any contract so far as it relates to the creation or transfer of an interest in land.

(2)   Section 65 does not affect the validity of any discharge or indemnity given by a person in consideration of the receipt by that person of compensation in settlement of any claim the person has.

(3)   Section 65 does not—

(a)   apply to liability which is excluded or discharged as mentioned in section 4(2)(a) (exception to liability to pay damages to relatives) of the Damages (Scotland) Act 2011, or

(b)   affect the operation of section 5 (discharge of liability to pay damages: exception for mesothelioma) of that Act.

(4)   Section 65 does not apply to the liability of an occupier of premises to a person who obtains access to the premises for recreational purposes if—

(a)   the person suffers loss or damage because of the dangerous state of the premises, and

(b) allowing the person access for those purposes is not within the purposes of the occupier's trade, business, craft or profession

67 Effect of an unfair term on the rest of a contract

Where a term of a consumer contract is not binding on the consumer as a result of this Part, the contract continues, so far as practicable, to have effect in every other respect.

68 Requirement for transparency

(1) A trader must ensure that a written term of a consumer contract, or a consumer notice in writing, is transparent.

(2) A consumer notice is transparent for the purposes of subsection (1) if it is expressed in plain and intelligible language and it is legible.

69 Contract terms that may have different meanings

(1) If a term in a consumer contract, or a consumer notice, could have different meanings, the meaning that is most favourable to the consumer is to prevail.

...

HOW ARE THE GENERAL RULES ENFORCED?

70 Enforcement of the law on unfair contract terms

(1) Schedule 3 confers functions on the Competition and Markets Authority and other regulators in relation to the enforcement of this Part.

(2) For provision about the investigatory powers that are available to those regulators for the purposes of that Schedule, see Schedule 5.

SUPPLEMENTARY PROVISIONS

71 Duty of court to consider fairness of term

(1) Subsection (2) applies to proceedings before a court which relate to a term of a consumer contract.

(2) The court must consider whether the term is fair even if none of the parties to the proceedings has raised that issue or indicated that it intends to raise it.

(3) But subsection (2) does not apply unless the court considers that it has before it sufficient legal and factual material to enable it to consider the fairness of the term.

76 Interpretation of Part 2

(1) In this Part—

"consumer contract" has the meaning given by section 61(3);

"consumer notice" has the meaning given by section 61(7);

"transparent" is to be construed in accordance with sections 64(3) and 68(2).

(2)   The following have the same meanings in this Part as they have in Part 1 —

"trader" (see section 2(2));

"consumer" (see section 2(3));

"goods" (see section 2(8));

"digital content" (see section 2(9)).

(3)   Section 2(4) (trader who claims an individual is not a consumer must prove it) applies in relation to this Part as it applies in relation to Part 1.

...

SCHEDULE 2 CONSUMER CONTRACT TERMS WHICH MAY BE REGARDED AS UNFAIR

Section 63

Part 1 List of Terms

(1)   A term which has the object or effect of excluding or limiting the trader's liability in the event of the death of or personal injury to the consumer resulting from an act or omission of the trader.

(2)   A term which has the object or effect of inappropriately excluding or limiting the legal rights of the consumer in relation to the trader or another party in the event of total or partial non-performance or inadequate performance by the trader of any of the contractual obligations, including the option of offsetting a debt owed to the trader against any claim which the consumer may have against the trader.

(3)   A term which has the object or effect of making an agreement binding on the consumer in a case where the provision of services by the trader is subject to a condition whose realisation depends on the trader's will alone.

(4)   A term which has the object or effect of permitting the trader to retain sums paid by the consumer where the consumer decides not to conclude or perform the contract, without providing for the consumer to receive compensation of an equivalent amount from the trader where the trader is the party cancelling the contract.

(5)   A term which has the object or effect of requiring that, where the consumer decides not to conclude or perform the contract, the consumer must pay the trader a disproportionately high sum in compensation or for services which have not been supplied.

(6)   A term which has the object or effect of requiring a consumer who fails to fulfil his obligations under the contract to pay a disproportionately high sum in compensation.

(7)   A term which has the object or effect of authorising the trader to dissolve the contract on a discretionary basis where the same facility is not granted to the consumer, or permitting the trader to retain the sums paid for services not yet supplied by the trader where it is the trader who dissolves the contract.

(8)   A term which has the object or effect of enabling the trader to terminate a contract of indeterminate duration without reasonable notice except where there are serious grounds for doing so.

(9)   A term which has the object or effect of automatically extending a contract of fixed duration where the consumer does not indicate otherwise, when the deadline fixed for the consumer to express a desire not to extend the contract is unreasonably early.

(10)   A term which has the object or effect of irrevocably binding the consumer to terms with which the consumer has had no real opportunity of becoming acquainted before the conclusion of the contract.

(11)   A term which has the object or effect of enabling the trader to alter the terms of the contract unilaterally without a valid reason which is specified in the contract.

(12)   A term which has the object or effect of permitting the trader to determine the characteristics of the subject matter of the contract after the consumer has become bound by it.

(13)   A term which has the object or effect of enabling the trader to alter unilaterally without a valid reason any characteristics of the goods, digital content or services to be provided.

(14)   A term which has the object or effect of giving the trader the discretion to decide the price payable under the contract after the consumer has become bound by it, where no price or method of determining the price is agreed when the consumer becomes bound.

(15)   A term which has the object or effect of permitting a trader to increase the price of goods, digital content or services without giving the consumer the right to cancel the contract if the final price is too high in relation to the price agreed when the contract was concluded.

(16)   A term which has the object or effect of giving the trader the right to determine whether the goods, digital content or services supplied are in conformity with the contract, or giving the trader the exclusive right to interpret any term of the contract.

(17)   A term which has the object or effect of limiting the trader's obligation to respect commitments undertaken by the trader's agents or making the trader's commitments subject to compliance with a particular formality.

(18)   A term which has the object or effect of obliging the consumer to fulfil all of the consumer's obligations where the trader does not perform the trader's obligations.

(19)   A term which has the object or effect of allowing the trader to transfer the trader's rights and obligations under the contract, where this may reduce the guarantees for the consumer, without the consumer's agreement.

(20)   A term which has the object or effect of excluding or hindering the consumer's right to take legal action or exercise any other legal remedy, in particular by—

(a)   requiring the consumer to take disputes exclusively to arbitration not covered by legal provisions,

(b)   unduly restricting the evidence available to the consumer, or

(c)   imposing on the consumer a burden of proof which, according to the applicable law, should lie with another party to the contract.

CONTRACTS (RIGHTS OF THIRD PARTIES) ACT 1999

1999 chapter 31

An Act to make provision for the enforcement of contractual terms by third parties.

1 Right of third party to enforce contractual term

(1)   Subject to the provisions of this Act, a person who is not a party to a contract (a "third party") may in his own right enforce a term of the contract if-

(a)   the contract expressly provides that he may, or

(b)   subject to subsection (2), the term purports to confer a benefit on him.

(2)   Subsection (1)(b) does not apply if on a proper construction of the contract it appears that the parties did not intend the term to be enforceable by the third party.

(3)   The third party must be expressly identified in the contract by name, as a member of a class or as answering a particular description but need not be in existence when the contract is entered into.

(4)   This section does not confer a right on a third party to enforce a term of a contract otherwise than subject to and in accordance with any other relevant terms of the contract.

(5)   For the purpose of exercising his right to enforce a term of the contract, there shall be available to the third party any remedy that would have been available to him in an action for breach of contract if he had been a party to the contract (and the rules relating to damages, injunctions, specific performance and other relief shall apply accordingly).

(6)   Where a term of a contract excludes or limits liability in relation to any matter references in this Act to the third party enforcing the term shall be construed as references to his availing himself of the exclusion or limitation.

(7)   In this Act, in relation to a term of a contract which is enforceable by a third party-

(a)   "the promisor" means the party to the contract against whom the term is enforceable by the third party, and

(b)   "the promisee" means the party to the contract by whom the term is enforceable against the promisor.

2 Variation and rescission of contract

(1)   Subject to the provisions of this section, where a third party has a right under section 1 to enforce a term of the contract, the parties to the contract may not, by agreement, rescind the contract, or vary it in such a way as to extinguish or alter his entitlement under that right, without his consent if-

    (a)   the third party has communicated his assent to the term to the promisor,

    (b)   the promisor is aware that the third party has relied on the term, or

    (c)   the promisor can reasonably be expected to have foreseen that the third party would rely on the term and the third party has in fact relied on it.

(2)   The assent referred to in subsection (1)(a)-

    (a)   may be by words or conduct, and

    (b)   if sent to the promisor by post or other means, shall not be regarded as communicated to the promisor until received by him.

(3)   Subsection (1) is subject to any express term of the contract under which-

    (a)   the parties to the contract may by agreement rescind or vary the contract without the consent of the third party, or

    (b)   the consent of the third party is required in circumstances specified in the contract instead of those set out in subsection (1)(a) to (c).

(4)   Where the consent of a third party is required under subsection (1) or (3), the court or arbitral tribunal may, on the application of the parties to the contract, dispense with his consent if satisfied-

    (a)   that his consent cannot be obtained because his whereabouts cannot reasonably be ascertained, or

    (b)   that he is mentally incapable of giving his consent.

(5)   The court or arbitral tribunal may, on the application of the parties to a contract, dispense with any consent that may be required under subsection (1)(c) if satisfied that it cannot reasonably be ascertained whether or not the third party has in fact relied on the term.

(6)   If the court or arbitral tribunal dispenses with a third party's consent, it may impose such conditions as it thinks fit, including a condition requiring the payment of compensation to the third party.

(7)   The jurisdiction conferred on the court by subsections (4) to (6) is exercisable by both the High Court and a county court.

3 Defences etc. available to promisor

(1)   Subsections (2) to (5) apply where, in reliance on section 1, proceedings for the enforcement of a term of a contract are brought by a third party.

(2)   The promisor shall have available to him by way of defence or set-off any matter that-

(a)   arises from or in connection with the contract and is relevant to the term, and

(b)   would have been available to him by way of defence or set-off if the proceedings had been brought by the promisee.

(3)   The promisor shall also have available to him by way of defence or set-off any matter if-

(a)   an express term of the contract provides for it to be available to him in proceedings brought by the third party, and

(b)   it would have been available to him by way of defence or set-off if the proceedings had been brought by the promisee.

(4)   The promisor shall also have available to him-

(a)   by way of defence or set-off any matter, and

(b)   by way of counterclaim any matter not arising from the contract,

that would have been available to him by way of defence or set-off or, as the case may be, by way of counterclaim against the third party if the third party had been a party to the contract.

(5)   Subsections (2) and (4) are subject to any express term of the contract as to the matters that are not to be available to the promisor by way of defence, set-off or counterclaim.

(6)   Where in any proceedings brought against him a third party seeks in reliance on section 1 to enforce a term of a contract (including, in particular, a term purporting to exclude or limit liability), he may not do so if he could not have done so (whether by reason of any particular circumstances relating to him or otherwise) had he been a party to the contract.

4 Enforcement of contract by promisee

Section 1 does not affect any right of the promisee to enforce any term of the contract.

5 Protection of promisor from double liability

Where under section 1 a term of a contract is enforceable by a third party, and the promisee has recovered from the promisor a sum in respect of-

(a)   the third party's loss in respect of the term, or

(b)   the expense to the promisee of making good to the third party the default of the promisor,

then, in any proceedings brought in reliance on that section by the third party, the court or arbitral tribunal shall reduce any award to the third party to such extent as it thinks appropriate to take account of the sum recovered by the promisee.

6 Exceptions

(1)   Section 1 confers no rights on a third party in the case of a contract on a bill of exchange, promissory note or other negotiable instrument.

(2)   Section 1 confers no rights on a third party in the case of any contract binding on a company and its members under [section 33 of the Companies Act 2006 (effect of company's constitution)].

[[(2A) Section 1 confers no rights on a third party in the case of any incorporation document of a limited liability partnership [or any agreement (express or implied) between the members of a limited liability partnership, or between a limited liability partnership and its members, that determines the mutual rights and duties of the members and their rights and duties in relation to the limited liability partnership.]]

(3) Section 1 confers no right on a third party to enforce-

    (a) any term of a contract of employment against an employee,

    (b) any term of a worker's contract against a worker (including a home worker), or

    (c) any term of a relevant contract against an agency worker.

(4) In subsection (3)-

    (a) "Contract of employment", "employee", "worker's contract", and "worker" have the meaning given by section 54 of the National Minimum Wage Act 1998,

    (b) "Home worker" has the meaning given by section 35(2) of that Act,

    (c) "Agency worker" has the same meaning as in section 34(1) of that Act, and

    (d) "Relevant contract" means a contract entered into, in a case where section 34 of that Act applies, by the agency worker as respects work falling within subsection (1)(a) of that section.

(5) Section 1 confers no rights on a third party in the case of-

    (a) a contract for the carriage of goods by sea, or

    (b) a contract for the carriage of goods by rail or road, or for the carriage of cargo by air, which is subject to the rules of the appropriate international transport convention,

except that a third party may in reliance on that section avail himself of an exclusion or limitation of liability in such a contract.

(6) In subsection (5) "contract for the carriage of goods by sea" means a contract of carriage-

    (a) contained in or evidenced by a bill of lading, sea waybill or a corresponding electronic transaction, or

    (b) under or for the purposes of which there is given an undertaking which is contained in a ship's delivery order or a corresponding electronic transaction.

(7) For the purposes of subsection (6)-

    (a) "bill of lading", "sea waybill" and "ship's delivery order" have the same meaning as in the Carriage of Goods by Sea Act 1992, and

    (b) a corresponding electronic transaction is a transaction within section 1(5) of that Act which corresponds to the issue, indorsement, delivery or transfer of a bill of lading, sea waybill or ship's delivery order.

(8) In subsection (5) "the appropriate international transport convention" means-

(a) in relation to a contract for the carriage of goods by rail, the Convention which has the force of law in the United Kingdom under [regulation 3 of the Railways (Convention on International Carriage by Rail) Regulations 2005],

(b) in relation to a contract for the carriage of goods by road, the Convention which has the force of law in the United Kingdom under section 1 of the Carriage of Goods by Road Act 1965, and

(c) in relation to a contract for the carriage of cargo by air-

    (i) the Convention which has the force of law in the United Kingdom under section 1 of the Carriage by Air Act 1961, or

    (ii) the Convention which has the force of law under section 1 of the Carriage by Air (Supplementary Provisions) Act 1962, or

    (iii) either of the amended Conventions set out in Part B of Schedule 2 or 3 to the Carriage by Air Acts (Application of Provisions) Order 1967.

7 Supplementary provisions relating to third party

(1) Section 1 does not affect any right or remedy of a third party that exists or is available apart from this Act.

(2) Section 2(2) of the Unfair Contract Terms Act 1977 (restriction on exclusion etc. of liability for negligence) shall not apply where the negligence consists of the breach of an obligation arising from a term of a contract and the person seeking to enforce it is a third party acting in reliance on section 1.

(3) In sections 5 and 8 of the Limitation Act 1980 the references to an action founded on a simple contract and an action upon a specialty shall respectively include references to an action brought in reliance on section 1 relating to a simple contract and an action brought in reliance on that section relating to a specialty.

(4) A third party shall not, by virtue of section 1(5) or 3(4) or (6), be treated as a party to the contract for the purposes of any other Act (or any instrument made under any other Act).

10 Short title, commencement and extent

(1) This Act may be cited as the Contracts (Rights of Third Parties) Act 1999.

LAW REFORM (FRUSTRATED CONTRACTS) ACT 1943

1943 chapter 40

An Act to amend the law relating to the frustration of contracts.

1 Adjustment of rights and liabilities of parties to frustrated contracts

(1) Where a contract governed by English law has become impossible of performance or been otherwise frustrated, and the parties thereto have for that reason been discharged from the

further performance of the contract, the following provisions of this section shall, subject to the provisions of section two of this Act, have effect in relation thereto.

(2)   All sums paid or payable to any party in pursuance of the contract before the time when the parties were so discharged (in this Act referred to as "the time of discharge") shall, in the case of sums so paid, be recoverable from him as money received by him for the use of the party by whom the sums were paid, and, in the case of sums so payable, cease to be so payable:

Provided that, if the party to whom the sums were so paid or payable incurred expenses before the time of discharge in, or for the purpose of, the performance of the contract, the court may, if it considers it just to do so having regard to all the circumstances of the case, allow him to retain or, as the case may be, recover the whole or any part of the sums so paid or payable, not being an amount in excess of the expenses so incurred.

(3)   Where any party to the contract has, by reason of anything done by any other party thereto in, or for the purpose of, the performance of the contract, obtained a valuable benefit (other than a payment of money to which the last foregoing subsection applies) before the time of discharge, there shall be recoverable from him by the said other party such sum (if any), not exceeding the value of the said benefit to the party obtaining it, as the court considers just, having regard to all the circumstances of the case and, in particular-

(a)   the amount of any expenses incurred before the time of discharge by the benefited party in, or for the purpose of, the performance of the contract, including any sums paid or payable by him to any other party in pursuance of the contract and retained or recoverable by that party under the last foregoing subsection, and

(b)   the effect, in relation to the said benefit, of the circumstances giving rise to the frustration of the contract.

(4)   In estimating, for the purposes of the foregoing provisions of this section, the amount of any expenses incurred by any party to the contract, the court may, without prejudice to the generality of the said provisions, include such sum as appears to be reasonable in respect of overhead expenses and in respect of any work or services performed personally by the said party.

(5)   In considering whether any sum ought to be recovered or retained under the foregoing provisions of this section by any party to the contract, the court shall not take into account any sums which have, by reason of the circumstances giving rise to the frustration of the contract, become payable to that party under any contract of insurance unless there was an obligation to insure imposed by an express term of the frustrated contract or by or under any enactment.

(6)   Where any person has assumed obligations under the contract in consideration of the conferring of a benefit by any other party to the contract upon any other person, whether a party to the contract or not, the court may, if in all the circumstances of the case it considers it just to do so, treat for the purposes of subsection (3) of this section any benefit so conferred as a benefit obtained by the person who has assumed the obligations as aforesaid.

2 Provision as to application of this Act

(1)   This Act shall apply to contracts, whether made before or after the commencement of this Act, as respects which the time of discharge is on or after the first day of July, nineteen hundred and forty-three, but not to contracts as respects which the time of discharge is before the said date.

(2)   This Act shall apply to contracts to which the Crown is a party in like manner as to contracts between subjects.

(3)   Where any contract to which this Act applies contains any provision which, upon the true construction of the contract, is intended to have effect in the event of circumstances arising which operate, or would but for the said provision operate, to frustrate the contract, or is intended to have effect whether such circumstances arise or not, the court shall give effect to the said provision and shall only give effect to the foregoing section of this Act to such extent, if any, as appears to the court to be consistent with the said provision.

(4)   Where it appears to the court that a part of any contract to which this Act applies can properly be severed from the remainder of the contract, being a part wholly performed before the time of discharge, or so performed except for the payment in respect of that part of the contract of sums which are or can be ascertained under the contract, the court shall treat that part of the contract as if it were a separate contract and had not been frustrated and shall treat the foregoing section of this Act as only applicable to the remainder of that contract.

(5)   This Act shall not apply-

    (a)   any charterparty, except a time charterparty or a charterparty by way of demise, or to any contract (other than a charterparty) for the carriage of goods by sea: or

    (b)   any contract of insurance, save as is provided by subsection (5) of the foregoing section; or

    (c)   to any contract to which [section 7 of the Sale of Goods Act 1979](which avoids contracts for the sale of specific goods which perish before the risk has passed to the buyer) applies, or to any other contract for the sale, or for the sale and delivery, of specific goods, where the contract is frustrated by reason of the fact that the goods have perished.

3 Short title and interpretation

(1)   This Act may be cited as the Law Reform (Frustrated Contracts) Act 1943.

(2)   In this Act the expression "court" means, in relation to any matter, the court or arbitrator by or before whom the matter falls to be determined.

MISREPRESENTATION ACT 1967

1967 chapter 7

An Act to amend the law relating to innocent misrepresentations and to amend sections 11 and 35 of the Sale of Goods Act 1893.

1 Removal of certain bars to rescission for innocent misrepresentation

Where a person has entered into a contract after a misrepresentation has been made to him, and-

(a)   the misrepresentation has become a term of the contract; or

(b)   the contract has been performed;

or both, then, if otherwise he would be entitled to rescind the contract without alleging fraud, he shall be so entitled, subject to the provisions of this Act, notwithstanding the matters mentioned in paragraphs (a) and (b) of this section.

2 Damages for misrepresentation

(1)   Where a person has entered into a contract after a misrepresentation has been made to him by another party thereto and as a result thereof he has suffered loss, then, if the person making the misrepresentation would be liable to damages in respect thereof had the misrepresentation been made fraudulently, that person shall be so liable notwithstanding that the misrepresentation was not made fraudulently, unless he proves that he had reasonable ground to believe and did believe up to the time the contract was made the facts represented were true.

(2)   Where a person has entered into a contract after a misrepresentation has been made to him otherwise than fraudulently, and he would be entitled, by reason of the misrepresentation, to rescind the contract, then, if it is claimed, in any proceedings arising out of the contract, that the contract ought to be or has been rescinded, the court or arbitrator may declare the contract subsisting and award damages in lieu of rescission, if of opinion that it would be equitable to do so, having regard to the nature of the misrepresentation and the loss that would be caused by it if the contract were upheld, as well as to the loss that rescission would cause to the other party.

(3)   Damages may be awarded against a person under subsection (2) of this section whether or not he is liable to damages under subsection (1) thereof, but where he is so liable any award under the said subsection (2) shall be taken into account in assessing his liability under the said subsection (1).

[3 Avoidance of provision excluding liability for misrepresentation

[(1)]   [If a contract contains a term which would exclude or restrict—

    (a)   any liability to which a party to a contract may be subject by reason of any misrepresentation made by him before the contract was made; or

    (b)   any remedy available to another party to the contract by reason of such a misrepresentation,

    that term shall be of no effect except in so far as it satisfies the requirement of reasonableness as stated in section 11(1) of the Unfair Contract Terms Act 1977; and it is for those claiming that the term satisfies that requirement to show that it does.]

[(2)   This section does not apply to a term in a consumer contract within the meaning of Part 2 of the Consumer Rights Act 2015 (but see the provision made about such contracts in section 62 of that Act).]

6 Short title, commencement and extent

(1)   This Act may be cited as the Misrepresentation Act 1967.

SALE OF GOODS ACT 1979

1979 chapter 54

An Act to consolidate the law relating to the sale of goods.

PART I CONTRACTS TO WHICH ACT APPLIES

(1)   This Act applies to contracts of sale of goods made on or after (but not to those made before) 1 January 1894.

(2)   In relation to contracts made on certain dates, this Act applies subject to the modification of certain of its sections as mentioned in Schedule 1 below.

(3)   Any such modification is indicated in the section concerned by a reference to Schedule 1 below.

(4)   Accordingly, where a section does not contain such a reference, this Act applies in relation to the contract concerned without such modification of the section.

(5)   Certain sections or subsections of this Act do not apply to a contract to which Chapter 2 of Part 1 of the Consumer Rights Act 2015 applies.

(6)   Where that is the case it is indicated in the section concerned.

2 Contract of sale

(1)   A contract of sale of goods is a contract by which the seller transfers or agrees to transfer the property in goods to the buyer for a money consideration, called the price.

(2)   There may be a contract of sale between one part owner and another.

(3)   A contract of sale may be absolute or conditional.

(4)   Where under a contract of sale the property in the goods is transferred from the seller to the buyer the contract is called a sale.

(5)   Where under a contract of sale the transfer of the property in the goods is to take place at a future time or subject to some condition later to be fulfilled the contract is called an agreement to sell.

(6)   An agreement to sell becomes a sale when the time elapses or the conditions are fulfilled subject to which the property in the goods is to be transferred.

3 Capacity to buy and sell

(1) Capacity to buy and sell is regulated by the general law concerning capacity to contract and to transfer and acquire property.

(2) Where necessaries are sold and delivered to a person who by reason of drunkenness is incompetent to contract, he must pay a reasonable price for them.

(3) In subsection (2) above "necessaries" means goods suitable to the condition in life of the minor or other person concerned and to his actual requirements at the time of the sale and delivery.

4 How contract of sale is made

(1) Subject to this and any other Act, a contract of sale may be made in writing (either with or without seal), or by word of mouth, or partly in writing and partly by word of mouth, or may be implied from the conduct of the parties.

(2) Nothing in this section affects the law relating to corporations.

6 GOODS WHICH HAVE PERISHED

Where there is a contract for the sale of specific goods, and the goods without the knowledge of the seller have perished at the time when the contract is made, the contract is void.

8 Ascertainment of price

(1) The price in a contract of sale may be fixed by the contract, or may be left to be fixed in a manner agreed by the contract, or may be determined by the course of dealing between the parties.

(2) Where the price is not determined as mentioned in sub-section (1) above the buyer must pay a reasonable price.

(3) What is a reasonable price is a question of fact dependent on the circumstances of each particular case.

11 When condition to be treated as warranty

[(1) This section does not apply to Scotland.]

(2) Where a contract of sale is subject to a condition to be fulfilled by the seller, the buyer may waive the condition, or may elect to treat the breach of the condition as a breach of warranty and not as a ground for treating the contract as repudiated.

(3) Whether a stipulation in a contract of sale is a condition, the breach of which may give rise to a right to treat the contract as repudiated, or a warranty, the breach of which may give rise to a claim for damages but not to a right to reject the goods and treat the contract as repudiated, depends in each case on the construction of the contract; and a stipulation may be a condition, though called a warranty in the contract.

(4) Subject to section 35A below where a contract of sale is not severable and the buyer has accepted the goods or part of them, the breach of a condition to be fulfilled by the seller can

only be treated as a breach of warranty, and not as a ground for rejecting the goods and treating the contract as repudiated, unless there is an express or implied term of the contract to that effect.

(4A) Subsection (4) does not apply to a contract to which Chapter 2 of Part 1 of the Consumer Rights Act 2015 applies (but see the provision made about such contracts in sections 19 to 22 of that Act).

(5) . . .

(6) Nothing in this section affects a condition or warranty whose fulfilment is excused by law by reason of impossibility or otherwise.

(7) Paragraph 2 of Schedule 1 below applies in relation to a contract made before 22 April 1967 or (in the application of this Act to Northern Ireland) 28 July 1967.

12 Implied terms about title, etc.

(1) In a contract of sale, other than one to which subsection (3) below applies, there is an implied [term] on the part of the seller that in the case of a sale he has a right to sell the goods, and in the case of an agreement to sell he will have such a right at the time when the property is to pass.

(2) In a contract of sale, other than one to which subsection (3) below applies, there is also an implied [term] that—

(a) the goods are free, and will remain free until the time when the property is to pass, from any charge or encumbrance not disclosed or known to the buyer before the contract is made, and

(b) the buyer will enjoy quiet possession of the goods except so far as it may be disturbed by the owner or other person entitled to the benefit of any charge or encumbrance so disclosed or known.

(3) This subsection applies to a contract of sale in the case of which there appears from the contract or is to be inferred from its circumstances an intention that the seller should transfer only such title as he or a third person may have.

(4) In a contract to which subsection (3) above applies there is an implied [term] that all charges or encumbrances known to the seller and not known to the buyer have been disclosed to the buyer before the contract is made.

(5) In a contract to which subsection (3) above applies there is also an implied [term] that none of the following will disturb the buyer's quiet possession of the goods, namely—

(a) the seller;

(b) in a case where the parties to the contract intend that the seller should transfer only such title as a third person may have, that person;

(c) anyone claiming through or under the seller or that third person otherwise than under a charge or encumbrance disclosed or known to the buyer before the contract is made.

[(5A) As regards England and Wales and Northern Ireland, the term implied by subsection (1) above is a condition and the terms implied by subsections (2), (4) and (5) above are warranties.]

(6)   Paragraph 3 of Schedule 1 below applies in relation to a contract made before 18 May 1973.

(7)   This section does not apply to a contract to which Chapter 2 of Part 1 of the Consumer Rights Act 2015 applies (but see the provision made about such contracts in section 17 of that Act).

13 Sale by description

(1)   Where there is a contract for the sale of goods by description, there is an implied [term] that the goods will correspond with the description.

[(1A) As regards England and Wales and Northern Ireland, the term implied by subsection (I) above is a condition.]

(2)   If the sale is by sample as well as by description it is not sufficient that the bulk of the goods corresponds with the sample if the goods do not also correspond with the description.

(3)   A sale of goods is not prevented from being a sale by description by reason only that, being exposed for sale or hire, they are selected by the buyer.

(4)   Paragraph 4 of Schedule 1 below applies in relation to a contract made before 18th May 1973.

(5)   This section does not apply to a contract to which Chapter 2 of Part 1 of the Consumer Rights Act 2015 applies (but see the provision made about such contracts in section 11 of that Act).

14 Implied terms about quality or fitness

(1)   Except as provided by this section and section 15 below and subject to any other enactment, there is no implied [term] about the quality or fitness for any particular purpose of goods supplied under a contract of sale.

[(2)   Where the seller sells goods in the course of a business, there is an implied term that the goods supplied under the contract are of satisfactory quality.

(2A)   For the purposes of this Act, goods are of satisfactory quality if they meet the standard that a reasonable person would regard as satisfactory, taking account of any description of the goods, the price (if relevant) and all the other relevant circumstances.

(2B)   For the purposes of this Act, the quality of goods includes their state and condition and the following (among others) are in appropriate cases aspects of the quality of goods—

     (a)   fitness for all the purposes for which goods of the kind in question are commonly supplied,

     (b)   appearance and finish,

     (c)   freedom from minor defects,

     (d)   safety, and

     (e)   durability.

(2C) The term implied by subsection (2) above does not extend to any matter making the quality of goods unsatisfactory—

(a) which is specifically drawn to the buyer's attention before the contract is made,

(b) where the buyer examines the goods before the contract is made, which that examination ought to reveal, or

(c) in the case of a contract for sale by sample, which would have been apparent on a reasonable examination of the sample.]

[(2D) Repealed by the Consumer Rights Act 2015

(2E) Repealed by the Consumer Rights Act 2015

(2F) Repealed by the Consumer Rights Act 2015

(3) Where the seller sells goods in the course of a business and the buyer, expressly or by implication, makes known—

(a) to the seller, or

(b) where the purchase price or part of it is payable by instalments and the goods were previously sold by a credit-broker to the seller, to that credit-broker,

any particular purpose for which the goods are being bought, there is an implied [term] that the goods supplied under the contract are reasonably fit for that purpose, whether or not that is a purpose for which such goods are commonly supplied, except where the circumstances show that the buyer does not rely, or that it is unreasonable for him to rely, on the skill or judgment of the seller or credit-broker.

(4) An implied [term] about quality or fitness for a particular purpose may be annexed to a contract of sale by usage.

(5) The preceding provisions of this section apply to a sale by a person who in the course of a business is acting as agent for another as they apply to a sale by a principal in the course of a business, except where that other is not selling in the course of a business and either the buyer knows that fact or reasonable steps are taken to bring it to the notice of the buyer before the contract is made.

[(6) As regards England and Wales and Northern Ireland, the terms implied by subsections (2) and (3) above are conditions.]

(7) Paragraph 5 of Schedule 1 below applies in relation to a contract made on or after 18 May 1973 and before the appointed day, and paragraph 6 in relation to one made before 18th May 1973.

(8) In subsection (7) above and paragraph 5 of Schedule 1 below references to the appointed day are to the day appointed for the purposes of those provisions by an order of the Secretary of State made by statutory instrument.

[(9) This section does not apply to a contract to which Chapter 2 of Part 1 of the Consumer Rights Act 2015 applies (but see the provision made about such contracts in sections 9, 10 and 18 of that Act).]

15 Sale by sample

(1)   A contract of sale is a contract for sale by sample where there is an express or implied term to that effect in the contract.

(2)   In the case of a contract for sale by sample there is an implied [term]—

   (a)   that the bulk will correspond with the sample in quality;

   (b)   . . .

   (c)   that the goods will be free from any defect, [making their quality unsatisfactory], which would not be apparent on reasonable examination of the sample.

[(3)   As regards England and Wales and Northern Ireland, the term implied by subsection (2) above is a condition.]

(4)   Paragraph 7 of Schedule 1 below applies in relation to a contract made before 18 May 1973.

[(5)   This section does not apply to a contract to which Chapter 2 of Part 1 of the Consumer Rights Act 2015 applies (but see the provision made about such contracts in sections 13 and 18 of that Act).]

[15A Modification of remedies for breach of condition in non-consumer cases

[(1)   Where in the case of a contract of sale—

   (a)   the buyer would, apart from this subsection, have the right to reject goods by reason of a breach on the part of the seller of a term implied by section 13, 14 or 15 above, but

   (b)   the breach is so slight that it would be unreasonable for him to reject them,

   the breach is not to be treated as a breach of condition but may be treated as a breach of warranty.

(2)   This section applies unless a contrary intention appears in, or is to be implied from, the contract.

(3)   It is for the seller to show that a breach fell within subsection (1)(b) above.

(4)   This section does not apply to Scotland.]

23 Sale under voidable title

When the seller of goods has a voidable title to them, but his title has not been avoided at the time of the sale, the buyer acquires a good title to the goods, provided he buys them in good faith and without notice of the seller's defect of title.

Repealed by Consumer Rights Act 2015

Seller's remedies

49 Action for price

(1)   Where, under a contract of sale, the property in the goods has passed to the buyer and he wrongfully neglects or refuses to pay for the goods according to the terms of the contract, the seller may maintain an action against him for the price of the goods.

(2)   Where, under a contract of sale, the price is payable on a day certain irrespective of delivery and the buyer wrongfully neglects or refuses to pay such price, the seller may maintain an action for the price, although the property in the goods has not passed and the goods have not been appropriated to the contract.

50 Damages for non-acceptance

(1)   Where the buyer wrongfully neglects or refuses to accept and pay for the goods, the seller may maintain an action against him for damages for non-acceptance.

(2)   The measure of damages is the estimated loss directly and naturally resulting, in the ordinary course of events, from the buyer's breach of contract.

(3)   Where there is an available market for the goods in question the measure of damages is prima facie to be ascertained by the difference between the contract price and the market or current price at the time or times when the goods ought to have been accepted or (if no time was fixed for acceptance) at the time of the refusal to accept.

Buyer's remedies

51 Damages for non-delivery

(1)   Where the seller wrongfully neglects or refuses to deliver the goods to the buyer, the buyer may maintain an action against the seller for damages for non-delivery.

(2)   The measure of damages is the estimated loss directly and naturally resulting, in the ordinary course of events, from the seller's breach of contract.

(3)   Where there is an available market for the goods in question the measure of damages is prima facie to be ascertained by the difference between the contract price and the market or current price of the goods at the time or times when they ought to have been delivered or (if no time was fixed) at the time of the refusal to deliver.

[(4)   This section does not apply to a contract to which Chapter 2 of Part 1 of the Consumer Rights Act 2015 applies (but see the provision made about such contracts in section 19 of that Act).]

52 Specific performance

(1)   In any action for breach of contract to deliver specific or ascertained goods the court may, if it thinks fit, on the plaintiff's application, by its judgment or decree direct that the contract shall be performed specifically, without giving the defendant the option of retaining the goods on payment of damages.

(2)   The plaintiff's application may be made at any time before judgment or decree.

(3)   The judgment or decree may be unconditional, or on such terms and conditions as to damages, payment of the price and otherwise as seem just to the court.

(4)   The provisions of this section shall be deemed to be supplementary to, and not in derogation of, the right of specific implement in Scotland.

[(5)   This section does not apply to a contract to which Chapter 2 of Part 1 of the Consumer Rights Act 2015 applies (but see the provision made about such contracts in section 19 of that Act).]

53 Remedy for breach of warranty

(1)   Where there is a breach of warranty by the seller, or where the buyer elects (or is compelled) to treat any breach of a condition on the part of the seller as a breach of warranty, the buyer is not by reason only of such breach of warranty entitled to reject the goods; but he may—

(a)   set up against the seller the breach of warranty in diminution or extinction of the price, or
(b)   maintain an action against the seller for damages for the breach of warranty.

(2)   The measure of damages for breach of warranty is the estimated loss directly and naturally resulting, in the ordinary course of events, from the breach of warranty.

(3)   In the case of breach of warranty of quality such loss is prima facie the difference between the value of the goods at the time of delivery to the buyer and the value they would have had if they had fulfilled the warranty.

(4)   The fact that the buyer has set up the breach of warranty in diminution or extinction of the price does not prevent him from maintaining an action for the same breach of warranty if he has suffered further damage.

[(4A) This section does not apply to a contract to which Chapter 2 of Part 1 of the Consumer Rights Act 2015 applies (but see the provision made about such contracts in section 19 of that Act).]

[(5)   This section does not apply to Scotland.]

55 Exclusion of implied terms

(1)   Where a right, duty or liability would arise under a contract of sale of goods by implication of law, it may (subject to the Unfair Contract Terms Act 1977) be negatived or varied by express agreement, or by the course of dealing between the parties, or by such usage as binds both parties to the contract.

[(1A) Subsection (1) does not apply to a contract to which Chapter 2 of Part 1 of the Consumer Rights Act 2015 applies (but see the provision made about such contracts in section 31 of that Act).]

(2)   An express [term] does not negative a [term] implied by this Act unless inconsistent with it.

(3)   Paragraph 11 of Schedule 1 below applies in relation to a contract made on or after 18th May 1973 and before 1st February 1978, and paragraph 12 in relation to one made before 18th May 1973

57 Auction sales

(1)   Where goods are put up for sale by auction in lots, each lot is prima facie deemed to be the subject of a separate contract of sale.

(2)   A sale by auction is complete when the auctioneer announces its completion by the fall of the hammer, or in other customary manner; and until the announcement is made any bidder may retract his bid.

(3)   A sale by auction may be notified to be subject to a reserve or upset price, and a right to bid may also be reserved expressly by or on behalf of the seller.

(4)   Where a sale by auction is not notified to be subject to a right to bid by or on behalf of the seller, it is not lawful for the seller to bid himself or to employ any person to bid at the sale, or for the auctioneer knowingly to take any bid from the seller or any such person.

(5)   A sale contravening subsection (4) above may be treated as fraudulent by the buyer.

(6)   Where, in respect of a sale by auction, a right to bid is expressly reserved (but not otherwise) the seller or any one person on his behalf may bid at the auction.

59 Reasonable time a question of fact

Where a reference is made in this Act to a reasonable time the question what is a reasonable time is a question of fact.

64 Short title and commencement

(1)   This Act may be cited as the Sale of Goods Act 1979.

SUPPLY OF GOODS AND SERVICES ACT 1982

1982 chapter 29

An Act to amend the law with respect to the terms to be implied in certain contracts for the transfer of the property in goods, in certain contracts for the hire of goods and in certain contracts for the supply of a service; and for connected purposes.

Part I Supply of Goods

Contracts for the transfer of property in goods

1 The contracts concerned

(1)   In this Act [in its application to England and Wales and Northern Ireland] a "[relevant contract for the transfer of goods]" means a contract under which one person transfers or agrees to transfer to another the property in goods, other than an excepted contract[, and other than a contract to which Chapter 2 of Part 1 of the Consumer Rights Act 2015 applies].

(2)   For the purposes of this section an excepted contract means any of the following: —

(a)   a contract of sale of goods;

(b)   a hire-purchase agreement;

(c)   . . .

(d)   a transfer or agreement to transfer which is made by deed and for which there is no consideration other than the presumed consideration imported by the deed;

(e)   a contract intended to operate by way of mortgage, pledge, charge or other security.

(3)   For the purposes of this Act [in its application to England and Wales and Northern Ireland] a contract is a [relevant contract for the transfer of goods] whether or not services are also provided or to be provided under the contract, and (subject to subsection (2) above) whatever is the nature of the consideration for the transfer or agreement to transfer.

2 Implied terms about title, etc.

(1)   In a [relevant contract for the transfer of goods], other than one to which subsection (3) below applies, there is an implied condition on the part of the transferor that in the case of a transfer of the property in the goods he has a right to transfer the property and in the case of an agreement to transfer the property in the goods he will have such a right at the time when the property is to be transferred.

(2)   In a [relevant contract for the transfer of goods], other than one to which subsection (3) below applies, there is also an implied warranty that—

(a)   the goods are free, and will remain free until the time when the property is to be transferred, from any charge or encumbrance not disclosed or known to the transferee before the contract is made, and

(b)   the transferee will enjoy quiet possession of the goods except so far as it may be disturbed by the owner or other person entitled to the benefit of any charge or encumbrance so disclosed or known.

(3)   This subsection applies to a [relevant contract for the transfer of goods] in the case of which there appears from the contract or is to be inferred from its circumstances an intention that the transferor should transfer only such title as he or a third person may have.

(4)   In a contract to which subsection (3) above applies there is an implied warranty that all charges or encumbrances known to the transferor and not known to the transferee have been disclosed to the transferee before the contract is made.

(5)   In a contract to which subsection (3) above applies there is also an implied warranty that none of the following will disturb the transferee's quiet possession of the goods, namely—

(a)   the transferor;

(b)   in a case where the parties to the contract intend that the transferor should transfer only such title as a third person may have, that person;

(c)   anyone claiming through or under the transferor or that third person otherwise than under a charge or encumbrance disclosed or known to the transferee before the contract is made.

3 Implied terms where transfer is by description

(1)   This section applies where, under a [relevant contract for the transfer of goods], the transferor transfers or agrees to transfer the property in the goods by description.

(2)   In such a case there is an implied condition that the goods will correspond with the description.

(3)   If the transferor transfers or agrees to transfer the property in the goods by sample as well as by description it is not sufficient that the bulk of the goods corresponds with the sample if the goods do not also correspond with the description.

(4)   A contract is not prevented from falling within subsection (1) above by reason only that, being exposed for supply, the goods are selected by the transferee.

4 Implied terms about quality or fitness

(1)   Except as provided by this section and section 5 below and subject to the provisions of any other enactment, there is no implied condition or warranty about the quality or fitness for any particular purpose of goods supplied under a [relevant contract for the transfer of goods].

[(2)   Where, under such a contract, the transferor transfers the property in goods in the course of a business, there is an implied condition that the goods supplied under the contract are of satisfactory quality.

(2A)   For the purposes of this section and section 5 below, goods are of satisfactory quality if they meet the standard that a reasonable person would regard as satisfactory, taking account of any description of the goods, the price (if relevant) and all the other relevant circumstances.

[(2B – 2D repealed by the Consumer Rights Act 2015]

(3)   The condition implied by subsection (2) above does not extend to any matter making the quality of goods unsatisfactory—

(a)   which is specifically drawn to the transferee's attention before the contract is made,

(b)   where the transferee examines the goods before the contract is made, which that examination ought to reveal, or

(c)   where the property in the goods is transferred by reference to a sample, which would have been apparent on a reasonable examination of the sample.]

(4)   Subsection (5) below applies where, under a [relevant contract for the transfer of goods], the transferor transfers the property in goods in the course of a business and the transferee, expressly or by implication, makes known—

(a)   to the transferor, or

(b)   where the consideration or part of the consideration for the transfer is a sum payable by instalments and the goods were previously sold by a credit-broker to the transferor, to that credit-broker,

any particular purpose for which the goods are being acquired.

(5)   In that case there is (subject to subsection (6) below) an implied condition that the goods supplied under the contract are reasonably fit for that purpose, whether or not that is a purpose for which such goods are commonly supplied.

(6)   Subsection (5) above does not apply where the circumstances show that the transferee does not rely, or that it is unreasonable for him to rely, on the skill or judgment of the transferor or credit-broker.

(7)   An implied condition or warranty about quality or fitness for a particular purpose may be annexed by usage to a [relevant contract for the transfer of goods].

(8)   The preceding provisions of this section apply to a transfer by a person who in the course of a business is acting as agent for another as they apply to a transfer by a principal in the course of a business, except where that other is not transferring in the course of a business and either the transferee knows that fact or reasonable steps are taken to bring it to the transferee's notice before the contract concerned is made.

(9)   . . .

5 Implied terms where transfer is by sample

(1)   This section applies where, under a [relevant contract for the transfer of goods], the transferor transfers or agrees to transfer the property in the goods by reference to a sample.

(2)   In such a case there is an implied condition—

(a)   that the bulk will correspond with the sample in quality; and

(b)   that the transferee will have a reasonable opportunity of comparing the bulk with the sample; and

(c)   that the goods will be free from any defect, [making their quality unsatisfactory], which would not be apparent on reasonable examination of the sample.

(3)   . . .

(4)   For the purposes of this section a transferor transfers or agrees to transfer the property in goods by reference to a sample where there is an express or implied term to that effect in the contract concerned.

[5A Modification of remedies for breach of statutory condition in non-consumer cases

(1)   Where in the case of a contract for the transfer of goods-

(a)   the transferee would, apart from this subsection, have the right to treat the contract as repudiated by reason of a breach on the part of the transferor of a term implied by section 3, 4 or 5(2)(a) or (c) above, but

(b)   the breach is so slight that it would be unreasonable for him to do so,

then, if the transferee does not deal as consumer, the breach is not to be treated as a breach of condition but may be treated as a breach of warranty.

(2)   This section applies unless a contrary intention appears in, or is to be implied from, the contract.

(3)   It is for the transferor to show that a breach fell within subsection (1)(b) above.]

Contracts for the hire of goods ...

11 Exclusion of implied terms, etc.

(1)   Where a right, duty or liability would arise under a [relevant contract for the transfer of goods] or a [relevant contract for the hire of goods] by implication of law, it may (subject to subsection (2) below and the 1977 Act) be negatived or varied by express agreement, or by the course of dealing between the parties, or by such usage as binds both parties to the contract.

(2)   An express condition or warranty does not negative a condition or warranty implied by the preceding provisions of this Act unless inconsistent with it.

(3)   Nothing in the preceding provisions of this Act prejudices the operation of any other enactment or any rule of law whereby any condition or warranty (other than one relating to quality or fitness) is to be implied in a [relevant contract for the transfer of goods] or a [relevant contract for the hire of goods].

PART II SUPPLY OF SERVICES

12 The contracts concerned

(1)   In this Act a " [relevant contract for the supply of a service]" means, subject to subsection (2) below, a contract under which a person ("the supplier") agrees to carry out a service[, other than a contract to which Chapter 4 of Part 1 of the Consumer Rights Act 2015 applies].

(2)   For the purposes of this Act, a contract of service or apprenticeship is not a [relevant contract for the supply of a service].

(3)   Subject to subsection (2) above, a contract is a [relevant contract for the supply of a service] for the purposes of this Act whether or not goods are also—

(a)   transferred or to be transferred, or

(b)   bailed or to be bailed by way of hire,

under the contract, and whatever is the nature of the consideration for which the service is to be carried out.

(4)   The Secretary of State may by order provide that one or more of sections 13 to 15 below shall not apply to services of a description specified in the order, and such an order may make different provision for different circumstances.

(5)   The power to make an order under subsection (4) above shall be exercisable by statutory instrument subject to annulment in pursuance of a resolution of either House of Parliament.

13 Implied term about care and skill

In a [relevant contract for the supply of a service] where the supplier is acting in the course of a business, there is an implied term that the supplier will carry out the service with reasonable care and skill.14 Implied term about time for performance

(1) Where, under a [relevant contract for the supply of a service] by a supplier acting in the course of a business, the time for the service to be carried out is not fixed by the contract, left to be fixed in a manner agreed by the contract or determined by the course of dealing between the parties, there is an implied term that the supplier will carry out the service within a reasonable time.

(2) What is a reasonable time is a question of fact.

15 Implied term about consideration

(1) Where, under a [relevant contract for the supply of a service], the consideration for the service is not determined by the contract, left to be determined in a manner agreed by the contract or determined by the course of dealing between the parties, there is an implied term that the party contracting with the supplier will pay a reasonable charge.

(2) What is a reasonable charge is a question of fact.

16 Exclusion of implied terms, etc.

(1) Where a right, duty or liability would arise under a [relevant contract for the supply of a service] by virtue of this Part of this Act, it may (subject to subsection (2) below and the 1977 Act) be negatived or varied by express agreement, or by the course of dealing between the parties, or by such usage as binds both parties to the contract.

(2) An express term does not negative a term implied by this Part of this Act unless inconsistent with it.

(3) Nothing in this Part of this Act prejudices—

   (a) any rule of law which imposes on the supplier a duty stricter than that imposed by section 13 or 14 above; or

   (b) subject to paragraph (a) above, any rule of law whereby any term not inconsistent with this Part of this Act is to be implied in a [relevant contract for the supply of a service].

(4) This Part of this Act has effect subject to any other enactment which defines or restricts the rights, duties or liabilities arising in connection with a service of any description.

20 Citation, transitional provisions, commencement and extent

(1) This Act may be cited as the Supply of Goods and Services Act 1982.

UNFAIR CONTRACT TERMS ACT 1977

1977 chapter 50

An Act to impose further limits on the extent to which under the law of England and Wales and Northern Ireland civil liability for breach of contract, or for negligence or other breach of duty, can be avoided by means of contract terms and otherwise, and under the law of Scotland civil liability can be avoided by means of contract terms.

1 Scope of Part I

(1) For the purposes of this Part of this Act, "negligence" means the breach-

 (a) of any obligation, arising from the express or implied terms of a contract, to take reasonable care or exercise reasonable skill in the performance of the contract;

 (b) of any common law duty to take reasonable care or exercise reasonable skill (but not any stricter duty);

 (c) of the common duty of care imposed by the Occupiers' Liability Act 1957 or the Occupiers' Liability Act (Northern Ireland) 1957.

(2) This Part of this Act is subject to Part III; and in relation to contracts, the operation of sections 3 and 7 is subject to the exceptions made by Schedule 1.

(3) In the case of both contract and tort, sections 2 to 7 apply (except where the contrary is stated in section 6(4)) only to business liability, that is liability for breach of obligations or duties arising-

 (a) from things done or to be done by a person in the course of a business (whether his own business or another's); or

 (b) from the occupation of premises used for business purposes of the occupier;

 and references to liability are to be read accordingly but liability of an occupier of premises for breach of an obligation or duty towards a person obtaining access to the premises for recreational or educational purposes, being liability for loss or damage suffered by reason of the dangerous state of the premises, is not a business liability of the occupier unless granting that person such access for the purposes concerned falls within the business purposes of the occupier.

(4) In relation to any breach of duty or obligation, it is immaterial for any purpose of this Part of this Act whether the breach was inadvertent or intentional, or whether liability for it arises directly or vicariously.

2 Negligence liability

(1) A person cannot by reference to any contract term or to a notice given to persons generally or to particular persons exclude or restrict his liability for death or personal injury resulting from negligence.

(2) In the case of other loss or damage, a person cannot so exclude or restrict his liability for negligence except in so far as the term or notice satisfies the requirement of reasonableness.

(3) Where a contract term or notice purports to exclude or restrict liability for negligence a person's agreement to or awareness of it is not of itself to be taken as indicating his voluntary acceptance of any risk.

(4) This section does not apply to—

 (a) a term in a consumer contract, or

 (b) a notice to the extent that it is a consumer notice,

(but see the provision made about such contracts and notices in sections 62 and 65 of the Consumer Rights Act 2015).

3 Liability arising in contract

(1)   This section applies as between contracting parties where one of them deals on the other's written standard terms of business.

(2)   As against that party, the other cannot by reference to any contract term —

    (a)   when himself in breach of contract, exclude or restrict any liability of his in respect of the breach; or

    (b)   claim to be entitled —

        (i)   to render a contractual performance substantially different from that which was reasonably expected of him, or

        (ii)   in respect of the whole or any part of his contractual obligation, to render no performance at all,

    except in so far as (in any of the cases mentioned above in this subsection) the contract term satisfies the requirement of reasonableness.

(3)   This section does not apply to a term in a consumer contract (but see the provision made about such contracts in section 62 of the Consumer Rights Act 2015).

6 Sale and hire purchase

(1)   Liability for breach of the obligations arising from —

    (a)   [section 12 of the Sale of Goods Act 1979] (seller's implied undertakings as to title, etc);

    (b)   section 8 of the Supply of Goods (Implied Terms) Act 1973 (the corresponding thing in relation to hire-purchase),

cannot be excluded or restricted by reference to any contract term.

(1A)   Liability for breach of the obligations arising from —

    (a)   section 13, 14 or 15 of the 1979 Act (seller's implied undertakings as to conformity of goods with description or sample, or as to their quality or fitness for a particular purpose);

    (b)   section 9, 10 or 11 of the 1973 Act (the corresponding things in relation to hire purchase),

cannot be excluded or restricted by reference to a contract term except in so far as the term satisfies the requirement of reasonableness.

(2)   Repealed by Consumer Rights Act 2015

(3)   Repealed by Consumer Rights Act 2015

(4)   The liabilities referred to in this section are not only the business liabilities defined by section 1(3), but include those arising under any contract of sale of goods or hire-purchase agreement.

(5)   This section does not apply to a consumer contract (but see the provision made about such contracts in section 31 of the Consumer Rights Act 2015).

9 Effect of breach

Repealed by the Consumer Rights Act 2015

11 The "reasonableness" test

(1)   In relation to a contract term, the requirement of reasonableness for the purposes of this Part of this Act, section 3 of the Misrepresentation Act 1967 and section 3 of the Misrepresentation Act (Northern Ireland) 1967 is that the term shall have been a fair and reasonable one to be included having regard to the circumstances which were, or ought reasonably to have been, known to or in the contemplation of the parties when the contract was made.

(2)   In determining for the purposes of section 6 or 7 above whether a contract term satisfies the requirement of reasonableness, regard shall be had in particular to the matters specified in Schedule 2 to this Act; but this subsection does not prevent the court or arbitrator from holding, in accordance with any rule of law, that a term which purports to exclude or restrict any relevant liability is not a term of the contract.

(3)   In relation to a notice (not being a notice having contractual effect), the requirement of reasonableness under this Act is that it should be fair and reasonable to allow reliance on it, having regard to all the circumstances obtaining when the liability arose or (but for the notice) would have arisen.

(4)   Where by reference to a contract term or notice a person seeks to restrict liability to a specified sum of money, and the question arises (under this or any other Act) whether the term or notice satisfies the requirement of reasonableness, regard shall be had in particular (but without prejudice to subsection (2) above in the case of contract terms) to—

(a)   the resources which he could expect to be available to him for the purpose of meeting the liability should it arise; and

(b)   how far it was open to him to cover himself by insurance.

(5)   It is for those claiming that a contract term or notice satisfies the requirement of reasonableness to show that it does.

12 "Dealing as a consumer"

Repealed by the Consumer Rights Act 2015

13 Varieties of exemption clause

(1)   To the extent that this Part of this Act prevents the exclusion or restriction of any liability it also prevents—

(a)   making the liability or its enforcement subject to restrictive or onerous conditions;

(b)   excluding or restricting any right or remedy in respect of the liability, or subjecting a person to any prejudice in consequence of his pursuing any such right or remedy;

(c)   excluding or restricting rules of evidence or procedure;

and (to that extent) sections 2, 6 and 7 also prevent excluding or restricting liability by reference to terms and notices which exclude or restrict the relevant obligation or duty.

(2) But an agreement in writing to submit present or future differences to arbitration is not to be treated under this Part of this Act as excluding or restricting any liability.

14 Interpretation of Part I

In this Part of this Act—

"business" includes a profession and the activities of any government department or local or public authority;

"consumer contract" has the same meaning as in the Consumer Rights Act 2015 (see section 61);

"consumer notice" has the same meaning as in the Consumer Rights Act 2015 (see section 61);

"goods" has the same meaning as in [the Sale of Goods Act 1979;

"hire-purchase agreement" has the same meaning as in the Consumer Credit Act 1974;

"negligence" has the meaning given by section 1(1);

"notice" includes an announcement, whether or not in writing, and any other communication or pretended communication; and

"personal injury" includes any disease and any impairment of physical or mental condition.

Schedule 2 "Guidelines" for Application of Reasonableness Test

The matters to which regard is to be had in particular for the purposes of sections 6(1A), 7(1A) and (4), 20 and 21 are any of the following which appear to be relevant—

(a) the strength of the bargaining positions of the parties relative to each other, taking into account (among other things) alternative means by which the customer's requirements could have been met;

(b) whether the customer received an inducement to agree to the term, or in accepting it had an opportunity of entering into a similar contract with other persons, but without having to accept a similar term;

(c) whether the customer knew or ought reasonably to have known of the existence and extent of the term (having regard, among other things, to any custom of the trade and any previous course of dealing between the parties);

(d) where the term excludes or restricts any relevant liability if some condition is not complied with, whether it was reasonable at the time of the contract to expect that compliance with that condition would be practicable;

(e) whether the goods were manufactured, processed or adapted to the special order of the customer.

UNFAIR TERMS IN CONSUMER CONTRACTS REGULATIONS 1999

Replaced by the Consumer Rights Act 2015

Part 3

Criminal Law

CORONERS AND JUSTICE ACT 2009

An Act to amend the law relating to coroners, to investigation of deaths and to certification and registration of deaths; to amend the criminal law; to make provision about criminal justice and about dealing with offenders; to make provision about the Commissioner for Victims and Witnesses; to make provision relating to the security of court and other buildings; to make provision about legal aid and about payments for legal services provided in connection with employment matters; to make provision for payments to be made by offenders in respect of benefits derived from the exploitation of material pertaining to offences; to amend the Data Protection Act 1998; and for connected purposes.

Partial defence to murder: loss of control

54 Partial defence to murder: loss of control

(1) Where a person ("D") kills or is a party to the killing of another ("V"), D is not to be convicted of murder if—

    (a) D's acts and omissions in doing or being a party to the killing resulted from D's loss of self-control,

    (b) the loss of self-control had a qualifying trigger, and

    (c) a person of D's sex and age, with a normal degree of tolerance and self-restraint and in the circumstances of D, might have reacted in the same or in a similar way to D.

(2) For the purposes of subsection (1)(a), it does not matter whether or not the loss of control was sudden.

(3) In subsection (1)(c) the reference to "the circumstances of D" is a reference to all of D's circumstances other than those whose only relevance to D's conduct is that they bear on D's general capacity for tolerance or self-restraint.

(4) Subsection (1) does not apply if, in doing or being a party to the killing, D acted in a considered desire for revenge.

(5) On a charge of murder, if sufficient evidence is adduced to raise an issue with respect to the defence under subsection (1), the jury must assume that the defence is satisfied unless the prosecution proves beyond reasonable doubt that it is not.

(6) For the purposes of subsection (5), sufficient evidence is adduced to raise an issue with respect to the defence if evidence is adduced on which, in the opinion of the trial judge, a jury, properly directed, could reasonably conclude that the defence might apply.

(7) A person who, but for this section, would be liable to be convicted of murder is liable instead to be convicted of manslaughter.

(8) The fact that one party to a killing is by virtue of this section not liable to be convicted of murder does not affect the question whether the killing amounted to murder in the case of any other party to it.

55 Meaning of "qualifying trigger"

(1)   This section applies for the purposes of section 54.

(2)   A loss of self-control had a qualifying trigger if subsection (3), (4) or (5) applies.

(3)   This subsection applies if D's loss of self-control was attributable to D's fear of serious violence from V against D or another identified person.

(4)   This subsection applies if D's loss of self-control was attributable to a thing or things done or said (or both) which—

   (a)   constituted circumstances of an extremely grave character, and

   (b)   caused D to have a justifiable sense of being seriously wronged.

(5)   This subsection applies if D's loss of self-control was attributable to a combination of the matters mentioned in subsections (3) and (4).

(6)   In determining whether a loss of self-control had a qualifying trigger—

   (a)   D's fear of serious violence is to be disregarded to the extent that it was caused by a thing which D incited to be done or said for the purpose of providing an excuse to use violence;

   (b)   a sense of being seriously wronged by a thing done or said is not justifiable if D incited the thing to be done or said for the purpose of providing an excuse to use violence;

   (c)   the fact that a thing done or said constituted sexual infidelity is to be disregarded.

(7)   In this section references to "D" and "V" are to be construed in accordance with section 54.

56 Abolition of common law defence of provocation

(1)   The common law defence of provocation is abolished and replaced by sections 54 and 55.

183 Short title

This Act may be cited as the Coroners and Justice Act 2009.

CRIMINAL ATTEMPTS ACT 1981

1981 chapter 47

An Act to amend the law of England and Wales as to attempts to commit offences and as to cases of conspiring to commit offences which, in the circumstances, cannot be committed; to repeal the provisions of section 4 of the Vagrancy Act 1824 which apply to suspected persons and reputed thieves; to make provision against unauthorised interference with vehicles; and for connected purposes.

1 Attempting to commit an offence

(1)   If, with intent to commit an offence to which this section applies, a person does an act which is more than merely preparatory to the commission of the offence, he is guilty of attempting to commit the offence.

(2)   A person may be guilty of attempting to commit an offence to which this section applies even though the facts are such that the commission of the offence is impossible.

(3)   In any case where—

(a)   apart from this subsection a person's intention would not be regarded as having amounted to an intent to commit an offence; but

(b)   if the facts of the case had been as he believed them to be, his intention would be so regarded,

then, for the purposes of subsection (1) above, he shall be regarded as having had an intent to commit that offence.

(4)   This section applies to any offence which, if it were completed, would be triable in England and Wales as an indictable offence, other than—

(a)   conspiracy (at common law or under section 1 of the Criminal Law Act 1977 or any other enactment);

(b)   aiding, abetting, counselling, procuring or suborning the commission of an offence;

(c)   offences under section 4(1) (assisting offenders) or 5(1) (accepting or agreeing to accept consideration for not disclosing information about an arrestable offence) of the Criminal Law Act 1967.

4 Trial and penalties

(1)   A person guilty by virtue of section 1 above of attempting to commit an offence shall—

(a)   if the offence attempted is murder or any other offence the sentence for which is fixed by law, be liable on conviction on indictment to imprisonment for life; and

(b)   if the offence attempted is indictable but does not fall within paragraph (a) above, be liable on conviction on indictment to any penalty to which he would have been liable on conviction on indictment of that offence; and

(c)   if the offence attempted is triable either way, be liable on summary conviction to any penalty to which he would have been liable on summary conviction of that offence.

(3)   Where, in proceedings against a person for an offence under section 1 above, there is evidence sufficient in law to support a finding that he did an act falling within subsection (1) of that section, the question whether or not his act fell within that subsection is a question of fact.

6 Effect of Part I on common law

(1)   The offence of attempt at common law and any offence at common law of procuring materials for crime are hereby abolished for all purposes not relating to acts done before the commencement of this Act.

(2)   Except as regards offences committed before the commencement of this Act, references in any enactment passed before this Act which fall to be construed as references to the offence of attempt at common law shall be construed as references to the offence under section 1 above.

12 Short title

This Act may be cited as the Criminal Attempts Act 1981.

CRIMINAL DAMAGE ACT 1971

1971 chapter 48

An Act to revise the law of England and Wales as to offences of damage to property, and to repeal or amend as respects the United Kingdom certain enactments relating to such offences; and for connected purposes.

1 Destroying or damaging property

(1)   A person who without lawful excuse destroys or damages any property belonging to another intending to destroy or damage any such property or being reckless as to whether any such property would be destroyed or damaged shall be guilty of an offence.

(2)   A person who without lawful excuse destroys or damages any property, whether belonging to himself or another—

(a)   intending to destroy or damage any property or being reckless as to whether any property would be destroyed or damaged; and

(b)   intending by the destruction or damage to endanger the life of another or being reckless as to whether the life of another would be thereby endangered;

shall be guilty of an offence.

(3)   An offence committed under this section by destroying or damaging property by fire shall be charged as arson.

2 Threats to destroy or damage property

A person who without lawful excuse makes to another a threat, intending that that other would fear it would be carried out,—

(a)   to destroy or damage any property belonging to that other or a third person; or

(b)   to destroy or damage his own property in a way which he knows is likely to endanger the life of that other or third person;

shall be guilty of an offence.

3 Possessing anything with intent to destroy or damage property

A person who has anything in his custody or under his control intending without lawful excuse to use it or cause or permit another to use it—

(a)   to destroy or damage any property belonging to some other person; or

(b)   to destroy or damage his own or the user's property in a way which he knows is likely to endanger the life of some other person;

shall be guilty of an offence.

4 Punishment of offences

(1)   A person guilty of arson under section 1 above or of an offence under section 1(2) above (whether arson or not) shall on conviction on indictment be liable to imprisonment for life.

(2)   A person guilty of any other offence under this Act shall on conviction on indictment be liable to imprisonment for a term not exceeding ten years.

5 "Without lawful excuse"

(1)   This section applies to any offence under section 1(1) above and any offence under section 2 or 3 above other than one involving a threat by the person charged to destroy or damage property in a way which he knows is likely to endanger the life of another or involving an intent by the person charged to use or cause or permit the use of something in his custody or under his control so to destroy or damage property.

(2)   A person charged with an offence to which this section applies, shall, whether or not he would be treated for the purposes of this Act as having a lawful excuse apart from this subsection, be treated for those purposes as having a lawful excuse—

(a)   if at the time of the act or acts alleged to constitute the offence he believed that the person or persons whom he believed to be entitled to consent to the destruction of or damage to the property in question had so consented, or would have so consented to it if he or they had known of the destruction or damage and its circumstances; or

(b)   if he destroyed or damaged or threatened to destroy or damage the property in question or, in the case of a charge of an offence under section 3 above, intended to use or cause or permit the use of something to destroy or damage it, in order to protect property belonging to himself or another or a right or interest in property which was or which he believed to be vested in himself or another, and at the time of the act or acts alleged to constitute the offence he believed—

(i)   that the property, right or interest was in immediate need of protection; and

(ii)   that the means of protection adopted or proposed to be adopted were or would be reasonable having regard to all the circumstances.

(3)   For the purposes of this section it is immaterial whether a belief is justified or not if it is honestly held.

(4)   For the purposes of subsection (2) above a right or interest in property includes any right or privilege in or over land, whether created by grant, licence or otherwise.

(5)   This section shall not be construed as casting doubt on any defence recognised by law as a defence to criminal charges.

10 Interpretation

(1) In this Act "property" means property of a tangible nature, whether real or personal, including money and—

(a) including wild creatures which have been tamed or are ordinarily kept in captivity, and any other wild creatures or their carcasses if, but only if, they have been reduced into possession which has not been lost or abandoned or are in the course of being reduced into possession; but

(b) not including mushrooms growing wild on any land or flowers, fruit or foliage of a plant growing wild on any land.

For the purposes of this subsection "mushroom" includes any fungus and "plant" includes any shrub or tree.

(2) Property shall be treated for the purposes of this Act as belonging to any person—

(a) having the custody or control of it;

(b) having in it any proprietary right or interest (not being an equitable interest arising only from an agreement to transfer or grant an interest); or

(c) having a charge on it.

(3) Where property is subject to a trust, the persons to whom it belongs shall be so treated as including any person having a right to enforce the trust.

(4) Property of a corporation sole shall be so treated as belonging to the corporation notwithstanding a vacancy in the corporation.

12 Short title and extent

(2) This Act may be cited as the Criminal Damage Act 1971.

CRIMINAL JUSTICE ACT 1967

1967 chapter 80

An Act to amend the law relating to the proceedings of criminal courts, including the law relating to evidence, and to the qualification of jurors, in such proceedings and to appeals in criminal cases; to reform existing methods and provide new methods of dealing with offenders; to make further provision for the treatment of offenders, the management of prisons and other institutions and the arrest of offenders unlawfully at large; to make further provision with respect to legal aid and advice in criminal proceedings; to amend the law relating to firearms and ammunition; to alter the penalties which may be imposed for certain offences; and for connected purposes.

8 Proof of criminal intent

A court or jury, in determining whether a person has committed an offence, —

(a) shall not be bound in law to infer that he intended or foresaw a result of his actions by reason only of its being a natural and probable consequence of those actions; but

(b) shall decide whether he did intend or foresee that result by reference to all the evidence, drawing such inferences from the evidence as appear proper in the circumstances.

CRIMINAL JUSTICE ACT 1988

An Act to make fresh provision for extradition; to amend the rules of evidence in criminal proceedings; to provide for the reference by the Attorney General of certain questions relating to sentencing to the Court of Appeal; to amend the law with regard to the jurisdiction and powers of criminal courts, the collection, enforcement and remission of fines imposed by coroners, juries, supervision orders, the detention of children and young persons, probation and the probation service, criminal appeals, anonymity in cases of rape and similar cases, orders under sections 4 and 11 of the Contempt of Court Act 1981 relating to trials on indictment, orders restricting the access of the public to the whole or any part of a trial on indictment or to any proceedings ancillary to such a trial and orders restricting the publication of any report of the whole or any part of a trial on indictment or any such ancillary proceedings, the alteration of names of petty sessions areas, officers of inner London magistrates' courts and the costs and expenses of prosecution witnesses and certain other persons; to make fresh provision for the payment of compensation by the Criminal Injuries Compensation Board; to make provision for the payment of compensation for a miscarriage of justice which has resulted in a wrongful conviction; to create an offence of torture and an offence of having an article with a blade or point in a public place; to create further offences relating to weapons; to create a summary offence of possession of an indecent photograph of a child; to amend the Police and Criminal Evidence Act 1984 in relation to searches, computer data about fingerprints and bail for persons in customs detention; to make provision in relation to the taking of body samples by the police in Northern Ireland; to amend the Bail Act 1976; to give a justice of the peace power to authorise entry and search of premises for offensive weapons; to provide for the enforcement of the Video Recordings Act 1984 by officers of a weights and measures authority and in Northern Ireland by officers of the Department of Economic Development; to extend to the purchase of easements and other rights over land the power to purchase land conferred on the Secretary of State by section 36 of the Prison Act 1952; and for connected purposes.

39 Common assault and battery to be summary offences

Common assault and battery shall be summary offences and a person guilty of either of them shall be liable to a fine not exceeding level 5 on the standard scale, to imprisonment for a term not exceeding six months, or to both.

CRIMINAL JUSTICE AND IMMIGRATION ACT 2008

2008 chapter 4

An Act to make further provision about criminal justice (including provision about the police) and dealing with offenders and defaulters; to make further provision about the management of offenders; to amend the criminal law; to make further provision for combatting crime and disorder; to make provision about the mutual recognition of financial penalties; to amend the Repatriation of Prisoners Act 1984; to make provision for a new immigration status in certain cases involving criminality; to make provision about the automatic deportation of criminals under the UK Borders Act 2007; to amend section 127 of the Criminal Justice and Public Order Act 1994 and to confer power to suspend the operation of that section; and for connected purposes.

Part V Criminal Law

76 Reasonable force for purposes of self-defence etc

(1) This section applies where in proceedings for an offence—

    (a) an issue arises as to whether a person charged with the offence ("D") is entitled to rely on a defence within subsection (2), and

    (b) the question arises whether the degree of force used by D against a person ("V") was reasonable in the circumstances.

(2) The defences are—

    (a) the common law defence of self-defence; -

    (aa) the common law defence of property; and

    (c) the defence provided by section 3(1) of the Criminal Law Act 1967 (c 58) or section 3(1) of the Criminal Law Act (Northern Ireland) 1967 (c 18 (NI)) (use of force in prevention of crime or making arrest).

(3) The question whether the degree of force used by D was reasonable in the circumstances is to be decided by reference to the circumstances as D believed them to be, and subsections (4) to (8) also apply in connection with deciding that question.

(4) If D claims to have held a particular belief as regards the existence of any circumstances—

    (a) the reasonableness or otherwise of that belief is relevant to the question whether D genuinely held it; but

    (b) if it is determined that D did genuinely hold it, D is entitled to rely on it for the purposes of subsection (3), whether or not—

        (i) it was mistaken, or

        (ii) (if it was mistaken) the mistake was a reasonable one to have made.

(5) But subsection (4)(b) does not enable D to rely on any mistaken belief attributable to intoxication that was voluntarily induced.

(5A) In a householder case, the degree of force used by D is not to be regarded as having been reasonable in the circumstances as D believed them to be if it was grossly disproportionate in those circumstances

(6) In a case other than a householder case, the degree of force used by D is not to be regarded as having been reasonable in the circumstances as D believed them to be if it was disproportionate in those circumstances.

(6A) In deciding the question mentioned in subsection (3), a possibility that D could have retreated is to be considered (so far as relevant) as a factor to be taken into account, rather than as giving rise to a duty to retreat

(7) In deciding the question mentioned in subsection (3) the following considerations are to be taken into account (so far as relevant in the circumstances of the case)—

  (a) that a person acting for a legitimate purpose may not be able to weigh to a nicety the exact measure of any necessary action; and

  (b) that evidence of a person's having only done what the person honestly and instinctively thought was necessary for a legitimate purpose constitutes strong evidence that only reasonable action was taken by that person for that purpose.

(8) Subsections (6A) and (7) are not to be read as preventing other matters from being taken into account where they are relevant to deciding the question mentioned in subsection (3).

(8A) For the purposes of this section "a householder case" is a case where -

  (a) the defence concerned is the common law defence of self defence,

  (b) the force concerned is force used by D while in or partly in a building, or part of a building, that is a dwelling or is forces accommodation (or is both),

  (c) D is not a trespasser at the time the force is used, and

  (d) at that time D believed V to be in, or entering, the building or part as a trespasser.

(8B) Where —

  (a) a part of a building is a dwelling where D dwells,

  (b) another part of the building is a place of work for D or another person who dwells in the first part, and

  (c) that other part is internally accessible from the first part, that other part, and any internal means of access between the two parts, are each treated for the purposes of subsection (8A) as a part of a building that is a dwelling.

(8C) Where —

(a) a part of a building is forces accommodation that is living or sleeping accommodation for D,

(b) another part of the building is a place of work for D or another person for whom the first part is living or sleeping accommodation, and

(c) that other part is internally accessible from the first part, that other part, and any internal means of access between the two parts, are each treated for the purposes of subsection (8A) as a part of a building that is forces accommodation.

(8D) Subsections (4) and (5) apply for the purposes of subsection (8A)(d) as they apply for the purposes of subsection (3).

(8E) The fact that a person derives title from a trespasser, or has the permission of a trespasser, does not prevent the person from being a trespasser for the purposes of subsection (8A).

(8F) In subsections (8A) to (8C) "building" includes a vehicle or vessel, and "forces accommodation" means service living accommodation for the purposes of Part 3 of the Armed Forces Act 2006 by virtue of section 96(1)(a) or (b) of that Act.

(9) This section is, except so far as making different provisions for householder cases, intended to clarify the operation of the existing defences mentioned in subsection (2).

(10) In this section—

(a) "legitimate purpose" means—

(i) the purpose of self-defence under the common law,

(ia) the purpose of defence of property under the common law, or

(iii) the prevention of crime or effecting or assisting in the lawful arrest of persons mentioned in the provisions referred to in subsection (2)(b);

(b) references to self-defence include acting in defence of another person; and

(c) references to the degree of force used are to the type and amount of force used.

CRIMINAL LAW ACT 1977

1977 chapter 45

An Act to amend the law of England and Wales with respect to criminal conspiracy; to make new provision in that law, in place of the provisions of the common law and the Statutes of Forcible Entry, for restricting the use or threat of violence for securing entry into any premises and for penalising unauthorised entry or remaining on premises in certain circumstances; otherwise to amend the criminal law, including the law with respect to the administration of criminal justice; to provide for the alteration of certain pecuniary and other limits; to amend section 9(4) of the Administration of Justice Act 1973, the Legal Aid Act 1974, the Rabies Act 1974 and the Diseases of Animals (Northern Ireland) Order 1975 and the law about juries and coroners' inquests; and for connected purposes.

1 The offence of conspiracy

[(1)   Subject to the following provisions of this Part of this Act, if a person agrees with any other person or persons that a course of conduct shall be pursued which, if the agreement is carried out in accordance with their intentions, either—

(a)   will necessarily amount to or involve the commission of any offence or offences by one or more of the parties to the agreement, or

(b)   would do so but for the existence of facts which render the commission of the offence or any of the offences impossible,

he is guilty of conspiracy to commit the offence or offences in question.]

(2)   Where liability for any offence may be incurred without knowledge on the part of the person committing it of any particular fact or circumstance necessary for the commission of the offence, a person shall nevertheless not be guilty of conspiracy to commit that offence by virtue of subsection (1) above unless he and at least one other party to the agreement intend or know that that fact or circumstance shall or will exist at the time when the conduct constituting the offence is to take place.

2 Exemptions from liability for conspiracy

(1)   A person shall not by virtue of section 1 above be guilty of conspiracy to commit any offence if he is an intended victim of that offence.

(2)   A person shall not by virtue of section 1 above be guilty of conspiracy to commit any offence or offences if the only other person or persons with whom he agrees are (both initially and at all times during the currency of the agreement) persons of any one or more of the following descriptions, that is to say—

(a)   his spouse;
(b)   a person under the age of criminal responsibility; and
(c)   an intended victim of that offence or of each of those offences.

(3)   A person is under the age of criminal responsibility for the purposes of subsection (2)(b) above so long as it is conclusively presumed, by virtue of section 50 of the Children and Young Persons Act 1933, that he cannot be guilty of any offence.

3 Penalties for conspiracy

(1)   A person guilty by virtue of section 1 above of conspiracy to commit any offence or offences shall be liable on conviction on indictment—

(a)   in a case falling within subsection (2) or (3) below, to imprisonment for a term related in accordance with that subsection to the gravity of the offence or offences in question (referred to below in this section as the relevant offence or offences); and

(b)   in any other case, to a fine.

Paragraph (b) above shall not be taken as prejudicing the application of [section 127 of the Powers of Criminal Courts (Sentencing) Act 2000] (general power of court to fine offender convicted on indictment) in a case falling within subsection (2) or (3) below.

(2)   Where the relevant offence or any of the relevant offences is an offence of any of the following descriptions, that is to say—

   (a)   murder, or any other offence the sentence for which is fixed by law;

   (b)   an offence for which a sentence extending to imprisonment for life is provided; or

   (c)   an indictable offence punishable with imprisonment for which no maximum term of imprisonment is provided,

   the person convicted shall be liable to imprisonment for life.

(3)   Where in a case other than one to which subsection (2) above applies the relevant offence or any of the relevant offences is punishable with imprisonment, the person convicted shall be liable to imprisonment for a term not exceeding the maximum term provided for that offence or (where more than one such offence is in question) for any one of those offences (taking the longer or the longest term as the limit for the purposes of this section where the terms provided differ).

In the case of an offence triable either way the references above in this subsection to the maximum term provided for that offence are references to the maximum term so provided on conviction on indictment.

FRAUD ACT 2006

2006 chapter 35

An Act to make provision for, and in connection with, criminal liability for fraud and obtaining services dishonestly.

1 Fraud

(1)   A person is guilty of fraud if he is in breach of any of the sections listed in subsection (2) (which provide for different ways of committing the offence).

(2)   The sections are—

   (a)   section 2 (fraud by false representation),
   (b)   section 3 (fraud by failing to disclose information), and
   (c)   section 4 (fraud by abuse of position).

(3)   A person who is guilty of fraud is liable—

   (a)   on summary conviction, to imprisonment for a term not exceeding 12 months or to a fine not exceeding the statutory maximum (or to both);

   (b)   on conviction on indictment, to imprisonment for a term not exceeding 10 years or to a fine (or to both).

2 Fraud by false representation

(1)   A person is in breach of this section if he—

(a)   dishonestly makes a false representation, and

(b)   intends, by making the representation—

(i)   to make a gain for himself or another, or
(ii)   to cause loss to another or to expose another to a risk of loss.

(2)   A representation is false if—

(a)   it is untrue or misleading, and
(b)   the person making it knows that it is, or might be, untrue or misleading.

(3)   "Representation" means any representation as to fact or law, including a representation as to the state of mind of—

(a)   the person making the representation, or
(b)   any other person.

(4)   A representation may be express or implied.

(5)   For the purposes of this section a representation may be regarded as made if it (or anything implying it) is submitted in any form to any system or device designed to receive, convey or respond to communications (with or without human intervention).

3 Fraud by failing to disclose information

A person is in breach of this section if he—

(a)   dishonestly fails to disclose to another person information which he is under a legal duty to disclose, and

(b)   intends, by failing to disclose the information—

(i)   to make a gain for himself or another, or
(ii)   to cause loss to another or to expose another to a risk of loss.

4 Fraud by abuse of position

(1)   A person is in breach of this section if he—

(a)   occupies a position in which he is expected to safeguard, or not to act against, the financial interests of another person,

(b)   dishonestly abuses that position, and

(c)   intends, by means of the abuse of that position—

(i)   to make a gain for himself or another, or
(ii)   to cause loss to another or to expose another to a risk of loss.

(2)   A person may be regarded as having abused his position even though his conduct consisted of an omission rather than an act.

5 "Gain" and "loss"

(1) The references to gain and loss in sections 2 to 4 are to be read in accordance with this section.

(2) "Gain" and "loss"—

   (a) extend only to gain or loss in money or other property;

   (b) include any such gain or loss whether temporary or permanent;

   and "property" means any property whether real or personal (including things in action and other intangible property).

(3) "Gain" includes a gain by keeping what one has, as well as a gain by getting what one does not have.

(4) "Loss" includes a loss by not getting what one might get, as well as a loss by parting with what one has.

16 Short title

This Act may be cited as the Fraud Act 2006.

HOMICIDE ACT 1957

1957, chapter 11

An Act to make for England and Wales (and for courts-martial wherever sitting) amendments of the law relating to homicide and the trial and punishment of murder, and for Scotland amendments of the law relating to the trial and punishment of murder and attempts to murder.

1 Abolition of "constructive malice"

(1) Where a person kills another in the course or furtherance of some other offence, the killing shall not amount to murder unless done with the same malice aforethought (express or implied) as is required for a killing to amount to murder when not done in the course or furtherance of another offence.

(2) For the purposes of the foregoing subsection, a killing done in the course or for the purpose of resisting an officer of justice, or of resisting or avoiding or preventing a lawful arrest, or of effecting or assisting an escape or rescue from legal custody, shall be treated as a killing in the course or furtherance of an offence.

2 Persons suffering from diminished responsibility

(1) A person ("D") who kills or is a party to the killing of another is not to be convicted of murder if D was suffering from an abnormality of mental functioning which—

   (a) arose from a recognised medical condition,

(b)   substantially impaired D's ability to do one or more of the things mentioned in subsection (1A), and

(c)   provides an explanation for D's acts and omissions in doing or being a party to the killing.

(1A)   Those things are—

(a)   to understand the nature of D's conduct;

(b)   to form a rational judgment;

(c)   to exercise self-control.

(1B)   For the purposes of subsection (1)(c), an abnormality of mental functioning provides an explanation for D's conduct if it causes, or is a significant contributory factor in causing, D to carry out that conduct.

(2)   On a charge of murder, it shall be for the defence to prove that the person charged is by virtue of this section not liable to be convicted of murder.

(3)   A person who but for this section would be liable, whether as principal or as accessory, to be convicted of murder shall be liable instead to be convicted of manslaughter.

17 Short title, repeal and extent

(1)   This Act may be cited as the Homicide Act 1957.

MISUSE OF DRUGS ACT 1971

1971 chapter 38

An Act to make new provision with respect to dangerous or otherwise harmful drugs and related matters, and for purposes connected therewith.

2 Controlled drugs and their classification for purposes of this Act

(1)   In this Act—

(a)   the expression "controlled drug" means any substance or product for the time being specified in Part I, II, or III of Schedule 2 to this Act; and

(b)   the expressions "Class A drug", "Class B drug" and "Class C drug" mean any of the substances and products for the time being specified respectively in Part I, Part II and Part III of that Schedule;

and the provisions of Part IV of that Schedule shall have effect with respect to the meanings of expressions used in that Schedule.

4 Restriction of production and supply of controlled drugs

(1)   Subject to any regulations under section 7 of this Act for the time being in force, it shall not be lawful for a person—

  (a)   to produce a controlled drug; or
  (b)   to supply or offer to supply a controlled drug to another.

(2)   Subject to section 28 of this Act, it is an offence for a person—

  (a)   to produce a controlled drug in contravention of subsection (1) above; or

  (b)   to be concerned in the production of such a drug in contravention of that subsection by another.

(3)   Subject to section 28 of this Act, it is an offence for a person—

  (a)   to supply or offer to supply a controlled drug to another in contravention of subsection (1) above; or

  (b)   to be concerned in the supplying of such a drug to another in contravention of that subsection; or

  (c)   to be concerned in the making to another in contravention of that subsection of an offer to supply such a drug.

5 Restriction of possession of controlled drugs

(1)   Subject to any regulations under section 7 of this Act for the time being in force, it shall not be lawful for a person to have a controlled drug in his possession.

(2)   Subject to section 28 of this Act and to subsection (4) below, it is an offence for a person to have a controlled drug in his possession in contravention of subsection (1) above.

(3)   Subject to section 28 of this Act, it is an offence for a person to have a controlled drug in his possession, whether lawfully or not, with intent to supply it to another in contravention of section 4(1) of this Act.

(4)   In any proceedings for an offence under subsection (2) above in which it is proved that the accused had a controlled drug in his possession, it shall be a defence for him to prove—

  (a)   that, knowing or suspecting it to be a controlled drug, he took possession of it for the purpose of preventing another from committing or continuing to commit an offence in connection with that drug and that as soon as possible after taking possession of it he took all such steps as were reasonably open to him to destroy the drug or to deliver it into the custody of a person lawfully entitled to take custody of it; or

  (b)   that, knowing or suspecting it to be a controlled drug, he took possession of it for the purpose of delivering it into the custody of a person lawfully entitled to take custody of it and that as soon as possible after taking possession of it he took all such steps as were reasonably open to him to deliver it into the custody of such a person.

[(5)   Subsection (4) above shall apply in the case of proceedings for an offence under section 19(1) of this Act consisting of an attempt to commit an offence under subsection (2) above as it applies in the case of proceedings for an offence under subsection (2), subject to the following modifications, that is to say—

(a)   for the references to the accused having in his possession, and to his taking possession of, a controlled drug there shall be substituted respectively references to his attempting to get, and to his attempting to take, possession of such a drug; and

(b)   in paragraphs (a) and (b) the words from "and that as soon as possible" onwards shall be omitted.]

(6)   Nothing in subsection (4) [or (5)] above shall prejudice any defence which it is open to a person charged with an offence under this section to raise apart from that subsection.

8 Occupiers etc of premises to be punishable for permitting certain activities to take place there

A person commits an offence if, being the occupier or concerned in the management of any premises, he knowingly permits or suffers any of the following activities to take place on those premises, that is to say—

(a)   producing or attempting to produce a controlled drug in contravention of section 4(1) of this Act;

(b)   supplying or attempting to supply a controlled drug to another in contravention of section 4(1) of this Act, or offering to supply a controlled drug to another in contravention of section 4(1);

(c)   preparing opium for smoking;

(d)   smoking cannabis, cannabis resin or prepared opium.

28 Proof of lack of knowledge etc to be a defence in proceedings for certain offences

(1)   This section applies to offences under any of the following provisions of this Act, that is to say section 4(2) and (3), section 5(2) and (3), section 6(2) and section 9.

(2)   Subject to subsection (3) below, in any proceedings for an offence to which this section applies it shall be a defence for the accused to prove that he neither knew of nor suspected nor had reason to suspect the existence of some fact alleged by the prosecution which it is necessary for the prosecution to prove if he is to be convicted of the offence charged.

(3)   Where in any proceedings for an offence to which this section applies it is necessary, if the accused is to be convicted of the offence charged, for the prosecution to prove that some substance or product involved in the alleged offence was the controlled drug which the prosecution alleges it to have been, and it is proved that the substance or product in question was that controlled drug, the accused—

(a)   shall not be acquitted of the offence charged by reason only of proving that he neither knew nor suspected nor had reason to suspect that the substance or product in question was the particular controlled drug alleged; but

(b)   shall be acquitted thereof—

(i)   if he proves that he neither believed nor suspected nor had reason to suspect that the substance or product in question was a controlled drug; or

(ii)   if he proves that he believed the substance or product in question to be a controlled drug, or a controlled drug of a description, such that, if it had in fact been that controlled drug or a controlled drug of that description, he would not at the material time have been committing any offence to which this section applies.

(4)   Nothing in this section shall prejudice any defence which it is open to a person charged with an offence to which this section applies to raise apart from this section

37 Interpretation

(1)   In this Act, except in so far as the context otherwise requires, the following expressions have the meanings hereby assigned to them respectively, that is to say:—

"produce", where the reference is to producing a controlled drug, means producing it by manufacture, cultivation or any other method, and "production" has a corresponding meaning;

"supplying" includes distributing;

(2)   References in this Act to misusing a drug are references to misusing it by taking it; and the reference in the foregoing provision to the taking of a drug is a reference to the taking of it by a human being by way of any form of self-administration, whether or not involving assistance by another.

(3)   For the purposes of this Act the things which a person has in his possession shall be taken to include any thing subject to his control which is in the custody of another.

40 Short title, extent and commencement

(1)   This Act may be cited as the Misuse of Drugs Act 1971.

OFFENCES AGAINST THE PERSON ACT 1861

1861 chapter 100 24 and 25 Vict

An Act to consolidate and amend the Statute Law of England and Ireland relating to Offences against the Person.

18 Wounding, or causing grievous bodily harm with intent to do grievous bodily harm, or to resist apprehension

Whosoever shall unlawfully and maliciously by any means whatsoever wound or cause any grievous bodily harm to any person . . . with intent . . . to do some . . . grievous bodily harm to any person, or with intent to resist or prevent the lawful apprehension or detainer of any person, shall be guilty of felony, and being convicted thereof shall be liable, . . . to be kept in penal servitude for life . . .

20 Inflicting bodily injury, with or without weapon

Whosoever shall unlawfully and maliciously wound or inflict any grievous bodily harm upon any other person, either with or without any weapon or instrument, [shall be guilty of an offence and liable, on conviction on indictment, to imprisonment for a term not exceeding 5 years.]

23 Maliciously administering poison, etc so as to endanger life or inflict grievous bodily harm

Whosoever shall unlawfully and maliciously administer to or cause to be administered to or taken by any other person any poison or other destructive or noxious thing, so as thereby to endanger the life of such person, or so as thereby to inflict upon such person any grievous bodily harm, shall be guilty of felony, and being convicted thereof shall be liable . . . to be kept in penal servitude for any term not exceeding ten years. .

24 Maliciously administering poison, etc with intent to injure, aggrieve, or annoy any other person

Whosoever shall unlawfully and maliciously administer to or cause to be administered to or taken by any other person any poison or other destructive or noxious thing, with intent to injure, aggrieve, or annoy such person, , [shall be guilty of an offence and liable, on conviction on indictment, to imprisonment for a term not exceeding 5 years.]

47 Assault occasioning bodily harm

Whosoever shall be convicted upon an indictment of any assault occasioning actual bodily harm shall be liable . . . [to imprisonment for a term not exceeding 5 years] . . .; and whosoever shall be convicted upon an indictment for a common assault shall be liable, at the discretion of the court, to be imprisoned for any term not exceeding [two years]

SEXUAL OFFENCES ACT 2003

2003 chapter 42

An Act to make new provision about sexual offences, their prevention and the protection of children from harm from other sexual acts, and for connected purposes.

Rape

1 Rape

(1)   A person (A) commits an offence if—

    (a)   he intentionally penetrates the vagina, anus or mouth of another person (B) with his penis,

    (b)   B does not consent to the penetration, and

    (c)   A does not reasonably believe that B consents.

(2)   Whether a belief is reasonable is to be determined having regard to all the circumstances, including any steps A has taken to ascertain whether B consents

(3)   Sections 75 and 76 apply to an offence under this section.

(4)   A person guilty of an offence under this section is liable, on conviction on indictment, to imprisonment for life.

Assault

2 Assault by penetration

(1)   A person (A) commits an offence if—

    (a)   he intentionally penetrates the vagina or anus of another person (B) with a part of his body or anything else,

    (b)   the penetration is sexual,

    (c)   B does not consent to the penetration, and

    (d)   A does not reasonably believe that B consents.

(2)   Whether a belief is reasonable is to be determined having regard to all the circumstances, including any steps A has taken to ascertain whether B consents.

(3)   Sections 75 and 76 apply to an offence under this section.

(4)   A person guilty of an offence under this section is liable, on conviction on indictment, to imprisonment for life.

3 Sexual assault

(1)   A person (A) commits an offence if—

    (a)   he intentionally touches another person (B),
    (b)   the touching is sexual,
    (c)   B does not consent to the touching, and
    (d)   A does not reasonably believe that B consents.

(2)   Whether a belief is reasonable is to be determined having regard to all the circumstances, including any steps A has taken to ascertain whether B consents.

(3)   Sections 75 and 76 apply to an offence under this section.

(4)   A person guilty of an offence under this section is liable—

    (a)   on summary conviction, to imprisonment for a term not exceeding 6 months or a fine not exceeding the statutory maximum or both;

    (b)   on conviction on indictment, to imprisonment for a term not exceeding 10 years.

4 Causing a person to engage in sexual activity without consent

(1)   A person (A) commits an offence if—

    (a)   he intentionally causes another person (B) to engage in an activity,

    (b)   the activity is sexual,

    (c)   B does not consent to engaging in the activity, and

    (d)   A does not reasonably believe that B consents.

(2)   Whether a belief is reasonable is to be determined having regard to all the circumstances, including any steps A has taken to ascertain whether B consents.

(3)   Sections 75 and 76 apply to an offence under this section.

(4)   A person guilty of an offence under this section, if the activity caused involved—

    (a)   penetration of B's anus or vagina,

    (b)   penetration of B's mouth with a person's penis,

    (c)   penetration of a person's anus or vagina with a part of B's body or by B with anything else, or

    (d)   penetration of a person's mouth with B's penis,

is liable, on conviction on indictment, to imprisonment for life.

74 "Consent"

For the purposes of this Part, a person consents if he agrees by choice, and has the freedom and capacity to make that choice.

75 Evidential presumptions about consent

(1)   If in proceedings for an offence to which this section applies it is proved—

    (a)   that the defendant did the relevant act,

    (b)   that any of the circumstances specified in subsection (2) existed, and

    (c)   that the defendant knew that those circumstances existed,

the complainant is to be taken not to have consented to the relevant act unless sufficient evidence is adduced to raise an issue as to whether he consented, and the defendant is to be taken not to have reasonably believed that the complainant consented unless sufficient evidence is adduced to raise an issue as to whether he reasonably believed it.

(2)   The circumstances are that—

    (a)   any person was, at the time of the relevant act or immediately before it began, using violence against the complainant or causing the complainant to fear that immediate violence would be used against him;

    (b)   any person was, at the time of the relevant act or immediately before it began, causing the complainant to fear that violence was being used, or that immediate violence would be used, against another person;

    (c)   the complainant was, and the defendant was not, unlawfully detained at the time of the relevant act;

(d)   the complainant was asleep or otherwise unconscious at the time of the relevant act;

(e)   because of the complainant's physical disability, the complainant would not have been able at the time of the relevant act to communicate to the defendant whether the complainant consented;

(f)   any person had administered to or caused to be taken by the complainant, without the complainant's consent, a substance which, having regard to when it was administered or taken, was capable of causing or enabling the complainant to be stupefied or overpowered at the time of the relevant act.

(3)   In subsection (2)(a) and (b), the reference to the time immediately before the relevant act began is, in the case of an act which is one of a continuous series of sexual activities, a reference to the time immediately before the first sexual activity began.

76 Conclusive presumptions about consent

(1)   If in proceedings for an offence to which this section applies it is proved that the defendant did the relevant act and that any of the circumstances specified in subsection (2) existed, it is to be conclusively presumed—

(a)   that the complainant did not consent to the relevant act, and

(b)   that the defendant did not believe that the complainant consented to the relevant act.

(2)   The circumstances are that—

(a)   the defendant intentionally deceived the complainant as to the nature or purpose of the relevant act;

(b)   the defendant intentionally induced the complainant to consent to the relevant act by impersonating a person known personally to the complainant.

77 Sections 75 and 76: relevant acts

In relation to an offence to which sections 75 and 76 apply, references in those sections to the relevant act and to the complainant are to be read as follows—

Offence	Relevant Act*
An offence under section 1 (rape).	The defendant intentionally penetrating, with his penis, the vagina, anus or mouth of another person ("the complainant").
An offence under section 2 (assault by penetration).	The defendant intentionally penetrating, with a part of his body or anything else, the vagina or anus of another person ("the complainant"), where the penetration is sexual.
An offence under section 3 (sexual assault).	The defendant intentionally touching another person ("the complainant"), where the touching is sexual.
An offence under section 4 (causing a person to engage in sexual activity without consent).	The defendant intentionally causing another person ("the complainant") to engage in an activity, where the activity is sexual.

78 "Sexual"

For the purposes of this Part (except section 71), penetration, touching or any other activity is sexual if a reasonable person would consider that—

(a)   whatever its circumstances or any person's purpose in relation to it, it is because of its nature sexual, or

(b)   because of its nature it may be sexual and because of its circumstances or the purpose of any person in relation to it (or both) it is sexual.

79 Part 1: general interpretation

(1)   The following apply for the purposes of this Part.

(2)   Penetration is a continuing act from entry to withdrawal.

(3)   References to a part of the body include references to a part surgically constructed (in particular, through gender reassignment surgery).

(8)   Touching includes touching—

    (a)   with any part of the body,
    (b)   with anything else,
    (c)   through anything,

and in particular includes touching amounting to penetration.

(9)   "Vagina" includes vulva.

143 Short title

This Act may be cited as the Sexual Offences Act 2003.

THEFT ACT 1968

1968 chapter 60

An Act to revise the law of England and Wales as to theft and similar or associated offences, and in connection therewith to make provision as to criminal proceedings by one party to a marriage against the other, and to make certain amendments extending beyond England and Wales in the Post Office Act 1953 and other enactments; and for other purposes connected therewith.

1 Basic definition of theft

(1)   A person is guilty of theft if he dishonestly appropriates property belonging to another with the intention of permanently depriving the other of it; and "thief" and "steal" shall be construed accordingly.

(2)   It is immaterial whether the appropriation is made with a view to gain, or is made for the thief's own benefit.

(3)   The five following sections of this Act shall have effect as regards the interpretation and operation of this section (and, except as otherwise provided by this Act, shall apply only for purposes of this section).

2 "Dishonestly"

(1)   A person's appropriation of property belonging to another is not to be regarded as dishonest—

    (a)   if he appropriates the property in the belief that he has in law the right to deprive the other of it, on behalf of himself or of a third person; or

    (b)   if he appropriates the property in the belief that he would have the other's consent if the other knew of the appropriation and the circumstances of it; or

    (c)   (except where the property came to him as trustee or personal representative) if he appropriates the property in the belief that the person to whom the property belongs cannot be discovered by taking reasonable steps.

(2)   A person's appropriation of property belonging to another may be dishonest notwithstanding that he is willing to pay for the property.

3 "Appropriates"

(1)   Any assumption by a person of the rights of an owner amounts to an appropriation, and this includes, where he has come by the property (innocently or not) without stealing it, any later assumption of a right to it by keeping or dealing with it as owner.

(2)   Where property or a right or interest in property is or purports to be transferred for value to a person acting in good faith, no later assumption by him of rights which he believed himself to be acquiring shall, by reason of any defect in the transferor's title, amount to theft of the property.

4 "Property"

(1)   "Property" includes money and all other property, real or personal, including things in action and other intangible property.

(2)   A person cannot steal land, or things forming part of land and severed from it by him or by his directions, except in the following cases, that it to say—

    (a)   when he is a trustee or personal representative, or is authorised by power of attorney, or as liquidator of a company, or otherwise, to sell or dispose of land belonging to another, and he appropriates the land or anything forming part of it by dealing with it in breach of the confidence reposed in him; or

    (b)   when he is not in possession of the land and appropriates anything forming part of the land by severing it or causing it to be severed, or after it has been severed; or

    (c)   when, being in possession of the land under a tenancy, he appropriates the whole or part of any fixture or structure let to be used with the land.

For purposes of this subsection "land" does not include incorporeal hereditaments; "tenancy" means a tenancy for years or any less period and includes an agreement for such a tenancy, but a person who after the end of a tenancy remains in possession as statutory tenant or otherwise is to be treated as having possession under the tenancy, and "let" shall be construed accordingly.

(3) A person who picks mushrooms growing wild on any land, or who picks flowers, fruit or foliage from a plant growing wild on any land, does not (although not in possession of the land) steal what he picks, unless he does it for reward or for sale or other commercial purpose.

For purposes of this subsection "mushroom" includes any fungus, and "plant" includes any shrub or tree.

(4) Wild creatures, tamed or untamed, shall be regarded as property; but a person cannot steal a wild creature not tamed nor ordinarily kept in captivity, or the carcase of any such creature, unless either it has been reduced into possession by or on behalf of another person and possession of it has not since been lost or abandoned, or another person is in course of reducing it into possession.

5 "Belonging to another"

(1) Property shall be regarded as belonging to any person having possession or control of it, or having in it any proprietary right or interest (not being an equitable interest arising only from an agreement to transfer or grant an interest).

(2) Where property is subject to a trust, the persons to whom it belongs shall be regarded as including any person having a right to enforce the trust, and an intention to defeat the trust shall be regarded accordingly as an intention to deprive of the property any person having that right.

(3) Where a person receives property from or on account of another, and is under an obligation to the other to retain and deal with that property or its proceeds in a particular way, the property or proceeds shall be regarded (as against him) as belonging to the other.

(4) Where a person gets property by another's mistake, and is under an obligation to make restoration (in whole or in part) of the property or its proceeds or of the value thereof, then to the extent of that obligation the property or proceeds shall be regarded (as against him) as belonging to the person entitled to restoration, and an intention not to make restoration shall be regarded accordingly as an intention to deprive that person of the property or proceeds.

6 "With the intention of permanently depriving the other of it"

(1) A person appropriating property belonging to another without meaning the other permanently to lose the thing itself is nevertheless to be regarded as having the intention of permanently depriving the other of it if his intention is to treat the thing as his own to dispose of regardless of the other's rights; and a borrowing or lending of it may amount to so treating it if, but only if, the borrowing or lending is for a period and in circumstances making it equivalent to an outright taking or disposal.

(2) Without prejudice to the generality of subsection (1) above, where a person, having possession or control (lawfully or not) of property belonging to another, parts with the property under a condition as to its return which he may not be able to perform, this (if done for purposes of his own and without the other's authority) amounts to treating the property as his own to dispose of regardless of the other's rights.

7 Theft

A person guilty of theft shall on conviction on indictment be liable to imprisonment for a term not exceeding seven years.

8 Robbery

(1)   A person is guilty of robbery if he steals, and immediately before or at the time of doing so, and in order to do so, he uses force on any person or puts or seeks to put any person in fear of being then and there subjected to force.

(2)   A person guilty of robbery, or of an assault with intent to rob, shall on conviction on indictment be liable to imprisonment for life.

9 Burglary

(1)   A person is guilty of burglary if—

(a)   he enters any building or part of a building as a trespasser and with intent to commit any such offence as is mentioned in subsection (2) below; or

(b)   having entered any building or part of a building as a trespasser he steals or attempts to steal anything in the building or that part of it or inflicts or attempts to inflict on any person therein any grievous bodily harm.

(2)   The offences referred to in subsection (1)(a) above are offences of stealing anything in the building or part of a building in question, of inflicting on any person therein any grievous bodily harm ... therein, and of doing unlawful damage to the building or anything therein.

[(3)   A person guilty of burglary shall on conviction on indictment be liable to imprisonment for a term not exceeding—

(a)   where the offence was committed in respect of a building or part of a building which is a dwelling, fourteen years;

(b)   in any other case, ten years.

(4)   References in subsections (1) and (2) above to a building, and the reference in subsection (3) above to a building which is a dwelling, shall apply also to an inhabited vehicle or vessel, and shall apply to any such vehicle or vessel at times when the person having a habitation in it is not there as well as at times when he is.]

10 Aggravated burglary

(1)   A person is guilty of aggravated burglary if he commits any burglary and at the time has with him any firearm or imitation firearm, any weapon of offence, or any explosive; and for this purpose—

(a)   "firearm" includes an airgun or air pistol, and "imitation firearm" means anything which has the appearance of being a firearm, whether capable of being discharged or not; and

(b)   "weapon of offence" means any article made or adapted for use for causing injury to or incapacitating a person, or intended by the person having it with him for such use; and

(c)   "explosive" means any article manufactured for the purpose of producing a practical effect by explosion, or intended by the person having it with him for that purpose.

(2)   A person guilty of aggravated burglary shall on conviction on indictment be liable to imprisonment for life.

21 Blackmail

(1)   A person is guilty of blackmail if, with a view to gain for himself or another or with intent to cause loss to another, he makes any unwarranted demand with menaces; and for this purpose a demand with menaces is unwarranted unless the person making it does so in the belief—

(a)   that he has reasonable grounds for making the demand; and

(b)   that the use of the menaces is a proper means of reinforcing the demand.

(2)   The nature of the act or omission demanded is immaterial, and it is also immaterial whether the menaces relate to action to be taken by the person making the demand.

(3)   A person guilty of blackmail shall on conviction on indictment be liable to imprisonment for a term not exceeding fourteen years.

34 Interpretation

(1)   Sections 4(1) and 5(1) of this Act shall apply generally for purposes of this Act as they apply for purposes of section 1.

(2)   For purposes of this Act—

(a)   "gain" and "loss" are to be construed as extending only to gain or loss in money or other property, but as extending to any such gain or loss whether temporary or permanent; and—

(i)   "gain" includes a gain by keeping what one has, as well as a gain by getting what one has not; and

(ii)   "loss" includes a loss by not getting what one might get, as well as a loss by parting with what one has;

(b)   "goods", except in so far as the context otherwise requires, includes money and every other description of property except land, and includes things severed from the land by stealing.

36 Short title, and general provisions as to Scotland and Northern Ireland

(1)   This Act may be cited as the Theft Act 1968.

THEFT ACT 1978

1978 chapter 31

An Act to replace section 16(2)(a) of the Theft Act 1968 with other provision against fraudulent conduct; and for connected purposes.

3 Making off without payment

(1)   Subject to subsection (3) below, a person who, knowing that payment on the spot for any goods supplied or service done is required or expected from him, dishonestly makes off without having paid as required or expected and with intent to avoid payment of the amount due shall be guilty of an offence.

(2)   For purposes of this section "payment on the spot" includes payment at the time of collecting goods on which work has been done or in respect of which service has been provided.

(3)   Subsection (1) above shall not apply where the supply of the goods or the doing of the service is contrary to law, or where the service done is such that payment is not legally enforceable.

4 Punishments

(1)   Offences under this Act shall be punishable either on conviction on indictment or on summary conviction.

(2)   A person convicted on indictment shall be liable —

(a)   for an offence under section 1 or section 2 of this Act, to imprisonment for a term not exceeding five years; and

(b)   for an offence under section 3 of this Act, to imprisonment for a term not exceeding two years.

Part 4

Equity & Trusts and Land Law

ADMINISTRATION OF JUSTICE ACT 1970

1970 chapter 31

An Act to make further provision about the courts (including assizes), their business, jurisdiction and procedure; to enable a High Court judge to accept appointment as arbitrator or umpire under an arbitration agreement; to amend the law respecting the enforcement of debt and other liabilities; to amend section 106 of the Rent Act 1968; and for miscellaneous purposes connected with the administration of justice.

Part IV Actions by Mortgagees for Possession

36 Additional powers of court in action by mortgagee for possession of dwelling-house

(1)   Where the mortgagee under a mortgage of land which consists of or includes a dwelling-house brings an action in which he claims possession of the mortgaged property, not being an action for foreclosure in which a claim for possession of the mortgaged property is also made, the court may exercise any of the powers conferred on it by subsection (2) below if it appears to the court that in the event of its exercising the power the mortgagor is likely to be able within a reasonable period to pay any sums due under the mortgage or to remedy a default consisting of a breach of any other obligation arising under or by virtue of the mortgage.

(2)   The court—

(a)   may adjourn the proceedings, or

(b)   on giving judgment, or making an order, for delivery of possession of the mortgaged property, or at any time before the execution of such judgment or order, may—

(i)   stay or suspend execution of the judgment or order, or

(ii)   postpone the date for delivery of possession,

for such period or periods as the court thinks reasonable.

(3)   Any such adjournment, stay, suspension or postponement as is referred to in subsection (2) above may be made subject to such conditions with regard to payment by the mortgagor of any sum secured by the mortgage or the remedying of any default as the court thinks fit.

(4)   The court may from time to time vary or revoke any condition imposed by virtue of this section.

[38A. This Part of this Act shall not apply to a mortgage securing an agreement which is a regulated agreement within the meaning of the Consumer Credit Act 1974.]

39 Interpretation of Part IV

(1)   In this Part of this Act—

"dwelling-house" includes any building or part thereof which is used as a dwelling;

"mortgage" includes a charge and "mortgagor" and "mortgagee" shall be construed accordingly;

"mortgagor" and "mortgagee" includes any person deriving title under the original mortgagor or mortgagee.

(2) The fact that part of the premises comprised in a dwelling-house is used as a shop or office or for business, trade or professional purposes shall not prevent the dwelling-house from being a dwelling-house for the purposes of this Part of this Act.

ADMINISTRATION OF JUSTICE ACT 1973

1973 chapter 15

An Act to amend the law relating to justices of the peace and to make further provision with respect to the administration of justice and matters connected therewith.

Part II Miscellaneous

8 Extension of powers of court in action by mortgagee of dwelling-house

(1) Where by a mortgage of land which consists of or includes a dwelling-house, or by any agreement between the mortgage under such a mortgage and the mortgagor, the mortgagor is entitled or is to be permitted to pay the principal sum secured by instalments or otherwise to defer payment of it in whole or in part, but provision is also made for earlier payment in the event of any default by the mortgagor or of a demand by the mortgagee or otherwise, then for purposes of section 36 of the Administration of Justice Act 1970 (under which a court has power to delay giving a mortgagee possession of the mortgaged property so as to allow the mortgagor a reasonable time to pay any sums due under the mortgage) a court may treat as due under the mortgage on account of the principal sum secured and of interest on it only such amounts as the mortgagor would have expected to be required to pay if there had been no such provision for earlier payment.

(2) A court shall not exercise by virtue of subsection (1) above the powers conferred by section 36 of the Administration of Justice Act 1970 unless it appears to the court not only that the mortgagor is likely to be able within a reasonable period to pay any amounts regarded (in accordance with subsection (1) above) as due on account of the principal sum secured, together with the interest on those amounts, but also that he is likely to be able by the end of that period to pay any further amounts that he would have expected to be required to pay by then on account of that sum and of interest on it if there had been no such provision as is Preferred to in subsection (1) above for earlier payment.

(3) Where subsection (1) above would apply to an action in which a mortgagee only claimed possession of the mortgaged property, and the mortgagee brings an action for foreclosure (with or without also claiming possession of the property), then section 36 of the Administration of Justice Act 1970 together with subsections (1) and (2) above shall apply as they would apply if it were an action in which the mortgagee only claimed possession of the mortgaged property, except that—

(a) section 36(2)(b) shall apply only in relation to any claim for possession; and

(b) section 36(5) shall not apply.

(4) For purposes of this section the expressions "dwelling-house", "mortgage", "mortgagee" and "mortgagor" shall be construed in the same way as for the purposes of Part IV of the Administration of Justice Act 1970.

CHARITIES ACT 2011

2011 chapter 25

An Act to consolidate the Charities Act 1993 and other enactments which relate to charities.

Part I Meaning of "Charity" and "Charitable Purpose"

1 Meaning of "Charity"

(1) For the purposes of the law of England and Wales, "charity" means an institution which—

   (a) is established for charitable purposes only, and

   (b) falls to be subject to the control of the High Court in the exercise of its jurisdiction with respect to charities.

(2) The definition of "charity" in subsection (1) does not apply for the purposes of an enactment if a different definition of that term applies for those purposes by virtue of that or any other enactment.

2 Meaning of "Charitable Purpose"

(1) For the purposes of the law of England and Wales, a charitable purpose is a purpose which—

   (a) falls within section 3(1), and

   (b) is for the public benefit (see section 4).

(2) Any reference in any enactment or document (in whatever terms)—

   (a) to charitable purposes, or

   (b) to institutions having purposes that are charitable under the law relating to charities in England and Wales, is to be read in accordance with subsection (1).

(3) Subsection (2) does not apply where the context otherwise requires.

(4) This section is subject to section 11 (which makes special provision for Chapter 2 of this Part onwards).

3 Descriptions of Purposes

(1) A purpose falls within this subsection if it falls within any of the following descriptions of purposes—

   (a) the prevention or relief of poverty;

   (b) the advancement of education;

(c)   the advancement of religion;

(d)   the advancement of health or the saving of lives;

(e)   the advancement of citizenship or community development;

(f)   the advancement of the arts, culture, heritage or science;

(g)   the advancement of amateur sport;

(h)   the advancement of human rights, conflict resolution or reconciliation or the promotion of religious or racial harmony or equality and diversity;

(i)   the advancement of environmental protection or improvement;

(j)   the relief of those in need because of youth, age, ill-health, disability, financial hardship or other disadvantage;

(k)   the advancement of animal welfare;

(l)   the promotion of the efficiency of the armed forces of the Crown or of the efficiency of the police, fire and rescue services or ambulance services;

(m)   any other purposes—

    (i)   that are not within paragraphs (a) to (l) but are recognised as charitable purposes by virtue of section 5 (recreational and similar trusts, etc.) or under the old law,

    (ii)   that may reasonably be regarded as analogous to, or within the spirit of, any purposes falling within any of paragraphs (a) to (l) or sub-paragraph (i), or

    (iii)   that may reasonably be regarded as analogous to, or within the spirit of, any purposes which have been recognised, under the law relating to charities in England and Wales, as falling within sub-paragraph (ii) or this sub-paragraph.

4 The Public Benefit Requirement

(1)   In this Act "the public benefit requirement" means the requirement in section 2(1)(b) that a purpose falling within section 3(1) must be for the public benefit if it is to be a charitable purpose.

(2)   In determining whether the public benefit requirement is satisfied in relation to any purpose falling within section 3(1), it is not to be presumed that a purpose of a particular description is for the public benefit.

(3)   In this Chapter any reference to the public benefit is a reference to the public benefit as that term is understood for the purposes of the law relating to charities in England and Wales.

(4)   Subsection (3) is subject to subsection (2).

CIVIL LIABILITY (CONTRIBUTION) ACT 1978

1978 chapter 47

An Act to make new provision for contribution between persons who are jointly or severally, or both jointly and severally, liable for the same damage and in certain other similar cases where two or more persons have paid or may be required to pay compensation for the same damage; and to amend the law relating to proceedings against persons jointly liable for the same debt or jointly or severally, or both jointly and severally, liable for the same damage.

Proceedings for contribution

1 Entitlement to contribution

(1)　Subject to the following provisions of this section, any person liable in respect of any damage suffered by another person may recover contribution from any other person liable in respect of the same damage (whether jointly with him or otherwise).

(2)　A person shall be entitled to recover contribution by virtue of subsection (1) above notwithstanding that he has ceased to be liable in respect of the damage in question since the time when the damage occurred, provided that he was so liable immediately before he made or was ordered or agreed to make the payment in respect of which the contribution is sought.

(3)　A person shall be liable to make contribution by virtue of subsection (1) above notwithstanding that he has ceased to be liable in respect of the damage in question since the time when the damage occurred, unless he ceased to be liable by virtue of the expiry of a period of limitation or prescription which extinguished the right on which the claim against him in respect of the damage was based.

(4)　A person who has made or agreed to make any payment in bona fide settlement or compromise of any claim made against him in respect of any damage (including a payment into court which has been accepted) shall be entitled to recover contribution in accordance with this section without regard to whether or not he himself is or ever was liable in respect of the damage, provided, however, that he would have been liable assuming that the factual basis of the claim against him could be established.

(5)　A judgment given in any action brought in any part of the United Kingdom by or on behalf of the person who suffered the damage in question against any person from whom contribution is sought under this section shall be conclusive in the proceedings for contribution as to any issue determined by that judgment in favour of the person from whom the contribution is sought.

(6)　References in this section to a person's liability in respect of any damage are references to any such liability which has been or could be established in an action brought against him in England and Wales by or on behalf of the person who suffered the damage; but it is immaterial whether any issue arising in any such action was or would be determined (in accordance with the rules of private international law) by reference to the law of a country outside England and Wales.

2 Assessment of contribution

(1)   Subject to subsection (3) below, in any proceedings for contribution under section 1 above the amount of the contribution recoverable from any person shall be such as may be found by the court to be just and equitable having regard to the extent of that person's responsibility for the damage in question.

(2)   Subject to subsection (3) below, the court shall have power in any such proceedings to exempt any person from liability to make contribution, or to direct that the contribution to be recovered from any person shall amount to a complete indemnity.

(3)   Where the amount of the damages which have or might have been awarded in respect of the damage in question in any action brought in England and Wales by or on behalf of the person who suffered it against the person from whom the contribution is sought was or would have been subject to—

(a)   any limit imposed by or under any enactment or by any agreement made before the damage occurred;

(b)   any reduction by virtue of section 1 of the Law Reform (Contributory Negligence) Act 1945 or section 5 of the Fatal Accidents Act 1976; or

(c)   any corresponding limit or reduction under the law of a country outside England and Wales;

the person from whom the contribution is sought shall not by virtue of any contribution awarded under section 1 above be required to pay in respect of the damage a greater amount than the amount of those damages as so limited or reduced.

6 Interpretation

(1)   A person is liable in respect of any damage for the purposes of this Act if the person who suffered it (or anyone representing his estate or dependants) is entitled to recover compensation from him in respect of that damage (whatever the legal basis of his liability, whether tort, breach of contract, breach of trust or otherwise).

(2)   References in this Act to an action brought by or on behalf of the person who suffered any damage include references to an action brought for the benefit of his estate or dependants.

(3)   In this Act "dependants" has the same meaning as in the Fatal Accidents Act 1976.

(4)   In this Act, except in section 1(5) above, "action" means an action brought in England and Wales.

CIVIL PARTNERSHIP ACT 2004

2004 chapter 33

An Act to make provision for and in connection with civil partnership.

Part 1 Introduction

1 Civil partnership

(1)   A civil partnership is a relationship between two people of the same sex ("civil partners")—

    (a)   which is formed when they register as civil partners of each other—

        (i)   in England or Wales (under Part 2),

        (ii)   in Scotland (under Part 3),

        (iii)   in Northern Ireland (under Part 4), or

        (iv)   outside the United Kingdom under an Order in Council made under Chapter 1 of Part 5 (registration at British consulates etc or by armed forces personnel), or

    (b)   which they are treated under Chapter 2 of Part 5 as having formed (at the time determined under that Chapter) by virtue of having registered an overseas relationship.

(2)   Subsection (1) is subject to the provisions of this Act under or by virtue of which a civil partnership is void.

(3)   A civil partnership ends only on death, dissolution or annulment.

(4)   The references in subsection (3) to dissolution and annulment are to dissolution and annulment having effect under or recognised in accordance with this Act.

(5)   References in this Act to an overseas relationship are to be read in accordance with Chapter 2 of Part 5.

Part 2 Civil partnership: England and Wales

Chapter 1 Registration

Formation, eligibility and parental etc consent

2 Formation of civil partnership by registration

(1)   For the purposes of section 1, two people are to be regarded as having registered as civil partners of each other once each of them has signed the civil partnership document—

    (a)   at the invitation of, and in the presence of, a civil partnership registrar, and

    (b)   in the presence of each other and two witnesses.

(2)   Subsection (1) applies regardless of whether subsections (3) and (4) are complied with.

(3) After the civil partnership document has been signed under subsection (1), it must also be signed, in the presence of the civil partners and each other, by—

    (a)   each of the two witnesses, and

    (b)   the civil partnership registrar.

(4) After the witnesses and the civil partnership registrar have signed the civil partnership document, the relevant registration authority must ensure that—

    (a)   the fact that the two people have registered as civil partners of each other, and

    (b)   any other information prescribed by regulations,

is recorded in the register as soon as is practicable.

(5) No religious service is to be used while the civil partnership registrar is officiating at the signing of a civil partnership document.

(6) "The civil partnership document" has the meaning given by section 7(1).

(7) "The relevant registration authority" means the registration authority in whose area the registration takes place.

3 Eligibility

(1) Two people are not eligible to register as civil partners of each other if—

    (a)   they are not of the same sex,
    (b)   either of them is already a civil partner or lawfully married,
    (c)   either of them is under 16, or
    (d)   they are within prohibited degrees of relationship.

(2) Part 1 of Schedule 1 contains provisions for determining when two people are within prohibited degrees of relationship.

4 Parental etc consent where proposed civil partner under 18

(1) The consent of the appropriate persons is required before a child and another person may register as civil partners of each other.

(2) Part 1 of Schedule 2 contains provisions for determining who are the appropriate persons for the purposes of this section.

(3) The requirement of consent under subsection (1) does not apply if the child is a surviving civil partner.

(4) Nothing in this section affects any need to obtain the consent of the High Court before a ward of court and another person may register as civil partners of each other.

(5) In this Part "child", except where used to express a relationship, means a person who is under 18.

CIVIL PROCEDURE ACT 1997

1997 chapter 12

An Act to amend the law about civil procedure in England and Wales; and for connected purposes.

7 Power of courts to make orders for preserving evidence, etc

(1)   The court may make an order under this section for the purpose of securing, in the case of any existing or proposed proceedings in the court—

    (a)   the preservation of evidence which is or may be relevant, or

    (b)   the preservation of property which is or may be the subject-matter of the proceedings or as to which any question arises or may arise in the proceedings.

(2)   A person who is, or appears to the court likely to be, a party to proceedings in the court may make an application for such an order.

(3)   Such an order may direct any person to permit any person described in the order, or secure that any person so described is permitted—

    (a)   to enter premises in England and Wales, and

    (b)   while on the premises, to take in accordance with the terms of the order any of the following steps.

(4)   Those steps are—

    (a)   to carry out a search for or inspection of anything described in the order, and

    (b)   to make or obtain a copy, photograph, sample or other record of anything so described.

(5)   The order may also direct the person concerned—

    (a)   to provide any person described in the order, or secure that any person so described is provided, with any information or article described in the order, and

    (b)   to allow any person described in the order, or secure that any person so described is allowed, to retain for safe keeping anything described in the order.

(6)   An order under this section is to have effect subject to such conditions as are specified in the order.

(7)   This section does not affect any right of a person to refuse to do anything on the ground that to do so might tend to expose him or his spouse to proceedings for an offence or for the recovery of a penalty.

(8)   In this section—

    •   "court" means the High Court, and

    •   "premises" includes any vehicle;

and an order under this section may describe anything generally, whether by reference to a class or otherwise.

COMMON LAW PROCEDURE ACT 1852

1852 chapter 76 15 and 16 Vict

An Act to amend the Process, Practice, and Mode of Pleading in the Superior Courts of Common Law at Westminster, and in the Superior Courts of the Counties Palatine of Lancaster and Durham.

210 Proceedings in ejectment by landlord for nonpayment of rent

In all cases between landlord and tenant, as often as it shall happen that one half year's rent shall be in arrear, and the landlord or lessor, to whom the same is due, hath right by law to re-enter for the nonpayment thereof, such landlord or lessor shall and may, without any formal demand or re-entry, serve a writ in ejectment for the recovery of the demised premises, . . ., which service . . . shall stand in the place and stead of a demand and re-entry; and in case of judgment against the defendant for nonappearance, if it shall be made appear to the court where the said action is depending, by affidavit, or be proved upon the trial in case the defendant appears, that half a year's rent was due before the said writ was served, and that no sufficient distress was to be found on the demised premises, countervailing the arrears then due, and that the lessor had power to re-enter, then and in every such case the lessor shall recover judgment and execution, in the same manner as if the rent in arrear had been legally demanded, and a re-entry made; and in case the lessee or his assignee, or other person claiming or deriving under the said lease, shall permit and suffer judgment to be had and recovered on such trial in ejectment, and execution to be executed thereon, without paying the rent and arrears, together with full costs, and without proceeding for relief in equity within six months after such execution executed, then and in such case the said lessee, his assignee, and all other persons claiming and deriving under the said lease, shall be barred and foreclosed from all relief or remedy in law or equity, other than by bringing error for reversal of such judgment, in case the same shall be erroneous; and the said landlord or lessor shall from thenceforth hold the said demised premises discharged from such lease; . . . provided that nothing herein contained shall extend to bar the right of any mortgagee of such lease, or any part thereof, who shall not be in possession, so as such mortgagee shall and do, within six months after such judgment obtained and execution executed pay all rent in arrear, and all costs and damages sustained by such lessor or person entitled to the remainder or reversion as aforesaid, and perform all the covenants and agreements which, on the part and behalf of the first lessee, are and ought to be performed.

211 Lessee proceeding in equity not to have injunction or relief without payment of rent and costs

In case the said lessee, his assignee, or other person claiming any right, title, or interest, in law or equity, of, in, or to the said lease, shall, within the time aforesaid, proceed for relief in any court of equity, such person shall not have or continue any injunction against the proceedings at law on such ejectment, unless he does or shall, within forty days next after a full and perfect answer shall be made by the claimant in such ejectment, bring into court, and lodge with the proper officer such sum and sums of money as the lessor or landlord shall in his answer swear to be due and in arrear over and above all just allowances, and also the costs taxed in the said suit, there to remain till the hearing of the cause, or to be paid out to the lessor or landlord on good security, subject to the decree of the court; and in case such proceedings for relief in equity shall be taken within the time aforesaid, and after execution is executed, the lessor or landlord shall be accountable only for so much and no more as he shall really and bona fide, without fraud, deceit, or wilful neglect, make of the demised premises from the time of his entering into the actual possession thereof; and if what shall be so made by the lessor or landlord happen to be less than the rent reserved on the said lease, then the said lessee or his assignee, before he shall be restored to his possession, shall pay such lessor or landlord, what the money so by him made fell short of the reserved rent for the time such lessor or landlord held the said lands.

212 Tenant paying all rent with costs, proceedings to cease

If the tenant or his assignee do or shall, at any time before the trial in such ejectment, pay or tender to the lessor or landlord, his executors or administrators, or his or their attorney in that cause, or pay into the court where the same cause is depending, all the rent and arrears, together with the costs, then and in such case, all further proceedings on the said ejectment shall cease and be discontinued; and if such lessee, his executors, administrators, or assigns, shall, upon such proceedings as aforesaid, be relieved in equity, he and they shall have, hold, and enjoy the demised lands, according to the lease thereof made, without any new lease.

CONSUMER CREDIT ACT 1974

1974 chapter 39

An Act to establish for the protection of consumers a new system, administered by the Director General of Fair Trading, of licensing and other control of traders concerned with the provision of credit, or the supply of goods on hire or hire-purchase, and their transactions in place of the present enactments regulating moneylenders, pawnbrokers and hire-purchase traders and their transactions, and for related matters.

Supplemental Provisions as to orders

135 Power to impose conditions, or suspend operation of order

(1)   If it considers it just to do so, the court may in an order made by it in relation to a regulated agreement include provisions–

    (a)   making the operation of any term of the order conditional on the doing of specified acts by any party to the proceedings;

    (b)   suspending the operation of any term of the order either—

        (i)   until such time as the court subsequently directs, or

        (ii)   until the occurrence of a specified act or omission.

CONSUMER CREDIT ACT 2006

2006 chapter 14

An Act to amend the Consumer Credit Act 1974; to extend the ombudsman scheme under the Financial Services and Markets Act 2000 to cover licensees under the Consumer Credit Act 1974; and for connected purposes.

Unfair relationships

19 Unfair relationships between creditors and debtors

After section 140 of the 1974 Act insert—

"Unfair relationships

140A Unfair relationships between creditors and debtors

(1)   The court may make an order under section 140B in connection with a credit agreement if it determines that the relationship between the creditor and the debtor arising out of the agreement (or the agreement taken with any related agreement) is unfair to the debtor because of one or more of the following—

   (a)   any of the terms of the agreement or of any related agreement;

   (b)   the way in which the creditor has exercised or enforced any of his rights under the agreement or any related agreement;

   (c)   any other thing done (or not done) by, or on behalf of, the creditor (either before or after the making of the agreement or any related agreement).

(2)   In deciding whether to make a determination under this section the court shall have regard to all matters it thinks relevant (including matters relating to the creditor and matters relating to the debtor).

(3)   For the purposes of this section the court shall (except to the extent that it is not appropriate to do so) treat anything done (or not done) by, or on behalf of, or in relation to, an associate or a former associate of the creditor as if done (or not done) by, or on behalf of, or in relation to, the creditor.

(4)   A determination may be made under this section in relation to a relationship notwithstanding that the relationship may have ended.

(5)   An order under section 140B shall not be made in connection with a credit agreement which is an exempt agreement by virtue of section 16(6C)."

20 Powers of court in relation to unfair relationships

After section 140A of the 1974 Act (inserted by section 19 of this Act) insert—

"140B Powers of court in relation to unfair relationships

(1)   An order under this section in connection with a credit agreement may do one or more of the following—

(a)   require the creditor, or any associate or former associate of his, to repay (in whole or in part) any sum paid by the debtor or by a surety by virtue of the agreement or any related agreement (whether paid to the creditor, the associate or the former associate or to any other person);

(b)   require the creditor, or any associate or former associate of his, to do or not to do (or to cease doing) anything specified in the order in connection with the agreement or any related agreement;

(c)   reduce or discharge any sum payable by the debtor or by a surety by virtue of the agreement or any related agreement;

(d)   direct the return to a surety of any property provided by him for the purposes of a security;

(e)   otherwise set aside (in whole or in part) any duty imposed on the debtor or on a surety by virtue of the agreement or any related agreement;

(f)   alter the terms of the agreement or of any related agreement;

(g)   direct accounts to be taken, or (in Scotland) an accounting to be made, between any persons.

(2)   An order under this section may be made in connection with a credit agreement only—

(a)   on an application made by the debtor or by a surety;

(b)   at the instance of the debtor or a surety in any proceedings in any court to which the debtor and the creditor are parties, being proceedings to enforce the agreement or any related agreement; or

(c)   at the instance of the debtor or a surety in any other proceedings in any court where the amount paid or payable under the agreement or any related agreement is relevant.

(3)   An order under this section may be made notwithstanding that its effect is to place on the creditor, or any associate or former associate of his, a burden in respect of an advantage enjoyed by another person.

(4)   An application under subsection (2)(a) may only be made—

(a)   in England and Wales, to the county court;
(b)   in Scotland, to the sheriff court;
(c)   in Northern Ireland, to the High Court (subject to subsection (6)).

(5)   In Scotland such an application may be made in the sheriff court for the district in which the debtor or surety resides or carries on business.

(6) In Northern Ireland such an application may be made to the county court if the credit agreement is an agreement under which the creditor provides the debtor with—

   (a)   fixed-sum credit not exceeding £15,000; or

   (b)   running-account credit on which the credit limit does not exceed £15,000.

(7) Without prejudice to any provision which may be made by rules of court made in relation to county courts in Northern Ireland, such rules may provide that an application made by virtue of subsection (6) may be made in the county court for the division in which the debtor or surety resides or carries on business.

(8) A party to any proceedings mentioned in subsection (2) shall be entitled, in accordance with rules of court, to have any person who might be the subject of an order under this section made a party to the proceedings.

(9) If, in any such proceedings, the debtor or a surety alleges that the relationship between the creditor and the debtor is unfair to the debtor, it is for the creditor to prove to the contrary."

21 Interpretation of ss. 140A and 140B of the 1974 Act

After section 140B of the 1974 Act (inserted by section 20 of this Act) insert—

"140C Interpretation of ss 140A and 140B

(1) In this section and in sections 140A and 140B 'credit agreement' means any agreement between an individual (the 'debtor') and any other person (the 'creditor') by which the creditor provides the debtor with credit of any amount.

(2) References in this section and in sections 140A and 140B to the creditor or to the debtor under a credit agreement include—

   (a)   references to the person to whom his rights and duties under the agreement have passed by assignment or operation of law;

   (b)   where two or more persons are the creditor or the debtor, references to any one or more of those persons.

(3) The definition of 'court' in section 189(1) does not apply for the purposes of sections 140A and 140B.

(4) References in sections 140A and 140B to an agreement related to a credit agreement (the 'main agreement') are references to—

   (a)   a credit agreement consolidated by the main agreement;

   (b)   a linked transaction in relation to the main agreement or to a credit agreement within paragraph (a);

   (c)   a security provided in relation to the main agreement, to a credit agreement within paragraph (a) or to a linked transaction within paragraph (b).

(5) In the case of a credit agreement which is not a regulated consumer credit agreement, for the purposes of subsection (4) a transaction shall be treated as being a linked transaction in relation to that agreement if it would have been such a transaction had that agreement been a regulated consumer credit agreement.

(6)   For the purposes of this section and section 140B the definitions of 'security' and 'surety' in section 189(1) apply (with any appropriate changes) in relation to—

(a)   a credit agreement which is not a consumer credit agreement as if it were a consumer credit agreement; and

(b)   a transaction which is a linked transaction by virtue of subsection (5).

(7)   For the purposes of this section a credit agreement (the 'earlier agreement') is consolidated by another credit agreement (the 'later agreement') if—

(a)   the later agreement is entered into by the debtor (in whole or in part) for purposes connected with debts owed by virtue of the earlier agreement; and

(b)   at any time prior to the later agreement being entered into the parties to the earlier agreement included—

(i)   the debtor under the later agreement; and

(ii)   the creditor under the later agreement or an associate or a former associate of his.

(8)   Further, if the later agreement is itself consolidated by another credit agreement (whether by virtue of this subsection or subsection (7)), then the earlier agreement is consolidated by that other agreement as well."

COUNTY COURTS ACT 1984

1984 chapter 28

An Act to consolidate certain enactments relating to county courts.

Forfeiture for non-payment of rent

138 Provisions as to forfeiture for non-payment of rent

(1)   This section has effect where a lessor is proceeding by action in a county court (being an action in which the county court has jurisdiction) to enforce against a lessee a right of re-entry or forfeiture in respect of any land for non-payment of rent.

(2)   If the lessee pays into court [or to the lessor] not less than 5 clear days before the return day all the rent in arrear and the costs of the action, the action shall cease, and the lessee shall hold the land according to the lease without any new lease.

(3)   If–

(a)   the action does not cease under subsection (2); and

(b)   the court at the trial is satisfied that the lessor is entitled to enforce the right of re-entry or forfeiture,

the court shall order possession of the land to be given to the lessor at the expiration of such period, not being less than 4 weeks from the date of the order, as the court thinks fit, unless within that period the lessee pays into court [or to the lessor] all the rent in arrear and the costs of the action.

(4)   The court may extend the period specified under subsection (3) at any time before possession of the land is recovered in pursuance of the order under that subsection.

(5)   . . . if –

   (a)   within the period specified in the order; or

   (b)   within that period as extended under subsection (4), the lessee pays into court [or to the lessor] – he shall hold the land according to the lease without any new lease.

      (i)   all the rent in arrear; and

      (ii)   the costs of the action,

(6)   Subsection (2) shall not apply where the lessor is proceeding in the same action to enforce a right of re-entry or forfeiture on any other ground as well as for non-payment of rent, or to enforce any other claim as well as the right of re-entry or forfeiture and the claim for arrears of rent.

[(9A)   Where the lessor recovers possession of the land at any time after the making of the order under subsection (3) (whether as a result of the enforcement of the order or otherwise) the lessee may, at any time within six months from the date on which the lessor recovers possession, apply to the court for relief; and on any such application the court may, if it thinks fit, grant to the lessee such relief, subject to such terms and conditions, as it thinks fit.

(9B)   Where the lessee is granted relief on an application under subsection (9A) he shall hold the land according to the lease without any new lease.

(9C)   An application under subsection (9A) may be made by a person with an interest under a lease of the land derived (whether immediately or otherwise) from the lessee's interest therein in like manner as if he were the lessee; and on any such application the court may make an order which (subject to such terms and conditions as the court thinks fit) vests the land in such a person, as lessee of the lessor, for the remainder of the term of the lease under which he has any such interest as aforesaid, or for any lesser term.

   In this subsection any reference to the land includes a reference to a part of the land.]

(10)   Nothing in this section or section 139 shall be taken to affect–

   (a)   the power of the court to make any order which it would otherwise have power to make as re-spects a right of re-entry or forfeiture on any ground other than non-payment of rent; or

   (b)   section 146(4) of the Law of Property Act 1925 (relief against forfeiture).

139 Provisions as to forfeiture for non-payment of rent

(1)   In a case where section 138 has effect, if–

   (a)   one-half-year's rent is in arrear at the time of the commencement of the action; and

   (b)   the lessor has a right to re-enter for non-payment of that rent; and

   (c)   *no sufficient distress is to be found on the premises countervailing the arrears then due,*

      [(c) the power under section 72(1) of the Tribunals, Courts and Enforcement Act 2007 (commercial rent arrears recovery) is exercisable to recover the arrears; and

(d)   there are not sufficient goods on the premises to recover the arrears by that power,]

the service of the summons in the action in the prescribed manner shall stand in lieu of a demand and re-entry.

(2)   Where a lessor has enforced against a lessee, by re-entry without action, a right of re-entry or forfeiture as respects any land for non-payment of rent, the lessee may . . . at any time within six months from the date on which the lessor re-entered apply to the county court for relief, and on any such application the court may, if it thinks fit, grant to the lessee such relief as the High Court could have granted.

[(3)   Subsections (9B) and (9C) of section 138 shall have effect in relation to an application under subsection (2) of this section as they have effect in relation to an application under subsection (9A) of that section.]

FAMILY LAW ACT 1996

1996 chapter 27

An Act to make provision with respect to: divorce and separation; legal aid in connection with mediation in disputes relating to family matters; proceedings in cases where marriages have broken down; rights of occupation of certain domestic premises; prevention of molestation; the inclusion in certain orders under the Children Act 1989 of provisions about the occupation of a dwelling-house; the transfer of tenancies between spouses and persons who have lived together as husband and wife; and for connected purposes.

Rights to occupy matrimonial [or civil partnership] home

30 Rights concerning [home where one spouse or civil partner] has no estate, etc

(1)   This section applies if—

   (a)   one spouse [or civil partner ('A')] is entitled to occupy a dwelling-house by virtue of—

      (i)   a beneficial estate or interest or contract; or
      (ii)   any enactment giving [A] the right to remain in occupation; and

   (b)   the other spouse [or civil partner ('B')] is not so entitled.

(2)   Subject to the provisions of this Part, [B] not so entitled has the following rights [home rights"]—

   (a)   if in occupation, a right not to be evicted or excluded from the dwelling-house or any part of it by [A] except with the leave of the court given by an order under section 33;

   (b)   if not in occupation, a right with the leave of the court so given to enter into and occupy the dwelling-house.

(3)   If [B] is entitled under this section to occupy a dwelling-house or any part of a dwelling-house, any payment or tender made or other thing done by [B] in or towards satisfaction of any liability of [A] in respect of rent, mortgage payments or other outgoings affecting the dwelling-

house is, whether or not it is made or done in pursuance of an order under section 40, as good as if made or done by [A].

(4)   [B's] occupation by virtue of this section—

(a)   is to be treated, for the purposes of the Rent (Agriculture) Act 1976 and the Rent Act 1977 (other than Part V and sections 103 to 106 of that Act), as occupation by [A as A's] residence, and

(b)   if [B occupies the dwelling-house as B's] only or principal home, is to be treated, for the purposes of the Housing Act 1985 [Part I of the Housing Act 1988 and Chapter I of Part V of the Housing Act 1996], as occupation by [A as A's] only or principal home.

(5)   If [B]—

(a)   is entitled under this section to occupy a dwelling-house or any part of a dwelling-house, and

(b)   makes any payment in or towards satisfaction of any liability of [A] in respect of mortgage payments affecting the dwelling-house,

the person to whom the payment is made may treat it as having been made by [A], but the fact that that person has treated any such payment as having been so made does not affect any claim of [B against A] to an interest in the dwelling-house by virtue of the payment.

(6)   If [B] is entitled under this section to occupy a dwelling-house or part of a dwelling-house by reason of an interest of [A] under a trust, all the provisions of subsections (3) to (5) apply in relation to the trustees as they apply in relation to [A].

(7)   This section does not apply to a dwelling-house which has at no time been, and [which –

(a)   was at no time intended by them to be, a matrimonial home of theirs; and

(b)   in the case of civil partners, has at no time been, and was at no time intended by them to be, a civil partnership home of theirs.]

(8)   [B's home rights] continue—

(a)   only so long as the marriage subsists, except to the extent that an order under section 33(5) otherwise provides; and

(b)   only so long as [A] is entitled as mentioned in subsection (1) to occupy the dwelling-house, except where provision is made by section 31 for those rights to be a charge on an estate or interest in the dwelling-house.

(9)   It is hereby declared that [a person]—

(a)   who has an equitable interest in a dwelling-house or in its proceeds of sale, but

(b)   is not [a person] in whom there is vested (whether solely or as joint tenant) a legal estate in fee simple or a legal term of years absolute in the dwelling-house,

is to be treated, only for the purpose of determining whether he has matrimonial home rights, as not being entitled to occupy the dwelling-house by virtue of that interest.

31 Effect of [home rights] as charge on dwelling-house

(1) Subsections (2) and (3) apply if, at any time during [a marriage or civil partnership, A] is entitled to occupy a dwelling-house by virtue of a beneficial estate or interest.

(2) [B's home rights] are a charge on the estate or interest.

(3) The charge created by subsection (2) has the same priority as if it were an equitable interest created at whichever is the latest of the following dates—

(a) the date on which [A] acquires the estate or interest;

(b) the date of the marriage [or the formation of the civil partnership]; and

(c) 1st January 1968 (the commencement date of the Matrimonial Homes Act 1967).

(4) Subsections (5) and (6) apply if, at any time when [B's home rights] are a charge on an interest of [A] under a trust, there are, apart from [A or B], no persons, living or unborn, who are or could become beneficiaries under the trust.

(5) The rights are a charge also on the estate or interest of the trustees for [A].

(6) The charge created by subsection (5) has the same priority as if it were an equitable interest created (under powers overriding the trusts) on the date when it arises.

(7) In determining for the purposes of subsection (4) whether there are any persons who are not, but could become, beneficiaries under the trust, there is to be disregarded any potential exercise of a general power of appointment exercisable by either or both [A and B] alone (whether or not the exercise of it requires the consent of another person).

(8) Even though [B's home rights] are a charge on an estate or interest in the dwelling-house, those rights are brought to an end by—

(a) the death of [A], or

(b) the termination (otherwise than by death) of the marriage [or civil partnership],unless the court directs otherwise by an order made under section 33(5).

(9) If—

(a) [B' home rights] are a charge on an estate or interest in the dwelling-house, and

(b) that estate or interest is surrendered to merge in some other estate or interest expectant on it in such circumstances that, but for the merger, the person taking the estate or interest would be bound by the charge,

the surrender has effect subject to the charge and the persons thereafter entitled to the other estate or interest are, for so long as the estate or interest surrendered would have endured if not so surrendered, to be treated for all purposes of this

Part as deriving title to the other estate or interest under [A] or, as the case may be, under the trustees for [A], by virtue of the surrender.

(10)   If the title to the legal estate by virtue of which a spouse is entitled to occupy a dwelling-house (including any legal estate held by trustees for [A]) is registered under the Land Registration Act 1925 or any enactment replaced by that Act—

(a)   registration of a land charge affecting the dwelling-house by virtue of this Part is to be effected by registering a notice under that Act; and

[(b)   [B's home rights] are not capable of falling within paragraph 2 of Schedule 1 or 3 to that Act.]

(12)   If—

(a)   [B's] home rights are a charge on the estate of [A] or of trustees of [A], and

(b)   that estate is the subject of a mortgage,

then if, after the date of the creation of the mortgage ("the first mortgage"), the charge is registered under section 2 of the Land Charges Act 1972, the charge is, for the purposes of section 94 of the Law of Property Act 1925 (which regulates the rights of mortgagees to make further advances ranking in priority to subsequent mortgages), to be deemed to be a mortgage subsequent in date to the first mortgage.

(13)   It is hereby declared that a charge under subsection (2) or (5) is not registrable under subsection (10) or under section 2 of the Land Charges Act 1972 unless it is a charge on a legal estate.

33 Occupation orders where applicant has estate or interest etc or has [home rights]

(1)   If—

(a)   a person ("the person entitled")–

(i)   is entitled to occupy a dwelling-house by virtue of a beneficial estate or interest or contract or by virtue of any enactment giving him the right to remain in occupation, or

(ii)   has [home rights] in relation to a dwelling-house, and

(b)   the dwelling-house–

(i)   is or at any time has been the home of the person entitled and of another person with whom he is associated, or

(ii)   was at any time intended by the person entitled and any such other person to be their home,

the person entitled may apply to the court for an order containing any of the provisions specified in subsections (3), (4) and (5).

(3)   An order under this section may–

(a)   enforce the applicant's entitlement to remain in occupation as against the other person ("the respondent");

(b)   require the respondent to permit the applicant to enter and remain in the dwelling-house or part of the dwelling-house;

(c)   regulate the occupation of the dwelling-house by either or both parties;

(d)   if the respondent is entitled as mentioned in subsection (1)(a)(i), prohibit, suspend or restrict the exercise by him of his right to occupy the dwelling-house;

(e)   if the respondent has [home rights] in relation to the dwelling-house and the applicant is the other spouse [or civil partner], restrict or terminate those rights;

(f)   require the respondent to leave the dwelling-house or part of the dwelling-house; or

(g)   exclude the respondent from a defined area in which the dwelling-house is included.

(4)   An order under this section may declare that the applicant is entitled as mentioned in subsection (1)(a)(i) or has [home rights].

(5)   If the applicant has [home rights] and the respondent is the other spouse [or civil partner], an order under this section made during the marriage [or civil partnership] may provide that those rights are not brought to an end by–

(a)   the death of the other spouse [or civil partner]; or

(b)   the termination (otherwise than by death) of the marriage [or civil partnership].

(6)   In deciding whether to exercise its powers under subsection (3) and (if so) in what manner, the court shall have regard to all the circumstances including–

(a)   the housing needs and housing resources of each of the parties and of any relevant child;

(b)   the financial resources of each of the parties;

(c)   the likely effect of any order, or of any decision by the court not to exercise its powers under subsection (3), on the health, safety or well-being of the parties and of any relevant child; and

(d)   the conduct of the parties in relation to each other and otherwise.

(7)   If it appears to the court that the applicant or any relevant child is likely to suffer significant harm attributable to conduct of the respondent if an order under this section containing one or more of the provisions mentioned in subsection (3) is not made, the court shall make the order unless it appears to it that–

(a)   the respondent or any relevant child is likely to suffer significant harm if the order is made; and

(b)   the harm likely to be suffered by the respondent or child in that event is as great as, or greater than, the harm attributable to conduct of the respondent which is likely to be suffered by the applicant or child if the order is not made.

(8)   The court may exercise its powers under subsection (5) in any case where it considers that in all the circumstances it is just and reasonable to do so.

(9)   An order under this section–

(a)   may not be made after the death of either of the parties mentioned in subsection (1); and

(b)   except in the case of an order made by virtue of subsection (5)(a), ceases to have effect on the death of either party.

(10)   An order under this section may, in so far as it has continuing effect, be made for a specified period, until the occurrence of a specified event or until further order.

INHERITANCE AND TRUSTEES' POWERS ACT 2014

2014 chapter 16

An Act to make further provision about the distribution of estates of deceased persons and to amend the law relating to the powers of trustees.

8 Power to Apply Income for Maintenance

In section 31 of the Trustee Act 1925 (power to apply income for maintenance and to accumulate surplus income during a minority), in subsection (1)—

(a)   in paragraph (i) for "as may, in all the circumstances, be reasonable," substitute " as the trustees may think fit, " and

(b)   omit the words from "Provided that" to the end.

9 Power of Advancement

(1)   Section 32 of the Trustee Act 1925 (power of advancement) is amended as follows.

(2)   In subsection (1), in the words before the proviso—

(a)   after "subject to a trust," insert " or transfer or apply any other property forming part of the capital of the trust property, " and

(b)   after "payment" insert " , transfer ".

(3)   In subsection (1), in paragraph (a) of the proviso—

(a)   for the words from the beginning to "amount" substitute " property (including any money) so paid, transferred or applied for the advancement or benefit of any person must not, altogether, represent more than ", and

(b)   omit "one-half of".

(4)   In paragraph (b) of that proviso for "the money so paid or applied" substitute " the money or other property   so paid, transferred or applied ".

(5)   In paragraph (c) of that proviso—

(a)   after "payment" (in both places) insert " , transfer ", and

(b)   for "paid" substitute " or other property paid, transferred ".

(6)   After subsection (1), insert—

"(1A)In exercise of the foregoing power trustees may pay, transfer or apply money or other property on the basis (express or implied) that it shall be treated as a proportionate part of the capital out of which it was paid, transferred or applied, for the purpose of bringing it into account in accordance with proviso (b) to subsection (1) of this section."

10 Application of Sections 8 and 9

(1)   Section 8 applies in accordance with subsections (4) and (5).

(2)   Section 9, apart from subsection (3)(b), applies in relation to trusts whenever created or arising.

(3)   Section 9(3)(b) applies in accordance with subsections (4) and (5).

(4)   Subject to subsection (5), the provisions mentioned in subsections (1) and (3) apply only in relation to trusts created or arising after the coming into force of those provisions.

(5)   Those provisions also apply in relation to an interest under a trust (not falling within subsection (4)) if the interest is created or arises as a result of the exercise, after the coming into force of those provisions, of any power.

INSOLVENCY ACT 1986

1986 chapter 45

An Act to consolidate the enactments relating to company insolvency and winding up (including the winding up of companies that are not insolvent, and of unregistered companies); enactments relating to the insolvency and bankruptcy of individuals; and other enactments bearing on those two subject matters, including the functions and qualification of insolvency practitioners, the public administration of insolvency, the penalisation and redress of malpractice and wrongdoing, and the avoidance of certain transactions at an undervalue.

Chapter IV

Administration by Trustee

305 General functions of trustee

(1)   This Chapter applies in relation to any bankruptcy where either—

    (a)   the appointment of a person as trustee of a bankrupt's estate takes effect, or

    (b)   the official receiver becomes trustee of a bankrupt's estate.

(2)   The function of the trustee is to get in, realise and distribute the bankrupt's estate in accordance with the following provisions of this Chapter; and in the carrying out of that function and in the management of the bankrupt's estate the trustee is entitled, subject to those provisions, to use his own discretion.

(3)   It is the duty of the trustee, if he is not the official receiver—

   (a)   to furnish the official receiver with such information,

   (b)   to produce to the official receiver, and permit inspection by the official receiver of, such books, papers and other records, and

   (c)   to give the official receiver such other assistance,

   as the official receiver may reasonably require for the purpose of enabling him to carry out his functions in relation to the bankruptcy.

(4)   The official name of the trustee shall be "the trustee of the estate of ...., a bankrupt" (inserting the name of the bankrupt); but he may be referred to as "the trustee in bankruptcy" of the particular bankrupt.

Acquisition, control and realisation of bankrupt's estate

306 Vesting of bankrupt's estate in trustee

(1)   The bankrupt's estate shall vest in the trustee immediately on his appointment taking effect or, in the case of the official receiver, on his becoming trustee.

(2)   Where any property which is, or is to be, comprised in the bankrupt's estate vests in the trustee (whether under this section or under any other provision of this Part), it shall so vest without any conveyance, assignment or transfer.

[335A Rights under trusts of land

(1)   Any application by a trustee of a bankrupt's estate under section 14 of the Trusts of Land and Appointment of Trustees Act 1996 (powers of court in relation to trusts of land) for an order under that section for the sale of land shall be made to the court having jurisdiction in relation to the bankruptcy.

(2)   On such an application the court shall make such order as it thinks just and reasonable having regard to—

   (a)   the interests of the bankrupt's creditors;

   (b)   where the application is made in respect of land which includes a dwelling house which is or has been the home of the bankrupt or the [bankrupt's spouse or civil partner or former spouse or former civil partner]—

      (i)   the conduct of the [spouse, civil partner, former spouse or former civil partner], so far as contributing to the bankruptcy,

      (ii)   the needs and financial resources of the [spouse, civil partner, former spouse or former civil partner, and

      (iii)   the needs of any children; and

   (c)   all the circumstances of the case other than the needs of the bankrupt.

(3) Where such an application is made after the end of the period of one year beginning with the first vesting under Chapter IV of this Part of the bankrupt's estate in a trustee, the court shall assume, unless the circumstances of the case are exceptional, that the interests of the bankrupt's creditors outweigh all other considerations.

(4) The powers conferred on the court by this section are exercisable on an application whether it is made before or after the commencement of this section.]

LAND CHARGES ACT 1972

1972 chapter 61

An Act to consolidate certain enactments relating to the registration of land charges and other instruments and matters affecting land.

Preliminary

1 The registers and the index

(1) The registrar shall continue to keep at the registry in the prescribed manner the following registers, namely—

    (a) a register of land charges;
    (b) a register of pending actions;
    (c) a register of writs and orders affecting land;
    (d) a register of deeds of arrangement affecting land;
    (e) a register of annuities,

and shall also continue to keep there an index whereby all entries made in any of those registers can readily be traced.

(2) Every application to register shall be in the prescribed form and shall contain the prescribed particulars.

[(3) Where any charge or other matter is registrable in more than one of the registers kept under this Act, it shall be sufficient if it is registered in one such register, and if it is so registered the person entitled to the benefit of it shall not be prejudicially affected by any provision of this Act as to the effect of non-registration in any other such register.

(3A) Where any charge or other matter is registrable in a register kept under this Act and was also, before the commencement of the Local Land Charges Act 1975, registrable in a local land charges register, then, if before the commencement of the said Act it was registered in the appropriate local land charges register, it shall be treated for the purposes of the provisions of this Act as to the effect of non-registration as if it had been registered in the appropriate register under this Act; and any certificate setting out the result of an official search of the appropriate local land charges register shall, in relation to it, have effect as if it were a certificate setting out the result of an official search under this Act.]

(4) Schedule 1 to this Act shall have effect in relation to the register of annuities.

(5)   An office copy of an entry in any register kept under this section shall be admissible in evidence in all proceedings and between all parties to the same extent as the original would be admissible.

(6)   Subject to the provisions of this Act, registration may be vacated pursuant to an order of the court.

[(6A)   The county courts have jurisdiction under subsection (6) above—

(a)   in the case of a land charge of Class C(i), C(ii) or D(i), if the amount does not exceed £30,000;

(b)   in the case of a land charge of Class C(iii), if it is for a specified capital sum of money not exceeding £30,000 or, where it is not for a specified capital sum, if the capital value of the land affected does not exceed £30,000;

(c)   in the case of a land charge of Class A, Class B, Class C(iv), Class D(ii), Class D(iii) or Class E if the capital value of the land affected does not exceed £30,000;

(d)   in the case of a land charge of Class F, if the land affected by it is the subject of an order made by the court under section 1 of the Matrimonial Homes Act 1983 [or section 33 of the Family Law Act 1996] or an application for an order under [either of those sections] relating to that land has been made to the court;

(e)   in a case where an application under section 23 of the Deeds of Arrangement Act 1914 could be entertained by the court.]

(6B)   [...] .

(7)   In this section "index" includes any device or combination of devices serving the purpose of an index.

Registration in register of land charges

2 The register of land charges

(1)   If a charge on or obligation affecting land falls into one of the classes described in this section, it may be registered in the register of land charges as a land charge of that class.

(2)   A Class A land charge is—

(a)   a rent or annuity or principal money payable by instalments or otherwise, with or without interest, which is not a charge created by deed but is a charge upon land (other than a rate) created pursuant to the application of some person under the provisions of any Act of Parliament, for securing to any person either the money spent by him or the costs, charges and expenses incurred by him under such Act, or the money advanced by him for repaying the money spent or the costs, charges and expenses incurred by another person under the authority of an Act of Parliament; or

(b)   a rent or annuity or principal money payable as mentioned in paragraph (a) above which is not a charge created by deed but is a charge upon land (other than a rate) created pursuant to the application of some person under any of the enactments mentioned in Schedule 2 to this Act.

(3)   A Class B land charge is a charge on land (not being a local land charge . . .) of any of the kinds described in paragraph (a) of subsection (2) above, created otherwise than pursuant to the application of any person.

(4)   A Class C land charge is any of the following [(not being a local land charge)], namely—

(i)   a puisne mortgage;

(ii)   a limited owner's charge;

(iii)   a general equitable charge;

(iv)   an estate contract;

and for this purpose—

(i)   a puisne mortgage is a legal mortgage which is not protected by a deposit of documents relating to the legal estate affected;

(ii)   a limited owner's charge is an equitable charge acquired by a tenant for life or statutory owner under [[the Inheritance Tax Act 1984] or under] any other statute by reason of the discharge by him of any [inheritance tax] or other liabilities and to which special priority is given by the statute;

(iii)   a general equitable charge is any equitable charge which—

(a)   is not secured by a deposit of documents relating to the legal estate affected; and

(b)   does not arise or affect an interest arising under a [trust of land] or a settlement; and

(c)   is not a charge given by way of indemnity against rents equitably apportioned or charged exclusively on land in exoneration of other land and against the breach or non-observance of covenants or conditions; and

(d)   is not included in any other class of land charge;

(iv)   an estate contract is a contract by an estate owner or by a person entitled at the date of the contract to have a legal estate conveyed to him to convey or create a legal estate, including a contract conferring either expressly or by statutory implication a valid option to purchase, a right of pre-emption or any other like right.

(5)   A Class D land charge is any of the following [(not being a local land charge)], namely—

(i)   an Inland Revenue Charge;

(ii)   a restrictive covenant;

(iii)   an equitable easement;

and for this purpose—

(i)   an Inland Revenue charge is a charge on land, being a charge acquired by the Board under [the Inheritance Tax Act 1984];

(ii)   a restrictive covenant is a covenant or agreement (other than a covenant or agreement between a lessor and a lessee) restrictive of the user of land and entered into on or after 1st January 1926;

(iii)   an equitable easement is an easement, right or privilege over or affecting land created or arising on or after 1st January 1926, and being merely an equitable interest.

(6)   A Class E land charge is an annuity created before 1st January 1926 and not registered in the register of annuities.

(7)   A Class F land charge is a charge affecting any land by virtue of the [Part IV of the Family Law Act 1996].

(8)   A charge or obligation created before 1st January 1926 can only be registered as a Class B land charge or a Class C land charge if it is acquired under a conveyance made on or after that date.

3 Registration of land charges

(1)   A land charge shall be registered in the name of the estate owner whose estate is intended to be affected.

[(1A) Where a person has died and a land charge created before his death would apart from his death have been registered in his name, it shall be so registered notwithstanding his death.]

(2)   A land charge registered before 1st January 1926 under any enactment replaced by the Land Charges Act 1925 in the name of a person other than the estate owner may remain so registered until it is registered in the name of the estate owner in the prescribed manner.

(3)   A puisne mortgage created before 1st January 1926 may be registered as a land charge before any transfer of the mortgage is made.

(4)   The expenses incurred by the person entitled to the charge in registering a land charge of Class A, Class B or Class C (other than an estate contract) or by the Board in registering an Inland Revenue charge shall be deemed to form part of the land charge, and shall be recoverable accordingly on the day for payment of any part of the land charge next after such expenses are incurred.

(5)   Where a land charge is not created by an instrument, short particulars of the effect of the charge shall be furnished with the application to register the charge.

(6)   An application to register an Inland Revenue charge shall state the [tax] in respect of which the charge is claimed and, so far as possible, shall define the land affected, and such particulars shall be entered or referred to in the register.

(7)   In the case of a land charge for securing money created by a company before 1st January 1970 or so created at any time as a floating charge, registration under [Part XII, or Chapter III of Part XXIII of the Companies Act 1985 (or corresponding earlier enactments)] shall be sufficient in place of registration under this Act, and shall have effect as if the land charge had been registered under this Act.

(8)   [The corresponding earlier enactments] referred to in subsection (7) above are section 93 of the Companies (Consolidation) Act 1908, section 79 of the Companies Act 1929 … [and sections 395 to 398 of the Companies Act 1985 [as originally enacted]].

4 Effect of land charges and protection of purchasers

(1)   A land charge of Class A (other than a land improvement charge registered after 31st December 1969) or of Class B shall, when registered, take effect as if it had been created by a deed of charge by way of legal mortgage, but without prejudice to the priority of the charge.

(2)   A land charge of Class A created after 31st December 1888 shall be void as against a purchaser of the land charged with it or of any interest in such land, unless the land charge is registered in the register of land charges before the completion of the purchase.

(3)   After the expiration of one year from the first conveyance occurring on or after 1st January 1889 of a land charge of Class A created before that date the person entitled to the land charge shall not be able to recover the land charge or any part of it as against a purchaser of the land charged with it or of any interest in the land, unless the land charge is registered in the register of land charges before the completion of the purchase.

(4)   If a land improvement charge was registered as a land charge of Class A before 1st January 1970, any body corporate which, but for the charge, would have power to advance money on the security of the estate or interest affected by it shall have that power notwithstanding the charge.

(5)   A land charge of Class B and a land charge of Class C (other than an estate contract) created or arising on or after 1st January 1926 shall be void as against a purchaser of the land charged with it, or of any interest in such land, unless the land charge is registered in the appropriate register before the completion of the purchase.

(6)   An estate contract and a land charge of Class D created or entered into on or after 1st January 1926 shall be void as against a purchaser for money or money's worth [(or, in the case of an Inland Revenue Charge, a purchaser within the meaning of [the Capital Transfer Tax Act 1984)]] of a legal estate in the land charged with it, unless the land charge is registered in the appropriate register before the completion of the purchase.

(7)   After the expiration of one year from the first conveyance occurring on or after 1st January 1926 of a land charge of Class B or Class C created before that date the person entitled to the land charge shall not be able to enforce or recover the land charge or any part of it as against a purchaser of the land charged with it, or of any interest in the land, unless the land charge is registered in the appropriate register before the completion of the purchase.

(8)   A land charge of Class F shall be void as against a purchaser of the land charged with it, or of any interest in such land, unless the land charge is registered in the appropriate register before the completion of the purchase.

17 Interpretation

(1)   In this Act, unless the context otherwise requires:—

"annuity" means a rent charge or an annuity for a life or lives or for any term of years or greater estate determinable on a life or on lives and created after 25th April 1855 and before 1st January 1926, but does not include an annuity created by a marriage settlement or will;

"the Board" means the Commissioners of Inland Revenue;

"conveyance" includes a mortgage, charge, lease, assent, vesting declaration, vesting instrument, release and every other assurance of property, or of an interest in property, by any instrument except a will, and "convey" has a corresponding meaning;

"court" means the High Court, or the county court in a case where that court has jurisdiction;

"deed of arrangement" has the same meaning as in the Deeds of Arrangement Act 1914;

"estate owner", "legal estate", "equitable interest", [...], "charge by way of legal mortgage", [and "will"] have the same meanings as in the Law of Property Act 1925;

"judgment" includes any order or decree having the effect of a judgment;

"land" includes land of any tenure and mines and minerals, whether or not severed from the surface, buildings or parts of buildings (whether the division is horizontal, vertical or made in any other way) and other corporeal hereditaments, also a manor, an advowson and a rent and other incorporeal hereditaments, and an easement, right, privilege or benefit in, over or derived from land, but not an undivided share in land, and "hereditament" means real property which, on an intestacy occurring before 1st January 1926, might have devolved on an heir;

"land improvement charge" means any charge under the M3 Improvement of Land Act 1864 or under any special improvement Act within the meaning of the Improvement of Land Act 1899;

"pending land action" means any action or proceeding pending in court relating to land or any interest in or charge on land;

"prescribed" means prescribed by rules made pursuant to this Act;

"purchaser" means any person (including a mortgagee or lessee) who, for valuable consideration, takes any interest in land or in a charge on land, and "purchase" has a corresponding meaning;

"registrar" means the Chief Land Registrar, "registry" means Her Majesty's Land Registry, and "registered land" has the same meaning as in the Land Registration Act 1925;

"tenant for life", "statutory owner", "vesting instrument" and "settlement" have the same meanings as in the Settled Land Act 1925.

(2)   [...]

(3)   Any reference in this Act to any enactment is a reference to it as amended by or under any other enactment, including this Act.

LAND REGISTRATION ACT 1925

1925 chapter 21 15 and 16 Geo 5

An Act to consolidate the Land Transfer Acts and the statute law relating to registered land.

Part VI **General Provisions as to Registration and the Effect Thereof**

70 Liability of registered land to overriding interests

(1)   All registered land shall, unless under the provisions of this Act the contrary is expressed on the register, be deemed to be subject to such of the following overriding interests as may be for the time being subsisting in reference thereto, and such interests shall not be treated as incumbrances within the meaning of this Act, (that is to say):—

    (a)   Rights of common, drainage rights, customary rights (until extinguished), public rights, profits a prendre, rights of sheep walk, rights of way, watercourses, rights of water, and other easements not being equitable easements required to be protected by notice on the register;

    (b)   Liability to repair highways by reason of tenure, quit-rents, crown rents, heriots, and other rents and charges (until extinguished) having their origin in tenure;

    (c)   Liability to repair the chancel of any church;

    (d)   Liability in respect of embankments, and sea and river walls;

    (e)   […] payments in lieu of tithe, and charges or annuities payable for the redemption of tithe rent charges;

    (f)   Subject to the provisions of this Act, rights acquired or in course of being acquired under the Limitation Acts;

    (g)   The rights of every person in actual occupation of the land or in receipt of the rents and profits thereof, save where enquiry is made of such person and the rights are not disclosed;

    (h)   In the case of a possessory, qualified, or good leasehold title, all estates, rights, interests, and powers excepted from the effect of registration;

    (i)   Rights under local land charges unless and until registered or protected on the register in the prescribed manner;

    (j)   Rights of fishing and sporting, seignorial and manorial rights of all descriptions (until extinguished), and franchises;

    [(k)   Leases granted for a term not exceeding twenty-one years;]

    [(kk)   PPP leases;]

(l)   In respect of land registered before the commencement of this Act, rights to mines and minerals, and rights of entry, search, and user, and other rights and reservations incidental to or required for the purpose of giving full effect to the enjoyment of rights to mines and minerals or of property in mines or minerals, being rights which, where the title was first registered before the first day of January, eighteen hundred and ninety-eight, were created before that date, and where the title was first registered after the thirty-first day of December, eighteen hundred and ninety-seven, were created before the date of first registration:

[(m)   any interest or right which is an overriding interest by virtue of paragraph 1(1) of Schedule 9 to the Coal Industry Act 1994:]

Provided that, where it is proved to the satisfaction of the registrar that any land registered or about to be registered is exempt from land tax, or tithe rent charge or payments in lieu of tithe, or from charges or annuities payable for the redemption of tithe rent charge, the registrar may notify the fact on the register in the prescribed manner.

(2)   Where at the time of first registration any easement, right, privilege, or benefit created by an instrument and appearing on the title adversely affects the land, the registrar shall enter a note thereof on the register.

(3)   Where the existence of any overriding interest mentioned in this section is proved to the satisfaction of the registrar or admitted, he may (subject to any prescribed exceptions) enter notice of the same or of a claim thereto on the register, but no claim to an easement, right, or privilege not created by an instrument shall be noted against the title to the servient land if the proprietor of such land (after the prescribed notice is given to him) shows sufficient cause to the contrary.

[3A]   Neither subsection (2) nor subsection (3) of this section shall apply in the case of a PPP lease.]

[(4)   Neither subsection (2) nor subsection (3) of this section shall apply in the case of any such interest or right as is mentioned in subsection (1)(m) of this subsection.]

Note: The Land Registration Act 1925 was repealed by the Land Registration Act 2002 s 135; Sch 13 as of 13 October 2004

LAND REGISTRATION ACT 2002

2002 chapter 9

An Act to make provision about land registration; and for connected purposes.

Part 2 First registration of title

Chapter 1 First registration

Voluntary registration

3 When title may be registered

(1)   This section applies to any unregistered legal estate which is an interest of any of the following kinds—

(a)   an estate in land,

(b)   a rent charge,

(c)   a franchise, and

(d)   a profit a prendre in gross.

(2)   Subject to the following provisions, a person may apply to the registrar to be registered as the proprietor of an unregistered legal estate to which this section applies if—

(a)   the estate is vested in him, or

(b)   he is entitled to require the estate to be vested in him.

(3)   Subject to subsection (4), an application under subsection (2) in respect of a leasehold estate may only be made if the estate was granted for a term of which more than seven years are unexpired.

(4)   In the case of an estate in land, subsection (3) does not apply if the right to possession under the lease is discontinuous.

(5)   A person may not make an application under subsection (2)(a) in respect of a leasehold estate vested in him as a mortgagee where there is a subsisting right of redemption.

(6)   A person may not make an application under subsection (2)(b) if his entitlement is as a person who has contracted to buy under a contract.

(7)   If a person holds in the same right both—

(a)   a lease in possession, and

(b)   a lease to take effect in possession on, or within a month of, the end of the lease in possession,

then, to the extent that they relate to the same land, they are to be treated for the purposes of this section as creating one continuous term.

Compulsory registration

4 When title must be registered

(1)   The requirement of registration applies on the occurrence of any of the following events—

    (a)   the transfer of a qualifying estate—

        (i)   for valuable or other consideration, by way of gift or in pursuance of an order of any court, or

        (ii)   by means of an assent (including a vesting assent);

    (b)   the transfer of an unregistered legal estate in land in circumstances where section 171A of the Housing Act 1985 (c 68) applies (disposal by landlord which leads to a person no longer being a secure tenant);

    (c)   the grant out of a qualifying estate of an estate in land—

        (i)   for a term of years absolute of more than seven years from the date of the grant, and

        (ii)   for valuable or other consideration, by way of gift or in pursuance of an order of any court;

    (d)   the grant out of a qualifying estate of an estate in land for a term of years absolute to take effect in possession after the end of the period of three months beginning with the date of the grant;

    (e)   the grant of a lease in pursuance of Part 5 of the Housing Act 1985 (the right to buy) out of an unregistered legal estate in land;

    (f)   the grant of a lease out of an unregistered legal estate in land in such circumstances as are mentioned in paragraph (b);

    (g)   the creation of a protected first legal mortgage of a qualifying estate.

(2)   For the purposes of subsection (1), a qualifying estate is an unregistered legal estate which is—

    (a)   a freehold estate in land, or

    (b)   a leasehold estate in land for a term which, at the time of the transfer, grant or creation, has more than seven years to run.

(3)   In subsection (1)(a), the reference to transfer does not include transfer by operation of law.

(4)   Subsection (1)(a) does not apply to—

    (a)   the assignment of a mortgage term, or

    (b)   the assignment or surrender of a lease to the owner of the immediate reversion where the term is to merge in that reversion.

(5)   Subsection (1)(c) does not apply to the grant of an estate to a person as a mortgagee.

(6)   For the purposes of subsection (1)(a) and (c), if the estate transferred or granted has a negative value, it is to be regarded as transferred or granted for valuable or other consideration.

(7) In subsection (1)(a) and (c), references to transfer or grant by way of gift include transfer or grant for the purpose of—

    (a) constituting a trust under which the settlor does not retain the whole of the beneficial interest, or

    (b) uniting the bare legal title and the beneficial interest in property held under a trust under which the settlor did not, on constitution, retain the whole of the beneficial interest.

(8) For the purposes of subsection (1)(g)—

    (a) a legal mortgage is protected if it takes effect on its creation as a mortgage to be protected by the deposit of documents relating to the mortgaged estate, and

    (b) a first legal mortgage is one which, on its creation, ranks in priority ahead of any other mortgages then affecting the mortgaged estate.

(9) In this section—

"land" does not include mines and minerals held apart from the surface;

"vesting assent" has the same meaning as in the Settled Land Act 1925 (c 18).

5 Power to extend section 4

(1) The Lord Chancellor may by order—

    (a) amend section 4 so as to add to the events on the occurrence of which the requirement of registration applies such relevant event as he may specify in the order, and

    (b) make such consequential amendments of any provision of, or having effect under, any Act as he thinks appropriate.

(2) For the purposes of subsection (1)(a), a relevant event is an event relating to an unregistered legal estate which is an interest of any of the following kinds—

    (a) an estate in land,
    (b) a rent charge,
    (c) a franchise, and
    (d) a profit a prendre in gross.

(3) The power conferred by subsection (1) may not be exercised so as to require the title to an estate granted to a person as a mortgagee to be registered.

(4) Before making an order under this section the Lord Chancellor must consult such persons as he considers appropriate.

6 Duty to apply for registration of title

(1) If the requirement of registration applies, the responsible estate owner, or his successor in title, must, before the end of the period for registration, apply to the registrar to be registered as the proprietor of the registrable estate.

(2) If the requirement of registration applies because of section 4(1)(g)—

    (a) the registrable estate is the estate charged by the mortgage, and

(b)   the responsible estate owner is the owner of that estate.

(3)   If the requirement of registration applies otherwise than because of section 4(1)(g)—

(a)   the registrable estate is the estate which is transferred or granted, and

(b)   the responsible estate owner is the transferee or grantee of that estate.

(4)   The period for registration is 2 months beginning with the date on which the relevant event occurs, or such longer period as the registrar may provide under subsection (5).

(5)   If on the application of any interested person the registrar is satisfied that there is good reason for doing so, he may by order provide that the period for registration ends on such later date as he may specify in the order.

(6)   Rules may make provision enabling the mortgagee under any mortgage falling within section 4(1)(g) to require the estate charged by the mortgage to be registered whether or not the mortgagor consents.

7 Effect of non-compliance with section 6

(1)   If the requirement of registration is not complied with, the transfer, grant or creation becomes void as regards the transfer, grant or creation of a legal estate.

(2)   On the application of subsection (1)—

(a)   in a case falling within section 4(1)(a) or (b), the title to the legal estate reverts to the transferor who holds it on a bare trust for the transferee, and

(b)   in a case falling within section 4(1)(c) to (g), the grant or creation has effect as a contract made for valuable consideration to grant or create the legal estate concerned.

(3)   If an order under section 6(5) is made in a case where subsection (1) has already applied, that application of the subsection is to be treated as not having occurred.

(4)   The possibility of reverter under subsection (1) is to be disregarded for the purposes of determining whether a fee simple is a fee simple absolute.

8 Liability for making good void transfers etc

If a legal estate is retransferred, regranted or recreated because of a failure to comply with the requirement of registration, the transferee, grantee or, as the case may be, the mortgagor—

(a)   is liable to the other party for all the proper costs of and incidental to the retransfer, regrant or recreation of the legal estate, and

(b)   is liable to indemnify the other party in respect of any other liability reasonably incurred by him because of the failure to comply with the requirement of registration.

Part 3 Dispositions of registered land

Registrable dispositions

27 Dispositions required to be registered

(1)   If a disposition of a registered estate or registered charge is required to be completed by registration, it does not operate at law until the relevant registration requirements are met.

(2)   In the case of a registered estate, the following are the dispositions which are required to be completed by registration—

   (a)   a transfer,

   (b)   where the registered estate is an estate in land, the grant of a term of years absolute—

      (i)   for a term of more than seven years from the date of the grant,

      (ii)   to take effect in possession after the end of the period of three months beginning with the date of the grant,

      (iii)   under which the right to possession is discontinuous,

      (iv)   in pursuance of Part 5 of the Housing Act 1985 (c 68) (the right to buy), or

      (v)   in circumstances where section 171A of that Act applies (disposal by landlord which leads to a person no longer being a secure tenant),

   (c)   where the registered estate is a franchise or manor, the grant of a lease,

   (d)   the express grant or reservation of an interest of a kind falling within section 1(2)(a) of the Law of Property Act 1925 (c 20), other than one which is capable of being registered under the Commons Registration Act 1965 (c 64),

   (e)   the express grant or reservation of an interest of a kind falling within section 1(2)(b) or (e) of the Law of Property Act 1925, and

   (f)   the grant of a legal charge.

(3)   In the case of a registered charge, the following are the dispositions which are required to be completed by registration—

   (a)   a transfer, and
   (b)   the grant of a sub-charge.

(4)   Schedule 2 to this Act (which deals with the relevant registration requirements) has effect.

(5)   This section applies to dispositions by operation of law as it applies to other dispositions, but with the exception of the following—

   (a)   a transfer on the death or bankruptcy of an individual proprietor,
   (b)   a transfer on the dissolution of a corporate proprietor, and
   (c)   the creation of a legal charge which is a local land charge.

(6)   Rules may make provision about applications to the registrar for the purpose of meeting registration requirements under this section.

(7)   In subsection (2)(d), the reference to express grant does not include grant as a result of the operation of section 62 of the Law of Property Act 1925 (c 20).

Effect of dispositions on priority

28 Basic rule

(1)   Except as provided by sections 29 and 30, the priority of an interest affecting a registered estate or charge is not affected by a disposition of the estate or charge.

(2)   It makes no difference for the purposes of this section whether the interest or disposition is registered.

29 Effect of registered dispositions: estates

(1)   If a registrable disposition of a registered estate is made for valuable consideration, completion of the disposition by registration has the effect of postponing to the interest under the disposition any interest affecting the estate immediately before the disposition whose priority is not protected at the time of registration.

(2)   For the purposes of subsection (1), the priority of an interest is protected—

   (a)   in any case, if the interest—

       (i)   is a registered charge or the subject of a notice in the register,

       (ii)   falls within any of the paragraphs of Schedule 3, or

       (iii)   appears from the register to be excepted from the effect of registration, and

   (b)   in the case of a disposition of a leasehold estate, if the burden of the interest is incident to the estate.

(3)   Subsection (2)(a)(ii) does not apply to an interest which has been the subject of a notice in the register at any time since the coming into force of this section.

(4)   Where the grant of a leasehold estate in land out of a registered estate does not involve a registrable disposition, this section has effect as if—

   (a)   the grant involved such a disposition, and
   (b)   the disposition were registered at the time of the grant.

30 Effect of registered dispositions: charges

(1)   If a registrable disposition of a registered charge is made for valuable consideration, completion of the disposition by registration has the effect of postponing to the interest under the disposition any interest affecting the charge immediately before the disposition whose priority is not protected at the time of registration.

(2)   For the purposes of subsection (1), the priority of an interest is protected—

   (a)   in any case, if the interest—

       (i)   is a registered charge or the subject of a notice in the register,
       (ii)   falls within any of the paragraphs of Schedule 3, or
       (iii)   appears from the register to be excepted from the effect of registration, and

(b)   in the case of a disposition of a charge which relates to a leasehold estate, if the burden of the interest is incident to the estate.

(3)   Subsection (2)(a)(ii) does not apply to an interest which has been the subject of a notice in the register at any time since the coming into force of this section.

Part 4 Notices and restrictions

Notices

32 Nature and effect

(1)   A notice is an entry in the register in respect of the burden of an interest affecting a registered estate or charge.

(2)   The entry of a notice is to be made in relation to the registered estate or charge affected by the interest concerned.

(3)   The fact that an interest is the subject of a notice does not necessarily mean that the interest is valid, but does mean that the priority of the interest, if valid, is protected for the purposes of sections 29 and 30.

33 Excluded interests

No notice may be entered in the register in respect of any of the following—

(a)   an interest under—

(i)   a trust of land, or
(ii)   a settlement under the Settled Land Act 1925 (c 18),

(b)   a leasehold estate in land which—

(i)   is granted for a term of years of three years or less from the date of the grant, and

(ii)   is not required to be registered,

(c)   a restrictive covenant made between a lessor and lessee, so far as relating to the demised premises,

(d)   an interest which is capable of being registered under the Commons Registration Act 1965 (c 64), and

(e)   an interest in any coal or coal mine, the rights attached to any such interest and the rights of any person under section 38, 49 or 51 of the Coal Industry Act 1994 (c 21).

34 Entry on application

(1)   A person who claims to be entitled to the benefit of an interest affecting a registered estate or charge may, if the interest is not excluded by section 33, apply to the registrar for the entry in the register of a notice in respect of the interest.

(2)   Subject to rules, an application under this section may be for—

(a)   an agreed notice, or
(b)   a unilateral notice.

(3)   The registrar may only approve an application for an agreed notice if—

    (a)   the applicant is the relevant registered proprietor, or a person entitled to be registered as such proprietor,

    (b)   the relevant registered proprietor, or a person entitled to be registered as such proprietor, consents to the entry of the notice, or

    (c)   the registrar is satisfied as to the validity of the applicant's claim.

(4)   In subsection (3), references to the relevant registered proprietor are to the proprietor of the registered estate or charge affected by the interest to which the application relates.

35 Unilateral notices

(1)   If the registrar enters a notice in the register in pursuance of an application under section 34(2)(b) ("a unilateral notice"), he must give notice of the entry to—

    (a)   the proprietor of the registered estate or charge to which it relates, and
    (b)   such other persons as rules may provide.

(2)   A unilateral notice must—

    (a)   indicate that it is such a notice, and
    (b)   identify who is the beneficiary of the notice.

(3)   The person shown in the register as the beneficiary of a unilateral notice, or such other person as rules may provide, may apply to the registrar for the removal of the notice from the register.

38 Registrable dispositions

Where a person is entered in the register as the proprietor of an interest under a disposition falling within section 27(2)(b) to (e), the registrar must also enter a notice in the register in respect of that interest.

Restrictions

40 Nature

(1)   A restriction is an entry in the register regulating the circumstances in which a disposition of a registered estate or charge may be the subject of an entry in the register.

(2)   A restriction may, in particular—

    (a)   prohibit the making of an entry in respect of any disposition, or a disposition of a kind specified in the restriction;

    (b)   prohibit the making of an entry—

        (i)   indefinitely,
        (ii)   for a period specified in the restriction, or
        (iii)   until the occurrence of an event so specified.

(3)   Without prejudice to the generality of subsection (2)(b)(iii), the events which may be specified include—

    (a)   the giving of notice,

(b)   the obtaining of consent, and

(c)   the making of an order by the court or registrar.

(4)   The entry of a restriction is to be made in relation to the registered estate or charge to which it relates.

41 Effect

(1)   Where a restriction is entered in the register, no entry in respect of a disposition to which the restriction applies may be made in the register otherwise than in accordance with the terms of the restriction, subject to any order under subsection (2).

(2)   The registrar may by order—

(a)   disapply a restriction in relation to a disposition specified in the order or dispositions of a kind so specified, or

(b)   provide that a restriction has effect, in relation to a disposition specified in the order or dispositions of a kind so specified, with modifications so specified.

(3)   The power under subsection (2) is exercisable only on the application of a person who appears to the registrar to have a sufficient interest in the restriction.

42 Power of registrar to enter

(1)   The registrar may enter a restriction in the register if it appears to him that it is necessary or desirable to do so for the purpose of—

(a)   preventing invalidity or unlawfulness in relation to dispositions of a registered estate or charge,

(b)   securing that interests which are capable of being overreached on a disposition of a registered estate or charge are overreached, or

(c)   protecting a right or claim in relation to a registered estate or charge.

(2)   No restriction may be entered under subsection (1)(c) for the purpose of protecting the priority of an interest which is, or could be, the subject of a notice.

(3)   The registrar must give notice of any entry made under this section to the proprietor of the registered estate or charge concerned, except where the entry is made in pursuance of an application under section 43.

(4)   For the purposes of subsection (1)(c), a person entitled to the benefit of a charging order relating to an interest under a trust shall be treated as having a right or claim in relation to the trust property.

43 Applications

(1)   A person may apply to the registrar for the entry of a restriction under section 42(1) if—

(a)   he is the relevant registered proprietor, or a person entitled to be registered as such proprietor,

    (b)   the relevant registered proprietor, or a person entitled to be registered as such proprietor, consents to the application, or

    (c)   he otherwise has a sufficient interest in the making of the entry.

(2)   Rules may—

    (a)   require the making of an application under subsection (1) in such circumstances, and by such person, as the rules may provide;

    (b)   make provision about the form of consent for the purposes of subsection (1)(b);

    (c)   provide for classes of person to be regarded as included in subsection (1)(c);

    (d)   specify standard forms of restriction.

(3)   If an application under subsection (1) is made for the entry of a restriction which is not in a form specified under subsection (2)(d), the registrar may only approve the application if it appears to him—

    (a)   that the terms of the proposed restriction are reasonable, and

    (b)   that applying the proposed restriction would—

        (i)   be straightforward, and
        (ii)   not place an unreasonable burden on him.

(4)   In subsection (1), references to the relevant registered proprietor are to the proprietor of the registered estate or charge to which the application relates.

44 Obligatory restrictions

(1)   If the registrar enters two or more persons in the register as the proprietor of a registered estate in land, he must also enter in the register such restrictions as rules may provide for the purpose of securing that interests which are capable of being overreached on a disposition of the estate are overreached.

(2)   Where under any enactment the registrar is required to enter a restriction without application, the form of the restriction shall be such as rules may provide.

Part 5 Charges

Relative priority

48 Registered charges

(1)   Registered charges on the same registered estate, or on the same registered charge, are to be taken to rank as between themselves in the order shown in the register.

(2)   Rules may make provision about—

    (a)   how the priority of registered charges as between themselves is to be shown in the register, and

    (b)   applications for registration of the priority of registered charges as between themselves.

Part 12 Miscellaneous and general

Miscellaneous

115 Rights of pre-emption

(1) A right of pre-emption in relation to registered land has effect from the time of creation as an interest capable of binding successors in title (subject to the rules about the effect of dispositions on priority).

(2) This section has effect in relation to rights of pre-emption created on or after the day on which this section comes into force.

116 Proprietary estoppel and mere equities

It is hereby declared for the avoidance of doubt that, in relation to registered land, each of the following—

(a) an equity by estoppel, and

(b) a mere equity,

has effect from the time the equity arises as an interest capable of binding successors in title (subject to the rules about the effect of dispositions on priority).

132 General interpretation

(1) In this Act—

"adjudicator" means the Adjudicator to Her Majesty's Land Registry;

"caution against first registration" means a caution lodged under section 15;

"cautions register" means the register kept under section 19(1);

"charge" means any mortgage, charge or lien for securing money or money's worth;

"demesne land" means land belonging to Her Majesty in right of the Crown which is not held for an estate in fee simple absolute in possession;

"land" includes—

(a) buildings and other structures,

(b) land covered with water, and

(c) mines and minerals, whether or not held with the surface;

"land registration rules" means any rules under this Act, other than rules under section 93, Part 11, section 121 or paragraph 1, 2 or 3 of Schedule 5;

"legal estate" has the same meaning as in the Law of Property Act 1925 (c 20);

"legal mortgage" has the same meaning as in the Law of Property Act 1925;

"mines and minerals" includes any strata or seam of minerals or substances in or under any land, and powers of working and getting any such minerals or substances;

"registrar" means the Chief Land Registrar;

"register" means the register of title, except in the context of cautions against first registration;

"registered" means entered in the register;

"registered charge" means a charge the title to which is entered in the register;

"registered estate" means a legal estate the title to which is entered in the register, other than a registered charge;

"registered land" means a registered estate or registered charge;

"registrable disposition" means a disposition which is required to be completed by registration under section 27;

"requirement of registration" means the requirement of registration under section 4;

"sub-charge" means a charge under section 23(2)(b);

"term of years absolute" has the same meaning as in the Law of Property Act 1925 (c 20);

"valuable consideration" does not include marriage consideration or a nominal consideration in money.

(2)   In subsection (1), in the definition of "demesne land", the reference to land belonging to Her Majesty does not include land in relation to which a freehold estate in land has determined, but in relation to which there has been no act of entry or management by the Crown.

(3)   In this Act—

   (a)   references to the court are to the High Court or a county court,

   (b)   references to an interest affecting an estate or charge are to an adverse right affecting the title to the estate or charge, and

   (c)   references to the right to object to an application to the registrar are to the right under section 73.

Schedule 1 Unregistered interests which override first registration

Leasehold estates in land

1   A leasehold estate in land granted for a term not exceeding seven years from the date of the grant, except for a lease the grant of which falls within section 4(1) (d), (e) or (f).

Interests of persons in actual occupation

2   An interest belonging to a person in actual occupation, so far as relating to land of which he is in actual occupation, except for an interest under a settlement under the Settled Land Act 1925 (c 18).

Easements and profits a prendre

3   A legal easement or profit a prendre.

Customary and public rights

4   A customary right.

5   A public right.

Local land charges

6   A local land charge.

Mines and minerals

7   An interest in any coal or coal mine, the rights attached to any such interest and the rights of any person under section 38, 49 or 51 of the Coal Industry Act 1994 (c 21).

8   In the case of land to which title was registered before 1898, rights to mines and minerals (and incidental rights) created before 1898.

9   In the case of land to which title was registered between 1898 and 1925 inclusive, rights to mines and minerals (and incidental rights) created before the date of registration of the title.

Miscellaneous

10   A franchise.

11   A manorial right.

12   A right to rent which was reserved to the Crown on the granting of any freehold estate (whether or not the right is still vested in the Crown).

13   A non-statutory right in respect of an embankment or sea or river wall.

14   A right to payment in lieu of tithe.

[16 A right in respect of the repair of a church chancel.]

Schedule 2 Registrable dispositions: registration requirements

Part 1 Registered estates

Introductory

1   This Part deals with the registration requirements relating to those dispositions of registered estates which are required to be completed by registration.

Transfer

2   (1)   In the case of a transfer of whole or part, the transferee, or his successor in title, must be entered in the register as the proprietor.

        (2)   In the case of a transfer of part, such details of the transfer as rules may provide must be entered in the register in relation to the registered estate out of which the transfer is made.

Lease of estate in land

3   (1)   This paragraph applies to a disposition consisting of the grant out of an estate in land of a term of years absolute.

      (2)   In the case of a disposition to which this paragraph applies—

          (a)   the grantee, or his successor in title, must be entered in the register as the proprietor of the lease, and

          (b)   a notice in respect of the lease must be entered in the register.

Lease of franchise or manor

4   (1)   This paragraph applies to a disposition consisting of the grant out of a franchise or manor of a lease for a term of more than seven years from the date of the grant.

      (2)   In the case of a disposition to which this paragraph applies—

          (a)   the grantee, or his successor in title, must be entered in the register as the proprietor of the lease, and

          (b)   a notice in respect of the lease must be entered in the register.

5   (1)   This paragraph applies to a disposition consisting of the grant out of a franchise or manor of a lease for a term not exceeding seven years from the date of the grant.

      (2)   In the case of a disposition to which this paragraph applies, a notice in respect of the lease must be entered in the register.

Creation of independently registrable legal interest

6   (1)   This paragraph applies to a disposition consisting of the creation of a legal rent charge or profit a prendre in gross, other than one created for, or for an interest equivalent to, a term of years absolute not exceeding seven years from the date of creation.

      (2)   In the case of a disposition to which this paragraph applies—

          (a)   the grantee, or his successor in title, must be entered in the register as the proprietor of the interest created, and

          (b)   a notice in respect of the interest created must be entered in the register.

      (3)   In sub-paragraph (1), the reference to a legal rent charge or profit a prendre in gross is to one falling within section 1(2) of the Law of Property Act 1925 (c 20).

Creation of other legal interest

7   (1)   This paragraph applies to a disposition which—

          (a)   consists of the creation of an interest of a kind falling within section 1(2)(a), (b) or (e) of the Law of Property Act 1925, and

          (b)   is not a disposition to which paragraph 4, 5 or 6 applies.

(2)   In the case of a disposition to which this paragraph applies—

    (a)   a notice in respect of the interest created must be entered in the register, and

    (b)   if the interest is created for the benefit of a registered estate, the proprietor of the registered estate must be entered in the register as its proprietor.

(3)   Rules may provide for sub-paragraph (2) to have effect with modifications in relation to a right of entry over or in respect of a term of years absolute.

Creation of legal charge

8   In the case of the creation of a charge, the chargee, or his successor in title, must be entered in the register as the proprietor of the charge.

Part 2 Registered charges

Introductory

9   This Part deals with the registration requirements relating to those dispositions of registered charges which are required to be completed by registration.

Transfer

10   In the case of a transfer, the transferee, or his successor in title, must be entered in the register as the proprietor.

Creation of sub-charge

11   In the case of the creation of a sub-charge, the sub-chargee, or his successor in title, must be entered in the register as the proprietor of the sub-charge.

Schedule 3 Unregistered interests which override registered dispositions

Leasehold estates in land

1   A leasehold estate in land granted for a term not exceeding seven years from the date of the grant, except for—

    (a)   a lease the grant of which falls within section 4(1)(d), (e) or (f);

    (b)   a lease the grant of which constitutes a registrable disposition.

Interests of persons in actual occupation

2   An interest belonging at the time of the disposition to a person in actual occupation, so far as relating to land of which he is in actual occupation, except for—

    (a)   an interest under a settlement under the Settled Land Act 1925 (c 18);

    (b)   an interest of a person of whom inquiry was made before the disposition and who failed to disclose the right when he could reasonably have been expected to do so;

(c)   an interest—

  (i)   which belongs to a person whose occupation would not have been obvious on a reasonably careful inspection of the land at the time of the disposition, and

  (ii)   of which the person to whom the disposition is made does not have actual knowledge at that time;

(d)   a leasehold estate in land granted to take effect in possession after the end of the period of three months beginning with the date of the grant and which has not taken effect in possession at the time of the disposition.

[2A(1) An interest which, immediately before the coming into force of this Schedule, was an overriding interest under section 70(1)(g) of the Land Registration Act 1925 by virtue of a person's receipt of rents and profits, except for an interest of a person of whom inquiry was made before the disposition and who failed to disclose the right when he could reasonably have been expected to do so.

  (2) Sub-paragraph (1) does not apply to an interest if at any time since the coming into force of this Schedule it has been an interest which, had the Land Registration Act 1925 (c 21) continued in force, would not have been an overriding interest under section 70(1)(g) of that Act by virtue of a person's receipt of rents and profits.]

Easements and profits a prendre

3 (1) A legal easement or profit a prendre, except for an easement, or a profit a prendre which is not registered under the Commons Registration Act 1965 (c 64) [Part 1 of the Commons Act 2006], which at the time of the disposition—

  (a)   is not within the actual knowledge of the person to whom the disposition is made, and

  (b)   would not have been obvious on a reasonably careful inspection of the land over which the easement or profit is exercisable.

  (2) The exception in sub-paragraph (1) does not apply if the person entitled to the easement or profit proves that it has been exercised in the period of one year ending with the day of the disposition.

Customary and public rights

4   A customary right.

5   A public right.

Local land charges

6   A local land charge.

Mines and minerals

7   An interest in any coal or coal mine, the rights attached to any such interest and the rights of any person under section 38, 49 or 51 of the Coal Industry Act 1994 (c 21).

8   In the case of land to which title was registered before 1898, rights to mines and minerals (and incidental rights) created before 1898.

9   In the case of land to which title was registered between 1898 and 1925 inclusive, rights to mines and minerals (and incidental rights) created before the date of registration of the title.

Miscellaneous

10   A franchise.

11   A manorial right.

12   A right to rent which was reserved to the Crown on the granting of any freehold estate (whether or not the right is still vested in the Crown).

13   A non-statutory right in respect of an embankment or sea or river wall.

14   A right to payment in lieu of tithe.

[16 A right in respect of the repair of a church chancel.]

Schedule 12 Transition

Implied indemnity covenants on transfers of pre-1996 leases

20   (1)   On a disposition of a registered leasehold estate by way of transfer, the following covenants are implied in the instrument effecting the disposition, unless the contrary intention is expressed—

         (a)   in the case of a transfer of the whole of the land comprised in the registered lease, the covenant in sub-paragraph (2), and

         (b)   in the case of a transfer of part of the land comprised in the lease—

             (i)   the covenant in sub-paragraph (3), and

             (ii)   where the transferor continues to hold land under the lease, the covenant in sub-paragraph (4).

  (2)   The transferee covenants with the transferor that during the residue of the term granted by the registered lease the transferee and the persons deriving title under him will—

         (a)   pay the rent reserved by the lease,

         (b)   comply with the covenants and conditions contained in the lease, and

         (c)   keep the transferor and the persons deriving title under him indemnified against all actions, expenses and claims on account of any failure to comply with paragraphs (a) and (b).

  (3)   The transferee covenants with the transferor that during the residue of the term granted by the registered lease the transferee and the persons deriving title under him will—

(a) where the rent reserved by the lease is apportioned, pay the rent apportioned to the part transferred,

(b) comply with the covenants and conditions contained in the lease so far as affecting the part transferred, and

(c) keep the transferor and the persons deriving title under him indemnified against all actions, expenses and claims on account of any failure to comply with paragraphs (a) and (b).

(4) The transferor covenants with the transferee that during the residue of the term granted by the registered lease the transferor and the persons deriving title under him will—

(a) where the rent reserved by the lease is apportioned, pay the rent apportioned to the part retained,

(b) comply with the covenants and conditions contained in the lease so far as affecting the part retained, and

(c) keep the transferee and the persons deriving title under him indemnified against all actions, expenses and claims on account of any failure to comply with paragraphs (a) and (b).

(5) This paragraph does not apply to a lease which is a new tenancy for the purposes of section 1 of the Landlord and Tenant (Covenants) Act 1995 (c 30).

LANDLORD AND TENANT ACT 1927

1927 chapter 36 17 and 18 Geo 5

An Act to provide for the payment of compensation for improvements and goodwill to tenants of premises used for business purposes, or the grant of a new lease in lieu thereof; and to amend the law of landlord and tenant.

Part II General Amendments of the Law of Landlord and Tenant

18 Provisions as to covenants to repair

(1) Damages for a breach of a covenant or agreement to keep or put premises in repair during the currency of a lease, or to leave or put premises in repair at the termination of a lease, whether such covenant or agreement is expressed or implied, and whether general or specific, shall in no case exceed the amount (if any) by which the value of the reversion (whether immediate or not) in the premises is diminished owing to the breach of such covenant or agreement as aforesaid; and in particular no damage shall be recovered for a breach of any such covenant or agreement to leave or put premises in repair at the termination of a lease, if it is shown that the premises, in whatever state of repair they might be, would at or shortly after the termination of the tenancy have been or be pulled down, or such structural alterations made therein as would render valueless the repairs covered by the covenant or agreement.

(2) A right of re-entry or forfeiture for a breach of any such covenant or agreement as aforesaid shall not be enforceable, by action or otherwise, unless the lessor proves that the fact that such

a notice as is required by section one hundred and forty-six of the Law of Property Act, 1925, had been served on the lessee was known either—

(a)   to the lessee; or

(b)   to an under-lessee holding under an under-lease which reserved a nominal reversion only to the lessee; or

(c)   to the person who last paid the rent due under the lease either on his own behalf or as agent for the lessee or under-lessee;

and that a time reasonably sufficient to enable the repairs to be executed had elapsed since the time when the fact of the service of the notice came to the knowledge of any such person.

Where a notice has been sent by registered post addressed to a person at his last known place of abode in the United Kingdom, then, for the purposes of this subsection, that person shall be deemed, unless the contrary is proved, to have had knowledge of the fact that the notice had been served as from the time at which the letter would have been delivered in the ordinary course of post.

This subsection shall be construed as one with section one hundred and forty-six of the Law of Property Act, 1925.

(3)   This section applies whether the lease was created before or after the commencement of this Act.

19 Provisions as to covenants not to assign, etc. without licence or consent

(1)   In all leases whether made before or after the commencement of this Act containing a covenant condition or agreement against assigning, underletting, charging or parting with the possession of demised premises or any part thereof without licence or consent, such covenant condition or agreement shall, notwithstanding any express provision to the contrary, be deemed to be subject—

(a)   to a proviso to the effect that such licence or consent is not to be unreasonably withheld, but this proviso does not preclude the right of the landlord to require payment of a reasonable sum in respect of any legal or other expenses incurred in connection with such licence or consent; and

(b)   (if the lease is for more than forty years, and is made in consideration wholly or partially of the erection, or the substantial improvement, addition or alteration of buildings, and the lessor is not a Government department or local or public authority, or a statutory or public utility company) to a proviso to the effect that in the case of any assignment, under-letting, charging or parting with the possession (whether by the holders of the lease or any under-tenant whether immediate or not) effected more than seven years before the end of the term no consent or licence shall be required, if notice in writing of the transaction is given to the lessor within six months after the transaction is effected.

[(1A)   Where the landlord and the tenant under a qualifying lease have entered into an agreement specifying for the purposes of this subsection—

(a)   any circumstances in which the landlord may withhold his licence or consent to an assignment of the demised premises or any part of them, or

(b)   any conditions subject to which any such licence or consent may be granted,

then the landlord—

(i)   shall not be regarded as unreasonably withholding his licence or consent to any such assignment if he withholds it on the ground (and it is the case) that any such circumstances exist, and

(ii)   if he gives any such licence or consent subject to any such conditions, shall not be regarded as giving it subject to unreasonable conditions;

and section 1 of the Landlord and Tenant Act 1988 (qualified duty to consent to assignment etc.) shall have effect subject to the provisions of this subsection.

(1B)   Subsection (1A) of this section applies to such an agreement as is mentioned in that subsection—

(a)   whether it is contained in the lease or not, and

(b)   whether it is made at the time when the lease is granted or at any other time falling before the application for the landlord's licence or consent is made.

(1C)   Subsection (1A) shall not, however, apply to any such agreement to the extent that any circumstances or conditions specified in it are framed by reference to any matter falling to be determined by the landlord or by any other person for the purposes of the agreement, unless under the terms of the agreement—

(a)   that person's power to determine that matter is required to be exercised reasonably, or

(b)   the tenant is given an unrestricted right to have any such determination reviewed by a person independent of both landlord and tenant whose identity is ascertainable by reference to the agreement,

and in the latter case the agreement provides for the determination made by any such independent person on the review to be conclusive as to the matter in question.

(1D)   In its application to a qualifying lease, subsection (1)(b) of this section shall not have effect in relation to any assignment of the lease.

(1E)   In subsections (1A) and (1D) of this section—

(a)   "qualifying lease" means any lease which is a new tenancy for the purposes of section 1 of the Landlord and Tenant (Covenants) Act 1995 other than a residential lease, namely a lease by which a building or part of a building is let wholly or mainly as a single private residence; and

(b)   references to assignment include parting with possession on assignment.]

(2)   In all leases whether made before or after the commencement of this Act containing a covenant condition or agreement against the making of improvements without a licence or consent, such covenant condition or agreement shall be deemed, notwithstanding any express provision to the

contrary, to be subject to a proviso that such licence or consent is not to be unreasonably withheld; but this proviso does not preclude the right to require as a condition of such licence or consent the payment of a reasonable sum in respect of any damage to or diminution in the value of the premises or any neighbouring premises belonging to the landlord, and of any legal or other expenses properly incurred in connection with such licence or consent nor, in the case of an improvement which does not add to the letting value of the holding, does it preclude the right to require as a condition of such licence or consent, where such a requirement would be reasonable, an undertaking on the part of the tenant to reinstate the premises in the condition in which they were before the improvement was executed.

(3)   In all leases whether made before or after the commencement of this Act containing a covenant condition or agreement against the alteration of the user of the demised premises, without licence or consent, such covenant condition or agreement shall, if the alteration does not involve any structural alteration of the premises, be deemed, notwithstanding any express provision to the contrary, to be subject to a proviso that no fine or sum of money in the nature of a fine, whether by way of increase of rent or otherwise, shall be payable for or in respect of such licence or consent; but this proviso does not preclude the right of the landlord to require payment of a reasonable sum in respect of any damage to or diminution in the value of the premises or any neighbouring premises belonging to him and of any legal or other expenses incurred in connection with such licence or consent.

Where a dispute as to the reasonableness of any such sum has been determined by a court of competent jurisdiction, the landlord shall be bound to grant the licence or consent on payment of the sum so determined to be reasonable.

(4)   This section shall not apply to leases of agricultural holdings within the meaning of the [Agricultural Holdings Act 1986][which are leases in relation to which that Act applies, or to farm business tenancies within the meaning of the Agricultural Tenancies Act 1995], and paragraph (b) of subsection (1), subsection (2) and subsection (3) of this section shall not apply to mining leases.

LANDLORD AND TENANT ACT 1954

1954 chapter 56

An Act to provide security of tenure for occupying tenants under certain leases of residential property at low rents and for occupying sub-tenants of tenants under such leases; to enable tenants occupying property for business, professional or certain other purposes to obtain new tenancies in certain cases; to amend and extend the Landlord and Tenant Act 1927, the Leasehold Property (Repairs) Act 1938, and section eighty-four of the Law of Property Act 1925; to confer jurisdiction on the County Court in certain disputes between landlords and tenants; to make provision for the termination of tenancies of derelict land; and for purposes connected with the matters aforesaid.

Part II Security of Tenure for Business, Professional and other Tenants

23 Tenancies to which Part II applies

(1)   Subject to the provisions of this Act, this Part of this Act applies to any tenancy where the property comprised in the tenancy is or includes premises which are occupied by the tenant and are so occupied for the purposes of a business carried on by him or for those and other purposes.

(2)   In this Part of this Act the expression "business" includes a trade, profession or employment and includes any activity carried on by a body of persons, whether corporate or unincorporate.

(3)   In the following provisions of this Part of this Act the expression "the holding", in relation to a tenancy to which this Part of this Act applies, means the property comprised in the tenancy, there being excluded any part thereof which is occupied neither by the tenant nor by a person employed by the tenant and so employed for the purposes of a business by reason of which the tenancy is one to which this Part of this Act applies.

(4)   Where the tenant is carrying on a business, in all or any part of the property comprised in a tenancy, in breach of a prohibition (however expressed) of use for business purposes which subsists under the terms of the tenancy and extends to the whole of that property, this Part of this Act shall not apply to the tenancy unless the immediate landlord or his predecessor in title has consented to the breach or the immediate landlord has acquiesced therein.

In this subsection the reference to a prohibition of use for business purposes does not include a prohibition of use for the purposes of a specified business, or of use for purposes of any but a specified business, but save as aforesaid includes a prohibition of use for the purposes of some one or more only of the classes of business specified in the definition of that expression in subsection (2) of this section.

Continuation and renewal of tenancies

24 Continuation of tenancies to which Part II applies and grant of new tenancies

(1)   A tenancy to which this Part of this Act applies shall not come to an end unless terminated in accordance with the provisions of this Part of this Act; and, subject to the provisions of section 29 of this Act, the tenant under such a tenancy may apply to the court for a new tenancy—

(a)   if the landlord has given notice under section 25 of this Act to terminate the tenancy, or

(b)   if the tenant has made a request for a new tenancy in accordance with section 26 of this Act.

(2)   The last foregoing subsection shall not prevent the coming to an end of a tenancy by notice to quit given by the tenant, by surrender or forfeiture, or by the forfeiture of a superior tenancy, unless—

(a)   in the case of a notice to quit, the notice was given before the tenant had been in occupation in right of the tenancy for one month; or

(b) in the case of an instrument of surrender, the instrument was executed before, or was executed in pursuance of an agreement made before, the tenant had been in occupation in right of the tenancy for one month.

(3) Notwithstanding anything in subsection (1) of this section,—

(a) where a tenancy to which this Part of this Act applies ceases to be such a tenancy, it shall not come to an end by reason only of the cesser, but if it was granted for a term of years certain and has been continued by subsection (1) of this section then (without prejudice to the termination thereof in accordance with any terms of the tenancy) it may be terminated by not less than three nor more than six months' notice in writing given by the landlord to the tenant;

(b) where, at a time when a tenancy is not one to which this Part of this Act applies, the landlord gives notice to quit, the operation of the notice shall not be affected by reason that the tenancy becomes one to which this Part of this Act applies after the giving of the notice.]

24A Rent while tenancy continues by virtue of s. 24

(1) The landlord of a tenancy to which this Part of this Act applies may,—

(a) if he has given notice under section 25 of this Act to terminate the tenancy; or

(b) if the tenant has made a request for a new tenancy in accordance with section 26 of this Act;

apply to the court to determine a rent which it would be reasonable for the tenant to pay while the tenancy continues by virtue of section 24 of this Act, and the court may determine a rent accordingly.

(2) A rent determined in proceedings under this section shall be deemed to be the rent payable under the tenancy from the date on which the proceedings were commenced or the date specified in the landlord's notice or the tenant's request, whichever is the later.

(3) In determining a rent under this section the court shall have regard to the rent payable under the terms of the tenancy, but otherwise subsections (1) and (2) of section 34 of this Act shall apply to the determination as they would apply to the determination of a rent under that section if a new tenancy from year to year of the whole of the property comprised in the tenancy were granted to the tenant by order of the court.]

25 Termination of tenancy by the landlord

(1) The landlord may terminate a tenancy to which this Part of this Act applies by a notice given to the tenant in the prescribed form specifying the date at which the tenancy is to come to an end (hereinafter referred to as "the date of termination"):

Provided that this subsection has effect subject to the provisions of Part IV of this Act as to the interim continuation of tenancies pending the disposal of applications to the court.

(2) Subject to the provisions of the next following subsection, a notice under this section shall not have effect unless it is given not more than twelve nor less than six months before the date of the termination specified therein.

(3)   In the case of a tenancy which apart from this Act could have been brought to an end by notice to quit given by the landlord—

(a)   the date of termination specified in a notice under this section shall not be earlier than the earliest date on which apart from this Part of this Act the tenancy could have been brought to an end by notice to quit given by the landlord on the date of the giving of the notice under this section; and

(b)   where apart from this Part of this Act more than six months' notice to quit would have been required to bring the tenancy to an end, the last foregoing subsection shall have effect with the substitution for twelve months of a period six months longer than the length of notice to quit which would have been required as aforesaid.

(4)   In the case of any other tenancy, a notice under this section shall not specify a date of termination earlier than the date on which apart from this Part of this Act the tenancy would have come to an end by effluxion of time.

(5)   A notice under this section shall not have effect unless it requires the tenant, within two months after the giving of the notice, to notify the landlord in writing whether or not, at the date of termination, the tenant will be willing to give up possession of the property comprised in the tenancy.

(6)   A notice under this section shall not have effect unless it states whether the landlord would oppose an application to the court under this Part of this Act for the grant of a new tenancy and, if so, also states on which of the grounds mentioned in section thirty of this Act he would do so.

26 Tenant's request for a new tenancy

(1)   A tenant's request for a new tenancy may be made where the tenancy under which he holds for the time being (hereinafter referred to as "the current tenancy") is a tenancy granted for a term of years certain exceeding one year, whether or not continued by section twenty-four of this Act, or granted for a term of years certain and thereafter from year to year.

(2)   A tenant's request for a new tenancy shall be for a tenancy beginning with such date, not more than twelve nor less than six months after the making of the request, as may be specified therein:

Provided that the said date shall not be earlier than the date on which apart from this Act the current tenancy would come to an end by effluxion of time or could be brought to an end by notice to quit given by the tenant.

(3)   A tenant's request for a new tenancy shall not have effect unless it is made by notice in the prescribed form given to the landlord and sets out the tenant's proposals as to the property to be comprised in the new tenancy (being either the whole or part of the property comprised in the current tenancy), as to the rent to be payable under the new tenancy and as to the other terms of the new tenancy.

(4)   A tenant's request for a new tenancy shall not be made if the landlord has already given notice under the last foregoing section to terminate the current tenancy, or if the tenant has already given notice to quit or notice under the next following section; and no such notice shall be given by the landlord or the tenant after the making by the tenant of a request for a new tenancy.

(5)   Where the tenant makes a request for a new tenancy in accordance with the foregoing provisions of this section, the current tenancy shall, subject to the provisions of subsection (2) of section thirty-six of this Act and the provisions of Part IV of this Act as to the interim continuation of tenancies, terminate immediately before the date specified in the request for the beginning of the new tenancy.

(6)   Within two months of the making of a tenant's request for a new tenancy the landlord may give notice to the tenant that he will oppose an application to the court for the grant of a new tenancy, and any such notice shall state on which of the grounds mentioned in section thirty of this Act the landlord will oppose the application.

27 Termination by tenant of tenancy for fixed term

(1)   Where the tenant under a tenancy to which this Part of this Act applies, being a tenancy granted for a term of years certain, gives to the immediate landlord, not later than three months before the date on which apart from this Act the tenancy would come to an end by effluxion of time, a notice in writing that the tenant does not desire the tenancy to be continued, section 24 of this Act shall not have effect in relation to the tenancy, unless the notice is given before the tenant has been in occupation in right of the tenancy for one month.

(2)   A tenancy granted for a term of years certain which is continuing by virtue of section 24 of this Act may be brought to an end on any quarter day by not less than three months' notice in writing given by the tenant to the immediate landlord, whether the notice is given after the date on which apart from this Act the tenancy would have come to an end or before that date, but not before the tenant has been in occupation in right of the tenancy for one month.]

Application to court for new tenancies

29 Order by court for grant of a new tenancy

(1)   Subject to the provisions of this Act, on an application under subsection (1) of section twenty-four of this Act for a new tenancy the court shall make an order for the grant of a tenancy comprising such property, at such rent and on such other terms, as are hereinafter provided.

(2)   Where such an application is made in consequence of a notice given by the landlord under section twenty-five of this Act, it shall not be entertained unless the tenant has duly notified the landlord that he will not be willing at the date of termination to give up possession of the property comprised in the tenancy.

(3)   No application under subsection (1) of section twenty-four of this Act shall be entertained unless it is made not less than two nor more than four months after the giving of the landlord's notice under section twenty-five of this Act or, as the case may be, after the making of the tenant's request for a new tenancy.

30 Opposition by landlord to application for new tenancy

(1)   The grounds on which a landlord may oppose an application under subsection (1) of section 24 of this Act are such of the following grounds as may be stated in the landlord's notice under section 25 of this Act or, as the case may be, under subsection (6) of section 26 thereof, that is to say: —

(a)   where under the current tenancy the tenant has any obligations as respects the repair and maintenance of the holding, that the tenant ought not to be granted a new tenancy in view of the state of repair of the holding, being a state resulting from the tenant's failure to comply with the said obligations;

(b)   that the tenant ought not to be granted a new tenancy in view of his persistent delay in paying rent which has become due;

(c)   that the tenant ought not to be granted a new tenancy in view of other substantial breaches by him of his obligations under the current tenancy, or for any other reason connected with the tenant's use or management of the holding;

(d)   that the landlord has offered and is willing to provide or secure the provision of alternative accommodation for the tenant, that the terms on which the alternative accommodation is available are reasonable having regard to the terms of the current tenancy and to all other relevant circumstances, and that the accommodation and the time at which it will be available are suitable for the tenant's requirements (including the requirement to preserve goodwill) having regard to the nature and class of his business and to the situation and extent of, and facilities afforded by, the holding;

(e)   where the current tenancy was created by the sub-letting of part only of the property comprised in a superior tenancy and the landlord is the owner of an interest in reversion expectant on the termination of that superior tenancy, that the aggregate of the rents reasonably obtainable on separate lettings of the holding and the remainder of that property would be substantially less than the rent reasonably obtainable on a letting of that property as a whole, that on the termination of the current tenancy the landlord requires possession of the holding for the purpose of letting or otherwise disposing of the said property as a whole, and that in view thereof the tenant ought not to be granted a new tenancy;

(f)   that on the termination of the current tenancy the landlord intends to demolish or reconstruct the premises comprised in the holding or a substantial part of those premises or to carry out substantial work of construction on the holding or part thereof and that he could not reasonably do so without obtaining possession of the holding;

(g)   subject as hereinafter provided, that on the termination of the current tenancy the landlord intends to occupy the holding for the purposes, or partly for the purposes, of a business to be carried on by him therein, or as his residence.

(2)   The landlord shall not be entitled to oppose an application on the ground specified in paragraph (g) of the last foregoing subsection if the interest of the landlord, or an interest which has merged in that interest and but for the merger would be the interest of the landlord, was purchased or created after the beginning of the period of five years which ends with the termination of the current tenancy, and at all times since the purchase or creation thereof the holding has been comprised in a tenancy or successive tenancies of the description specified in subsection (1) of section 23 of this Act.

(3)   Where the landlord has a controlling interest in a company any business to be carried on by the company shall be treated for the purposes of subsection (1)(g) of this section as a business to be carried on by him.

For the purposes of this subsection, a person has a controlling interest in a company if and only if either—

(a)   he is a member of it and able, without the consent of any other person, to appoint or remove the holders of at least a majority of the directorships; or

(b)   he holds more than one-half of its equity share capital, there being disregarded any shares held by him in a fiduciary capacity or as nominee for another person;

and in this subsection "company" and "share" have the meanings assigned to them by section 455(1) of the M1Companies Act 1948 and "equity share capital" the meaning assigned to it by section 154(5) of that Act.]

31 Dismissal of application for new tenancy where landlord successfully opposes

(1)   If the landlord opposes an application under subsection (1) of section twenty-four of this Act on grounds on which he is entitled to oppose it in accordance with the last foregoing section and establishes any of those grounds to the satisfaction of the court, the court shall not make an order for the grant of a new tenancy.

(2)   Where in a case not falling within the last foregoing subsection the landlord opposes an application under the said subsection (1) on one or more of the grounds specified in paragraphs (d), (e) and (f) of subsection (1) of the last foregoing section but establishes none of those grounds to the satisfaction of the court, then if the court would have been satisfied of any of those grounds if the date of termination specified in the landlord's notice or, as the case may be, the date specified in the tenant's request for a new tenancy as the date from which the new tenancy is to begin, had been such later date as the court may determine, being a date not more than one year later than the date so specified,—

(a)   the court shall make a declaration to that effect, stating of which of the said grounds the court would have been satisfied as aforesaid and specifying the date determined by the court as aforesaid, but shall not make an order for the grant of a new tenancy;

(b)   if, within fourteen days after the making of the declaration, the tenant so requires the court shall make an order substituting the said date for the date specified in the said landlord's notice or tenant's request, and thereupon that notice or request shall have effect accordingly.

31A Grant of new tenancy in some cases where s. 30(1)(f) applies

(1)   Where the landlord opposes an application under section 24(1) of this Act on the ground specified in paragraph (f) of section 30(1) of this Act the court shall not hold that the landlord could not reasonably carry out the demolition, reconstruction or work of construction intended without obtaining possession of the holding if—

(a)   the tenant agrees to the inclusion in the terms of the new tenancy of terms giving the landlord access and other facilities for carrying out the work intended and, given that access and those facilities, the landlord could reasonably carry out the work without obtaining possession of the holding and without interfering to a substantial extent or for a substantial time with the use of the holding for the purposes of the business carried on by the tenant; or

(b)   the tenant is willing to accept a tenancy of an economically separable part of the holding and either paragraph (a) of this section is satisfied with respect to that part or possession of the remainder of the holding would be reasonably sufficient to enable the landlord to carry out the intended work.

(2)   For the purposes of subsection (1)(b) of this section a part of a holding shall be deemed to be an economically separate part if, and only if, the aggregate of the rents which, after the completion of the intended work, would be reasonably obtainable on separate lettings of that part and the remainder of the premises affected by or resulting from the work would not be substantially less than the rent which would then be reasonably obtainable on a letting of those premises as a whole.]

32 Property to be comprised in new tenancy

(1)   Subject to the following provisions of this section, an order under section 29 of this Act for the grant of a new tenancy shall be an order for the grant of a new tenancy of the holding; and in the absence of agreement between the landlord and the tenant as to the property which constitutes the holding the court shall in the order designate that property by reference to the circumstances existing at the date of the order.

(1A)   Where the court, by virtue of paragraph (b) of section 31A(1) of this Act, makes an order under section 29 of this Act for the grant of a new tenancy in a case where the tenant is willing to accept a tenancy of part of the holding, the order shall be an order for the grant of a new tenancy of that part only.

(2)   The foregoing provisions of this section shall not apply in a case where the property comprised in the current tenancy includes other property besides the holding and the landlord requires any new tenancy ordered to be granted under section 29 of this Act to be a tenancy of the whole of the property comprised in the current tenancy; but in any such case—

(a)   any order under the said section 29 for the grant of a new tenancy shall be an order for the grant of a new tenancy of the whole of the property comprised in the current tenancy, and

(b)   references in the following provisions of this Part of this Act to the holding shall be construed as references to the whole of that property.

(3)   Where the current tenancy includes rights enjoyed by the tenant in connection with the holding, those rights shall be included in a tenancy ordered to be granted under section 29 of this Act, except as otherwise agreed between the landlord and the tenant or, in default of such agreement, determined by the court.]

33 Duration of new tenancy

Where on an application under this Part of this Act the court makes an order for the grant of a new tenancy, the new tenancy shall be such tenancy as may be agreed between the landlord and the tenant, or, in default of such an agreement, shall be such a tenancy as may be determined by the court to be reasonable in all the circumstances, being, if it is a tenancy for a term of years certain, a tenancy for a term not exceeding fourteen years, and shall begin on the coming to an end of the current tenancy.

34 Rent under new tenancy

(1) The rent payable under a tenancy granted by order of the court under this Part of this Act shall be such as may be agreed between the landlord and the tenant or as, in default of such agreement, may be determined by the court to be that at which, having regard to the terms of the tenancy (other than those relating to rent), the holding might reasonably be expected to be let in the open market by a willing lessor, there being disregarded—

 (a) any effect on rent of the fact that the tenant has or his predecessors in title have been in occupation of the holding,

 (b) any goodwill attached to the holding by reason of the carrying on thereat of the business of the tenant (whether by him or by a predecessor of his in that business),

 (c) any effect on rent of an improvement to which this paragraph applies,

 (d) in the case of a holding comprising licensed premises, any addition to its value attributable to the licence, if it appears to the court that having regard to the terms of the current tenancy and any other relevant circumstances the benefit of the licence belongs to the tenant.

(2) Paragraph (c) of the foregoing subsection applies to any improvement carried out by a person who at the time it was carried out was the tenant, but only if it was carried out otherwise than in pursuance of an obligation to his immediate landlord and either it was carried out during the current tenancy or the following conditions are satisfied, that is to say,—

 (a) that it was completed not more than twenty-one years before the application for the new tenancy was made; and

 (b) that the holding or any part of it affected by the improvement has at all times since the completion of the improvement been comprised in tenancies of the description specified in section 23(1) of this Act; and

 (c) that at the termination of each of those tenancies the tenant did not quit.

(3) Where the rent is determined by the court the court may, if it thinks fit, further determine that the terms of the tenancy shall include such provision for varying the rent as may be specified in the determination.]

[(4) It is hereby declared that the matters which are to be taken into account by the court in determining the rent include any effect on rent of the operation of the provisions of the Landlord and Tenant (Covenants) Act 1995.]

35 Other terms of new tenancy

[(1)] The terms of a tenancy granted by order of the court under this Part of this Act (other than terms as to the duration thereof and as to the rent payable thereunder) shall be such as may be agreed between the landlord and the tenant or as, in default of such agreement, may be determined by the court; and in determining those terms the court shall have regard to the terms of the current tenancy and to all relevant circumstances.

[[2] In subsection (1) of this section the reference to all relevant circumstances includes (without prejudice to the generality of that reference) a reference to the operation of the provisions of the Landlord and Tenant (Covenants) Act 1995.]

37 Compensation where order for new tenancy precluded on certain grounds

(1)   Where on the making of an application under section 24 of this Act the court is precluded (whether by subsection (1) or subsection (2) of section 31 of this Act) from making an order for the grant of a new tenancy by reason of any of the grounds specified in paragraphs (e), (f) and (g) of subsection (1) of section 30 of this Act and not of any grounds specified in any other paragraph of that subsection, or where no other ground is specified in the landlord's notice under section 25 of this Act or, as the case may be, under section 26(6) thereof, than those specified in the said paragraphs (e), (f) and (g) and either no application under the said section 24 is made or such an application is withdrawn, then, subject to the provisions of this Act, the tenant shall be entitled on quitting the holding to recover from the landlord by way of compensation an amount determined in accordance with the following provisions of this section.

(2)   [Subject to subsections (5A) to [(5E)]] of this section] the said amount shall be as follows, that is to say, —

(a)   where the conditions specified in the next following subsection are satisfied it shall be [the product of the appropriate multiplier and] twice the rateable value of the holding,

(b)   in any other case it shall be [the product of the appropriate multiplier and] the rateable value of the holding.

(3)   The said conditions are—

(a)   that, during the whole of the fourteen years immediately preceding the termination of the current tenancy, premises being or comprised in the holding have been occupied for the purposes of a business carried on by the occupier or for those and other purposes;

(b)   that, if during those fourteen years there was a change in the occupier of the premises, the person who was the occupier immediately after the change was the successor to the business carried on by the person who was the occupier immediately before the change.

(4)   Where the court is precluded from making an order for the grant of a new tenancy under this Part of this Act in the circumstances mentioned in subsection (1) of this section, the court shall on the application of the tenant certify that fact.

(5)   For the purposes of subsection (2) of this section the rateable value of the holding shall be determined as follows: —

(a)   where in the valuation list in force at the date on which the landlord's notice under section 25 or, as the case may be, subsection (6) of section 26 of this Act is given a value is then shown as the annual value (as hereinafter defined) of the holding, the rateable value of the holding shall be taken to be that value;

(b)   where no such value is so shown with respect to the holding but such a value or such values is or are so shown with respect to premises comprised in or comprising the holding or part of it, the rateable value of the holding shall be taken to be such value as is found by a proper apportionment or aggregation of the value or values so shown;

(c)   where the rateable value of the holding cannot be ascertained in accordance with the foregoing paragraphs of this subsection, it shall be taken to be the value which, apart from any exemption from assessment to rates, would on a proper assessment be the value to be entered in the said valuation list as the annual value of the holding;

and any dispute arising, whether in proceedings before the court or otherwise, as to the determination for those purposes of the rateable value of the holding shall be referred to the Commissioners of Inland Revenue for decision by a valuation officer.

An appeal shall lie to the Lands Tribunal from any decision of a valuation officer under this subsection, but subject thereto any such decision shall be final.

[(5A) If part of the holding is domestic property, as defined in section 66 of the Local Government Finance Act 1988,—

(a)   the domestic property shall be disregarded in determining the rateable value of the holding under subsection (5) of this section; and

(b)   if, on the date specified in subsection (5)(a) of this section, the tenant occupied the whole or any part of the domestic property, the amount of compensation to which he is entitled under subsection (1) of this section shall be increased by the addition of a sum equal to his reasonable expenses in removing from the domestic property.

(5B)   Any question as to the amount of the sum referred to in paragraph (b) of subsection (5A) of this section shall be determined by agreement between the landlord and the tenant or, in default of agreement, by the court.

(5C)   If the whole of the holding is domestic property, as defined in section 66 of the Local Government Finance Act 1988, for the purposes of subsection (2) of this section the rateable value of the holding shall be taken to be an amount equal to the rent at which it is estimated the holding might reasonably be expected to let from year to year if the tenant undertook to pay all usual tenant's rates and taxes and to bear the cost of the repairs and insurance and the other expenses (if any) necessary to maintain the holding in a state to command that rent.

(5D)   The following provisions shall have effect as regards a determination of an amount mentioned in subsection (5C) of this section—

(a)   the date by reference to which such a determination is to be made is the date on which the landlord's notice under section 25 or, as the case may be, subsection (6) of section 26 of this Act is given;

(b)   any dispute arising, whether in proceedings before the court or otherwise, as to such a determination shall be referred to the Commissioners of Inland Revenue for decision by a valuation officer;

(c)   an appeal shall lie to the Lands Tribunal from such a decision but, subject to that, such a decision shall be final.]

[(5E) Any deduction made under paragraph 2A of Schedule 6 to the Local Government Finance Act 1988 (deduction from valuation of hereditaments used for breeding horses etc.) shall be disregarded, to the extent that it relates to the holding, in determining the rateable value of the holding under subsection (5) of this section.]

(6) The Commissioners of Inland Revenue may by statutory instrument make rules prescribing the procedure in connection with references under this section.

(7) In this section—

- the reference to the termination of the current tenancy is a reference to the date of termination specified in the landlord's notice under section 25 of this Act or, as the case may be, the date specified in the tenant's request for a new tenancy as the date from which the new tenancy is to begin;

- the expression "annual value" means rateable value except that where the rateable value differs from the net annual value the said expression means net annual value;

- the expression "valuation officer" means any officer of the Commissioners of Inland Revenue for the time being authorised by a certificate of the Commissioners to act in relation to a valuation list.]

[(8) In subsection (2) of this section "the appropriate multiplier" means such multiplier as the Secretary of State may by order made by statutory instrument prescribe [and different multipliers may be so prescribed in relation to different cases].

(9) A statutory instrument containing an order under subsection (8) of this section shall be subject to annulment in pursuance of a resolution of either House of Parliament.]

[38 Restriction on agreements excluding provisions of Part II

(1) Any agreement relating to a tenancy to which this Part of this Act applies (whether contained in the instrument creating the tenancy or not) shall be void (except as provided by subsection (4) of this section) in so far as it purports to preclude the tenant from making an application or request under this Part of this Act or provides for the termination or the surrender of the tenancy in the event of his making such an application or request or for the imposition of any penalty or disability on the tenant in that event.

(2) Where—

(a) during the whole of the five years immediately preceding the date on which the tenant under a tenancy to which this Part of this Act applies is to quit the holding, premises being or comprised in the holding have been occupied for the purposes of a business carried on by the occupier or for those and other purposes, and

(b) if during those five years there was a change in the occupier of the premises, the person who was the occupier immediately after the change was the successor to the business carried on by the person who was the occupier immediately before the change,

any agreement (whether contained in the instrument creating the tenancy or not and whether made before or after the termination of that tenancy) which purports to exclude or reduce compensation under the last foregoing section shall to that extent be void, so however that this subsection shall not affect any agreement as to the amount of any such compensation which is made after the right to compensation has accrued.

(3)   In a case not falling within the last foregoing subsection the right to compensation conferred by the last foregoing section may be excluded or modified by agreement.

(4)   The court may—

(a)   on the joint application of the persons who will be the landlord and the tenant in relation to a tenancy to be granted for a term of years certain which will be a tenancy to which this Part of this Act applies, authorise an agreement excluding in relation to that tenancy the provisions of sections 24 to 28 of this Act; and

(b)   on the joint application of the persons who are the landlord and the tenant in relation to a tenancy to which this Part of this Act applies, authorise an agreement for the surrender of the tenancy on such date or in such circumstances as may be specified in the agreement and on such terms (if any) as may be so specified;

if the agreement is contained in or endorsed on the instrument creating the tenancy or such other instrument as the court may specify; and an agreement contained in or endorsed on an instrument in pursuance of an authorisation given under this subsection shall be valid notwithstanding anything in the preceding provisions of this section.]

LANDLORD AND TENANT ACT 1985

1985 chapter 70

An Act to consolidate certain provisions of the law of landlord and tenant formerly found in the Housing Acts, together with the Landlord and Tenant Act 1962, with amendments to give effect to recommendations of the Law Commission.

Repairing obligations

11 Repairing obligations in short leases

(1)   In a lease to which this section applies (as to which, see sections 13 and 14) there is implied a covenant by the lessor—

(a)   to keep in repair the structure and exterior of the dwelling-house (including drains, gutters and external pipes),

(b)   to keep in repair and proper working order the installations in the dwelling-house for the supply of water, gas and electricity and for sanitation (including basins, sinks, baths and sanitary conveniences, but not other fixtures, fittings and appliances for making use of the supply of water, gas or electricity), and

(c)   to keep in repair and proper working order the installations in the dwelling-house for space heating and heating water.

[(1A) If a lease to which this section applies is a lease of a dwelling-house which forms part only of a building, then, subject to subsection (1B), the covenant implied by subsection (1) shall have effect as if—

    (a)   the reference in paragraph (a) of that subsection to the dwelling-house included a reference to any part of the building in which the lessor has an estate or interest; and

    (b)   any reference in paragraphs (b) and (c) of that subsection to an installation in the dwelling-house included a reference to an installation which, directly or indirectly, serves the dwelling-house and which either—

        (i)   forms part of any part of a building in which the lessor has an estate or interest; or

        (ii)   is owned by the lessor or under his control.

(1B)   Nothing in subsection (1A) shall be construed as requiring the lessor to carry out any works or repairs unless the disrepair (or failure to maintain in working order) is such as to affect the lessee's enjoyment of the dwelling-house or of any common parts, as defined in section 60(1) of the Landlord and Tenant Act 1987, which the lessee, as such, is entitled to use.]

(2)   The covenant implied by subsection (1) ("the lessor's repairing covenant") shall not be construed as requiring the lessor—

    (a)   to carry out works or repairs for which the lessee is liable by virtue of his duty to use the premises in a tenant-like manner, or would be so liable but for an express covenant on his part,

    (b)   to rebuild or reinstate the premises in the case of destruction or damage by fire, or by tempest, flood or other inevitable accident, or

    (c)   to keep in repair or maintain anything which the lessee is entitled to remove from the dwelling-house.

(3)   In determining the standard of repair required by the lessor's repairing covenant, regard shall be had to the age, character and prospective life of the dwelling-house and the locality in which it is situated.

[(3A) In any case where—

    (a)   the lessor's repairing covenant has effect as mentioned in subsection (1A), and

    (b)   in order to comply with the covenant the lessor needs to carry out works or repairs otherwise than in, or to an installation in, the dwelling-house, and

    (c)   the lessor does not have a sufficient right in the part of the building or the installation concerned to enable him to carry out the required works or repairs,

then, in any proceedings relating to a failure to comply with the lessor's repairing covenant, so far as it requires the lessor to carry out the works or repairs in question, it shall be a defence for the lessor to prove that he used all reasonable endeavours to obtain, but was unable to obtain, such rights as would be adequate to enable him to carry out the works or repairs.]

(4)   A covenant by the lessee for the repair of the premises is of no effect so far as it relates to the matters mentioned in subsection (1)(a) to (c), except so far as it imposes on the lessee any of the requirements mentioned in subsection (2)(a) or (c).

(5)   The reference in subsection (4) to a covenant by the lessee for the repair of the premises includes a covenant—

(a)   to put in repair or deliver up in repair,

(b)   to paint, point or render0,

(c)   to pay money in lieu of repairs by the lessee, or

(d)   to pay money on account of repairs by the lessor.

(6)   In a lease in which the lessor's repairing covenant is implied there is also implied a covenant by the lessee that the lessor, or any person authorised by him in writing, may at reasonable times of the day and on giving 24 hours' notice in writing to the occupier, enter the premises comprised in the lease for the purpose of viewing their condition and state of repair.

12 Restriction on contracting out of s. 11

(1)   A covenant or agreement, whether contained in a lease to which section 11 applies or in an agreement collateral to such a lease, is void in so far as it purports—

(a)   to exclude or limit the obligations of the lessor or the immunities of the lessee under that section, or

(b)   to authorise any forfeiture or impose on the lessee any penalty, disability or obligation in the event of his enforcing or relying upon those obligations or immunities,

unless the inclusion of the provision was authorised by the county court.

(2)   The county court may, by order made with the consent of the parties, authorise the inclusion in a lease, or in an agreement collateral to a lease, of provisions excluding or modifying in relation to the lease, the provisions of section 11 with respect to the repairing obligations of the parties if it appears to the court that it is reasonable to do so, having regard to all the circumstances of the case, including the other terms and conditions of the lease.

13 Leases to which s. 11 applies: general rule

(1)   Section 11 (repairing obligations) applies to a lease of a dwelling-house granted on or after 24th October 1961 for a term of less than seven years.

(2)   In determining whether a lease is one to which section 11 applies—

(a)   any part of the term which falls before the grant shall be left out of account and the lease shall be treated as a lease for a term commencing with the grant,

(b)   a lease which is determinable at the option of the lessor before the expiration of seven years from the commencement of the term shall be treated as a lease for a term of less than seven years, and

(c)   a lease (other than a lease to which paragraph (b) applies) shall not be treated as a lease for a term of less than seven years if it confers on the lessee an option for renewal for a term which, together with the original term, amounts to seven years or more.

(3)   This section has effect subject to—

section 14 (leases to which section 11 applies: exceptions), and

section 32(2) (provisions not applying to tenancies within Part II of the Landlord and Tenant Act 1954).

14 Leases to which s. 11 applies: exceptions

(1)   Section 11 (repairing obligations) does not apply to a new lease granted to an existing tenant, or to a former tenant still in possession, if the previous lease was not a lease to which section 11 applied (and, in the case of a lease granted before 24th October 1961, would not have been if it had been granted on or after that date).

(2)   In subsection (1)—

"existing tenant" means a person who is when, or immediately before, the new lease is granted, the lessee under another lease of the dwelling-house;

"former tenant is still in possession" means a person who—

(a)   was the lessee under another lease of the dwelling-house which terminated at some time before the new lease was granted, and

(b)   between the termination of that other lease and the grant of the new lease was continuously in possession of the dwelling-house or of the rents and profits of the dwelling-house; and

"the previous lease" means the other lease referred to in the above definitions.

(3)   Section 11 does not apply to a lease of a dwelling-house which is a tenancy of an agricultural holding within the meaning of the [Agricultural Holdings Act 1986][and in relation to which that Act applies or to a farm business tenancy within the meaning of the Agricultural Tenancies Act 1995].

(4)   Section 11 does not apply to a lease granted on or after 3rd October 1980 to—

a local authority,

[a National Park Authority],

a new town corporation,

an urban development corporation,

the Development Board for Rural Wales,

a [registered social landlord],

a co-operative housing association, or

an educational institution or other body specified, or of a class specified, by regulations under section 8 of the Rent Act 1977 [or paragraph 8 of Schedule 1 to the Housing Act 1988] (bodies making student lettings)

[a housing action trust established under Part III of the Housing Act 1988].

(5)   Section 11 does not apply to a lease granted on or after 3rd October 1980 to—

(a)   Her Majesty in right of the Crown (unless the lease is under the management of the Crown Estate Commissioners), or

(b)   a government department or a person holding in trust for Her Majesty for the purposes of a government department.

17 Specific performance of landlord's repairing obligations

(1)   In proceedings in which a tenant of a dwelling alleges a breach on the part of his landlord of a repairing covenant relating to any part of the premises in which the dwelling is comprised, the court may order specific performance of the covenant whether or not the breach relates to a part of the premises let to the tenant and notwithstanding any equitable rule restricting the scope of the remedy, whether on the basis of a lack of mutuality or otherwise.

(2)   In this section—

(a)   "tenant" includes a statutory tenant,

(b)   in relation to a statutory tenant the reference to the premises let to him is to the premises of which he is a statutory tenant,

(c)   "landlord", in relation to a tenant, includes any person against whom the tenant has a right to enforce a repairing covenant, and

(d)   "repairing covenant" means a covenant to repair, maintain, renew, construct or replace any property.

LANDLORD AND TENANT ACT 1988

1988 chapter 26

An Act to make new provision for imposing statutory duties in connection with covenants in tenancies against assigning, underletting, charging or parting with the possession of premises without consent.

1 Qualified duty to consent to assigning, underletting etc of premises

(1)   This section applies in any case where— .

(a)   a tenancy includes a covenant on the part of the tenant not to enter into one or more of the following transactions, that is—

(i)   assigning,
(ii)   underletting,
(iii)   charging, or
(iv)   parting with the possession of,

the premises comprised in the tenancy or any part of the premises without the consent of the landlord or some other person, but

(b)   the covenant is subject to the qualification that the consent is not to be unreasonably withheld (whether or not it is also subject to any other qualification).

(2)   In this section and section 2 of this Act—

(a) references to a proposed transaction are to any assignment, underletting, charging or parting with possession to which the covenant relates, and

(b) references to the person who may consent to such a transaction are to the person who under the covenant may consent to the tenant entering into the proposed transaction.

(3) Where there is served on the person who may consent to a proposed transaction a written application by the tenant for consent to the transaction, he owes a duty to the tenant within a reasonable time—

(a) to give consent, except in a case where it is reasonable not to give consent,

(b) to serve on the tenant written notice of his decision whether or not to give consent specifying in addition—

(i) if the consent is given subject to conditions, the conditions,
(ii) if the consent is withheld, the reasons for withholding it.

(4) Giving consent subject to any condition that is not a reasonable condition does not satisfy the duty under subsection (3)(a) above.

(5) For the purposes of this Act it is reasonable for a person not to give consent to a proposed transaction only in a case where, if he withheld consent and the tenant completed the transaction, the tenant would be in breach of a covenant.

(6) It is for the person who owed any duty under subsection (3) above—

(a) if he gave consent and the question arises whether he gave it within a reasonable time, to show that he did,

(b) if he gave consent subject to any condition and the question arises whether the condition was a reasonable condition, to show that it was,

(c) if he did not give consent and the question arises whether it was reasonable for him not to do so, to show that it was reasonable,

and, if the question arises whether he served notice under that subsection within a reasonable time, to show that he did.

LANDLORD AND TENANT (COVENANTS) ACT 1995

1995 chapter 30

An Act to make provision for persons bound by covenants of a tenancy to be released from such covenants on the assignment of the tenancy, and to make other provision with respect to rights and liabilities arising under such covenants; to restrict in certain circumstances the operation of rights of re-entry, forfeiture and disclaimer; and for connected purposes.

Preliminary

1 Tenancies to which the Act applies

(1) Sections 3 to 16 and 21 apply only to new tenancies.

(2)   Sections 17 to 20 apply to both new and other tenancies.

(3)   For the purposes of this section a tenancy is a new tenancy if it is granted on or after the date on which this Act comes into force otherwise than in pursuance of—

    (a)   an agreement entered into before that date, or

    (b)   an order of a court made before that date.

    Note: This came into force on 1 January 1996.

(4)   Subsection (3) has effect subject to section 20(1) in the case of overriding leases granted under section 19.

(5)   Without prejudice to the generality of subsection (3), that subsection applies to the grant of a tenancy where by virtue of any variation of a tenancy there is a deemed surrender and regrant as it applies to any other grant of a tenancy.

(6)   Where a tenancy granted on or after the date on which this Act comes into force is so granted in pursuance of an option granted before that date, the tenancy shall be regarded for the purposes of subsection (3) as granted in pursuance of an agreement entered into before that date (and accordingly is not a new tenancy), whether or not the option was exercised before that date.

(7)   In subsection (6) "option" includes right of first refusal.

2 Covenants to which the Act applies

(1)   This Act applies to a landlord covenant or a tenant covenant of a tenancy—

    (a)   whether or not the covenant has reference to the subject matter of the tenancy, and

    (b)   whether the covenant is express, implied or imposed by law,

but does not apply to a covenant falling within subsection (2).

(2)   Nothing in this Act affects any covenant imposed in pursuance of—

    (a)   section 35 or 155 of the Housing Act 1985 (covenants for repayment of discount on early disposals);

    (b)   paragraph 1 of Schedule 6A to that Act (covenants requiring redemption of landlord's share); or

    (c)   [section 11 or 13 of the Housing Act 1996 or]paragraph 1 or 3 of Schedule 2 to the Housing Associations Act 1985 (covenants for repayment of discount on early disposals or for restricting disposals).

Transmission of covenants

3 Transmission of benefit and burden of covenants

(1)   The benefit and burden of all landlord and tenant covenants of a tenancy—

    (a)   shall be annexed and incident to the whole, and to each and every part, of the premises demised by the tenancy and of the reversion in them, and

(b)   shall in accordance with this section pass on an assignment of the whole or any part of those premises or of the reversion in them.

(2)   Where the assignment is by the tenant under the tenancy, then as from the assignment the assignee—

    (a)   becomes bound by the tenant covenants of the tenancy except to the extent that—

        (i)   immediately before the assignment they did not bind the assignor, or

        (ii)   they fall to be complied with in relation to any demised premises not comprised in the assignment; and

    (b)   becomes entitled to the benefit of the landlord covenants of the tenancy except to the extent that they fall to be complied with in relation to any such premises.

(3)   Where the assignment is by the landlord under the tenancy, then as from the assignment the assignee—

    (a)   becomes bound by the landlord covenants of the tenancy except to the extent that—

        (i)   immediately before the assignment they did not bind the assignor, or

        (ii)   they fall to be complied with in relation to any demised premises not comprised in the assignment; and

    (b)   becomes entitled to the benefit of the tenant covenants of the tenancy except to the extent that they fall to be complied with in relation to any such premises.

(4)   In determining for the purposes of subsection (2) or (3) whether any covenant bound the assignor immediately before the assignment, any waiver or release of the covenant which (in whatever terms) is expressed to be personal to the assignor shall be disregarded.

(5)   Any landlord or tenant covenant of a tenancy which is restrictive of the user of land shall, as well as being capable of enforcement against an assignee, be capable of being enforced against any other person who is the owner or occupier of any demised premises to which the covenant relates, even though there is no express provision in the tenancy to that effect.

(6)   Nothing in this section shall operate—

    (a)   in the case of a covenant which (in whatever terms) is expressed to be personal to any person, to make the covenant enforceable by or (as the case may be) against any other person; or

    (b)   to make a covenant enforceable against any person if, apart from this section, it would not be enforceable against him by reason of its not having been registered under the [Land Registration Act 2002] or the Land Charges Act 1972.

(7)   To the extent that there remains in force any rule of law by virtue of which the burden of a covenant whose subject matter is not in existence at the time when it is made does not run with the land affected unless the covenantor covenants on behalf of himself and his assigns, that rule of law is hereby abolished in relation to tenancies.

4 Transmission of rights of re-entry

The benefit of a landlord's right of re-entry under a tenancy—

(a)   shall be annexed and incident to the whole, and to each and every part, of the reversion in the premises demised by the tenancy, and

(b)   shall pass on assignment of the whole or any part of the reversion in those premises.

Release of covenants on assignment

5 Tenant released from covenants on assignment of tenancy

(1)   This section applies where a tenant assigns premises demised to him under a tenancy.

(2)   If the tenant assigns the whole of the premises demised to him, he—

(a)   is released from the tenant covenants of the tenancy; and

(b)   ceases to be entitled to the benefit of the landlord covenants of the tenancy as from the assignment.

(3)   If the tenant assigns part only of the premises demised to him, then as from the assignment he—

(a)   is released from the tenant covenants of the tenancy; and

(b)   ceases to be entitled to the benefit of the landlord covenants of the tenancy, only to the extent that those covenants fall to be complied with in relation to that part of the demised premises.

(4)   This section applies as mentioned in subsection (1) whether or not the tenant is tenant of the whole of the premises comprised in the tenancy.

6 Landlord may be released from covenants on assignment of reversion

(1)   This section applies where a landlord assigns the reversion in premises of which he is the landlord under a tenancy.

(2)   If the landlord assigns the reversion in the whole of the premises of which he is the landlord—

(a)   he may apply to be released from the landlord covenants of the tenancy in accordance with section 8; and

(b)   if he is so released from all of those covenants, he ceases to be entitled to the benefit of the tenant covenants of the tenancy as from the assignment.

(3)   If the landlord assigns the reversion in part only of the premises of which he is the landlord—

(a)   he may apply to be so released from the landlord covenants of the tenancy to the extent that they fall to be complied with in relation to that part of those premises; and

(b)   if he is, to that extent, so released from all of those covenants, then as from the assignment he ceases to be entitled to the benefit of the tenant covenants only to the extent that they fall to be complied with in relation to that part of those premises.

(4)   This section applies as mentioned in subsection (1) whether or not the landlord is landlord of the whole of the premises comprised in the tenancy.

7 Former landlord may be released from covenants on assignment of reversion

(1)   This section applies where—

    (a)   a landlord assigns the reversion in premises of which he is the landlord under a tenancy, and

    (b)   immediately before the assignment a former landlord of the premises remains bound by a landlord covenant of the tenancy ("the relevant covenant").

(2)   If immediately before the assignment the former landlord does not remain the landlord of any other premises demised by the tenancy, he may apply to be released from the relevant covenant in accordance with section 8.

(3)   In any other case the former landlord may apply to be so released from the relevant covenant to the extent that it falls to be complied with in relation to any premises comprised in the assignment.

(4)   If the former landlord is so released from every landlord covenant by which he remained bound immediately before the assignment, he ceases to be entitled to the benefit of the tenant covenants of the tenancy.

(5)   If the former landlord is so released from every such landlord covenant to the extent that it falls to be complied with in relation to any premises comprised in the assignment, he ceases to be entitled to the benefit of the tenant covenants of the tenancy to the extent that they fall to be so complied with.

(6)   This section applies as mentioned in subsection (1)—

    (a)   whether or not the landlord making the assignment is landlord of the whole of the premises comprised in the tenancy; and

    (b)   whether or not the former landlord has previously applied (whether under section 6 or this section) to be released from the relevant covenant.

8 Procedure for seeking release from a covenant under section 6 or 7

(1)   For the purposes of section 6 or 7 an application for the release of a covenant to any extent is made by serving on the tenant, either before or within the period of four weeks beginning with the date of the assignment in question, a notice informing him of—

    (a)   the proposed assignment or (as the case may be) the fact that the assignment has taken place, and

    (b)   the request for the covenant to be released to that extent.

(2)   Where an application for the release of a covenant is made in accordance with subsection (1), the covenant is released to the extent mentioned in the notice if—

(a) the tenant does not, within the period of four weeks beginning with the day on which the notice is served, serve on the landlord or former landlord a notice in writing objecting to the release, or

(b) the tenant does so serve such a notice but the court, on the application of the landlord or former landlord, makes a declaration that it is reasonable for the covenant to be so released, or

(c) the tenant serves on the landlord or former landlord a notice in writing consenting to the release and, if he has previously served a notice objecting to it, stating that that notice is withdrawn.

(3) Any release from a covenant in accordance with this section shall be regarded as occurring at the time when the assignment in question takes place.

(4) In this section—

(a) "the tenant" means the tenant of the premises comprised in the assignment in question (or, if different parts of those premises are held under the tenancy by different tenants, each of those tenants);

(b) any reference to the landlord or the former landlord is a reference to the landlord referred to in section 6 or the former landlord referred to in section 7, as the case may be; and

(c) "the court" means a county court.

Excluded assignments

11 Assignments in breach of covenant or by operation of law

(1) This section provides for the operation of sections 5 to 10 in relation to assignments in breach of a covenant of a tenancy or assignments by operation of law ("excluded assignments").

(2) In the case of an excluded assignment subsection (2) or (3) of section 5—

(a) shall not have the effect mentioned in that subsection in relation to the tenant as from that assignment, but

(b) shall have that effect as from the next assignment (if any) of the premises assigned by him which is not an excluded assignment.

(3) In the case of an excluded assignment subsection (2) or (3) of section 6 or 7—

(a) shall not enable the landlord or former landlord to apply for such a release as is mentioned in that subsection as from that assignment, but

(b) shall apply on the next assignment (if any) of the reversion assigned by the landlord which is not an excluded assignment so as to enable the landlord or former landlord to apply for any such release as from that subsequent assignment.

(4) Where subsection (2) or (3) of section 6 or 7 does so apply—

(a) any reference in that section to the assignment (except where it relates to the time as from which the release takes effect) is a reference to the excluded assignment; but

(b) in that excepted case and in section 8 as it applies in relation to any application under that section made by virtue of subsection (3) above, any reference to the assignment or proposed assignment is a reference to any such subsequent assignment as is mentioned in that subsection.

(5) In the case of an excluded assignment section 9—

(a) shall not enable the tenant or landlord and his assignee to apply for an agreed apportionment to become binding in accordance with section 10 as from that assignment, but

(b) shall apply on the next assignment (if any) of the premises or reversion assigned by the tenant or landlord which is not an excluded assignment so as to enable him and his assignee to apply for such an apportionment to become binding in accordance with section 10 as from that subsequent assignment.

(6) Where section 9 does so apply—

(a) any reference in that section to the assignment or the assignee under it is a reference to the excluded assignment and the assignee under that assignment; but

(b) in section 10 as it applies in relation to any application under section 9 made by virtue of subsection (5) above, any reference to the assignment or proposed assignment is a reference to any such subsequent assignment as is mentioned in that subsection.

(7) If any such subsequent assignment as is mentioned in subsection (2), (3) or (5) above comprises only part of the premises assigned by the tenant or (as the case may be) only part of the premises the reversion in which was assigned by the landlord on the excluded assignment—

(a) the relevant provision or provisions of section 5, 6, 7 or 9 shall only have the effect mentioned in that subsection to the extent that the covenants or covenant in question fall or falls to be complied with in relation to that part of those premises; and

(b) that subsection may accordingly apply on different occasions in relation to different parts of those premises.

Joint liability under covenants

14 Abolition of indemnity covenants implied by statute

The following provisions (by virtue of which indemnity covenants are implied on the assignment of a tenancy) shall cease to have effect—

(a) subsections (1)(C) and (D) of section 77 of the Law of Property Act 1925; and

(b) subsections (1)(b) and (2) of section 24 of the Land Registration Act 1925.

Enforcement of covenants

15 Enforcement of covenants

(1) Where any tenant covenant of a tenancy, or any right of re-entry contained in a tenancy, is enforceable by the reversioner in respect of any premises demised by the tenancy, it shall also be so enforceable by—

(a)   any person (other than the reversioner) who, as the holder of the immediate reversion in those premises, is for the time being entitled to the rents and profits under the tenancy in respect of those premises, or

(b)   any mortgagee in possession of the reversion in those premises who is so entitled.

(2)   Where any landlord covenant of a tenancy is enforceable against the reversioner in respect of any premises demised by the tenancy, it shall also be so enforceable against any person falling within subsection (1)(a) or (b).

(3)   Where any landlord covenant of a tenancy is enforceable by the tenant in respect of any premises demised by the tenancy, it shall also be so enforceable by any mortgagee in possession of those premises under a mortgage granted by the tenant.

(4)   Where any tenant covenant of a tenancy, or any right of re-entry contained in a tenancy, is enforceable against the tenant in respect of any premises demised by the tenancy, it shall also be so enforceable against any such mortgagee.

(5)   Nothing in this section shall operate—

(a)   in the case of a covenant which (in whatever terms) is expressed to be personal to any person, to make the covenant enforceable by or (as the case may be) against any other person; or

(b)   to make a covenant enforceable against any person if, apart from this section, it would not be enforceable against him by reason of its not having been registered under the Land Registration Act 1925 or the Land Charges Act 1972.

(6)   In this section—

"mortgagee" and "mortgage" include "chargee" and "charge" respectively;

"the reversioner", in relation to a tenancy, means the holder for the time being of the interest of the landlord under the tenancy.

Liability of former tenant etc in respect of covenants

16 Tenant guaranteeing performance of covenant by assignee

(1)   Where on an assignment a tenant is to any extent released from a tenant covenant of a tenancy by virtue of this Act ("the relevant covenant"), nothing in this Act (and in particular section 25) shall preclude him from entering into an authorised guarantee agreement with respect to the performance of that covenant by the assignee.

(2)   For the purposes of this section an agreement is an authorised guarantee agreement if—

(a)   under it the tenant guarantees the performance of the relevant covenant to any extent by the assignee; and

(b)   it is entered into in the circumstances set out in subsection (3); and

(c)   its provisions conform with subsections (4) and (5).

(3)   Those circumstances are as follows—

(a)   by virtue of a covenant against assignment (whether absolute or qualified) the assignment cannot be effected without the consent of the landlord under the tenancy or some other person;

(b)   any such consent is given subject to a condition (lawfully imposed) that the tenant is to enter into an agreement guaranteeing the performance of the covenant by the assignee; and

(c)   the agreement is entered into by the tenant in pursuance of that condition.

(4)   An agreement is not an authorised guarantee agreement to the extent that it purports—

(a)   to impose on the tenant any requirement to guarantee in any way the performance of the relevant covenant by any person other than the assignee; or

(b)   to impose on the tenant any liability, restriction or other requirement (of whatever nature) in relation to any time after the assignee is released from that covenant by virtue of this Act.

(5) Subject to subsection (4), an authorised guarantee agreement may—

(a) impose on the tenant any liability as sole or principal debtor in respect of any obligation owed by the assignee under the relevant covenant;

(b) impose on the tenant liabilities as guarantor in respect of the assignee's performance of that covenant which are no more onerous than those to which he would be subject in the event of his being liable as sole or principal debtor in respect of any obligation owed by the assignee under that covenant;

(c) require the tenant, in the event of the tenancy assigned by him being disclaimed, to enter into a new tenancy of the premises comprised in the assignment—

(i) whose term expires not later than the term of the tenancy assigned by the tenant, and

(ii) whose tenant covenants are no more onerous than those of that tenancy;

(d) make provision incidental or supplementary to any provision made by virtue of any of paragraphs (a) to (c).

(6) Where a person ("the former tenant") is to any extent released from a covenant of a tenancy by virtue of section 11(2) as from an assignment and the assignor under the assignment enters into an authorised guarantee agreement with the landlord with respect to the performance of that covenant by the assignee under the assignment—

(a) the landlord may require the former tenant to enter into an agreement under which he guarantees, on terms corresponding to those of that authorised guarantee agreement, the performance of that covenant by the assignee under the assignment; and

(b) if its provisions conform with subsections (4) and (5), any such agreement shall be an authorised guarantee agreement for the purposes of this section; and

(c) in the application of this section in relation to any such agreement—

(i) subsections (2)(b) and (c) and (3) shall be omitted, and

(ii) any reference to the tenant or to the assignee shall be read as a reference to the former tenant or to the assignee under the assignment.

(7) For the purposes of subsection (1) it is immaterial that—

(a) the tenant has already made an authorised guarantee agreement in respect of a previous assignment by him of the tenancy referred to in that subsection, it having been subsequently revested in him following a disclaimer on behalf of the previous assignee, or

(b) the tenancy referred to in that subsection is a new tenancy entered into by the tenant in pursuance of an authorised guarantee agreement;

and in any such case subsections (2) to (5) shall apply accordingly.

(8) It is hereby declared that the rules of law relating to guarantees (and in particular those relating to the release of sureties) are, subject to its terms, applicable in relation to any authorised guarantee agreement as in relation to any other guarantee agreement.

17 Restriction on liability of former tenant or his guarantor for rent or service charge etc

(1) This section applies where a person ("the former tenant") is as a result of an assignment no longer a tenant under a tenancy but—

    (a) (in the case of a tenancy which is a new tenancy) he has under an authorised guarantee agreement guaranteed the performance by his assignee of a tenant covenant of the tenancy under which any fixed charge is payable; or

    (b) (in the case of any tenancy) he remains bound by such a covenant.

(2) The former tenant shall not be liable under that agreement or (as the case may be) the covenant to pay any amount in respect of any fixed charge payable under the covenant unless, within the period of six months beginning with the date when the charge becomes due, the landlord serves on the former tenant a notice informing him—

    (a) that the charge is now due; and

    (b) that in respect of the charge the landlord intends to recover from the former tenant such amount as is specified in the notice and (where payable) interest calculated on such basis as is so specified.

(3) Where a person ("the guarantor") has agreed to guarantee the performance by the former tenant of such a covenant as is mentioned in subsection (1), the guarantor shall not be liable under the agreement to pay any amount in respect of any fixed charge payable under the covenant unless, within the period of six months beginning with the date when the charge becomes due, the landlord serves on the guarantor a notice informing him—

    (a) that the charge is now due; and

    (b) that in respect of the charge the landlord intends to recover from the guarantor such amount as is specified in the notice and (where payable) interest calculated on such basis as is so specified.

(4) Where the landlord has duly served a notice under subsection (2) or (3), the amount (exclusive of interest) which the former tenant or (as the case may be) the guarantor is liable to pay in respect of the fixed charge in question shall not exceed the amount specified in the notice unless—

    (a) his liability in respect of the charge is subsequently determined to be for a greater amount,

    (b) the notice informed him of the possibility that that liability would be so determined, and

    (c) within the period of three months beginning with the date of the determination, the landlord serves on him a further notice informing him that the landlord intends to recover that greater amount from him (plus interest, where payable).

(5) For the purposes of subsection (2) or (3) any fixed charge which has become due before the date on which this Act comes into force shall be treated as becoming due on that date; but neither of those subsections applies to any such charge if before that date proceedings have been instituted by the landlord for the recovery from the former tenant of any amount in respect of it.

(6)   In this section—

"fixed charge", in relation to a tenancy, means—

(a)   rent,

(b)   any service charge as defined by section 18 of the Landlord and Tenant Act 1985 (the words "of a dwelling" being disregarded for this purpose), and

(c)   any amount payable under a tenant covenant of the tenancy providing for the payment of a liquidated sum in the event of a failure to comply with any such covenant;

"landlord", in relation to a fixed charge, includes any person who has a right to enforce payment of the charge.

18 Restriction of liability of former tenant or his guarantor where tenancy subsequently varied

(1)   This section applies where a person ("the former tenant") is as a result of an assignment no longer a tenant under a tenancy but—

(a)   (in the case of a new tenancy) he has under an authorised guarantee agreement guaranteed the performance by his assignee of any tenant covenant of the tenancy; or

(b)   (in the case of any tenancy) he remains bound by such a covenant.

(2)   The former tenant shall not be liable under the agreement or (as the case may be) the covenant to pay any amount in respect of the covenant to the extent that the amount is referable to any relevant variation of the tenant covenants of the tenancy effected after the assignment.

(3)   Where a person ("the guarantor") has agreed to guarantee the performance by the former tenant of a tenant covenant of the tenancy, the guarantor (where his liability to do so is not wholly discharged by any such variation of the tenant covenants of the tenancy) shall not be liable under the agreement to pay any amount in respect of the covenant to the extent that the amount is referable to any such variation.

(4)   For the purposes of this section a variation of the tenant covenants of a tenancy is a "relevant variation" if either—

(a)   the landlord has, at the time of the variation, an absolute right to refuse to allow it; or

(b)   the landlord would have had such a right if the variation had been sought by the former tenant immediately before the assignment by him but, between the time of that assignment and the time of the variation, the tenant covenants of the tenancy have been so varied as to deprive the landlord of such a right.

(5)   In determining whether the landlord has or would have had such a right at any particular time regard shall be had to all the circumstances (including the effect of any provision made by or under any enactment).

(6)   Nothing in this section applies to any variation of the tenant covenants of a tenancy effected before the date on which this Act comes into force.

(7)   In this section "variation" means a variation whether effected by deed or otherwise.

Overriding leases

19 Right of former tenant or his guarantor to overriding lease

(1)   Where in respect of any tenancy ("the relevant tenancy") any person ("the claimant") makes full payment of an amount which he has been duly required to pay in accordance with section 17, together with any interest payable, he shall be entitled (subject to and in accordance with this section) to have the landlord under that tenancy grant him an overriding lease of the premises demised by the tenancy.

(2)   For the purposes of this section "overriding lease" means a tenancy of the reversion expectant on the relevant tenancy which—

    (a)   is granted for a term equal to the remainder of the term of the relevant tenancy plus three days or the longest period (less than three days) that will not wholly displace the landlord's reversionary interest expectant on the relevant tenancy, as the case may require; and

    (b)   subject to subsections (3) and (4) and to any modifications agreed to by the claimant and the landlord) otherwise contains the same covenants as the relevant tenancy, as they have effect immediately before the grant of the lease.

(3)   An overriding lease shall not be required to reproduce any covenant of the relevant tenancy to the extent that the covenant is (in whatever terms) expressed to be a personal covenant between the landlord and the tenant under that tenancy.

(4)   If any right, liability or other matter arising under a covenant of the relevant tenancy falls to be determined or otherwise operates (whether expressly or otherwise) by reference to the commencement of that tenancy—

    (a)   the corresponding covenant of the overriding lease shall be so framed that that right, liability or matter falls to be determined or otherwise operates by reference to the commencement of that tenancy; but

    (b)   the overriding lease shall not be required to reproduce any covenant of that tenancy to the extent that it has become spent by the time that that lease is granted.

(5)   A claim to exercise the right to an overriding lease under this section is made by the claimant making a request for such a lease to the landlord; and any such request—

    (a)   must be made to the landlord in writing and specify the payment by virtue of which the claimant claims to be entitled to the lease ("the qualifying payment"); and

    (b)   must be so made at the time of making the qualifying payment or within the period of 12 months beginning with the date of that payment.

(6)   Where the claimant duly makes such a request—

    (a)   the landlord shall (subject to subsection (7)) grant and deliver to the claimant an overriding lease of the demised premises within a reasonable time of the request being received by the landlord; and

(b)   the claimant—

    (i)   shall thereupon deliver to the landlord a counterpart of the lease duly executed by the claimant, and

    (ii)   shall be liable for the landlord's reasonable costs of and incidental to the grant of the lease.

(7)   The landlord shall not be under any obligation to grant an overriding lease of the demised premises under this section at a time when the relevant tenancy has been determined; and a claimant shall not be entitled to the grant of such a lease if at the time when he makes his request—

(a)   the landlord has already granted such a lease and that lease remains in force; or

(b)   another person has already duly made a request for such a lease to the landlord and that request has been neither withdrawn nor abandoned by that person.

(8)   Where two or more requests are duly made on the same day, then for the purposes of subsection (7)—

(a)   a request made by a person who was liable for the qualifying payment as a former tenant shall be treated as made before a request made by a person who was so liable as a guarantor; and

(b)   a request made by a person whose liability in respect of the covenant in question commenced earlier than any such liability of another person shall be treated as made before a request made by that other person.

(9)   Where a claimant who has duly made a request for an overriding lease under this section subsequently withdraws or abandons the request before he is granted such a lease by the landlord, the claimant shall be liable for the landlord's reasonable costs incurred in pursuance of the request down to the time of its withdrawal or abandonment; and for the purposes of this section—

(a)   a claimant's request is withdrawn by the claimant notifying the landlord in writing that he is withdrawing his request; and

(b)   a claimant is to be regarded as having abandoned his request if—

    (i)   the landlord has requested the claimant in writing to take, within such reasonable period as is specified in the landlord's request, all or any of the remaining steps required to be taken by the claimant before the lease can be granted, and

    (ii)   the claimant fails to comply with the landlord's request, and is accordingly to be regarded as having abandoned it at the time when that period expires.

(10)   Any request or notification under this section may be sent by post.

(11)   The preceding provisions of this section shall apply where the landlord is the tenant under an overriding lease granted under this section as they apply where no such lease has been granted; and accordingly there may be two or more such leases interposed between the first such lease and the relevant tenancy.

20 Overriding leases: supplementary provisions

(1)   For the purposes of section 1 an overriding lease shall be a new tenancy only if the relevant tenancy is a new tenancy.

(2)   Every overriding lease shall state—

(a)   that it is a lease granted under section 19, and

(b)   whether it is or is not a new tenancy for the purposes of section 1;

and any such statement shall comply with such requirements as may be prescribed by rules made in pursuance of section 144 of the Land Registration Act 1925 (power to make general rules).

(3)   A claim that the landlord has failed to comply with subsection (6)(a) of section 19 may be made the subject of civil proceedings in like manner as any other claim in tort for breach of statutory duty; and if the claimant under that section fails to comply with subsection (6)(b)(i) of that section he shall not be entitled to exercise any of the rights otherwise exercisable by him under the overriding lease.

(4)   An overriding lease—

(a)   shall be deemed to be authorised as against the persons interested in any mortgage of the landlord's interest (however created or arising); and

(b)   shall be binding on any such persons;

and if any such person is by virtue of such a mortgage entitled to possession of the documents of title relating to the landlord's interest—

(i)   the landlord shall within one month of the execution of the lease deliver to that person the counterpart executed in pursuance of section 19(6)(b)(i); and

(ii)   if he fails to do so, the instrument creating or evidencing the mortgage shall apply as if the obligation to deliver a counterpart were included in the terms of the mortgage as set out in that instrument.

(5)   It is hereby declared—

(a)   that the fact that an overriding lease takes effect subject to the relevant tenancy shall not constitute a breach of any covenant of the lease against subletting or parting with possession of the premises demised by the lease or any part of them; and

(b)   that each of sections 16, 17 and 18 applies where the tenancy referred to in subsection (1) of that section is an overriding lease as it applies in other cases falling within that subsection.

(6)   No tenancy shall be registrable under the Land Charges Act 1972 or be taken to be an estate contract within the meaning of that Act by reason of any right or obligation that may arise under section 19, and any right arising from a request made under that section shall not be an overriding interest within the meaning of the Land Registration Act 1925; but any such request shall be registrable under the Land Charges Act 1972, or may be the subject of a notice or caution under the Land Registration Act 1925, as if it were an estate contract.

(7)   In this section—

(a)   "mortgage" includes "charge"; and

(b)   any expression which is also used in section 19 has the same meaning as in that section.

Supplemental

23 Effects of becoming subject to liability under, or entitled to benefit of, covenant etc

(1)   Where as a result of an assignment a person becomes, by virtue of this Act, bound by or entitled to the benefit of a covenant, he shall not by virtue of this Act have any liability or rights under the covenant in relation to any time falling before the assignment.

(2)   Subsection (1) does not preclude any such rights being expressly assigned to the person in question.

(3)   Where as a result of an assignment a person becomes, by virtue of this Act, entitled to a right of re-entry contained in a tenancy, that right shall be exercisable in relation to any breach of a covenant of the tenancy occurring before the assignment as in relation to one occurring thereafter, unless by reason of any waiver or release it was not so exercisable immediately before the assignment.

24 Effects of release from liability under, or loss of benefit of, covenant

(1)   Any release of a person from a covenant by virtue of this Act does not affect any liability of his arising from a breach of the covenant occurring before the release.

(2)   Where—

(a)   by virtue of this Act a tenant is released from a tenant covenant of a tenancy, and

(b)   immediately before the release another person is bound by a covenant of the tenancy imposing any liability or penalty in the event of a failure to comply with that tenant covenant, then, as from the release of the tenant, that other person is released from the covenant mentioned in paragraph (b) to the same extent as the tenant is released from that tenant covenant.

(3)   Where a person bound by a landlord or tenant covenant of a tenancy—

(a)   assigns the whole or part of his interest in the premises demised by the tenancy, but

(b)   is not released by virtue of this Act from the covenant (with the result that subsection (1) does not apply),the assignment does not affect any liability of his arising from a breach of the covenant occurring before the assignment.

(4)   Where by virtue of this Act a person ceases to be entitled to the benefit of a covenant, this does not affect any rights of his arising from a breach of the covenant occurring before he ceases to be so entitled.

25 Agreement void if it restricts operation of the Act

(1) Any agreement relating to a tenancy is void to the extent that—

(a) it would apart from this section have effect to exclude, modify or otherwise frustrate the operation of any provision of this Act, or

(b) it provides for—

(i) the termination or surrender of the tenancy, or

(ii) the imposition on the tenant of any penalty, disability or liability, in the event of the operation of any provision of this Act, or

(c) it provides for any of the matters referred to in paragraph (b)(i) or (ii) and does so (whether expressly or otherwise) in connection with, or in consequence of, the operation of any provision of this Act.

(2) To the extent that an agreement relating to a tenancy constitutes a covenant (whether absolute or qualified) against the assignment, or parting with the possession, of the premises demised by the tenancy or any part of them—

(a) the agreement is not void by virtue of subsection (1) by reason only of the fact that as such the covenant prohibits or restricts any such assignment or parting with possession; but

(b) paragraph (a) above does not otherwise affect the operation of that subsection in relation to the agreement (and in particular does not preclude its application to the agreement to the extent that it purports to regulate the giving of, or the making of any application for, consent to any such assignment or parting with possession).

(3) In accordance with section 16(1) nothing in this section applies to any agreement to the extent that it is an authorised guarantee agreement; but (without prejudice to the generality of subsection (1) above) an agreement is void to the extent that it is one falling within section 16(4)(a) or (b).

(4) This section applies to an agreement relating to a tenancy whether or not the agreement is—

(a) contained in the instrument creating the tenancy; or
(b) made before the creation of the tenancy.

26 Miscellaneous savings etc

(1) Nothing in this Act is to be read as preventing—

(a) a party to a tenancy from releasing a person from a landlord covenant or a tenant covenant of the tenancy; or

(b) the parties to a tenancy from agreeing to an apportionment of liability under such a covenant.

(2) Nothing in this Act affects the operation of section 3(3A) of the Landlord and Tenant Act 1985 (preservation of former landlord's liability until tenant notified of new landlord).

(3)   No apportionment which has become binding in accordance with section 10 shall be affected by any order or decision made under or by virtue of any enactment not contained in this Act which relates to apportionment.

28 Interpretation

(1)   In this Act (unless the context otherwise requires) —

"assignment" includes equitable assignment and in addition (subject to section 11) assignment in breach of a covenant of a tenancy or by operation of law;

"authorised guarantee agreement" means an agreement which is an authorised guarantee agreement for the purposes of section 16;

"collateral agreement", in relation to a tenancy, means any agreement collateral to the tenancy, whether made before or after its creation;

"consent" includes licence;

"covenant" includes term, condition and obligation, and references to a covenant (or any description of covenant) of a tenancy include a covenant (or a covenant of that description) contained in a collateral agreement;

"landlord" and "tenant", in relation to a tenancy, mean the person for the time being entitled to the reversion expectant on the term of the tenancy and the person so entitled to that term respectively;

"landlord covenant", in relation to a tenancy, means a covenant falling to be complied with by the landlord of premises demised by the tenancy;

"new tenancy" means a tenancy which is a new tenancy for the purposes of section 1;

"reversion" means the interest expectant on the termination of a tenancy;

"tenancy" means any lease or other tenancy and includes —

(a)   a sub-tenancy, and

(b)   an agreement for a tenancy,

but does not include a mortgage term;

"tenant covenant", in relation to a tenancy, means a covenant falling to be complied with by the tenant of premises demised by the tenancy.

(2)   For the purposes of any reference in this Act to a covenant falling to be complied with in relation to a particular part of the premises demised by a tenancy, a covenant falls to be so complied with if —

(a)   it in terms applies to that part of the premises, or

(b)   in its practical application it can be attributed to that part of the premises (whether or not it can also be so attributed to other individual parts of those premises).

(3)   Subsection (2) does not apply in relation to covenants to pay money; and, for the purposes of any reference in this Act to a covenant falling to be complied with in relation to a particular part of the premises demised by a tenancy, a covenant of a tenancy which is a covenant to pay money falls to be so complied with if —

(a)   the covenant in terms applies to that part; or

(b)   the amount of the payment is determinable specifically by reference—

    (i)   to that part, or

    (ii)   to anything falling to be done by or for a person as tenant or occupier of that part (if it is a tenant covenant), or

    (iii)   to anything falling to be done by or for a person as landlord of that part (if it is a landlord covenant).

(4)   Where two or more persons jointly constitute either the landlord or the tenant in relation to a tenancy, any reference in this Act to the landlord or the tenant is a reference to both or all of the persons who jointly constitute the landlord or the tenant, as the case may be (and accordingly nothing in section 13 applies in relation to the rights and liabilities of such persons between themselves).

(5)   References in this Act to the assignment by a landlord of the reversion in the whole or part of the premises demised by a tenancy are to the assignment by him of the whole of his interest (as owner of the reversion) in the whole or part of those premises.

(6)   For the purposes of this Act—

(a)   any assignment (however effected) consisting in the transfer of the whole of the landlord's interest (as owner of the reversion) in any premises demised by a tenancy shall be treated as an assignment by the landlord of the reversion in those premises even if it is not effected by him; and

(b)   any assignment (however effected) consisting in the transfer of the whole of the tenant's interest in any premises demised by a tenancy shall be treated as an assignment by the tenant of those premises even if it is not effected by him.

30 Consequential amendments and repeals

(1)   The enactments specified in Schedule 1 are amended in accordance with that Schedule, the amendments being consequential on the provisions of this Act.

(2)   The enactments specified in Schedule 2 are repealed to the extent specified.

(3)   Subsections (1) and (2) do not affect the operation of—

(a)   section 77 of, or Part IX or X of Schedule 2 to, the Law of Property Act 1925, or

(b)   section 24(1)(b) or (2) of the Land Registration Act 1925,

in relation to tenancies which are not new tenancies.

(4)   In consequence of this Act nothing in the following provisions, namely—

(a)   sections 78 and 79 of the Law of Property Act 1925 (benefit and burden of covenants relating to land), and

(b)   sections 141 and 142 of that Act (running of benefit and burden of covenants with reversion),

shall apply in relation to new tenancies.

(5) The Lord Chancellor may by order made by statutory instrument make, in the case of such enactments as may be specified in the order, such amendments or repeals in, or such modifications of, those enactments as appear to him to be necessary or expedient in consequence of any provision of this Act.

(6) Any statutory instrument made under subsection (5) shall be subject to annulment in pursuance of a resolution of either House of Parliament.

LAW OF PROPERTY (MISCELLANEOUS PROVISIONS) ACT 1989

1989 chapter 34

An Act to make new provision with respect to deeds and their execution and contracts for the sale or other disposition of interests in land; and to abolish the rule of law known as the rule in Bain v. Fothergill.

1 Deeds and their execution

(1) Any rule of law which—

   (a) restricts the substances on which a deed may be written;

   (b) requires a seal for the valid execution of an instrument as a deed by an individual; or

   (c) requires authority by one person to another to deliver an instrument as a deed on his behalf to be given by deed,

   is abolished.

(2) An instrument shall not be a deed unless—

   (a) it makes it clear on its face that it is intended to be a deed by the person making it or, as the case may be, by the parties to it (whether by describing itself as a deed or expressing itself to be executed or signed as a deed or otherwise); and

   (b) it is validly executed as a deed—

      [(i) by that person or a person authorised to execute it in the name or on behalf of that person, or

      (ii) by one or more of those parties or a person authorised to execute it in the name or on behalf of one or more of those parties].

[(2A) For the purposes of subsection (2)(a) above, an instrument shall not be taken to make it clear on its face that it is intended to be a deed merely because it is executed under seal.]

(3) An instrument is validly executed as a deed by an individual if, and only if—

   (a) it is signed—

      (i) by him in the presence of a witness who attests the signature; or

        (ii)   at his direction and in his presence and the presence of two witnesses who each attest the signature; and

    (b)   it is delivered as a deed . . ..

(4)   In subsections (2) and (3) above "sign", in relation to an instrument, includes—

    [(a)   an individual signing the name of the person or party on whose behalf he executes the instrument; and

    (b)   making one's mark on the instrument,

    and "signature" is to be construed accordingly].

[(4A) Subsection (3) above applies in the case of an instrument executed by an individual in the name or on behalf of another person whether or not that person is also an individual.]

(5)   Where [a relevant lawyer, or an agent or employee of a relevant lawyer], in the course of or in connection with a transaction . . ., purports to deliver an instrument as a deed on behalf of a party to the instrument, it shall be conclusively presumed in favour of a purchaser that he is authorised so to deliver the instrument.

(6)   In subsection (5) above—

    ["purchaser" has the same meaning] as in the Law of Property Act 1925;

    ["relevant lawyer" means a person who, for the purposes of the Legal Services Act 2007, is an authorised person in relation to an activity which constitutes a reserved instrument activity (within the meaning of that Act);]

. . .

(7)   Where an instrument under seal that constitutes a deed is required for the purposes of an Act passed before this section comes into force, this section shall have effect as to signing, sealing or delivery of an instrument by an individual in place of any provision of that Act as to signing, sealing or delivery.

(8)   The enactments mentioned in Schedule 1 to this Act (which in consequence of this section require amendments other than those provided by subsection (7) above) shall have effect with the amendments specified in that Schedule.

(9)   Nothing in subsection (1)(b), (2), (3), (7) or (8) above applies in relation to deeds required or authorised to be made under—

    (a)   the seal of the county palatine of Lancaster;

    (b)   the seal of the Duchy of Lancaster; or

    (c)   the seal of the Duchy of Cornwall.

(10)   The references in this section to the execution of a deed by an individual do not include execution by a corporation sole and the reference in subsection (7) above to signing, sealing or delivery by an individual does not include signing, sealing or delivery by such a corporation.

(11)   Nothing in this section applies in relation to instruments delivered as deeds before this section comes into force.

2 Contracts for sale etc of land to be made by signed writing

(1)   A contract for the sale or other disposition of an interest in land can only be made in writing and only by incorporating all the terms which the parties have expressly agreed in one document or, where contracts are exchanged, in each.

(2)   The terms may be incorporated in a document either by being set out in it or by reference to some other document.

(3)   The document incorporating the terms or, where contracts are exchanged, one of the documents incorporating them (but not necessarily the same one) must be signed by or on behalf of each party to the contract.

(4)   Where a contract for the sale or other disposition of an interest in land satisfies the conditions of this section by reason only of the rectification of one or more documents in pursuance of an order of a court, the contract shall come into being, or be deemed to have come into being, at such time as may be specified in the order.

(5)   This section does not apply in relation to—

    (a)   a contract to grant such a lease as is mentioned in section 54(2) of the Law Property Act 1925 (short leases);

    (b)   a contract made in the course of a public auction; or

    [(c)   a contract regulated under the Financial Services and Markets Act 2000, other than a regulated mortgage contract[, a regulated home reversion plan or a regulated home purchase plan] [a regulated home reversion plan, a regulated home purchase plan or a regulated sale and rent back agreement];]

and nothing in this section affects the creation or operation of resulting, implied or constructive trusts.

(6)   In this section—

"disposition" has the same meaning as in the Law of Property Act 1925;

"interest in land" means any estate, interest or charge in or over land . . .

["regulated mortgage contract"[, "regulated home reversion plan" and "regulated home purchase plan"] [, "regulated home purchase plan" and "regulated sale and rent back agreement"] must be read with—

    (a)   section 22 of the Financial Services and Markets Act 2000,

    (b)   any relevant order under that section, and

    (c)   Schedule 22 to that Act].

(7)   Nothing in this section shall apply in relation to contracts made before this section comes into force.

LAW OF PROPERTY ACT 1925

1925 chapter 20 15 and 16 Geo 5

An Act to consolidate the enactments relating to conveyancing and the law of property in England and Wales.

Part I General Principles as to Legal Estates, Equitable Interests and Powers

1 Legal estates and equitable interests

(1)   The only estates in land which are capable of subsisting or of being conveyed or created at law are—

    (a)   An estate in fee simple absolute in possession;

    (b)   A term of years absolute.

(2)   The only interests or charges in or over land which are capable of subsisting or of being conveyed or created at law are—

    (a)   An easement, right, or privilege in or over land for an interest equivalent to an estate in fee simple absolute in possession or a term of years absolute;

    (b)   A rentcharge in possession issuing out of or charged on land being either perpetual or for a term of years absolute;

    (c)   A charge by way of legal mortgage;

    (d)   […] and any other similar charge on land which is not created by an instrument;

    (e)   Rights of entry exercisable over or in respect of a legal term of years absolute, or annexed, for any purpose, to a legal rent charge.

(3)   All other estates, interests, and charges in or over land take effect as equitable interests.

(4)   The estates, interests, and charges which under this section are authorised to subsist or to be conveyed or created at law are (when subsisting or conveyed or created at law) in this Act referred to as "legal estates," and have the same incidents as legal estates subsisting at the commencement of this Act; and the owner of a legal estate is referred to as "an estate owner" and his legal estate is referred to as his estate.

(5)   A legal estate may subsist concurrently with or subject to any other legal estate in the same land in like manner as it could have done before the commencement of this Act.

(6)   A legal estate is not capable of subsisting or of being created in an undivided share in land or of being held by an infant.

(7)   Every power of appointment over, or power to convey or charge land or any interest therein, whether created by a statute or other instrument or implied by law, and whether created before or after the commencement of this Act (not being a power vested in a legal mortgagee or an estate owner in right of his estate and exercisable by him or by another person in his name and on his behalf), operates only in equity.

(8)   Estates, interests, and charges in or over land which are not legal estates are in this Act referred to as "equitable interests," and powers which by this Act are to operate in equity only are in this Act referred to as "equitable powers."

(9)   The provisions in any statute or other instrument requiring land to be conveyed to uses shall take effect as directions that the land shall (subject to creating or reserving thereout any legal estate authorised by this Act which may be required) be conveyed to a person of full age upon the requisite trusts.

(10)   The repeal of the Statute of Uses (as amended) does not affect the operation thereof in regard to dealings taking effect before the commencement of this Act.

2 Conveyances overreaching certain equitable interests and powers

(1)   A conveyance to a purchaser of a legal estate in land shall overreach any equitable interest or power affecting that estate, whether or not he has notice thereof, if—

    (i)   the conveyance is made under the powers conferred by the Settled Land Act, 1925, or any additional powers conferred by a settlement, and the equitable interest or power is capable of being overreached thereby, and the statutory requirements respecting the payment of capital money arising under the settlement are complied with;

    (ii)   the conveyance is made by [trustees of land] and the equitable interest or power is at the date of the conveyance capable of being overreached by such trustees under the provisions of subsection (2) of this section or independently of that subsection, and [the requirements of section 27 of this Act respecting the payment of capital money arising on such a conveyance] are complied with;

    (iii)   the conveyance is made by a mortgagee or personal representative in the exercise of his paramount powers, and the equitable interest or power is capable of being overreached by such conveyance, and any capital money arising from the transaction is paid to the mortgagee or personal representative;

    (iv)   the conveyance is made under an order of the court and the equitable interest or power is bound by such order, and any capital money arising from the transaction is paid into, or in accordance with the order of, the court.

[(1A) An equitable interest in land subject to a trust of land which remains in, or is to revert to, the settlor shall (subject to any contrary intention) be overreached by the conveyance if it would be so overreached were it an interest under the trust.]

(2)   [Where the legal estate affected is subject to [a trust of land], then if at the date of a conveyance made after the commencement of this Act [by the trustees], the trustees (whether original or substituted) are either]—

    (a)   two or more individuals approved or appointed by the court or the successors in office of the individuals so approved or appointed; or

    (b)   a trust corporation,

    [any equitable interest or power having priority [to the trust]] shall, notwithstanding any stipulation to the contrary, be overreached by the conveyance, and shall, according to its priority, take effect as if created or arising by means of a primary trust affecting the proceeds of sale and the income of the land until sale.

(3) The following equitable interests and powers are excepted from the operation of subsection (2) of this section, namely—

    (i) Any equitable interest protected by a deposit of documents relating to the legal estate affected;

    (ii) The benefit of any covenant or agreement restrictive of the user of land;

    (iii) Any easement, liberty, or privilege over or affecting land and being merely an equitable interest (in this Act referred to as an "equitable easement");

    (iv) The benefit of any contract (in this Act referred to as an "estate contract") to convey or create a legal estate, including a contract conferring either expressly or by statutory implication a valid option to purchase, a right of pre-emption, or any other like right;

    (v) Any equitable interest protected by registration under the Land Charges Act, 1925[1], other than—

        (a) an annuity within the meaning of Part II. of that Act;
        (b) a limited owner's charge or a general equitable charge within the meaning of that Act.

(4) Subject to the protection afforded by this section to the purchaser of a legal estate, nothing contained in this section shall deprive a person entitled to an equitable charge of any of his rights or remedies for enforcing the same.

(5) So far as regards the following interests, created before the commencement of this Act (which accordingly are not within the provisions of the Land Charges Act, 1925[1]), namely—

    (a) the benefit of any covenant or agreement restrictive of the user of the land;

    (b) any equitable easement;

    (c) the interest under a puisne mortgage within the meaning of the Land Charges Act, 1925, unless and until acquired under a transfer made after the commencement of this Act;

    (d) the benefit of an estate contract, unless and until the same is acquired under a conveyance made after the commencement of this Act;

a purchaser of a legal estate shall only take subject thereto if he has notice thereof, and the same are not overreached under the provisions contained or in the manner referred to in this section.

14 Interests of persons in possession

This Part of this Act shall not prejudicially affect the interest of any person in possession or in actual occupation of land to which he may be entitled in right of such possession or occupation.

27 Purchaser not to be concerned with the trusts of the proceeds of sale which are to be paid to two or more trustees or to a trust corporation

[(1)   A purchaser of a legal estate from trustees of land shall not be concerned with the trusts affecting the land, the net income of the land or the proceeds of sale of the land whether or not those trusts are declared by the same instrument as that by which the trust of land is created.]

[(2)   Notwithstanding anything to the contrary in the instrument (if any) creating a [trust] of land or in [any trust affecting the net proceeds of sale of the land if it is sold], the proceeds of sale or other capital money shall not be paid to or applied by the direction of fewer than two persons as [trustees], except where the trustee is a trust corporation, but this subsection does not affect the right of a sole personal representative as such to give valid receipts for, or direct the application of, proceeds of sale or other capital money, nor, except where capital money arises on the transaction, render it necessary to have more than one trustee.]

31 Trust [...] of mortgaged property where right of redemption is barred

(1)   Where any property, vested in trustees by way of security, becomes, by virtue of the statutes of limitation, or of an order for foreclosure or otherwise, discharged from the right of redemption, it shall be held by them [in trust—

   (a)   to apply the income from the property in the same manner as interest paid on the mortgage debt would have been applicable; and

   (b)   if the property is sold, to apply the net proceeds of sale, after payment of costs and expenses, in the same manner as repayment of the mortgage debt would have been applicable.]

[(2)   Subsection (1) of this section] operates without prejudice to any rule of law relating to the apportionment of capital and income between tenant for life and remainderman.

(3)   [...]

[(4)   Where—

   (a)   the mortgage money is capital money for the purposes of the Settled Land Act 1925;

   (b)   land other than any forming the whole or part of the property mentioned in subsection (1) of this section is, or is deemed to be, subject to the settlement; and

   (c)   the tenant for life or statutory owner requires the trustees to execute with respect to land forming the whole or part of that property a vesting deed such as would have been required in relation to the land if it had been acquired on a purchase with capital money,

   the trustees shall execute such a vesting deed.]

(5)   This section applies whether the right of redemption was discharged before or after the first day of January, nineteen hundred and twelve, but has effect without prejudice to any dealings or arrangements made before that date.

33 Application of Part 1 to personal representatives

The provisions of this Part of this Act relating to [trustees of land] apply to personal representatives holding [land in trust], but without prejudice to their rights and powers for purposes of administration.

Undivided Shares and Joint Ownership

34 Effect of future dispositions to tenants in common

(1)   An undivided share in land shall not be capable of being created except as provided by the Settled Land Act, 1925, or as hereinafter mentioned.

(2)   Where, after the commencement of this Act, land is expressed to be conveyed to any persons in undivided shares and those persons are of full age, the conveyance shall (notwithstanding anything to the contrary in this Act) operate as if the land had been expressed to be conveyed to the grantees, or, if there are more than four grantees, to the four first named in the conveyance, as joint tenants [in trust for the persons interested in the land]:

Provided that, where the conveyance is made by way of mortgage the land shall vest in the grantees or such four of them as aforesaid for a term of years absolute (as provided by this Act) as joint tenants subject to cesser on redemption in like manner as if the mortgage money had belonged to them on a joint account, but without prejudice to the beneficial interests in the mortgage money and interest.

(3)   A devise bequest or testamentary appointment, coming into operation after the commencement of this Act, of land to two or more persons in undivided shares shall operate as a devise bequest or appointment of the land to [. . .] the personal representatives of the testator, and [. . .] (but without prejudice to the rights and powers of the personal representatives for purposes of administration) [in trust for the persons interested in the land].

[(3A) In subsections (2) and (3) of this section references to the persons interested in the land include persons interested as trustees or personal representatives (as well as persons beneficially interested).]

36 Joint tenancies

(1)   Where a legal estate (not being settled land) is beneficially limited to or held in trust for any persons as joint tenants, the same shall be held [in trust], in like manner as if the persons beneficially entitled were tenants in common, but not so as to sever their joint tenancy in equity.

(2)   No severance of a joint tenancy of a legal estate, so as to create a tenancy in common in land, shall be permissible, whether by operation of law or otherwise, but this subsection does not affect the right of a joint tenant to release his interest to the other joint tenants, or the right to sever a joint tenancy in an equitable interest whether or not the legal estate is vested in the joint tenants:

Provided that, where a legal estate (not being settled land) is vested in joint tenants beneficially, and any tenant desires to sever the joint tenancy in equity, he shall give to the other joint tenants a notice in writing of such desire or do such other acts or things as would, in the case of personal estate, have been effectual to sever the tenancy in equity, and thereupon [the land shall be held in trust on terms] which would have been requisite for giving effect to the beneficial interests if there had been an actual severance.

[Nothing in this Act affects the right of a survivor of joint tenants, who is solely and beneficially interested, to deal with his legal estate as if it were not held [in trust].]

(3)   Without prejudice to the right of a joint tenant to release his interest to the other joint tenants no severance of a mortgage term or trust estate, so as to create a tenancy in common, shall be permissible.

37 Rights of husband and wife

A husband and wife shall, for all purposes of acquisition of any interest in property, under a disposition made or coming into operation after the commencement of this Act, be treated as two persons.

Transitional Provisions

39 Transitional provisions in First Schedule

For the purpose of effecting the transition from the law existing prior to the commencement of the Law of Property Act, 1922, to the law enacted by that Act (as amended), the provisions set out in the First Schedule to this Act shall have effect—

(1)   for converting existing legal estates, interests and charges not capable under the said Act of taking effect as legal interests into equitable interests;

(2)   for discharging, getting in or vesting outstanding legal estates;

(3)   for making provision with respect to legal estates vested in infants;

(4)   for subjecting land held in undivided shares to [trusts];

(5)   for dealing with party structures and open spaces held in common;

(6)   [...]

(7)   for converting existing freehold mortgages into mortgages by demise;

(8)   for converting existing leasehold mortgages into mortgages by sub-demise.

Part II Contracts, Conveyances and other Instruments

Contracts

40 Contracts for sale, of land to be in writing etc.

No action may be brought upon any contract for the sale or other disposition of land or any interest in land unless the agreement upon which such action is brought, or some memorandum or note thereof, is in writing, and signed by the party to be charged or by some other person thereunder by him lawfully authorised.

This section does not apply to contracts whether made before or after the commencement of this Act and does not affect the law relating to past performance or sales by the court.

Note: Repealed by the Law of Property (Miscellaneous Provisions) Act 1989 s 2, except for contracts made before 27 September 1989.

41 Stipulations not of the essence of a contract

Stipulations in a contract, as to time or otherwise, which according to rules of equity are not deemed to be or to have become of the essence of the contract, are also construed and have effect at law in accordance with the same rules.

52 Conveyances to be by deed

(1)   All conveyances of land or of any interest therein are void for the purpose of conveying or creating a legal estate unless made by deed.

(2)   This section does not apply to—

(a)   assents by a personal representative;

(b)   disclaimers made in accordance with [sections 178 to 180 or sections 315 to 319 of the Insolvency Act 1986], or not required to be evidenced in writing;

(c)   surrenders by operation of law, including surrenders which may, by law, be effected without writing;

(d)   leases or tenancies or other assurances not required by law to be made in writing;

(e)   receipts [other than those falling within section 115 below];

(f)   vesting orders of the court or other competent authority;

(g)   conveyances taking effect by operation of law.

53 Instruments required to be in writing

(1)   Subject to the provision hereinafter contained with respect to the creation of interests in land by parol—

(a)   no interest in land can be created or disposed of except by writing signed by the person creating or conveying the same, or by his agent thereunto lawfully authorised in writing, or by will, or by operation of law;

(b)   a declaration of trust respecting any land or any interest therein must be manifested and proved by some writing signed by some person who is able to declare such trust or by his will;

(c)   a disposition of an equitable interest or trust subsisting at the time of the disposition, must be in writing signed by the person disposing of the same, or by his agent thereunto lawfully authorised in writing or by will.

(2)   This section does not affect the creation or operation of resulting, implied or constructive trusts.

54 Creation of interests in land by parol

(1) All interests in land created by parol and not put in writing and signed by the persons so creating the same, or by their agents thereunto lawfully authorised in writing, have, notwithstanding any consideration having been given for the same, the force and effect of interests at will only.

(2) Nothing in the foregoing provisions of this Part of this Act shall affect the creation by parol of leases taking effect in possession for a term not exceeding three years (whether or not the lessee is given power to extend the term) at the best rent which can be reasonably obtained without taking a fine.

56 Persons taking who are not parties and as to indentures

(1) A person may take an immediate or other interest in land or other property, or the benefit of any condition, right of entry, covenant or agreement over or respecting land or other property, although he may not be named as a party to the conveyance or other instrument.

(2) A deed between parties, to effect its objects, has the effect of an indenture though not indented or expressed to be an indenture.

60 Abolition of technicalities in regard to conveyances and deeds

(1) A conveyance of freehold land to any person without words of limitation, or any equivalent expression, shall pass to the grantee the fee simple or other the whole interest which the grantor had power to convey in such land, unless a contrary intention appears in the conveyance.

(2) A conveyance of freehold land to a corporation sole by his corporate designation without the word "successors" shall pass to the corporation the fee simple or other the whole interest which the grantor had power to convey in such land, unless a contrary intention appears in the conveyance.

(3) In a voluntary conveyance a resulting trust for the grantor shall not be implied merely by reason that the property is not expressed to be conveyed for the use or benefit of the grantee.

(4) The foregoing provisions of this section apply only to conveyances and deeds executed after the commencement of this Act:

Provided that in a deed executed after the thirty-first day of December, eighteen hundred and eighty-one, it is sufficient—

(a) In the limitation of an estate in fee simple, to use the words "in fee simple," without the word "heirs";

[…]

61 Construction of expressions used in deeds and other instruments

In all deeds, contracts, wills, orders and other instruments executed, made or coming into operation after the commencement of this Act, unless the context otherwise requires—

(a) "Month" means calendar month;
(b) "Person" includes a corporation;

(c)   The singular includes the plural and vice versa;

(d)   The masculine includes the feminine and vice versa.

62 General words implied in conveyances

(1)   A conveyance of land shall be deemed to include and shall by virtue of this Act operate to convey, with the land, all buildings, erections, fixtures, commons, hedges, ditches, fences, ways, waters, water-courses, liberties, privileges, easements, rights, and advantages whatsoever, appertaining or reputed to appertain to the land, or any part thereof, or, at the time of conveyance, demised, occupied, or enjoyed with, or reputed or known as part or parcel of or appurtenant to the land or any part thereof.

(2)   A conveyance of land, having houses or other buildings thereon, shall be deemed to include and shall by virtue of this Act operate to convey, with the land, houses, or other buildings, all outhouses, erections, fixtures, cellars, areas, courts, courtyards, cisterns, sewers, gutters, drains, ways, passages, lights, watercourses, liberties, privileges, easements, rights, and advantages whatsoever, appertaining or reputed to appertain to the land, houses, or other buildings conveyed, or any of them, or any part thereof, or, at the time of conveyance, demised, occupied, or enjoyed with, or reputed or known as part or parcel of or appurtenant to, the land, houses, or other buildings conveyed, or any of them, or any part thereof.

(3)   A conveyance of a manor shall be deemed to include and shall by virtue of this Act operate to convey, with the manor, all pastures, feedings, wastes, warrens, commons, mines, minerals, quarries, furzes, trees, woods, underwoods, coppices, and the ground and soil thereof, fishings, fisheries, fowlings, courts leet, courts baron, and other courts, view of frankpledge and all that to view of frankpledge doth belong, mills, mulctures, customs, tolls, duties, reliefs, heriots, fines, sums of money, amerciaments, waifs, estrays, chief-rents, quitrents, rents charge, rents seck, rents of assize, fee farm rents, services, royalties jurisdictions, franchises, liberties, privileges, easements, profits, advantages, rights, emoluments, and hereditaments whatsoever, to the manor appertaining or reputed to appertain, or, at the time of conveyance, demised, occupied, or enjoyed with the same, or reputed or known as part, parcel, or member thereof.

For the purposes of this subsection the right to compensation for manorial incidents on the extinguishment thereof shall be deemed to be a right appertaining to the manor.

(4)   This section applies only if and as far as a contrary intention is not expressed in the conveyance, and has effect subject to the terms of the conveyance and to the provisions therein contained.

(5)   This section shall not be construed as giving to any person a better title to any property, right, or thing in this section mentioned than the title which the conveyance gives to him to the land or manor expressed to be conveyed, or as conveying to him any property, right, or thing in this section mentioned, further or otherwise than as the same could have been conveyed to him by the conveying parties.

(6)   This section applies to conveyances made after the thirty-first day of December, eighteen hundred and eighty-one.

65 Reservation of legal estates

(1) A reservation of a legal estate shall operate at law without any execution of the conveyance by the grantee of the legal estate out of which the reservation is made, or any regrant by him, so as to create the legal estate reserved, and so as to vest the same in possession in the person (whether being the grantor or not) for whose benefit the reservation is made.

(2) A conveyance of a legal estate expressed to be made subject to another legal estate not in existence immediately before the date of the conveyance, shall operate as a reservation, unless a contrary intention appears.

(3) This section applies only to reservations made after the commencement of this Act.

Covenants

77 Implied covenants in conveyances subject to rents

77 In addition to the covenants implied under [Part I of the Law of Property (Miscellaneous Provisions) Act 1994], there shall in the several cases in this section mentioned, be deemed to be included and implied, a covenant to the effect in this section stated, by and with such persons as are hereinafter mentioned, that is to say:—

(A) In a conveyance for valuable consideration, other than a mortgage, of the entirety of the land affected by a rent charge, a covenant by the grantee or joint and several covenants by the grantees, if more than one, with the conveying parties and with each of them, if more than one, in the terms set out in Part VII of the Second Schedule to this Act. Where a rent charge has been apportioned in respect of any land, with the consent of the owner of the rent charge, the covenants in this paragraph shall be implied in the conveyance of that land in like manner as if the apportioned rent charge were the rent charge referred to, and the document creating the rentcharge related solely to that land:

...

(C) In a conveyance for valuable consideration, other than a mortgage, of the entirety of the land comprised in a lease, for the residue of the term or interest created by the lease, a covenant by the assignee or joint and several covenants by the assignees (if more than one) with the conveying parties and with each of them (if more than one) in the terms set out in Part IX of the Second Schedule to this Act. Where a rent has been apportioned in respect of any land, with the consent of the lessor, the covenants in this paragraph shall be implied in the conveyance of that land in like manner as if the apportioned rent were the original rent reserved, and the lease related solely to that land:

[(2) Where in a conveyance for valuable consideration, other than a mortgage, part of land affected by a rent charge is, without the consent of the owner of the rent charge, expressed to be conveyed subject to or charged with the entire rent, paragraph (B)(i) of subsection (1) of this section shall apply as if, in paragraph (i) of Part VIII of the Second Schedule to this Act—

(a) any reference to the apportioned rent were to the entire rent; and
(b) the words "(other than the covenant to pay the entire rent)" were omitted.

(2A)   Where in a conveyance for valuable consideration, other than a mortgage, part of land affected by a rent charge is, without the consent of the owner of the rent charge, expressed to be conveyed discharged or exonerated from the entire rent, paragraph (B)(ii) of subsection (1) of this section shall apply as if, in paragraph (ii) of Part VIII of the Second Schedule to this Act—

(a)   any reference to the balance of the rent were to the entire rent; and

(b)   the words ", other than the covenant to pay the entire rent," were omitted.]

(3)   In this section "conveyance" does not include a demise by way of lease at a rent.

(4)   Any covenant which would be implied under this section by reason of a person conveying or being expressed to convey as beneficial owner may, by express reference to this section, be implied, with or without variation, in a conveyance, whether or not for valuable consideration, by a person who conveys or is expressed to convey as settlor, or as trustee, or as mortgagee, or as personal representative of a deceased person, [. . .] or under an order of the court.

(5)   The benefit of a covenant implied as aforesaid shall be annexed and incident to, and shall go with, the estate or interest of the implied covenantee, and shall be capable of being enforced by every person in whom that estate or interest is, for the whole or any part thereof, from time to time vested.

(6)   A covenant implied as aforesaid may be varied or extended by deed, and, as so varied or extended, shall, as far as may be, operate in the like manner, and with all the like incidents, effects and consequences, as if such variations or extensions were directed in this section to be implied.

(7)   In particular any covenant implied under this section may be extended by providing that—

(a)   the land conveyed; or

(b)   the part of the land affected by the rent charge which remains vested in the covenantor;

shall, as the case may require, stand charged with the payment of all money which may become payable under the implied covenant.

(8)   This section applies only to conveyances made after the commencement of this Act.

78 Benefit of covenants relating to land

(1)   A covenant relating to any land of the covenantee shall be deemed to be made with the covenantee and his successors in title and the persons deriving title under him or them, and shall have effect as if such successors and other persons were expressed.

For the purposes of this subsection in connexion with covenants restrictive of the user of land "successors in title" shall be deemed to include the owners and occupiers for the time being of the land of the covenantee intended to be benefited.

(2)   This section applies to covenants made after the commencement of this Act, but the repeal of section fifty-eight of the Conveyancing Act, 1881, does not affect the operation of covenants to which that section applied.

Note: Section 78 does not apply to tenancies created after 1 January 1996: see Landlord and Tenant (Covenants) Act 1995 s 1(3).

79 Burden of covenants relating to land

(1)   A covenant relating to any land of a covenantor or capable of being bound by him, shall, unless a contrary intention is expressed, be deemed to be made by the covenantor on behalf of himself his successors in title and the persons deriving title under him or them, and, subject as aforesaid, shall have effect as if such successors and other persons were expressed.

This subsection extends to a covenant to do some act relating to the land, notwithstanding that the subject-matter may not be in existence when the covenant is made.

(2)   For the purposes of this section in connexion with covenants restrictive of the user of land "successors in title" shall be deemed to include the owners and occupiers for the time being of such land.

(3)   This section applies only to covenants made after the commencement of this Act.

Note: Section 79 does not apply to tenancies created after 1 January 1996: see Landlord and Tenant (Covenants) Act 1995 s 1(3).

84 Power to discharge or modify restrictive covenants affecting land

(1)   [the Lands Tribunal] shall (without prejudice to any concurrent jurisdiction of the court) have power from time to time, on the application of any person interested in any freehold land affected by any restriction arising under covenant or otherwise as to the user thereof or the building thereon, by order wholly or partially to discharge or modify any such restriction [. . .] on being satisfied—

(a)   that by reason of changes in the character of the property or the neighbourhood or other circumstances of the case which [the Lands Tribunal] may deem material, the restriction ought to be deemed obsolete, or

[(aa)   that [in a case falling within subsection (1A) below] the continued existence thereof would impede [some reasonable user] of the land for public or private purposes [. . .] or, as the case may be, would unless modified so impede such user; or]

(b)   that the persons of full age and capacity for the time being or from time to time entitled to the benefit of the restriction, whether in respect of estates in fee simple or any lesser estates or interests in the property to which the benefit of the restriction is annexed, have agreed, either expressly or by implication, by their acts or omissions, to the same being discharged or modified; or

(c)   that the proposed discharge or modification will not injure the persons entitled to the benefit of the restriction:

[and an order discharging or modifying a restriction under this subsection may direct the applicant to pay to any person entitled to the benefit of the restriction such sum by way of consideration as the Tribunal may think it just to award under one, but not both, of the following heads, that is to say, either—

(i)   a sum to make up for any loss or disadvantage suffered by that person in consequence of the discharge or modification; or

      (ii)   a sum to make up for any effect which the restriction had, at the time when it was imposed, in reducing the consideration then received for the land affected by it.]

[(1A) Subsection (1) (*aa*) above authorises the discharge or modification of a restriction by reference to its impeding some reasonable user of land in any case in which the Lands Tribunal is satisfied that the restriction, in impeding that user, either—

      (a)   does not secure to persons entitled to the benefit of it any practical benefits of substantial value or advantage to them; or

      (b)   is contrary to the public interest;

and that money will be an adequate compensation for the loss or disadvantage (if any) which any such person will suffer from the discharge or modification.]

[(1B) In determining whether a case is one falling within subsection (1A) above, and in determining whether (in any such case or otherwise) a restriction ought to be discharged or modified, the Lands Tribunal shall take into account the development plan and any declared or ascertainable pattern for the grant or refusal of planning permissions in the relevant areas, as well as the period at which and context in which the restriction was created or imposed and any other material circumstances.]

[(1C) It is hereby declared that the power conferred by this section to modify a restriction includes power to add such further provisions restricting the user of or the building on the land affected as appear to the Lands Tribunal to be reasonable in view of the relaxation of the existing provisions, and as may be accepted by the applicant; and the Lands Tribunal may accordingly refuse to modify a restriction without some such addition.]

(2)   The court shall have power on the application of any person interested—

      (a)   To declare whether or not in any particular case any freehold land is [or would in any given event be] affected by a restriction imposed by any instrument; or

      (b)   To declare what, upon the true construction of any instrument purporting to impose a restriction, is the nature and extent of the restriction thereby imposed and whether the same is [or would in any given event be] enforceable and if so by whom.

[Neither subsections (7) and (11) of this section nor, unless the contrary is expressed, any later enactment providing for this section not to apply to any restrictions shall affect the operation of this subsection or the operation for purposes of this subsection of any other provisions of this section.]

(3)   [The Lands Tribunal] shall, before making any order under this section, direct such enquiries, if any, to be made of any [government department or] local authority, and such notices, if any, whether by way of advertisement or otherwise, to be given to such of the persons who appear to be entitled to the benefit of the restriction intended to be discharged, modified, or dealt with as, having regard to any enquiries notices or other proceedings previously made, given or taken, [the Lands Tribunal] may think fit.

[(3A) On an application to the Lands Tribunal under this section the Lands Tribunal shall give any necessary directions as to the persons who are or are not to be admitted (as appearing to be entitled to the benefit of the restriction) to oppose the application, and no appeal shall lie against any such direction; but rules under the Lands Tribunal Act 1949 shall make provision whereby, in cases in which there arises on such an application (whether or not in connection with the admission of persons to oppose) any such question as is referred to in subsection (2) (*a*) or (*b*) of this section, the proceedings on the application can and, if the rules so provide, shall be suspended to enable the decision of the court to be obtained on that question by an application under that subsection, or by means of a case stated by the Lands Tribunal, or otherwise, as may be provided by those rules or by rules of court.]

[(4)   …]

(5)   Any order made under this section shall be binding on all persons, whether ascertained or of full age or capacity or not, then entitled or thereafter capable of becoming entitled to the benefit of any restriction, which is thereby discharged, modified, or dealt with, and whether such persons are parties to the proceedings or have been served with notice or not [. . .]

(6)   An order may be made under this section notwithstanding that any instrument which is alleged to impose the restriction intended to be discharged, modified, or dealt with, may not have been produced to the court or [the Lands Tribunal], and the court or [the Lands Tribunal] may act on such evidence of that instrument as it may think sufficient.

(7)   This section applies to restrictions whether subsisting at the commencement of this Act or imposed thereafter, but this section does not apply where the restriction was imposed on the occasion of a disposition made gratuitously or for a nominal consideration for public purposes.

(8)   This section applies whether the land affected by the restrictions is registered or not […]

(9)   Where any proceedings by action or otherwise are taken to enforce a restrictive covenant, any person against whom the proceedings are taken, may in such proceedings apply to the court for an order giving leave to apply to [the Lands Tribunal] under this section, and staying the proceedings in the meantime.

(10)   […]

(11)   This section does not apply to restrictions imposed by the Commissioners of Works under any statutory power for the protection of any Royal Park or Garden or to restrictions of a like character imposed upon the occasion of any enfranchisement effected before the commencement of this Act in any manor vested in His Majesty in right of the Crown or the Duchy of Lancaster, nor [subject to subsection (11A) below] to restrictions created or imposed—

(a)   for Naval, Military or Air Force purposes,

[(b)   for civil aviation purposes under the powers of the Air Navigation Act 1920, of section 19 or 23 of the Civil Aviation Act 1949 or of section 30 or 41 of the Civil Aviation Act 1982.]

[(11A)Subsection (11) of this section—

(a)   shall exclude the application of this section to a restriction falling within subsection (11)(*a*), and not created or imposed in connection with the use of any land as an aerodrome, only so long as the restriction is enforceable by or on behalf of the Crown; and

(b)   shall exclude the application of this section to a restriction falling within subsection (11)(*b*), or created or imposed in connection with the use of any land as an aerodrome, only so long as the restriction is enforceable by or on behalf of the Crown or any public or international authority.]

(12)   Where a term of more than [forty] years is created in land (whether before or after the commencement of this Act) this section shall, after the expiration of [twenty-five] years of the term, apply to restrictions affecting such leasehold land in like manner as it would have applied had the land been freehold:

Provided that this subsection shall not apply to mining leases.

Part III Mortgages, Rent charges, and Powers of Attorney

Mortgages

85 Mode of mortgaging freeholds

(1)   A mortgage of an estate in fee simple shall only be capable of being effected at law either by a demise for a term of years absolute, subject to a provision for cesser on redemption, or by a charge by deed expressed to be by way of legal mortgage:

Provided that a first mortgagee shall have the same right to the possession of documents as if his security included the fee simple.

(2)   Any purported conveyance of an estate in fee simple by way of mortgage made after the commencement of this Act shall (to the extent of the estate of the mortgagor) operate as a demise of the land to the mortgagee for a term of years absolute, without impeachment for waste, but subject to cesser on redemption, in manner following, namely:—

(a)   A first or only mortgagee shall take a term of three thousand years from the date of the mortgage:

(b)   A second or subsequent mortgagee shall take a term (commencing from the date of the mortgage) one day longer than the term vested in the first or other mortgagee whose security ranks immediately before that of such second or subsequent mortgagee:

and, in this subsection, any such purported conveyance as aforesaid includes an absolute conveyance with a deed of defeasance and any other assurance which, but for this subsection, would operate in effect to vest the fee simple in a mortgagee subject to redemption.

(3)   [Subsection (2) does not apply to registered land, but, subject to that, this section applies whether or not the land is registered land and whether or not] the mortgage is expressed to be made by way of trust for sale or otherwise.

(4)   Without prejudice to the provisions of this Act respecting legal and equitable powers, every power to mortgage or to lend money on mortgage of an estate in fee simple shall be construed as a power to mortgage the estate for a term of years absolute, without impeachment for waste, or by a charge by way of legal mortgage or to lend on such security.

(5)   In its application to instruments made after the coming into force of section 1 of the Law of Property (Miscellaneous Provisions) Act 1989 subsection (1) above shall have effect as if for the

words "under seal, and a bond or obligation under seal," there were substituted the words "bond or obligation executed as a deed in accordance with section 1 of the Law of Property (Miscellaneous Provisions) Act 1989".]

86 Mode of mortgaging leaseholds

(1)   A mortgage of a term of years absolute shall only be capable of being effected at law either by a subdemise for a term of years absolute, less by one day at least than the term vested in the mortgagor, and subject to a provision for cesser on redemption, or by a charge by deed expressed to be by way of legal mortgage; and where a licence to subdemise by way of mortgage is required, such licence shall not be unreasonably refused:

Provided that a first mortgagee shall have the same right to the possession of documents as if his security had been effected by assignment.

(2)   Any purported assignment of a term of years absolute by way of mortgage made after the commencement of this Act shall (to the extent of the estate of the mortgagor) operate as a subdemise of the leasehold land to the mortgagee for a term of years absolute, but subject to cesser on redemption, in manner following, namely:—

(a)   The term to be taken by a first or only mortgagee shall be ten days less than the term expressed to be assigned:

(b)   The term to be taken by a second or subsequent mortgagee shall be one day longer than the term vested in the first or other mortgagee whose security ranks immediately before that of the second or subsequent mortgagee, if the length of the last mentioned term permits, and in any case for a term less by one day at least than the term expressed to be assigned:

and, in this subsection, any such purported assignment as aforesaid includes an absolute assignment with a deed of defeasance and any other assurance which, but for this subsection, would operate in effect to vest the term of the mortgagor in a mortgagee subject to redemption.

(3)   [Subsection (2) does not apply to registered land, but, subject to that, this section applies whether or not the land is registered land and whether or not] the mortgage is made by way of sub-mortgage of a term of years absolute, or is expressed to be by way of trust for sale or otherwise.

(4)   Without prejudice to the provisions of this Act respecting legal and equitable powers, every power to mortgage for or to lend money on mortgage of a term of years absolute by way of assignment shall be construed as a power to mortgage the term by subdemise for a term of years absolute or by a charge by way of legal mortgage, or to lend on such security.

87 Charges by way of legal mortgage

(1)   Where a legal mortgage of land is created by a charge by deed expressed to be by way of legal mortgage, the mortgagee shall have the same protection, powers and remedies (including the right to take proceedings to obtain possession from the occupiers and the persons in receipt of rents and profits, or any of them) as if—

(a)   where the mortgage is a mortgage of an estate in fee simple, a mortgage term for three thousand years without impeachment of waste had been thereby created in favour of the mortgagee; and

(b)   where the mortgage is a mortgage of a term of years absolute, a sub-term less by one day than the term vested in the mortgagor had been thereby created in favour of the mortgagee.

(2)   Where an estate vested in a mortgagee immediately before the commencement of this Act has by virtue of this Act been converted into a term of years absolute or sub-term, the mortgagee may, by a declaration in writing to that effect signed by him, convert the mortgage into a charge by way of legal mortgage, and in that case the mortgage term shall be extinguished in the inheritance or in the head term as the case may be, and the mortgagee shall have the same protection, powers and remedies (including the right to take proceedings to obtain possession from the occupiers and the persons in receipt of rents and profits or any of them) as if the mortgage term or sub-term had remained subsisting.

The power conferred by this subsection may be exercised by a mortgagee notwithstanding that he is a trustee or personal representative.

(3)   Such declaration shall not affect the priority of the mortgagee or his right to retain possession of documents, nor affect his title to or right over any fixtures or chattels personal comprised in the mortgage.

[(4)   Subsection (1) of this section shall not be taken to be affected by section 23(1)(a) of the Land Registration Act 2002 (under which owner's powers in relation to a registered estate do not include power to mortgage by demise or sub-demise).]

91 Sale of mortgaged property in action for redemption or foreclosure

(1)   Any person entitled to redeem mortgaged property may have a judgment or order for sale instead of for redemption in an action brought by him either for redemption alone, or for sale alone, or for sale or redemption in the alternative.

(2)   In any action, whether for foreclosure, or for redemption, or for sale, or for the raising and payment in any manner of mortgage money, the court, on the request of the mortgagee, or of any person interested either in the mortgage money or in the right of redemption, and, notwithstanding that—

(a)   any other person dissents; or
(b)   the mortgagee or any person so interested does not appear in the action;

and without allowing any time for redemption or for payment of any mortgage money, may direct a sale of the mortgaged property, on such terms as it thinks fit, including the deposit in court of a reasonable sum fixed by the court to meet the expenses of sale and to secure performance of the terms.

(3)   But, in an action brought by a person interested in the right of redemption and seeking a sale, the court may, on the application of any defendant, direct the plaintiff to give such security for costs as the court thinks fit, and may give the conduct of the sale to any defendant, and may give such directions as it thinks fit respecting the costs of the defendants or any of them.

(4)   In any case within this section the court may, if it thinks fit, direct a sale without previously determining the priorities of incumbrancers.

(5)   This section applies to actions brought either before or after the commencement of this Act.

(6)   In this section "mortgaged property" includes the estate or interest which a mortgagee would have had power to convey if the statutory power of sale were applicable.

(7)   For the purposes of this section the court may, in favour of a purchaser, make a vesting order conveying the mortgaged property, or appoint a person to do so, subject or not to any incumbrance, as the court may think fit; or, in the case of an equitable mortgage, may create and vest a mortgage term in the mortgagee to enable him to carry out the sale as if the mortgage had been made by deed by way of legal mortgage.

[(8)   The county court has jurisdiction under this section where the amount owing in respect of the mortgage or charge at the commencement of the proceedings does not exceed [£30,000].]

94 Tacking and further advances

(1)   After the commencement of this Act, a prior mortgagee shall have a right to make further advances to rank in priority to subsequent mortgages (whether legal or equitable)—

(a)   if an arrangement has been made to that effect with the subsequent mortgagees; or

(b)   if he had no notice of such subsequent mortgages at the time when the further advance was made by him; or

(c)   whether or not he had such notice as aforesaid, where the mortgage imposes an obligation on him to make such further advances.

This subsection applies whether or not the prior mortgage was made expressly for securing further advances.

(2)   In relation to the making of further advances after the commencement of this Act a mortgagee shall not be deemed to have notice of a mortgage merely by reason that it was registered as a land chargeor in a local deeds registry, if it was not so registered at the [time when the original mortgage was created] or when the last search (if any) by or on behalf of the mortgagee was made, whichever last happened.

This subsection only applies where the prior mortgage was made expressly for securing a current account or other further advances.

(3)   Save in regard to the making of further advances as aforesaid, the right to tack is hereby abolished:

Provided that nothing in this Act shall affect any priority acquired before the commencement of this Act by tacking, or in respect of further advances made without notice of a subsequent incumbrance or by arrangement with the subsequent incumbrancer.

(4)   This section applies to mortgages of land made before or after the commencement of this Act, but not to charges [registered under the Land Registration Act, 1925, or any enactment replaced by that Act [on registered land]] .

95 Obligation to transfer instead of reconveying, and as to right to take possession

(1)   Where a mortgagor is entitled to redeem, then subject to compliance with the terms on compliance with which he would be entitled to require a reconveyance or surrender, he shall be entitled to require the mortgagee, instead of reconveying or surrendering, to assign the mortgage debt and convey the mortgaged property to any third person, as the mortgagor directs; and the mortgagee shall be bound to assign and convey accordingly.

(2)   The rights conferred by this section belong to and are capable of being enforced by each incumbrancer, or by the mortgagor, notwithstanding any intermediate incumbrance; but a requisition of an incumbrancer prevails over a requisition of the mortgagor, and, as between incumbrancers, a requisition of a prior incumbrancer prevails over a requisition of a subsequent incumbrancer.

(3)   The foregoing provisions of this section do not apply in the case of a mortgagee being or having been in possession.

(4)   Nothing in this Act affects prejudicially the right of a mortgagee of land whether or not his charge is secured by a legal term of years absolute to take possession of the land, but the taking of possession by the mortgagee does not convert any legal estate of the mortgagor into an equitable interest.

(5)   This section applies to mortgages made either before or after the commencement of this Act, and takes effect notwithstanding any stipulation to the contrary.

97 Priorities as between puisne mortgages

Every mortgage affecting a legal estate in land made after the commencement of this Act, whether legal or equitable (not being a mortgage protected by the deposit of documents relating to the legal estate affected) shall rank according to its date of registration as a land charge pursuant to the Land Charges Act 1925.

98 Actions for possession by mortgagors

(1)   A mortgagor for the time being entitled to the possession or receipt of the rents and profits of any land, as to which the mortgagee has not given notice of his intention to take possession or to enter into the receipt of the rents and profits thereof, may sue for such possession, or for the recovery of such rents or profits, or to prevent or recover damages in respect of any trespass or other wrong relative thereto, in his own name only, unless the cause of action arises upon a lease or other contract made by him jointly with any other person.

(2)   This section does not prejudice the power of a mortgagor independently of this section to take proceedings in his own name only, either in right of any legal estate vested in him or otherwise.

(3)   This section applies whether the mortgage was made before or after the commencement of this Act.

99 Leasing powers of mortgagor and mortgagee in possession

(1) A mortgagor of land while in possession shall, as against every incumbrancer, have power to make from time to time any such lease of the mortgaged land, or any part thereof, as is by this section authorised.

(2) A mortgagee of land while in possession shall, as against all prior incumbrancers, if any, and as against the mortgagor, have power to make from time to time any such lease as aforesaid.

(3) The leases which this section authorises are—

(i) agricultural or occupation leases for any term not exceeding twenty-one years, or, in the case of a mortgage made after the commencement of this Act, fifty years; and

(ii) building leases for any term not exceeding ninety-nine years, or, in the case of a mortgage made after the commencement of this Act, nine hundred and ninety-nine years.

(4) Every person making a lease under this section may execute and do all assurances and things necessary or proper in that behalf.

(5) Every such lease shall be made to take effect in possession not later than twelve months after its date.

(6) Every such lease shall reserve the best rent that can reasonably be obtained, regard being had to the circumstances of the case, but without any fine being taken.

(7) Every such lease shall contain a covenant by the lessee for payment of the rent, and a condition of re-entry on the rent not being paid within a time therein specified not exceeding thirty days.

(8) A counterpart of every such lease shall be executed by the lessee and delivered to the lessor, of which execution and delivery the execution of the lease by the lessor shall, in favour of the lessee and all persons deriving title under him, be sufficient evidence.

(9) Every such building lease shall be made in consideration of the lessee, or some person by whose direction the lease is granted, having erected, or agreeing to erect within not more than five years from the date of the lease, buildings, new or additional, or having improved or repaired buildings, or agreeing to improve or repair buildings within that time, or having executed, or agreeing to execute within that time, on the land leased, an improvement for or in connexion with building purposes.

(10) In any such building lease a peppercorn rent, or a nominal or other rent less than the rent ultimately payable, may be made payable for the first five years, or any less part of the term.

(11) In case of a lease by the mortgagor, he shall, within one month after making the lease, deliver to the mortgagee, or, where there are more than one, to the mortgagee first in priority, a counterpart of the lease duly executed by the lessee, but the lessee shall not be concerned to see that this provision is complied with.

(12) A contract to make or accept a lease under this section may be enforced by or against every person on whom the lease if granted would be binding.

(13) [Subject to subsection (13A) below] this section applies only if and as far as a contrary intention is not expressed by the mortgagor and mortgagee in the mortgage deed, or otherwise in

writing, and has effect subject to the terms of the mortgage deed or of any such writing and to the provisions therein contained.

[(13A) Subsection (13) of this section—

(a)   shall not enable the application of any provision of this section to be excluded or restricted in relation to any mortgage of agricultural land made after 1st March 1948 but before 1st September 1995, and

(b)   shall not enable the power to grant a lease of an agricultural holding to which, by virtue of section 4 of the Agricultural Tenancies Act 1995, the Agricultural Holdings Act 1986 will apply, to be excluded or restricted in relation to any mortgage of agricultural land made on or after 1st September 1995.

(13B) In subsection (13A) of this section—

"agricultural holding" has the same meaning as in the Agricultural Holdings Act 1986; and

"agricultural land" has the same meaning as in the Agriculture Act 1947.]

(14)   The mortgagor and mortgagee may, by agreement in writing, whether or not contained in the mortgage deed, reserve to or confer on the mortgagor or the mortgagee, or both, any further or other powers of leasing or having reference to leasing; and any further or other powers so reserved or conferred shall be exercisable, as far as may be, as if they were conferred by this Act, and with all the like incidents, effects, and consequences:

Provided that the powers so reserved or conferred shall not prejudicially affect the rights of any mortgagee interested under any other mortgage subsisting at the date of the agreement, unless that mortgagee joins in or adopts the agreement.

(15)   Nothing in this Act shall be construed to enable a mortgagor or mortgagee to make a lease for any longer term or on any other conditions than such as could have been granted or imposed by the mortgagor, with the concurrence of all the incumbrancers, if this Act and the enactments replaced by this section had not been passed:

Provided that, in the case of a mortgage of leasehold land, a lease granted under this section shall reserve a reversion of not less than one day.

(16)   Subject as aforesaid, this section applies to any mortgage made after the thirty-first day of December, eighteen hundred and eighty-one, but the provisions thereof, or any of them, may, by agreement in writing made after that date between mortgagor and mortgagee, be applied to a mortgage made before that date, so nevertheless that any such agreement shall not prejudicially affect any right or interest of any mortgagee not joining in or adopting the agreement.

(17)   The provisions of this section referring to a lease shall be construed to extend and apply, as far as circumstances admit, to any letting, and to an agreement, whether in writing or not, for leasing or letting.

(18)   For the purposes of this section "mortgagor" does not include an incumbrancer deriving title under the original mortgagor.

(19)   The powers of leasing conferred by this section shall, after a receiver of the income of the mortgaged property or any part thereof has been appointed by a mortgagee under his statutory power, and so long as the receiver acts, be exercisable by such mortgagee instead of by the mortgagor, as respects any land affected by the receivership, in like manner as if such mortgagee were in possession of the land, and the mortgagee may, by writing, delegate any of such powers to the receiver.

101 Powers incident to estate or interest of mortgagee

(1)   A mortgagee, where the mortgage is made by deed, shall, by virtue of this Act, have the following powers, to the like extent as if they had been in terms conferred by the mortgage deed, but not further (namely):

(i)   A power, when the mortgage money has become due, to sell, or to concur with any other person in selling, the mortgaged property, or any part thereof, either subject to prior charges or not, and either together or in lots, by public auction or by private contract, subject to such conditions respecting title, or evidence of title, or other matter, as the mortgagee thinks fit, with power to vary any contract for sale, and to buy in at an auction, or to rescind any contract for sale, and to re-sell, without being answerable for any loss occasioned thereby; and

(ii)   A power, at any time after the date of the mortgage deed, to insure and keep insured against loss or damage by fire any building, or any effects or property of an insurable nature, whether affixed to the freehold or not, being or forming part of the property which or an estate or interest wherein is mortgaged, and the premiums paid for any such insurance shall be a charge on the mortgaged property or estate or interest, in addition to the mortgage money, and with the same priority, and with interest at the same rate, as the mortgage money; and

(iii)   A power, when the mortgage money has become due, to appoint a receiver of the income of the mortgaged property, or any part thereof; or, if the mortgaged property consists of an interest in income, or of a rentcharge or an annual or other periodical sum, a receiver of that property or any part thereof; and

(iv)   A power, while the mortgagee is in possession, to cut and sell timber and other trees ripe for cutting, and not planted or left standing for shelter or ornament, or to contract for any such cutting and sale, to be completed within any time not exceeding twelve months from the making of the contract.

[(1A)   Subsection (1)(i) is subject to section 21 of the Commonhold and Leasehold Reform Act 2002 (no disposition of part-units).]

(2)   Where the mortgage deed is executed after the thirty-first day of December, nineteen hundred and eleven, the power of sale aforesaid includes the following powers as incident thereto (namely):—

(i)   A power to impose or reserve or make binding, as far as the law permits, by covenant, condition, or otherwise, on the unsold part of the mortgaged property or any part thereof, or on the purchaser and any property sold, any restriction or reservation with respect to building on or other user of land, or with respect to mines and minerals, or for the purpose of the more beneficial working thereof, or with respect to any other thing:

(ii) A power to sell the mortgaged property, or any part thereof, or all or any mines and minerals apart from the surface:—

(a) With or without a grant or reservation of rights of way, rights of water, easements, rights, and privileges for or connected with building or other purposes in relation to the property remaining in mortgage or any part thereof, or to any property sold: and

(b) With or without an exception or reservation of all or any of the mines and minerals in or under the mortgaged property, and with or without a grant or reservation of powers or working, wayleaves, or rights of way, rights of water and drainage and other powers, easements, rights, and privileges for or connected with mining purposes in relation to the property remaining unsold or any part thereof, or to any property sold: and

(c) With or without covenants by the purchaser to expend money on the land sold.

(3) The provisions of this Act relating to the foregoing powers, comprised either in this section, or in any other section regulating the exercise of those powers, may be varied or extended by the mortgage deed, and, as so varied or extended, shall, as far as may be, operate in the like manner and with all the like incidents, effects, and consequences, as if such variations or extensions were contained in this Act.

(4) This section applies only if and as far as a contrary intention is not expressed in the mortgage deed, and has effect subject to the terms of the mortgage deed and to the provisions therein contained.

(5) Save as otherwise provided, this section applies where the mortgage deed is executed after the thirty-first day of December, eighteen hundred and eighty-one.

(6) The power of sale conferred by this section includes such power of selling the estate in fee simple or any leasehold reversion as is conferred by the provisions of this Act relating to the realisation of mortgages.

103 Regulation of exercise of power of sale

A mortgagee shall not exercise the power of sale conferred by this Act unless and until—

(i) Notice requiring payment of the mortgage money has been served on the mortgagor or one of two or more mortgagors, and default has been made in payment of the mortgage money, or of part thereof, for three months after such service; or

(ii) Some interest under the mortgage is in arrear and unpaid for two months after becoming due; or

(iii) There has been a breach of some provision contained in the mortgage deed or in this Act, or in an enactment replaced by this Act, and on the part of the mortgagor, or of some person concurring in making the mortgage, to be observed or performed, other than and besides a covenant for payment of the mortgage money or interest thereon.

105 Application of proceeds of sale

The money which is received by the mortgagee, arising from the sale, after discharge of prior incumbrances to which the sale is not made subject, if any, or after payment into court under this Act of a sum to meet any prior incumbrance, shall be held by him in trust to be applied by him, first, in payment of all costs, charges, and expenses properly incurred by him as incident to the sale or any attempted sale, or otherwise; and secondly, in discharge of the mortgage money, interest, and costs, and other money, if any, due under the mortgage; and the residue of the money so received shall be paid to the person entitled to the mortgaged property, or authorised to give receipts for the proceeds of the sale thereof.

Part IV Equitable Interests and Things in Action

136 Legal assignments of things in action

(1)   Any absolute assignment by writing under the hand of the assignor (not purporting to be by way of charge only) of any debt or other legal thing in action, of which express notice in writing has been given to the debtor, trustee or other person from whom the assignor would have been entitled to claim such debt or thing in action, is effectual in law (subject to equities having priority over the right of the assignee) to pass and transfer from the date of such notice—

(a)   the legal right to such debt or thing in action;

(b)   all legal and other remedies for the same; and

(c)   the power to give a good discharge for the same without the concurrence of the assignor:

Provided that, if the debtor, trustee or other person liable in respect of such debt or thing in action has notice—

(a)   that the assignment is disputed by the assignor or any person claiming under him; or

(b)   of any other opposing or conflicting claims to such debt or thing in action; he may, if he thinks fit, either call upon the persons making claim thereto to interplead concerning the same, or pay the debt or other thing in action into court under the provisions of the Trustee Act, 1925.

(2)   This section does not affect the provisions of the Policies of Assurance Act, 1867.

[(3)   The county court has jurisdiction (including power to receive payment of money or securities into court) under the proviso to subsection (1) of this section where the amount or value of the debt or thing in action does not exceed [£30,000].]

Part V Leases and Tenancies

141 Rent and benefit of lessee's covenants to run with the reversion

(1)   Rent reserved by a lease, and the benefit of every covenant or provision therein contained, having reference to the subject-matter thereof, and on the lessee's part to be observed or performed, and every condition of re-entry and other condition therein contained, shall be annexed and incident to and shall go with the reversionary estate in the land, or in any part thereof, immediately expectant on the term granted by the lease, notwithstanding severance of that reversionary estate, and without prejudice to any liability affecting a covenantor or his estate.

(2)   Any such rent, covenant or provision shall be capable of being recovered, received, enforced, and taken advantage of, by the person from time to time entitled, subject to the term, to the income of the whole or any part, as the case may require, of the land leased.

(3)   Where that person becomes entitled by conveyance or otherwise, such rent, covenant or provision may be recovered, received, enforced or taken advantage of by him notwithstanding that he becomes so entitled after the condition of re-entry or forfeiture has become enforceable, but this subsection does not render enforceable any condition of re-entry or other condition waived or released before such person becomes entitled as aforesaid.

(4)   This section applies to leases made before or after the commencement of this Act, but does not affect the operation of—

   (a)   any severance of the reversionary estate; or

   (b)   any acquisition by conveyance or otherwise of the right to receive or enforce any rent covenant or provision;

effected before the commencement of this Act.

Note:Section 141 does not apply to tenancies created after 1 January 1996: see Landlord and Tenant (Covenants) Act 1995 s 1(3).

142 Obligation of lessor's covenants to run with reversion

(1)   The obligation under a condition or of a covenant entered into by a lessor with reference to the subject-matter of the lease shall, if and as far as the lessor has power to bind the reversionary estate immediately expectant on the term granted by the lease, be annexed and incident to and shall go with that reversionary estate, or the several parts thereof, notwithstanding severance of that reversionary estate, and may be taken advantage of and enforced by the person in whom the term is from time to time vested by conveyance, devolution in law, or otherwise; and, if and as far as the lessor has power to bind the person from time to time entitled to that reversionary estate, the obligation aforesaid may be taken advantage of and enforced against any person so entitled.

(2)   This section applies to leases made before or after the commencement of this Act, whether the severance of the reversionary estate was effected before or after such commencement:

Provided that, where the lease was made before the first day of January eighteen hundred and eighty-two, nothing in this section shall affect the operation of any severance of the reversionary estate effected before such commencement.

This section takes effect without prejudice to any liability affecting a covenantor or his estate.

Note:Section 142 does not apply to tenancies created after 1 January 1996: see Landlord and Tenant (Covenants) Act 1995 s 1(3).

146 Restrictions on and relief against forfeiture of leases and underleases

(1)   A right of re-entry or forfeiture under any proviso or stipulation in a lease for a breach of any covenant or condition in the lease shall not be enforceable, by action or otherwise, unless and until the lessor serves on the lessee a notice—

(a)   specifying the particular breach complained of; and

(b)   if the breach is capable of remedy, requiring the lesse-e to remedy the breach; and

(c)   in any case, requiring the lessee to make compensation in money for the breach;

and the lessee fails, within a reasonable time thereafter, to remedy the breach, if it is capable of remedy, and to make reasonable compensation in money, to the satisfaction of the lessor, for the breach.

(2)   Where a lessor is proceeding, by action or otherwise, to enforce such a right of re-entry or forfeiture, the lessee may, in the lessor's action, if any, or in any action brought by himself, apply to the court for relief; and the court may grant or refuse relief, as the court, having regard to the proceedings and conduct of the parties under the foregoing provisions of this section, and to all the other circumstances, thinks fit; and in case of relief may grant it on such terms, if any, as to costs, expenses, damages, compensation, penalty, or otherwise, including the granting of an injunction to restrain any like breach in the future, as the court, in the circumstances of each case, thinks fit.

(3)   A lessor shall be entitled to recover as a debt due to him from a lessee, and in addition to damages (if any), all reasonable costs and expenses properly incurred by the lessor in the employment of a solicitor and surveyor or valuer, or otherwise, in reference to any breach giving rise to a right of re-entry or forfeiture which, at the request of the lessee, is waived by the lessor, or from which the lessee is relieved, under the provisions of this Act.

(4)   Where a lessor is proceeding by action or otherwise to enforce a right of re-entry or forfeiture under any covenant, proviso, or stipulation in a lease, or for non-payment of rent, the court may, on application by any person claiming as under-lessee any estate or interest in the property comprised in the lease or any part thereof, either in the lessor's action (if any) or in any action brought by such person for that purpose, make an order vesting, for the whole term of the lease or any less term, the property comprised in the lease or any part thereof in any person entitled as under-lessee to any estate or interest in such property upon such conditions as to execution of any deed or other document, payment of rent, costs, expenses, damages, compensation, giving security, or otherwise, as the court in the circumstances of each case may think fit, but in no case shall any such under-lessee be entitled to require a lease to be granted to him for any longer term than he had under his original sub-lease.

(5)   For the purposes of this section—

(a)   "Lease" includes an original or derivative under-lease; also an agreement for a lease where the lessee has become entitled to have his lease granted; also a grant at a fee farm rent, or securing a rent by condition;

(b)   "Lessee" includes an original or derivative under-lessee, and the persons deriving title under a lessee; also a grantee under any such grant as aforesaid and the persons deriving title under him;

(c)   "Lessor" includes an original or derivative under-lessor, and the persons deriving title under a lessor; also a person making such grant as aforesaid and the persons deriving title under him;

(d)   "Under-lease" includes an agreement for an under-lease where the under-lessee has become entitled to have his underlease granted;

(e)   "Under-lessee" includes any person deriving title under an under-lessee.

(6)   This section applies although the proviso or stipulation under which the right of re-entry or forfeiture accrues is inserted in the lease in pursuance of the directions of any Act of Parliament.

(7)   For the purposes of this section a lease limited to continue as long only as the lessee abstains from committing a breach of covenant shall be and take effect as a lease to continue for any longer term for which it could subsist, but determinable by a proviso for re-entry on such a breach.

(8)   This section does not extend—

(i)   To a covenant or condition against assigning, underletting, parting with the possession, or disposing of the land leased where the breach occurred before the commencement of this Act; or

(ii)   In the case of a mining lease, to a covenant or condition for allowing the lessor to have access to or inspect books, accounts, records, weighing machines or other things, or to enter or inspect the mine or the workings thereof.

(9)   This section does not apply to a condition for forfeiture on the bankruptcy of the lessee or on taking in execution of the lessee's interest if contained in a lease of—

(a)   Agricultural or pastoral land;

(b)   Mines or minerals;

(c)   A house used or intended to be used as a public-house or beershop;

(d)   A house let as a dwelling-house, with the use of any furniture, books, works of art, or other chattels not being in the nature of fixtures;

(e)   Any property with respect to which the personal qualifications of the tenant are of importance for the preservation of the value or character of the property, or on the ground of neighbourhood to the lessor, or to any person holding under him.

(10)   Where a condition of forfeiture on the bankruptcy of the lessee or on taking in execution of the lessee's interest is contained in any lease, other than a lease of any of the classes mentioned in the last sub-section, then—

(a)   if the lessee's interest is sold within one year from the bankruptcy or taking in execution, this section applies to the forfeiture condition aforesaid;

(b)   if the lessee's interest is not sold before the expiration of that year, this section only applies to the forfeiture condition aforesaid during the first year from the date of the bankruptcy or taking in execution.

(11)   This section does not, save as otherwise mentioned, affect the law relating to re-entry or forfeiture or relief in case of non-payment of rent.

(12)   This section has effect notwithstanding any stipulation to the contrary.

[(13)   The county court has jurisdiction under this section—[. . .].]

147 Relief against notice to effect decorative repairs

(1)   After a notice is served on a lessee relating to the internal decorative repairs to a house or other building, he may apply to the court for relief, and if, having regard to all the circumstances of the case (including in particular the length of the lessee's term or interest remaining unexpired), the court is satisfied that the notice is unreasonable, it may, by order, wholly or partially relieve the lessee from liability for such repairs.

(2)   This section does not apply: —

    (i)   where the liability arises under an express covenant or agreement to put the property in a decorative state of repair and the covenant or agreement has never been performed;

    (ii)   to any matter necessary or proper—

        (a)   for putting or keeping the property in a sanitary condition, or
        (b)   for the maintenance or preservation of the structure;

    (iii)   to any statutory liability to keep a house in all respects reasonably fit for human habitation;

    (iv)   to any covenant or stipulation to yield up the house or other building in a specified state of repair at the end of the term.

(3)   In this section "lease" includes an underlease and an agreement for a lease, and "lessee" has a corresponding meaning and includes any person liable to effect the repairs.

(4)   This section applies whether the notice is served before or after the commencement of this Act, and has effect notwithstanding any stipulation to the contrary.

[(5)   The county court has jurisdiction under this section [...].]

149 Abolition of interesse termini, and as to reversionary leases and leases for lives

(6)   Any lease or underlease, at a rent, or in consideration of a fine, for life or lives or for any term of years determinable with life or lives, or on the marriage of the lessee, [or on the formation of a civil partnership between the lessee and another person,] or any contract therefore, made before or after the commencement of this Act, or created by virtue of Part V of the Law of Property Act 1922, shall take effect as a lease, underlease or contract therefore, for a term of ninety years determinable [after (as the case may be) the death or marriage of, or the formation of a civil partnership by, the original lessee or the survivor of the original lessees,] by at least one month's notice in writing given to determine the same on one of the quarter days applicable to the tenancy, either by the lessor or the persons deriving title under him, to the person entitled to the leasehold interest, or if no such person is in existence by affixing the same to the premises, or by the lessee or other persons in whom the leasehold interest is vested to the lessor or the persons deriving title under him:

Provided that–

(a)   this subsection shall not apply to any term taking effect in equity under a settlement or created out of an equitable interest under a settlement for mortgage, indemnity, or other like purposes;

(b)   the person in whom the leasehold interest is vested by virtue of Part V of the Law of Property Act 1922 shall, for the purposes of this subsection, be deemed an original lessee;

(c)   if the lease, underlease, or contract therefor is made determinable on the dropping of the lives of persons other than or besides the lessees, then the notice shall be capable of being served after the death of any person or of the survivor of any persons (whether or not including the lessees) on the cesser of whose life or lives the lease, underlease, or contract is made determinable, instead of after the death of the original lessee or of the survivor of the original lessees;

(d)   if there are no quarter days specially applicable to the tenancy, notice may be given to determine the tenancy on one of the usual quarter days.

Part XI Miscellaneous Notices

196 Regulations respecting notices

(1)   Any notice required or authorised to be served or given by this Act shall be in writing.

(2)   Any notice required or authorised by this Act to be served on a lessee or mortgagor shall be sufficient, although only addressed to the lessee or mortgagor by that designation, without his name, or generally to the persons interested, without any name, and notwithstanding that any person to be affected by the notice is absent, under disability, unborn, or unascertained.

(3)   Any notice required or authorised by this Act to be served shall be sufficiently served if it is left at the last-known place of abode or business in the United Kingdom of the lessee, lessor, mortgagee, mortgagor, or other person to be served, or, in case of a notice required or authorised to be served on a lessee or mortgagor, is affixed or left for him on the land or any house or building comprised in the lease or mortgage, or, in case of a mining lease, is left for the lessee at the office or counting-house of the mine.

(4)   Any notice required or authorised by this Act to be served shall also be sufficiently served, if it is sent by post in a registered letter addressed to the lessee, lessor, mortgagee, mortgagor, or other person to be served, by name, at the aforesaid place of abode or business, office, or counting-house, and if that letter is not returned [by the postal operator (within the meaning of the Postal Services Act 2000) concerned] undelivered; and that service shall be deemed to be made at the time at which the registered letter would in the ordinary course be delivered.

(5)   The provisions of this section shall extend to notices required to be served by any instrument affecting property executed or coming into operation after the commencement of this Act unless a contrary intention appears.

(6)   This section does not apply to notices served in proceedings in the court.

198 Registration under the Land Charges Act, 1925, to be notice

(1)   The registration of any instrument or matter [in any register kept under the Land Charges Act 1972 or any local land charges register], shall be deemed to constitute actual notice of such instrument or matter, and of the fact of such registration, to all persons and for all purposes connected with the land affected, as from the date of registration or other prescribed date and so long as the registration continues in force.

(2)   This section operates without prejudice to the provisions of this Act respecting the making of further advances by a mortgagee, and applies only to instruments and matters required or authorised to be registered [in any such register].

199 Restrictions on constructive notice

(1)   A purchaser shall not be prejudicially affected by notice of—

(i)   any instrument or matter capable of registration under the provisions of the Land Charges Act, 1925, or any enactment which it replaces, which is void or not enforceable as against him under that Act or enactment, by reason of the non-registration thereof;

(ii)   any other instrument or matter or any fact or thing unless—

(a)   it is within his own knowledge, or would have come to his knowledge if such inquiries and inspections had been made as ought reasonably to have been made by him; or

(b)   in the same transaction with respect to which a question of notice to the purchaser arises, it has come to the knowledge of his counsel, as such, or of his solicitor or other agent, as such, or would have come to the knowledge of his solicitor or other agent, as such, if such inquiries and inspections had been made as ought reasonably to have been made by the solicitor or other agent.

(2)   Paragraph (ii) of the last subsection shall not exempt a purchaser from any liability under, or any obligation to perform or observe, any covenant, condition, provision, or restriction contained in any instrument under which his title is derived, mediately or immediately; and such liability or obligation may be enforced in the same manner and to the same extent as if that paragraph had not been enacted.

(3)   A purchaser shall not by reason of anything in this section be affected by notice in any case where he would not have been so affected if this section had not been enacted.

(4)   This section applies to purchases made either before or after the commencement of this Act.

Part XII Construction, Jurisdiction, and General Provisions

205 General definitions

(1)   In this Act unless the context otherwise requires, the following expressions have the meanings hereby assigned to them respectively, that is to say:—

(i)   "Bankruptcy" includes liquidation by arrangement; also in relation to a corporation means the winding up thereof;

(ii)   "Conveyance" includes a mortgage, charge, lease, assent, vesting declaration, vesting instrument, disclaimer, release and every other assurance of property or of an interest therein by any instrument, except a will; "convey" has a corresponding meaning; and "disposition" includes a conveyance and also a devise, bequest, or an appointment of property contained in a will; and "dispose of" has a corresponding meaning;

(iii)   "Building purposes" include the erecting and improving of, and the adding to, and the repairing of buildings; and a "building lease" is a lease for building purposes or purposes connected therewith;

[(iiiA) [...]]

(iv)   "Death duty" means estate duty [. . .] and every other duty leviable or payable on a death;

(v)   "Estate owner" means the owner of a legal estate, but an infant is not capable of being an estate owner;

(vi)   "Gazette" means the London Gazette;

(vii)   "Incumbrance" includes a legal or equitable mortgage and a trust for securing money, and a lien, and a charge of a portion, annuity, or other capital or annual sum; and "incumbrancer" has a meaning corresponding with that of incumbrance, and includes every person entitled to the benefit of an incumbrance, or to require payment or discharge thereof;

(viii) "Instrument" does not include a statute, unless the statute creates a settlement;

(ix)   "Land" includes land of any tenure, and mines and minerals, whether or not held apart from the surface, buildings or parts of buildings (whether the division is horizontal, vertical or made in any other way) and other corporeal hereditaments; also a manor, an advowson, and a rent and other incorporeal hereditaments, and an easement, right, privilege, or benefit in, over, or derived from land; [. . .] and "mines and minerals" include any strata or seam of minerals or substances in or under any land, and powers of working and getting the same, [. . .]; and "manor" includes a lordship, and reputed manor or lordship; and "hereditament" means any real property which on an intestacy occurring before the commencement of this Act might have devolved upon an heir;

(x)   "Legal estates" mean the estates, interests and charges, in or over land (subsisting or created at law) which are by this Act authorised to subsist or to be created as legal estates; "equitable interests" mean all the other interests and charges in or over land [. . .]; an equitable interest "capable of subsisting as a legal estate" means such as could validly subsist or be created as a legal estate under this Act;

(xi)   "Legal powers" include the powers vested in a chargee by way of legal mortgage or in an estate owner under which a legal estate can be transferred or created; and "equitable powers" mean all the powers in or over land under which equitable interests or powers only can be transferred or created;

(xii)   "Limitation Acts" mean the Real Property Limitation Acts, 1833, 1837 and 1874, and "limitation" includes a trust;

[(xiii) [...]]

(xiv)   A "mining lease" means a lease for mining purposes, that is, the searching for, winning, working, getting, making merchantable, carrying away, or disposing of mines and minerals, or purposes connected therewith, and includes a grant or licence for mining purposes;

(xv)   [...]

(xvi)   "Mortgage" includes any charge or lien on any property for securing money or money's worth; "legal mortgage" means a mortgage by demise or subdemise or a charge by way of legal mortgage and "legal mortgagee" has a corresponding meaning; "mortgage money" means money or money's worth secured by a mortgage; "mortgagor" includes any person from time to time deriving title under the original mortgagor or entitled to redeem a mortgage according to his estate interest or right in the mortgaged property; "mortgagee" includes a chargee by way of legal mortgage and any person from time to time deriving title under the original mortgagee; and "mortgagee in possession" is, for the purposes of this Act, a mortgagee who, in right of the mortgage, has entered into and is in possession of the mortgaged property; and "right of redemption" includes an option to repurchase only if the option in effect creates a right of redemption;

(xvii)   "Notice" includes constructive notice;

(xviii)   "Personal representative" means the executor, original or by representation, or administrator for the time being of a deceased person, and as regards any liability for the payment of death duties includes any person who takes possession of or intermeddles with the property of a deceased person without the authority of the personal representatives or the court;

(xix)   "Possession" includes receipt of rents and profits or the right to receive the same, if any; and "income" includes rents and profits;

(xx)   "Property" includes any thing in action, and any interest in real or personal property;

(xxi)   "Purchaser" means a purchaser in good faith for valuable consideration and includes a lessee, mortgagee or other person who for valuable consideration acquires an interest in property except that in Part I of this Act and elsewhere where so expressly provided "purchaser" only means a person who acquires an interest in or charge on property for money or money's worth; and in reference to a legal estate includes a chargee by way of legal mortgage; and where the context so requires "purchaser" includes an intending purchaser; "purchase" has a meaning corresponding with that of "purchaser"; and "valuable consideration" includes marriage [, and formation of a civil partnership,] but does not include a nominal consideration in money;

(xxii)   "Registered land" has the same meaning as in the [Land Registration Act 2002;][...]

(xxiii)   "Rent" includes a rent service or a rent charge, or other rent, toll, duty, royalty, or annual or periodical payment in money or money's worth, reserved or issuing out of or charged upon land, but does not include mortgage interest; "rent charge" includes a fee farm rent; "fine" includes a premium or foregift and any payment, consideration, or benefit in the nature of a fine, premium or foregift; "lessor" includes an underlessor and a person deriving title under a lessor or underlessor; and "lessee" includes an underlessee and a person deriving title under a lessee or underlessee, and "lease" includes an underlease or other tenancy;

(xxiv) "Sale" includes an extinguishment of manorial incidents, but in other respects means a sale properly so called;

(xxv) "Securities" include stocks, funds and shares;

(xxvi) "Tenant for life," "statutory owner," "settled land," "settlement," "vesting deed," "subsidiary vesting deed," "vesting order," "vesting instrument," "trust instrument," "capital money," and "trustees of the settlement" have the same meanings as in the Settled Land Act, 1925;

(xxvii) "Term of years absolute" means a term of years (taking effect either in possession or in reversion whether or not at a rent) with or without impeachment for waste, subject or not to another legal estate, and either certain or liable to determination by notice, re-entry, operation of law, or by a provision for cesser on redemption, or in any other event (other than the dropping of a life, or the determination of a determinable life interest); but does not include any term of years determinable with life or lives or with the cesser of a determinable life interest, nor, if created after the commencement of this Act, a term of years which is not expressed to take effect in possession within twenty-one years after the creation thereof where required by this Act to take effect within that period; and in this definition the expression "term of years" includes a term for less than a year, or for a year or years and a fraction of a year or from year to year;

(xxviii)"Trust Corporation" means the Public Trustee or a corporation either appointed by the court in any particular case to be a trustee or entitled by rules made under subsection (3) of section four of the Public Trustee Act, 1906, to act as custodian trustee;

(xxix) "Trust for sale," in relation to land, means an immediate [. . .] trust for sale, whether or not exercisable at the request or with the consent of any person [. . .]; "trustees for sale" mean the persons (including a personal representative) holding land on trust for sale; [. . .]

(xxx) "United Kingdom" means Great Britain and Northern Ireland;

(xxxi) "Will" includes codicil.

[(1A) Any reference in this Act to money being paid into court shall be construed as referring to the money being paid into the [Senior Courts] or any other court that has jurisdiction, and any reference in this Act to the court, in a context referring to the investment or application of money paid into court, shall be construed, in the case of money paid into the [Senior Courts], as referring to the High Court, and in the case of money paid into another court, as referring to that other court.]

(2) Where an equitable interest in or power over property arises by statute or operation of law, references to the creation of an interest or power include references to any interest or power so arising.

(3) References to registration under the Land Charges Act, 1925, apply to any registration made under any other statute which is by the Land Charges Act, 1925, to have effect as if the registration had been made under that Act.

LEASEHOLD PROPERTY (REPAIRS) ACT 1938

1938 chapter 34 1 and 2 Geo 6

An Act to amend the law as to the enforcement by landlords of obligations to repair and similar obligations arising under leases.

1 Restriction on enforcement of repairing covenants in long leases of small houses

(1) Where a lessor serves on a lessee under subsection (1) of section one hundred and forty-six of the Law of Property Act, 1925, a notice that relates to a breach of a covenant or agreement to keep or put in repair during the currency of the lease [all or any of the property comprised in the lease], and at the date of the service of the notice [three] years or more of the term of the lease remain unexpired, the lessee may within twenty-eight days from that date serve on the lessor a counter-notice to the effect that he claims the benefit of this Act.

(2) A right to damages for a breach of such a covenant as aforesaid shall not be enforceable by action commenced at any time at which [three] years or more of the term of the lease remain unexpired unless the lessor has served on the lessee not less than one month before the commencement of the action such a notice as is specified in subsection (1) of section one hundred and forty-six of the Law of Property Act, 1925, and where a notice is served under this subsection, the lessee may, within twenty-eight days from the date of the service thereof, serve on the lessor a counter-notice to the effect that he claims the benefit of this Act.

(3) Where a counter-notice is served by a lessee under this section, then, notwithstanding anything in any enactment or rule of law, no proceedings, by action or otherwise, shall be taken by the lessor for the enforcement of any right of re-entry or forfeiture under any proviso or stipulation in the lease for breach of the covenant or agreement in question, or for damages for breach thereof, otherwise than with the leave of the court.

(4) A notice served under subsection (1) of section one hundred and forty-six of the Law of Property Act, 1925, in the circumstances specified in subsection (1) of this section, and a notice served under subsection (2) of this section shall not be valid unless it contains a statement, in characters not less conspicuous than those used in any other part of the notice, to the effect that the lessee is entitled under this Act to serve on the lessor a counter-notice claiming the benefit of this Act, and a statement in the like characters specifying the time within which, and the manner in which, under this Act a counter-notice may be served and specifying the name and address for service of the lessor.

(5) Leave for the purposes of this section shall not be given unless the lessor proves—

    (a) that the immediate remedying of the breach in question is requisite for preventing substantial diminution in the value of his reversion, or that the value thereof has been substantially diminished by the breach;

    (b) that the immediate remedying of the breach is required for giving effect in relation to the [premises] to the purposes of any enactment, or of any byelaw or other provision having effect under an enactment, [or for giving effect to any order of a court or requirement of any authority under any enactment or any such byelaw or other provision as aforesaid];

(c)   in a case in which the lessee is not in occupation of the whole of the [premises as respects which the covenant or agreement is proposed to be enforced], that the immediate remedying of the breach is required in the interests of the occupier of [those premises] or of part thereof;

(d)   that the breach can be immediately remedied at an expense that is relatively small in comparison with the much greater expense that would probably be occasioned by postponement of the necessary work; or

(e)   special circumstances which in the opinion of the court, render it just and equitable that leave should be given.

(6)   The court may, in granting or in refusing leave for the purposes of this section, impose such terms and conditions on the lessor or on the lessee as it may think fit.

LIMITATION ACT 1980

1980 chapter 58

An Act to consolidate the Limitation Acts 1939 to 1980.

19 Time limit for actions to recover rent

(1)   No action shall be brought, *or distress made* [and the power conferred by section 72(1) of the Tribunals, Courts and Enforcement Act 2007 shall not be exercisable], to recover arrears of rent, or damages in respect of arrears of rent, after the expiration of six years from the date on which the arrears became due.

21 Time limit for actions in respect of trust property

(1)   No period of limitation prescribed by this Act shall apply to an action by a beneficiary under a trust, being an action—

(a)   in respect of any fraud or fraudulent breach of trust to which the trustee was a party or privy; or

(b)   to recover from the trustee trust property or the proceeds of trust property in the possession of the trustee, or previously received by the trustee and converted to his use.

(2)   Where a trustee who is also a beneficiary under the trust receives or retains trust property or its proceeds as his share on a distribution of trust property under the trust, his liability in any action brought by virtue of subsection (1)(b) above to recover that property or its proceeds after the expiration of the period of limitation prescribed by this Act for bringing an action to recover trust property shall be limited to the excess over his proper share.

This subsection only applies if the trustee acted honestly and reasonably in making the distribution

(3)   Subject to the preceding provisions of this section, an action by a beneficiary to recover trust property or in respect of any breach of trust, not being an action for which a period of limitation is prescribed by any other provision of this Act, shall not be brought after the expiration of six years from the date on which the right of action accrued.

For the purposes of this subsection, the right of action shall not be treated as having accrued to any beneficiary entitled to a future interest in the trust property until the interest fell into possession.

(4) No beneficiary as against whom there would be a good defence under this Act shall derive any greater or other benefit from a judgment or order obtained by any other beneficiary that he could have obtained if he had brought the action and this Act had been pleaded in defence.

22 Time limit for actions claiming personal estate of a deceased person

Subject to section 21(1) and (2) of this Act—

(a) no action in respect of any claim to the personal estate of a deceased person or to any share or interest in any such estate (whether under a will or on intestacy) shall be brought after the expiration of twelve years from the date on which the right to receive the share or interest accrued; and

(b) no action to recover arrears of interest in respect of any legacy, or damages in respect of such arrears, shall be brought after the expiration of six years from the date on which the interest became due.

Actions for an account

23 Time limit in respect of actions for an account

An action for an account shall not be brought after the expiration of any time limit under this Act which is applicable to the claim which is the basis of the duty to account.

Part II Extension or Exclusion of Ordinary Time Limits

Disability

28 Extension of limitation period in case of disability

(1) Subject to the following provisions of this section, if on the date when any right of action accrued for which a period of limitation is prescribed by this Act, the person to whom it accrued was under a disability, the action may be brought at any time before the expiration of six years from the date when he ceased to be under a disability or died (whichever first occurred) notwithstanding that the period of limitation has expired.

(2) This section shall not affect any case where the right of action first accrued to some person (not under a disability) through whom the person under a disability claims.

(3) When a right of action which has accrued to a person under a disability accrues, on the death of that person while still under a disability, to another person under a disability, no further extension of time shall be allowed by reason of the disability of the second person.

(4) No action to recover land or money charged on land shall be brought by virtue of this section by any person after the expiration of thirty years from the date on which the right of action accrued to that person or some person through whom he claims.

[(4A) If the action is one to which section 4A of this Act applies, subsection (1) above shall have effect—

    (a)   in the case of an action for libel or slander, as if for the words from "at any time" to "occurred)" there were substituted the words "by him at any time before the expiration of one year from the date on which he ceased to be under a disability"; and

    (b)   in the case of an action for slander of title, slander of goods or other malicious falsehood, as if for the words "six years" there were substituted the words "one year".]

Fraud, concealment and mistake

32 Postponement of limitation period in case of fraud, concealment or mistake

(1)   Subject to [subsection (3)][subsections (3) and (4A)] below, where in the case of any action for which a period of limitation is prescribed by this Act, either—

    (a)   the action is based upon the fraud of the defendant; or

    (b)   any fact relevant to the plaintiff's right of action has been deliberately concealed from him by the defendant; or

    (c)   the action is for relief from the consequences of a mistake;

the period of limitation shall not begin to run until the plaintiff has discovered the fraud, concealment or mistake (as the case may be) or could with reasonable diligence have discovered it.

References in this subsection to the defendant include references to the defendant's agent and to any person through whom the defendant claims and his agent.

(2)   For the purposes of subsection (1) above, deliberate commission of a breach of duty in circumstances in which it is unlikely to be discovered for some time amounts to deliberate concealment of the facts involved in that breach of duty.

(3)   Nothing in this section shall enable any action—

    (a)   to recover, or recover the value of, any property; or

    (b)   to enforce any charge against, or set aside any transaction affecting, any property;

to be brought against the purchaser of the property or any person claiming through him in any case where the property has been purchased for valuable consideration by an innocent third party since the fraud or concealment or (as the case may be) the transaction in which the mistake was made took place.

(4)   A purchaser is an innocent third party for the purposes of this section—

    (a)   in the case of fraud or concealment of any fact relevant to the plaintiff's right of action, if he was not a party to the fraud or (as the case may be) to the concealment of that fact and did not at the time of the purchase know or have reason to believe that the fraud or concealment had taken place; and

    (b)   in the case of mistake, if he did not at that time of the purchase know or have reason to believe that the mistake had been made.

[(4A) Subsection (1) above shall not apply in relation to the time limit prescribed by section 11A(3) of this Act or in relation to that time limit as applied by virtue of section 12(1) of this Act.]

[(5) Sections 14A and 14B of this Act shall not apply to any action to which subsection (1)(b) above applies (and accordingly the period of limitation referred to in that subsection, in any case to which either of those sections would otherwise apply, is the period applicable under section 2 of this Act).]

36 Equitable jurisdiction and remedies

(1) The following time limits under this Act, that is to say—

(a) the time limit under section 2 for actions founded on tort;

[(aa) the time limit under section 4A for actions for libel or slander, or for slander of title, slander of goods or other malicious falsehood;]

(b) the time limit under section 5 for actions founded on simple contract;

(c) the time limit under section 7 for actions to enforce awards where the submission is not by an instrument under seal;

(d) the time limit under section 8 for actions on a specialty;

(e) the time limit under section 9 for actions to recover a sum recoverable by virtue of any enactment; and

(f) the time limit under section 24 for actions to enforce a judgment;

shall not apply to any claim for specific performance of a contract or for an injunction or for other equitable relief, except in so far as any such time limit may be applied by the court by analogy in like manner as the corresponding time limit under any enactment repealed by the Limitation Act 1939 was applied before 1st July 1940.

(2) Nothing in this Act shall affect any equitable jurisdiction to refuse relief on the ground of acquiescence or otherwise.

MATRIMONIAL CAUSES ACT 1973

1973 chapter 18

An Act to consolidate certain enactments relating to matrimonial proceedings, maintenance agreements, and declarations of legitimacy, validity of marriage and British nationality, with amendments to give effect to recommendations of the Law Commission.

Part II Financial Relief for Parties to Marriage and Children of Family

Financial provision and property adjustment orders

21 Financial provision and property adjustment orders

(1) The financial provision orders for the purposes of this Act are the orders for periodical or lump sum provision available (subject to the provisions of this Act) under section 23 below for the

purpose of adjusting the financial position of the parties to a marriage and any children of the family in connection with proceedings for divorce, nullity of marriage or judicial separation and under section 27(6) below on proof of neglect by one party to a marriage to provide, or to make a proper contribution towards, reasonable maintenance for the other or a child of the family, that is to say—

(a)   any order for periodical payments in favour of a party to a marriage under section 23(1)(a) or 27(6)(a) or in favour of a child of the family under section 23(1)(d), (2) or (4) or 27(6)(d);

(b)   any order for secured periodical payments in favour of a party to a marriage under section 23(1)(b) or 27(6)(b) or in favour of a child of the family under section 23(1)(e), (2) or (4) or 27(6)(e); and

(c)   any order for lump sum provision in favour of a party to a marriage under section 23(1)(c) or 27(6)(c) or in favour of a child of the family under section 23(1)(f), (2) or (4) or 27(6)(f);

and references in this Act (except in paragraphs 17(1) and 23 of Schedule 1 below) to periodical payments orders, secured periodical payments orders, and orders for the payment of a lump sum are references to all or some of the financial provision orders requiring the sort of financial provision in question according as the context of each reference may require.

(2)   The property adjustment orders for the purposes of this Act are the orders dealing with property rights available (subject to the provisions of this Act) under section 24 below for the purpose of adjusting the financial position of the parties to a marriage and any children of the family on or after the grant of a decree of divorce, nullity of marriage or judicial separation, that is to say—

(a)   any order under subsection (1)(a) of that section for a transfer of property;

(b)   any order under subsection (1)(b) of that section for a settlement of property; and

(c)   any order under subsection (1)(c) or (d) of that section for a variation of settlement.

22 Maintenance pending suit

On a petition for divorce, nullity of marriage or judicial separation, the court may make an order for maintenance pending suit, that is to say, an order requiring either party to the marriage to make to the other such periodical payments for his or her maintenance and for such term, being a term beginning not earlier than the date of the presentation of the petition and ending with the date of the determination of the suit, as the court thinks reasonable.

23 Financial provision orders in connection with divorce proceedings, etc

(1)   On granting a decree of divorce, a decree of nullity of marriage or a decree of judicial separation or at any time thereafter (whether, in the case of a decree of divorce or of nullity of marriage, before or after the decree is made absolute), the court may make any one or more of the following orders, that is to say—

(a)   an order that either party to the marriage shall make to the other such periodical payments, for such term, as may be specified in the order;

(b)   an order that either party to the marriage shall secure to the other to the satisfaction of the court such periodical payments, for such term, as may be so specified;

(c)   an order that either party to the marriage shall pay to the other such lump sum or sums as may be so specified;

(d)   an order that a party to the marriage shall make to such person as may be specified in the order for the benefit of a child of the family, or to such a child, such periodical payments, for such term, as may be so specified;

(e)   an order that a party to the marriage shall secure to such person as may be so specified for the benefit of such a child, or to such a child, to the satisfaction of the court, such periodical payments, for such term, as may be so specified;

(f)   an order that a party to the marriage shall pay to such person as may be so specified for the benefit of such a child, or to such a child, such lump sum as may be so specified;

subject, however, in the case of an order under paragraph (d), (e) or (f) above, to the restrictions imposed by section 29(1) and (3) below on the making of financial provision orders in favour of children who have attained the age of eighteen.

(2)   The court may also, subject to those restrictions, make any one or more of the orders mentioned in subsection (1)(d), (e) and (f) above—

(a)   in any proceedings for divorce, nullity of marriage or judicial separation, before granting a decree; and

(b)   where any such proceedings are dismissed after the beginning of the trial, either forthwith or within a reasonable period after the dismissal.

(3)   Without prejudice to the generality of subsection (1)(c) or (f) above—

(a)   an order under this section that a party to a marriage shall pay a lump sum to the other party may be made for the purpose of enabling that other party to meet any liabilities or expenses reasonably incurred by him or her in maintaining himself or herself or any child of the family before making an application for an order under this section in his or her favour;

(b)   an order under this section for the payment of a lump sum to or for the benefit of a child of the family may be made for the purpose of enabling any liabilities or expenses reasonably incurred by or for the benefit of that child before the making of an application for an order under this section in his favour to be met; and

(c)   an order under this section for the payment of a lump sum may provide for the payment of that sum by instalments of such amount as may be specified in the order and may require the payment of the instalments to be secured to the satisfaction of the court.

(4)   The power of the court under subsection (1) or (2)(a) above to make an order in favour of a child of the family shall be exercisable from time to time; and where the court makes an order in favour of a child under subsection (2)(b) above, it may from time to time, subject to the restrictions mentioned in subsection (1) above, make a further order in his favour of any of the kinds mentioned in subsection (1)(d), (e)or (f) above.

(5) Without prejudice to the power to give a direction under section 30 below for the settlement of an instrument by conveyancing counsel, where an order is made under subsection (1)(a), (b) or (c) above on or after granting a decree of divorce or nullity of marriage, neither the order nor any settlement made in pursuance of the order shall take effect unless the decree has been made absolute.

[[6) Where the court—

(a) makes an order under this section for the payment of a lump sum; and

(b) directs—

(i) that payment of that sum or any part of it shall be deferred; or
(ii) that that sum or any part of it shall be paid by instalments,

the court may order that the amount deferred or the instalments shall carry interest at such rate as may be specified by the order from such date, not earlier than the date of the order, as may be so specified, until the date when payment of it is due.]

24 Property adjustment orders in connection with divorce proceedings, etc

(1) On granting a decree of divorce, a decree of nullity of marriage or a decree of judicial separation or at any time thereafter (whether, in the case of a decree of divorce or of nullity of marriage, before or after the decree is made absolute), the court may make any one or more of the following orders, that is to say—

(a) an order that a party to the marriage shall transfer to the other party, to any child of the family or to such person as may be specified in the order for the benefit of such a child such property as may be so specified, being property to which the first-mentioned party is entitled, either in possession or reversion;

(b) an order that a settlement of such property as may be so specified, being property to which a party to the marriage is so entitled, be made to the satisfaction of the court for the benefit of the other party to the marriage and of the children of the family or either or any of them;

(c) an order varying for the benefit of the parties to the marriage and of the children of the family or either or any of them any ante-nuptial or post-nuptial settlement (including such a settlement made by will or codicil) made on the parties to the marriage [,other than one in the form of a pension arrangement (within the meaning of section 25D below)];

(d) an order extinguishing or reducing the interest of either of the parties to the marriage under any such settlement [, other than one in the form of a pension arrangement (within the meaning of section 25D below)];

subject, however, in the case of an order under paragraph (a) above, to the restrictions imposed by section 29(1) and (3) below on the making of orders for a transfer of property in favour of children who have attained the age of eighteen.

(2) The court may make an order under subsection (1)(c) above notwithstanding that there are no children of the family.

(3)   Without prejudice to the power to give a direction under section 30 below for the settlement of an instrument by conveyancing counsel, where an order is made under this section on or after granting a decree of divorce or nullity of marriage, neither the order nor any settlement made in pursuance of the order shall take effect unless the decree has been made absolute.

[25 Matters to which court is to have regard in deciding how to exercise its powers under ss. 23, 24 and 24A

(1)   It shall be the duty of the court in deciding whether to exercise its powers under section 23, 24 [, 24A or 24B] above and, if so, in what manner, to have regard to all the circumstances of the case, first consideration being given to the welfare while a minor of any child of the family who has not attained the age of eighteen.

(2)   As regards the exercise of the powers of the court under section 23(1)(a), (b) or (c), 24 [, 24A or 24B] above in relation to a party to the marriage, the court shall in particular have regard to the following matters—

(a)   the income, earning capacity, property and other financial resources which each of the parties to the marriage has or is likely to have in the foreseeable future, including in the case of earning capacity any increase in that capacity which it would in the opinion of the court be reasonable to expect a party to the marriage to take steps to acquire;

(b)   the financial needs, obligations and responsibilities which each of the parties to the marriage has or is likely to have in the foreseeable future;

(c)   the standard of living enjoyed by the family before the breakdown of the marriage;

(d)   the age of each party to the marriage and the duration of the marriage;

(e)   any physical or mental disability of either of the parties to the marriage;

(f)   the contributions which each of the parties has made or is likely in the foreseeable future to make to the welfare of the family, including any contribution by looking after the home or caring for the family;

(g)   the conduct of each of the parties, if that conduct is such that it would in the opinion of the court be inequitable to disregard it;

(h)   in the case of proceedings for divorce or nullity of marriage, the value to each of the parties to the marriage of any benefit ... which, by reason of the dissolution or annulment of the marriage, that party will lose the chance of acquiring.

(3)   As regards the exercise of the powers of the court under section 23(1)(d), (e) or (f), (2) or (4), 24 or 24A above in relation to a child of the family, the court shall in particular have regard to the following matters—

(a)   the financial needs of the child;

(b)   the income, earning capacity (if any), property and other financial resources of the child;

(c)   any physical or mental disability of the child;

(d)   the manner in which he was being and in which the parties to the marriage expected him to be educated or trained;

(e)   the considerations mentioned in relation to the parties to the marriage in paragraphs (*a*), (*b*), (*c*) and (*e*) of subsection (2) above.

(4)   As regards the exercise of the powers of the court under section 23(1)(*d*), (*e*) or (*f*), (2) or (4), 24 or 24A above against a party to a marriage in favour of a child of the family who is not the child of that party, the court shall also have regard—

(a)   to whether that party assumed any responsibility for the child's maintenance, and, if so, to the extent to which, and the basis upon which, that party assumed such responsibility and to the length of time for which that party discharged such responsibility;

(b)   to whether in assuming and discharging such responsibility that party did so knowing that the child was not his or her own;

(c)   to the liability of any other person to maintain the child.]

26 Commencement of proceedings for ancillary relief, etc

(1)   Where a petition for divorce, nullity of marriage or judicial separation has been presented, then, subject to subsection (2) below, proceedings for maintenance pending suit under section 22 above, for a financial provision order under section 23 above, or for a property adjustment order may be begun, subject to and in accordance with rules of court, at any time after the presentation of the petition.

(2)   Rules of court may provide, in such cases as may be prescribed by the rules—

(a)   that applications for any such relief as is mentioned in subsection (1) above shall be made in the petition or answer; and

(b)   that applications for any such relief which are not so made, or are not made until after the expiration of such period following the presentation of the petition or filing of the answer as may be so prescribed, shall be made only with the leave of the court.

MATRIMONIAL PROCEEDINGS AND PROPERTY ACT 1970

An Act to make fresh provision for empowering the court in matrimonial proceedings to make orders ordering either spouse to make financial provision for, or transfer property to, the other spouse or a child of the family, orders for the variation of ante-nuptial and post-nuptial settlements, orders for the custody and education of children and orders varying, discharging or suspending orders made in such proceedings; to make other amendments of the law relating to matrimonial proceedings; to abolish the right to claim restitution of conjugal rights; to declare what interest in property is acquired by a spouse who contributes to its improvement; to make provision as to a spouse's rights of occupation under section 1 of the Matrimonial Homes Act 1967 in certain cases; to extend section 17 of the Married Women's Property Act 1882 and section 7 of the Matrimonial Causes (Property and Maintenance) Act 1958; to amend the law about the property of a person whose marriage is the subject of a decree of judicial separation dying intestate; to abolish the agency of necessity of a wife; and for purposes connected with the matters aforesaid.

Provisions relating to property of married persons

37 Contributions by spouse in money or money's worth to the improvement of property

It is hereby declared that where a husband or wife contributes in money or money's worth to the improvement of real or personal property in which or in the proceeds of sale of which either or both of them has or have a beneficial interest, the husband or wife so contributing shall, if the contribution is of a substantial nature and subject to any agreement between them to the contrary express or implied, be treated as having then acquired by virtue of his or her contribution a share or an enlarged share, as the case may be, in that beneficial interest of such an extent as may have been then agreed or, in default of such agreement, as may seem in all the circumstances just to any court before which the question of the existence or extent of the beneficial interest of the husband or wife arises (whether in proceedings between them or in any other proceedings).

PERPETUITIES AND ACCUMULATIONS ACT 1964

1964 chapter 55

An Act to modify the law of England and Wales relating to the avoidance of future interests in property on grounds of remoteness and governing accumulations of income from property.

Perpetuities

1 Power to specify perpetuity period

(1)   Subject to section 9(2) of this Act and subsection (2) below, where the instrument by which any disposition is made so provides, the perpetuity period applicable to the disposition under the rule against perpetuities, instead of being of any other duration, shall be of a duration equal to such number of years not exceeding eighty as is specified in that behalf in the instrument.

(2)   Subsection (1) above shall not have effect where the disposition is made in exercise of a special power of appointment, but where a period is specified under that subsection in the instrument creating such a power the period shall apply in relation to any disposition under the power as it applies in relation to the power itself.

3 Uncertainty as to remoteness

(1)   Where, apart from the provisions of this section and sections 4 and 5 of this Act, a disposition would be void on the ground that the interest disposed of might not become vested until too remote a time, the disposition shall be treated, until such time (if any) as it becomes established that the vesting must occur, if at all, after the end of the perpetuity period, as if the disposition were not subject to the rule against perpetuities; and its becoming so established shall not affect the validity of anything previously done in relation to the interest disposed of by way of advancement, application of intermediate income or otherwise.

(2)   Where, apart from the said provisions, a disposition consisting of the conferring of a general power of appointment would be void on the ground that the power might not become exercisable until too remote a time, the disposition shall be treated, until such time (if any) as it becomes established that the power will not be exercisable within the perpetuity period, as if the disposition were not subject to the rule against perpetuities.

(3)   Where, apart from the said provisions, a disposition consisting of the conferring of any power, option or other right would be void on the ground that the right might be exercised at too remote a time, the disposition shall be treated as regards any exercise of the right within the perpetuity period as if it were not subject to the rule against perpetuities and, subject to the said provisions, shall be treated as void for remoteness only if, and so far as, the right is not fully exercised within that period.

(4)   Where this section applies to a disposition and the duration of the perpetuity period is not determined by virtue of section 1 or 9(2) of this Act, it shall be determined as follows:—

(a)   where any persons falling within subsection (5) below are individuals in being and ascertainable at the commencement of the perpetuity period the duration of the period shall be determined by reference to their lives and no others, but so that the lives of any description of persons falling within paragraph (b) or (c) of that subsection shall be disregarded if the number of persons of that description is such as to render it impracticable to ascertain the date of death of the survivor;

(b)   where there are no lives under paragraph (a) above the period shall be twenty-one years.

(5)   The said persons are as follows:—

(a)   the person by whom the disposition was made;

(b)   a person to whom or in whose favour the disposition was made, that is to say—

(i)   in the case of a disposition to a class of persons, any member or potential member of the class;

(ii)   in the case of an individual disposition to a person taking only on certain conditions being satisfied, any person as to whom some of the conditions are satisfied and the remainder may in time be satisfied;

(iii)   in the case of a special power of appointment exercisable in favour of members of a class, any member or potential member of the class;

(iv)   in the case of a special power of appointment exercisable in favour of one person only, that person or, where the object of the power is ascertainable only on certain conditions being satisfied, any person as to whom some of the conditions are satisfied and the remainder may in time be satisfied;

(v)   in the case of any power, option or other right, the person on whom the right is conferred;

(c)   a person having a child or grandchild within sub-paragraphs (i) to (iv) of paragraph (b) above, or any of whose children or grandchildren, if subsequently born, would by virtue of his or her descent fall within those sub-paragraphs;

(d)   any person on the failure or determination of whose prior interest the disposition is limited to take effect.

4 Reduction of age and exclusion of class members to avoid remoteness

(1) Where a disposition is limited by reference to the attainment by any person or persons of a specified age exceeding twenty-one years, and it is apparent at the time the disposition is made or becomes apparent at a subsequent time—

    (a) that the disposition would, apart from this section, be void for remoteness, but

    (b) that it would not be so void if the specified age had been twenty-one years,

    the disposition shall be treated for all purposes as if, instead of being limited by reference to the age in fact specified, it had been limited by reference to the age nearest to that age which would, if specified instead, have prevented the disposition from being so void.

(2) Where in the case of any disposition different ages exceeding twenty-one years are specified in relation to different persons—

    (a) the reference in paragraph (b) of subsection (1) above to the specified age shall be construed as a reference to all the specified ages, and

    (b) that subsection shall operate to reduce each such age so far as is necessary to save the disposition from being void for remoteness.

(3) Where the inclusion of any persons, being potential members of a class or unborn persons who at birth would become members or potential members of the class, prevents the foregoing provisions of this section from operating to save a disposition from being void for remoteness, those persons shall thenceforth be deemed for all the purposes of the disposition to be excluded from the class, and the said provisions shall thereupon have effect accordingly.

(4) Where, in the case of a disposition to which subsection (3) above does not apply, it is apparent at the time the disposition is made or becomes apparent at a subsequent time that, apart from this subsection, the inclusion of any persons, being potential members of a class or unborn persons who at birth would become members or potential members of the class, would cause the disposition to be treated as void for remoteness, those persons shall, unless their exclusion would exhaust the class, thenceforth be deemed for all the purposes of the disposition to be excluded from the class.

(5) Where this section has effect in relation to a disposition to which section 3 above applies, the operation of this section shall not affect the validity of anything previously done in relation to the interest disposed of by way of advancement, application of intermediate income or otherwise.

(6) ...

[(7) For the avoidance of doubt it is hereby declared that a question arising under section 3 of this Act or subsection 1(a) above of whether a disposition would be void apart from this section is to be determined as if subsection (6) above had been a separate section of this Act.]

Supplemental

15 Short title, interpretation and extent

(1)   This Act may be cited as the Perpetuities and Accumulations Act 1964.

(2)   In this Act—

"disposition" includes the conferring of a power of appointment and any other disposition of an interest in or right over property, and references to the interest disposed of shall be construed accordingly;

"in being" means living or en ventre sa mere;

"power of appointment" includes any discretionary power to transfer a beneficial interest in property without the furnishing of valuable consideration;

"will" includes a codicil;

and for the purposes of this Act a disposition contained in a will shall be deemed to be made at the death of the testator.

(3)   For the purposes of this Act a person shall be treated as a member of a class if in his case all the conditions identifying a member of the class are satisfied, and shall be treated as a potential member if in his case some only of those conditions are satisfied but there is a possibility that the remainder will in time be satisfied.

(4)   Nothing in this Act shall affect the operation of the rule of law rendering void for remoteness certain dispositions under which property is limited to be applied for purposes other than the benefit of any person or class of persons in cases where the property may be so applied after the end of the perpetuity period.

(5)   The foregoing sections of this Act shall apply (except as provided in section 8(2) above) only in relation to instruments taking effect after the commencement of this Act, and in the case of an instrument made in the exercise of a special power of appointment shall apply only where the instrument creating the power takes effect after that commencement:

Provided that section 7 above shall apply in all cases for construing the foregoing reference to a special power of appointment.

(6)   This Act shall apply in relation to a disposition made otherwise than by an instrument as if the disposition had been contained in an instrument taking effect when the disposition was made.

(7)   This Act binds the Crown.

(8)   ...

PERPETUITIES AND ACCUMULATIONS ACT 2009

2009 chapter 18

An Act to amend the law relating to the avoidance of future interests on grounds of remoteness and the law relating to accumulations of income.

Application of rule against perpetuities

1 Application of the rule

(1)   The rule against perpetuities applies (and applies only) as provided by this section.

(2)   If an instrument limits property in trust so as to create successive estates or interests the rule applies to each of the estates or interests.

(3)   If an instrument limits property in trust so as to create an estate or interest which is subject to a condition precedent and which is not one of successive estates or interests, the rule applies to the estate or interest.

(4)   If an instrument limits property in trust so as to create an estate or interest subject to a condition subsequent the rule applies to—

   (a)   any right of re-entry exercisable if the condition is broken, or

   (b)   any equivalent right exercisable in the case of property other than land if the condition is broken.

(5)   If an instrument which is a will limits personal property so as to create successive interests under the doctrine of executory bequests, the rule applies to each of the interests.

(6)   If an instrument creates a power of appointment the rule applies to the power.

(7)   For the purposes of subsection (2) an estate or interest includes an estate or interest—

   (a)   which arises under a right of reverter on the determination of a determinable fee simple, or

   (b)   which arises under a resulting trust on the determination of a determinable interest.

(8)   This section has effect subject to the exceptions made by section 2 and to any exceptions made under section 3.

(9)   In section 4(3) of the Law of Property Act 1925 (c. 20) (rights of entry affecting a legal estate) omit the words from "but" to the end.

2 Exceptions to rule's application

(1)   This section contains exceptions to the application of the rule against perpetuities.

(2)   The rule does not apply to an estate or interest created so as to vest in a charity on the occurrence of an event if immediately before the occurrence an estate or interest in the property concerned is vested in another charity.

(3)   The rule does not apply to a right exercisable by a charity on the occurrence of an event if immediately before the occurrence an estate or interest in the property concerned is vested in another charity.

(4)   The rule does not apply to an interest or right arising under a relevant pension scheme.

(5)   The exception in subsection (4) does not apply if the interest or right arises under—

   (a)   an instrument nominating benefits under the scheme, or

   (b)   an instrument made in the exercise of a power of advancement arising under the scheme.

Perpetuity period

5 Perpetuity period

(1) The perpetuity period is 125 years (and no other period).

(2) Subsection (1) applies whether or not the instrument referred to in section 1(2) to (6) specifies a perpetuity period; and a specification of a perpetuity period in that instrument is ineffective.

Perpetuities: miscellaneous

7 Wait and see rule

(1) Subsection (2) applies if (apart from this section and section 8) an estate or interest would be void on the ground that it might not become vested until too remote a time.

(2) In such a case—

(a) until such time (if any) as it becomes established that the vesting must occur (if at all) after the end of the perpetuity period the estate or interest must be treated as if it were not subject to the rule against perpetuities, and

(b) if it becomes so established, that does not affect the validity of anything previously done (whether by way of advancement, application of intermediate income or otherwise) in relation to the estate or interest.

(3) Subsection (4) applies if (apart from this section) any of the following would be void on the ground that it might be exercised at too remote a time—

(a) a right of re-entry exercisable if a condition subsequent is broken;

(b) an equivalent right exercisable in the case of property other than land if a condition subsequent is broken;

(c) a special power of appointment.

(4) In such a case—

(a) the right or power must be treated as regards any exercise of it within the perpetuity period as if it were not subject to the rule against perpetuities, and

(b) the right or power must be treated as void for remoteness only if and so far as it is not fully exercised within the perpetuity period.

(5) Subsection (6) applies if (apart from this section) a general power of appointment would be void on the ground that it might not become exercisable until too remote a time.

(6) Until such time (if any) as it becomes established that the power will not be exercisable within the perpetuity period, it must be treated as if it were not subject to the rule against perpetuities.

8 Exclusion of class members to avoid remoteness

(1)   This section applies if—

    (a)   it is apparent at the time an instrument takes effect or becomes apparent at a later time that (apart from this section) the inclusion of certain persons as members of a class would cause an estate or interest to be treated as void for remoteness, and

    (b)   those persons are potential members of the class or unborn persons who at birth would become members or potential members of the class.

(2)   From the time it is or becomes so apparent those persons must be treated for all the purposes of the instrument as excluded from the class unless their exclusion would exhaust the class.

(3)   If this section applies in relation to an estate or interest to which section 7 applies, this section does not affect the validity of anything previously done (whether by way of advancement, application of intermediate income or otherwise) in relation to the estate or interest.

(4)   For the purposes of this section—

    (a)   a person is a member of a class if in that person's case all the conditions identifying a member of the class are satisfied, and

    (b)   a person is a potential member of a class if in that person's case some only of those conditions are satisfied but there is a possibility that the remainder will in time be satisfied.

12 Pre-commencement instruments: period difficult to ascertain

(1)   If—

    (a)   an instrument specifies for the purposes of property limited in trust a perpetuity period by reference to the lives of persons in being when the instrument takes effect,

    (b)   the trustees believe that it is difficult or not reasonably practicable for them to ascertain whether the lives have ended and therefore whether the perpetuity period has ended, and

    (c)   they execute a deed stating that they so believe and that subsection (2) is to apply to the instrument,

that subsection applies to the instrument.

(2)   If this subsection applies to an instrument—

    (a)   the instrument has effect as if it specified a perpetuity period of 100 years (and no other period);

    (b)   the rule against perpetuities has effect as if the only perpetuity period applicable to the instrument were 100 years;

    (c)   sections 6 to 11 of this Act are to be treated as if they applied (and always applied) in relation to the instrument;

    (d)   sections 1 to 12 of the Perpetuities and Accumulations Act 1964 (c. 55) are to be treated as if they did not apply (and never applied) in relation to the instrument.

(3)   A deed executed under this section cannot be revoked.

Application of statutory provisions

15 Application of this Act

(1)   Sections 1, 2, 4 to 11, 13 and 14 apply in relation to an instrument taking effect on or after the commencement day, except that—

    (a)   those sections do not apply in relation to a will executed before that day, and

    (b)   those sections apply in relation to an instrument made in the exercise of a special power of appointment only if the instrument creating the power takes effect on or after that day.

(2)   Section 12 applies (except as provided by subsection (3)) in relation to—

    (a)   a will executed before the commencement day (whether or not it takes effect before that day);

    (b)   an instrument, other than a will, taking effect before that day.

(3)   Section 12 does not apply if—

    (a)   the terms of the trust were exhausted before the commencement day, or

    (b)   before that day the property became held on trust for charitable purposes by way of a final disposition of the property.

(4)   The commencement day is the day appointed under section 22(2).

16 Limitation of 1964 Act to existing instruments

In section 15 of the Perpetuities and Accumulations Act 1964 (c. 55) the following subsections are inserted after subsection (5) (which makes provision as to the instruments to which the Act applies)—

"(5A) The foregoing sections of this Act shall not apply in relation to an instrument taking effect on or after the day appointed under section 22(2) of the Perpetuities and Accumulations Act 2009 (commencement), but this shall not prevent those sections applying in relation to an instrument so taking effect if—

    (a)   it is a will executed before that day, or

    (b)   it is an instrument made in the exercise of a special power of appointment, and the instrument creating the power took effect before that day.

(5B)   Subsection (5A) above shall not affect the operation of sections 4(6) and 11(2) above."

General

18 Rule as to duration not affected

This Act does not affect the rule of law which limits the duration of non-charitable purpose trusts.

PROTECTION FROM EVICTION ACT 1977

1977 chapter 43

An Act to consolidate section 16 of the Rent Act 1957 and Part III of the Rent Act 1965, and related enactments.

1 Unlawful eviction and harassment of occupier

(1)   In this section "residential occupier", in relation to any premises, means a person occupying the premises as a residence, whether under a contract or by virtue of any enactment or rule of law giving him the right to remain in occupation or restricting the right of any other person to recover possession of the premises.

(2)   If any person unlawfully deprives the residential occupier of any premises of his occupation of the premises or any part thereof, or attempts to do so, he shall be guilty of an offence unless he proves that he believed, and had reasonable cause to believe, that the residential occupier had ceased to reside in the premises.

(3)   If any person with intent to cause the residential occupier of any premises—

    (a)   to give up the occupation of the premises or any part thereof; or

    (b)   to refrain from exercising any right or pursuing any remedy in respect of the premises or part thereof;

does acts [likely] to interfere with the peace or comfort of the residential occupier or members of his household, or persistently withdraws or withholds services reasonably required for the occupation of the premises as a residence, he shall be guilty of an offence.

[(3A) Subject to subsection (3B) below, the landlord of a residential occupier or an agent of the landlord shall be guilty of an offence if—

    (a)   he does acts likely to interfere with the peace or comfort of the residential occupier or members of his household, or

    (b)   he persistently withdraws or withholds services reasonably required for the occupation of the premises in question as a residence,

and (in either case) he knows, or has reasonable cause to believe, that the conduct is likely to cause the residential occupier to give up the occupation of the whole or part of the premises or to refrain from exercising any right or pursuing any remedy in respect of the whole or any part of the premises.

(3B)   A person shall not be guilty of an offence under subsection (3A) above if he proves that he had reasonable grounds for doing the acts or withdrawing or withholding the services in question.

(3C)   In subsection (3A) above "landlord", in relation to a residential occupier of any premises, means the person who, but for—

    (a)   the residential occupier's right to remain in occupation of the premises, or

(b)   a restriction on the person's right to recover possession of the premises, would be entitled to occupation of the premises and any superior landlord under whom that person derives title.]

2 Restriction on re-entry without due process of law

Where any premises are let as a dwelling on a lease which is subject to a right of re-entry or forfeiture it shall not be lawful to enforce that right otherwise than by proceedings in the court while any person is lawfully residing in the premises or part of them.

5 Validity of notices to quit

(1)   [Subject to subsection (1B) below] no notice by a landlord or a tenant to quit any premises let (whether before or after the commencement of this Act) as a dwelling shall be valid unless—

(a)   it is in writing and contains such information as may be prescribed, and

(b)   it is given not less than 4 weeks before the date on which it is to take effect.

[(1A)   Subject to subsection (1B) below, no notice by a licensor or licensee to determine a periodic licence to occupy premises as a dwelling (whether the licence was granted before or after the passing of this Act) shall be valid unless—

(a)   it is in writing and contains such information as may be prescribed, and

(b)   it is given not less than 4 weeks before the date on which it is to take effect.

(1B)   Nothing in subsection (1) or subsection (1A) above applies to –

(a)   premises let on an excluded tenancy which is entered into on or after the date on which the Housing Act 1988 came into force unless it is entered into pursuant to a contract made before that date; or

(b)   premises occupied under an excluded licence.

TRADE UNION AND LABOUR RELATIONS (CONSOLIDATION) ACT 1992

1992 chapter 52

An Act to consolidate the enactments relating to collective labour relations, that is to say, to trade unions, employers' associations, industrial relations and industrial action.

No compulsion to work

236 No compulsion to work

No court shall, whether by way of—

(a)   an order for specific performance or specific implement of a contract of employment, or

(b)   an injunction or interdict restraining a breach or threatened breach of such a contract, compel an employee to do any work or attend at any place for the doing of any work.

TREASURE ACT 1996

1996 chapter 24

An Act to abolish treasure trove and to make fresh provision in relation to treasure.

Meaning of "treasure"

1 Meaning of "treasure"

(1)   Treasure is—

    (a)   any object at least 300 years old when found which—

        (i)   is not a coin but has metallic content of which at least 10 per cent by weight is precious metal;

        (ii)   when found, is one of at least two coins in the same find which are at least 300 years old at that time and have that percentage of precious metal; or

        (iii)   when found, is one of at least ten coins in the same find which are at least 300 years old at that time;

    (b)   any object at least 200 years old when found which belongs to a class designated under section 2(1);

    (c)   any object which would have been treasure trove if found before the commencement of section 4;

    (d)   any object which, when found, is part of the same find as—

        (i)   an object within paragraph (a), (b) or (c) found at the same time or earlier; or

        (ii)   an object found earlier which would be within paragraph (a) or (b) if it had been found at the same time.

(2)   Treasure does not include objects which are—

    (a)   unworked natural objects, or

    (b)   minerals as extracted from a natural deposit,

or which belong to a class designated under section 2(2).

2 Power to alter meaning

(1)   The Secretary of State may by order, for the purposes of section 1(1)(b), designate any class of object which he considers to be of outstanding historical, archaeological or cultural importance.

(2)   The Secretary of State may by order, for the purposes of section 1(2), designate any class of object which (apart from the order) would be treasure.

(3) – (4)...

3 Supplementary

(1)   This section supplements section 1.

(2)   "Coin" includes any metal token which was, or can reasonably be assumed to have been, used or intended for use as or instead of money.

(3)   "Precious metal" means gold or silver.

(4)   When an object is found, it is part of the same find as another object if—

(a)   they are found together,

(b)   the other object was found earlier in the same place where they had been left together,

(c)   the other object was found earlier in a different place, but they had been left together and had become separated before being found.

(5)   If the circumstances in which objects are found can reasonably be taken to indicate that they were together at some time before being found, the objects are to be presumed to have been left together, unless shown not to have been.

(6)   An object which can reasonably be taken to be at least a particular age is to be presumed to be at least that age, unless shown not to be.

(7)   An object is not treasure if it is wreck within the meaning of Part IX of the Merchant Shipping Act 1995.

Ownership of treasure

4 Ownership of treasure which is found

(1)   When treasure is found, it vests, subject to prior interests and rights—

(a)   in the franchisee, if there is one;

(b)   otherwise, in the Crown.

(2)   Prior interests and rights are any which, or which derive from any which—

(a)   were held when the treasure was left where it was found, or

(b)   if the treasure had been moved before being found, were held when it was left where it was before being moved.

(3)   If the treasure would have been treasure trove if found before the commencement of this section, neither the Crown nor any franchisee has any interest in it or right over it except in accordance with this Act.

(4)   This section applies—

(a)   whatever the nature of the place where the treasure was found, and

(b)   whatever the circumstances in which it was left (including being lost or being left with no intention of recovery).

5 Meaning of "franchisee"

(1)   The franchisee for any treasure is the person who—

    (a)   was, immediately before the commencement of section 4, or

    (b)   apart from this Act, as successor in title, would have been, the franchisee of the Crown in right of treasure trove for the place where the treasure was found.

(2)   It is as franchisees in right of treasure trove that Her Majesty and the Duke of Cornwall are to be treated as having enjoyed the rights to treasure trove which belonged respectively to the Duchy of Lancaster and the Duchy of Cornwall immediately before the commencement of section 4.

6 Treasure vesting in the Crown

(1)   Treasure vesting in the Crown under this Act is to be treated as part of the hereditary revenues of the Crown to which section 1 of the Civil List Act 1952 applies (surrender of hereditary revenues to the Exchequer).

(2)   Any such treasure may be transferred, or otherwise disposed of, in accordance with directions given by the Secretary of State.

(3)   The Crown's title to any such treasure may be disclaimed at any time by the Secretary of State.

(4)   ...

Coroners' jurisdiction

7 Jurisdiction of coroners

(1)   The jurisdiction of coroners which is referred to in section 30 of the Coroners Act 1988 (treasure) is exercisable in relation to anything which is treasure for the purposes of this Act.

(2)   That jurisdiction is not exercisable for the purposes of the law relating to treasure trove in relation to anything found after the commencement of section 4.

(3)   The Act of 1988 and anything saved by virtue of section 36(5) of that Act (saving for existing law and practice etc.) has effect subject to this section.

(4)   An inquest held by virtue of this section is to be held without a jury, unless the coroner orders otherwise.

8 Duty of finder to notify coroner

(1)   A person who finds an object which he believes or has reasonable grounds for believing is treasure must notify the coroner for the district in which the object was found before the end of the notice period.

(2)   The notice period is fourteen days beginning with—

    (a)   the day after the find; or

    (b)   if later, the day on which the finder first believes or has reason to believe the object is treasure.

(3) Any person who fails to comply with subsection (1) is guilty of an offence and liable on summary conviction to—

    (a)   imprisonment for a term not exceeding three months;

    (b)   a fine of an amount not exceeding level 5 on the standard scale; or

    (c)   both.

(4) In proceedings for an offence under this section, it is a defence for the defendant to show that he had, and has continued to have, a reasonable excuse for failing to notify the coroner.

(5) If the office of coroner for a district is vacant, the person acting as coroner for that district is the coroner for the purposes of subsection (1).

9 Procedure for inquests

(1) In this section, "inquest" means an inquest held under section 7.

(2) A coroner proposing to conduct an inquest must notify—

    (a)   the British Museum, if his district is in England; or

    (b)   the National Museum of Wales, if it is in Wales.

(3) Before conducting the inquest, the coroner must take reasonable steps to notify—

    (a)   any person who it appears to him may have found the treasure; and

    (b)   any person who, at the time the treasure was found, occupied land which it appears to him may be where it was found.

(4) During the inquest the coroner must take reasonable steps to notify any such person not already notified.

(5) Before or during the inquest, the coroner must take reasonable steps—

    (a)   to obtain from any person notified under subsection (3) or (4) the names and addresses of interested persons; and

    (b)   to notify any interested person whose name and address he obtains.

(6) The coroner must take reasonable steps to give any interested person notified under subsection (3), (4) or (5) an opportunity to examine witnesses at the inquest.

(7) In subsections (5) and (6), "interested person" means a person who appears to the coroner to be likely to be concerned with the inquest—

    (a)   as the finder of the treasure or otherwise involved in the find;

    (b)   as the occupier, at the time the treasure was found, of the land where it was found, or

    (c)   as having had an interest in that land at that time or since.

Rewards, codes of practice and report

10 Rewards

(1) This section applies if treasure—

    (a) has vested in the Crown under section 4; and

    (b) is to be transferred to a museum.

(2) The Secretary of State must determine whether a reward is to be paid by the museum before the transfer.

(3) If the Secretary of State determines that a reward is to be paid, he must also determine, in whatever way he thinks fit—

    (a) the treasure's market value;

    (b) the amount of the reward;

    (c) to whom the reward is to be payable; and

    (d) if it is to be payable to more than one person, how much each is to receive.

(4) The total reward must not exceed the treasure's market value.

(5) The reward may be payable to—

    (a) the finder or any other person involved in the find;

    (b) the occupier of the land at the time of the find;

    (c) any person who had an interest in the land at that time, or has had such an interest at any time since then.

(6) Payment of the reward is not enforceable against a museum or the Secretary of State.

(7) In a determination under this section, the Secretary of State must take into account anything relevant in the code of practice issued under section 11.

(8) This section also applies in relation to treasure which has vested in a franchisee under section 4, if the franchisee makes a request to the Secretary of State that it should.

TRUSTEE ACT 1925

1925 chapter 19 15 and 16 Geo 5

An Act to consolidate certain enactments relating to trustees in England and Wales.

Part II General Powers of Trustees and Personal Representatives

General Powers

14 Power of trustees to give receipts

(1) The receipt in writing of a trustee for any money, securities, [investments] or other personal property or effects payable, transferable, or deliverable to him under any trust or power shall be a sufficient discharge to the person paying, transferring, or delivering the same and shall

effectually exonerate him from seeing to the application or being answerable for any loss or misapplication thereof.

(2)   This section does not, except where the trustee is a trust corporation, enable a sole trustee to give a valid receipt for—

[(a)   proceeds of sale or other capital money arising under a trust of land;]

(b)   capital money arising under the Settled Land Act, 1925.

(3)   This section applies notwithstanding anything to the contrary in the instrument, if any, creating the trust.

[25 Delegation of trustee's functions by power of attorney

(1)   Notwithstanding any rule of law or equity to the contrary, a trustee may, by power of attorney, delegate the execution or exercise of all or any of the trusts, powers and discretions vested in him as trustee either alone or jointly with any other person or persons.

(2)   A delegation under this section—

(a)   commences as provided by the instrument creating the power or, if the instrument makes no provision as to the commencement of the delegation, with the date of the execution of the instrument by the donor; and

(b)   continues for a period of twelve months or any shorter period provided by the instrument creating the power.

(3)   The persons who may be donees of a power of attorney under this section include a trust corporation.

(4)   Before or within seven days after giving a power of attorney under this section the donor shall give written notice of it (specifying the date on which the power comes into operation and its duration, the donee of the power, the reason why the power is given and, where some only are delegated, the trusts, powers and discretions delegated) to—

(a)   each person (other than himself), if any, who under any instrument creating the trust has power (whether alone or jointly) to appoint a new trustee; and

(b)   each of the other trustees, if any;

but failure to comply with this subsection shall not, in favour of a person dealing with the donee of the power, invalidate any act done or instrument executed by the donee.

(5)   A power of attorney given under this section by a single donor—

(a)   in the form set out in subsection (6) of this section; or

(b)   in a form to the like effect but expressed to be made under this subsection,

shall operate to delegate to the person identified in the form as the single donee of the power the execution and exercise of all the trusts, powers and discretions vested in the donor as trustee (either alone or jointly with any other person or persons) under the single trust so identified.

(6)   The form referred to in subsection (5) of this section is as follows—

"THIS GENERAL TRUSTEE POWER OF ATTORNEY is made on [*date*] by [*name of one donor*] of [*address of donor*] as trustee of [*name or details of one trust*].

I appoint [*name of one donee*] of [*address of donee*] to be my attorney [if desired, the date on which the delegation commences or the period for which it continues (or both)] in accordance with section 25(5) of the Trustee Act 1925. [To be executed as a deed]".

(7)   The donor of a power of attorney given under this section shall be liable for the acts or defaults of the donee in the same manner as if they were the acts or defaults of the donor.

(8)   For the purpose of executing or exercising the trusts or powers delegated to him, the donee may exercise any of the powers conferred on the donor as trustee by statute or by the instrument creating the trust, including power, for the purpose of the transfer of any inscribed stock, himself to delegate to an attorney power to transfer, but not including the power of delegation conferred by this section.

(9)   The fact that it appears from any power of attorney given under this section, or from any evidence required for the purposes of any such power of attorney or otherwise, that in dealing with any stock the donee of the power is acting in the execution of a trust shall not be deemed for any purpose to affect any person in whose books the stock is inscribed or registered with any notice of the trust.

(10)   This section applies to a personal representative, tenant for life and statutory owner as it applies to a trustee except that subsection (4) shall apply as if it required the notice there mentioned to be given—

(a)   in the case of a personal representative, to each of the other personal representatives, if any, except any executor who has renounced probate;

(b)   in the case of a tenant for life, to the trustees of the settlement and to each person, if any, who together with the person giving the notice constitutes the tenant for life; and

(c)   in the case of a statutory owner, to each of the persons, if any, who together with the person giving the notice constitute the statutory owner and, in the case of a statutory owner by virtue of section 23(1)(a) of the Settled Land Act 1925, to the trustees of the settlement.]

Maintenance, Advancement and Protective Trusts

31 Power to apply income for maintenance and to accumulate surplus income during a minority

(1)   Where any property is held by trustees in trust for any person for any interest whatsoever, whether vested or contingent, then, subject to any prior interests or charges affecting that property—

(i)   during the infancy of any such person, if his interest so long continues, the trustees may, at their sole discretion, pay to his parent or guardian, if any, or otherwise apply for or towards his maintenance, education, or benefit, the whole or such part, if any, of the income of that property as may, in all the circumstances, be reasonable, whether or not there is—

> (a)   any other fund applicable to the same purpose; or
>
> (b)   any person bound by law to provide for his maintenance or education; and

(ii)   if such person on attaining the age of [eighteen years] has not a vested interest in such income, the trustees shall thenceforth pay the income of that property and of any accretion thereto under subsection (2) of this section to him, until he either attains a vested interest therein or dies, or until failure of his interest:

Provided that, in deciding whether the whole or any part of the income of the property is during a minority to be paid or applied for the purposes aforesaid, the trustees shall have regard to the age of the infant and his requirements and generally to the circumstances of the case, and in particular to what other income, if any, is applicable for the same purposes; and where trustees have notice that the income of more than one fund is applicable for those purposes, then, so far as practicable, unless the entire income of the funds is paid or applied as aforesaid or the court otherwise directs, a proportionate part only of the income of each fund shall be so paid or applied.

(2)   During the infancy of any such person, if his interest so long continues, the trustees shall accumulate all the residue of that income [by investing it, and any profits from so investing it] from time to time in authorised investments, and shall hold those accumulations as follows:—

(i)   If any such person—

> (a)   attains the age of [eighteen years], or marries under that age, and his interest in such income during his infancy or until his marriage is a vested interest or;
>
> (b)   on attaining the age of [eighteen years] or on marriage under that age becomes entitled to the property from which such income arose in fee simple, absolute or determinable, or absolutely, or for an entailed interest;

the trustees shall hold the accumulations in trust for such person absolutely, but without prejudice to any provision with respect thereto contained in any settlement by him made under any statutory powers during his infancy, and so that the receipt of such person after marriage, and though still an infant shall be a good discharge, and

(ii)   In any other case the trustees shall, notwithstanding that such person had a vested interest in such income, hold the accumulations as an accretion to the capital of the property from which such accumulations arose, and as one fund with such capital for all purposes, and so that, if such property is settled land, such accumulations shall be held upon the same trusts as if the same were capital money arising therefrom; but the trustees may, at any time during the infancy of such person if his interest so long continues, apply those accumulations, or any part thereof, as if they were income arising in the then current year.

(3)   This section applies in the case of a contingent interest only if the limitation or trust carries the intermediate income of the property, but it applies to a future or contingent legacy by the parent of, or a person standing in loco parentis to, the legatee, if and for such period as, under the general law, the legacy carries interest for the maintenance of the legatee, and in any such case as last aforesaid the rate of interest shall (if the income available is sufficient, and subject to any rules of court to the contrary) be five pounds per centum per annum.

(4)   This section applies to a vested annuity in like manner as if the annuity were the income of property held by trustees in trust to pay the income thereof to the annuitant for the same period for which the annuity is payable, save that in any case accumulations made during the infancy of the annuitant shall be held in trust for the annuitant or his personal representatives absolutely.

(5)   This section does not apply where the instrument, if any, under which the interest arises came into operation before the commencement of this Act.

32 Power of advancement

(1)   Trustees may at any time or times pay or apply any capital money subject to a trust, for the advancement or benefit, in such manner as they may, in their absolute discretion, think fit, of any person entitled to the capital of the trust property or of any share thereof, whether absolutely or contingently on his attaining any specified age or on the occurrence of any other event, or subject to a gift over on his death under any specified age or on the occurrence of any other event, and whether in possession or in remainder or reversion, and such payment or application may be made notwithstanding that the interest of such person is liable to be defeated by the exercise of a power of appointment or revocation, or to be diminished by the increase of the class to which he belongs:

Provided that—

(a)   the money so paid or applied for the advancement or benefit of any person shall not exceed altogether in amount one-half of the presumptive or vested share or interest of that person in the trust property; and

(b)   if that person is or becomes absolutely and indefeasibly entitled to a share in the trust property the money so paid or applied shall be brought into account as part of such share; and

(c)   no such payment or application shall be made so as to prejudice any person entitled to any prior life or other interest, whether vested or contingent, in the money paid or applied unless such person is in existence and of full age and consents in writing to such payment or application.

[(2)   This section does not apply to capital money arising under the Settled Land Act 1925.]

(3)   This section does not apply to trusts constituted or created before the commencement of this Act.

33 Protective trusts

(1)   Where any income, including an annuity or other periodical income payment, is directed to be held on protective trusts for the benefit of any person (in this section called "the principal beneficiary") for the period of his life or for any less period, then, during that period (in this section called the "trust period") the said income shall, without prejudice to any prior interest, be held on the following trusts, namely:—

(i)   Upon trust for the principal beneficiary during the trust period or until he, whether before or after the termination of any prior interest, does or attempts to do or suffers any act or thing, or until any event happens, other than an advance under any statutory or express power, whereby, if the said income were payable during the trust period to the principal beneficiary absolutely during that period, he would be deprived of the right to receive the same or any part thereof, in any of which cases, as well as on the termination of the trust period, whichever first happens, this trust of the said income shall fail or determine;

(ii)   If the trust aforesaid fails or determines during the subsistence of the trust period, then, during the residue of that period, the said income shall be held upon trust for the application thereof for the maintenance or support, or otherwise for the benefit, of all or any one or more exclusively of the other or others of the following persons (that is to say) —

(a)   the principal beneficiary and his or her wife or husband, if any, and his or her children or more remote issue, if any; or

(b)   if there is no wife or husband or issue of the principal beneficiary in existence, the principal beneficiary and the persons who would, if he were actually dead, be entitled to the trust property or the income thereof or to the annuity fund, if any, or arrears of the annuity, as the case may be;

as the trustees in their absolute discretion, without being liable to account for the exercise of such discretion, think fit.

(2)   This section does not apply to trusts coming into operation before the commencement of this Act, and has effect subject to any variation of the implied trusts aforesaid contained in the instrument creating the trust.

(3)   Nothing in this section operates to validate any trust which would, if contained in the instrument creating the trust, be liable to be set aside.

[(4)   In relation to the dispositions mentioned in section 19(1) of the Family Law Reform Act 1987, this section shall have effect as if any reference (however expressed) to any relationship between two persons were construed in accordance with section 1 of that Act.]

Part III Appointment and Discharge of Trustees

34 Limitation of the number of trustees

(1)   Where, at the commencement of this Act, there are more than four trustees of a settlement of land, or more than four trustees holding land on trust for sale, no new trustees shall (except where as a result of the appointment the number is reduced to four or less) be capable of being appointed until the number is reduced to less than four, and thereafter the number shall not be increased beyond four.

(2)   In the case of settlements and dispositions [creating trusts of land] made or coming into operation after the commencement of this Act—

(a)   the number of trustees thereof shall not in any case exceed four, and where more than four persons are named as such trustees, the four first named (who are able and willing to act) shall alone be the trustees, and the other persons named shall not be trustees unless appointed on the occurrence of a vacancy;

(b)   the number of the trustees shall not be increased beyond four.

(3)   This section only applies to settlements and dispositions of land, and the restrictions imposed on the number of trustees do not apply—

(a)   in the case of land vested in trustees for charitable, ecclesiastical, or public purposes; or

(b)   where the net proceeds of the sale of the land are held for like purposes; or

(c)   to the trustees of a term of years absolute limited by a settlement on trusts for raising money, or of a like term created under the statutory remedies relating to annual sums charged on land.

36 Power of appointing new or additional trustees

(1)   Where a trustee, either original or substituted, and whether appointed by a court or otherwise, is dead, or remains out of the United Kingdom for more than twelve months, or desires to be discharged from all or any of the trusts or powers reposed in or conferred on him, or refuses or is unfit to act therein, or is incapable of acting therein, or is an infant, then, subject to the restrictions imposed by this Act on the number of trustees,—

(a)   the person or persons nominated for the purpose of appointing new trustees by the instrument, if any, creating the trust; or

(b)   if there is no such person, or no such person able and willing to act, then the surviving or continuing trustees or trustee for the time being, or the personal representatives of the last surviving or continuing trustee;

may, by writing, appoint one or more other persons (whether or not being the persons exercising the power) to be a trustee or trustees in the place of the trustee so deceased remaining out of the United Kingdom, desiring to be discharged, refusing, or being unfit or being incapable, or being an infant, as aforesaid.

(2)   Where a trustee has been removed under a power contained in the instrument creating the trust, a new trustee or new trustees may be appointed in the place of the trustee who is removed, as if he were dead, or, in the case of a corporation, as if the corporation desired to be discharged from the trust, and the provisions of this section shall apply accordingly, but subject to the restrictions imposed by this Act on the number of trustees.

(3)   Where a corporation being a trustee is or has been dissolved, either before or after the commencement of this Act, then, for the purposes of this section and of any enactment replaced thereby, the corporation shall be deemed to be and to have been from the date of the dissolution incapable of acting in the trusts or powers reposed in or conferred on the corporation.

(4)   The power of appointment given by subsection (1) of this section or any similar previous enactment to the personal representatives of a last surviving or continuing trustee shall be and shall be deemed always to have been exercisable by the executors for the time being (whether original or by representation) of such surviving or continuing trustee who have proved the will of their testator or by the administrators for the time being of such trustee without the concurrence of any executor who has renounced or has not proved.

(5)   But a sole or last surviving executor intending to renounce, or all the executors where they all intend to renounce, shall have and shall be deemed always to have had power, at any time

before renouncing probate, to exercise the power of appointment given by this section, or by any similar previous enactment, if willing to act for that purpose and without thereby accepting the office of executor.

[(6)   Where, in the case of any trust, there are not more than three trustees—]

(a)   the person or persons nominated for the purpose of appointing new trustees by the instrument, if any, creating the trust; or

(b)   if there is no such person, or no such person able and willing to act, then the trustee or trustees for the time being;

may, by writing appoint another person or other persons to be an additional trustee or additional trustees, but it shall not be obligatory to appoint any additional trustee, unless the instrument, if any, creating the trust, or any statutory enactment provides to the contrary, nor shall the number of trustees be increased beyond four by virtue of any such appointment.

[(6A) A person who is either—

(a)   both a trustee and attorney for the other trustee (if one other), or for both of the other trustees (if two others), under a registered power; or

(b)   attorney under a registered power for the trustee (if one) or for both or each of the trustees (if two or three),

may, if subsection (6B) of this section is satisfied in relation to him, make an appointment under subsection (6)(b) of this section on behalf of the trustee or trustees.

(6B)   This subsection is satisfied in relation to an attorney under a registered power for one or more trustees if (as attorney under the power)—

(a)   he intends to exercise any function of the trustee or trustees by virtue of section 1(1) of the Trustee Delegation Act 1999; or

(b)   he intends to exercise any function of the trustee or trustees in relation to any land, capital proceeds of a conveyance of land or income from land by virtue of its delegation to him under section 25 of this Act or the instrument (if any) creating the trust.

(6C)   In subsections (6A) and (6B) of this section "registered power" means [an enduring power of attorney or lasting power of attorney registered under the Mental Capacity Act 2005].

(6D)   Subsection (6A) of this section—

(a)   applies only if and so far as a contrary intention is not expressed in the instrument creating the power of attorney (or, where more than one, any of them) or the instrument (if any) creating the trust; and

(b)   has effect subject to the terms of those instruments.]

(7)   Every new trustee appointed under this section as well before as after all the trust property becomes by law, or by assurance, or otherwise, vested in him, shall have the same powers, authorities, and discretions, and may in all respects act as if he had been originally appointed a trustee by the instrument, if any, creating the trust.

(8) The provisions of this section relating to a trustee who is dead include the case of a person nominated trustee in a will but dying before the testator, and those relative to a continuing trustee include a refusing or retiring trustee, if willing to act in the execution of the provisions of this section.

[(9) Where a trustee [lacks capacity to exercise] his functions as trustee and is also entitled in possession to some beneficial interest in the trust property, no appointment of a new trustee in his place shall be made by virtue of paragraph (b) of subsection (1) of this section unless leave to make the appointment has been given by [the Court of Protection].]

37 Supplemental provisions as to appointment of trustees

(1) On the appointment of a trustee for the whole or any part of trust property—

(a) the number of trustees may, subject to the restrictions imposed by this Act on the number of trustees, be increased; and

(b) a separate set of trustees, not exceeding four, may be appointed for any part of the trust property held on trusts distinct from those relating to any other part or parts of the trust property, notwithstanding that no new trustees or trustee are or is to be appointed for other parts of the trust property, and any existing trustee may be appointed or remain one of such separate set of trustees, or, if only one trustee was originally appointed, then, save as hereinafter provided, one separate trustee may be so appointed; and

(c) it shall not be obligatory, save as hereinafter provided, to appoint more than one new trustee where only one trustee was originally appointed, or to fill up the original number of trustees where more than two trustees were originally appointed, but, except where only one trustee was originally appointed, and a sole trustee when appointed will be able to give valid receipts for all capital money, a trustee shall not be discharged from his trust unless there will be either a trust corporation or at least two [persons] to act as trustees to perform the trust; and

(d) any assurance or thing requisite for vesting the trust property, or any part thereof, in a sole trustee, or jointly in the persons who are the trustees, shall be executed or done.

(2) Nothing in this Act shall authorise the appointment of a sole trustee, not being a trust corporation, where the trustee, when appointed, would not be able to give valid receipts for all capital money arising under the trust.

38 Evidence as to a vacancy in a trust

(1) A statement, contained in any instrument coming into operation after the commencement of this Act by which a new trustee is appointed for any purpose connected with land, to the effect that a trustee has remained out of the United Kingdom for more than twelve months or refuses or is unfit to act, or is incapable of acting, or that he is not entitled to a beneficial interest in the trust property in possession, shall, in favour of a purchaser of a legal estate, be conclusive evidence of the matter stated.

(2) In favour of such purchaser any appointment of a new trustee depending on that statement, and any vesting declaration, express or implied, consequent on the appointment, shall be valid.

39 Retirement of trustee without a new appointment

(1)   Where a trustee is desirous of being discharged from the trust, and after his discharge there will be either a trust corporation or at least two [persons] to act as trustees to perform the trust, then, if such trustee as aforesaid by deed declares that he is desirous of being discharged from the trust, and if his co-trustees and such other person, if any, as is empowered to appoint trustees, by deed consent to the discharge of the trustee, and to the vesting in the co-trustees alone of the trust property, the trustee desirous of being discharged shall be deemed to have retired from the trust, and shall, by the deed, be discharged there from under this Act, without any new trustee being appointed in his place.

(2)   Any assurance or thing requisite for vesting the trust property in the continuing trustees alone shall be executed or done.

40 Vesting of trust property in new or continuing trustees

(1)   Where by a deed a new trustee is appointed to perform any trust, then—

  (a)   if the deed contains a declaration by the appointor to the effect that any estate or interest in any land subject to the trust, or in any chattel so subject, or the right to recover or receive any debt or other thing in action so subject, shall vest in the persons who by virtue of the deed become or are the trustees for performing the trust, the deed shall operate, without any conveyance or assignment, to vest in those persons as joint tenants and for the purposes of the trust the estate interest or right to which the declaration relates; and

  (b)   if the deed is made after the commencement of this Act and does not contain such a declaration, the deed shall, subject to any express provision to the contrary therein contained, operate as if it had contained such a declaration by the appointor extending to all the estates interests and rights with respect to which a declaration could have been made.

(2)   Where by a deed a retiring trustee is discharged under [section 39 of this Act or section 19 of the Trusts of Land and Appointment of Trustees Act 1996] without a new trustee being appointed, then—

  (a)   if the deed contains such a declaration as aforesaid by the retiring and continuing trustees, and by the other person, if any, empowered to appoint trustees, the deed shall, without any conveyance or assignment, operate to vest in the continuing trustees alone, as joint tenants, and for the purposes of the trust, the estate, interest, or right to which the declaration relates; and

  (b)   if the deed is made after the commencement of this Act and does not contain such a declaration, the deed shall, subject to any express provision to the contrary therein contained, operate as if it had contained such a declaration by such persons as aforesaid extending to all the estates, interests and rights with respect to which a declaration could have been made.

(3)   An express vesting declaration, whether made before or after the commencement of this Act, shall, notwithstanding that the estate, interest or right to be vested is not expressly referred to,

and provided that the other statutory requirements were or are complied with, operate and be deemed always to have operated (but without prejudice to any express provision to the contrary contained in the deed of appointment or discharge) to vest in the persons respectively referred to in subsections (1) and (2) of this section, as the case may require, such estates, interests and rights as are capable of being and ought to be vested in those persons.

(4)   This section does not extend—

(a)   to land conveyed by way of mortgage for securing money subject to the trust, except land conveyed on trust for securing debentures or debenture stock;

(b)   to land held under a lease which contains any covenant, condition or agreement against assignment or disposing of the land without licence or consent, unless, prior to the execution of the deed containing expressly or impliedly the vesting declaration, the requisite licence or consent has been obtained, or unless, by virtue of any statute or rule of law, the vesting declaration, express or implied, would not operate as a breach of covenant or give rise to a forfeiture;

(c)   to any share, stock, annuity or property which is only transferable in books kept by a company or other body, or in manner directed by or under an Act of Parliament.

In this subsection "lease" includes an underlease and an agreement for a lease or underlease.

(5)   For purposes of registration of the deed in any registry, the person or persons making the declaration expressly or impliedly, shall be deemed the conveying party or parties, and the conveyance shall be deemed to be made by him or them under a power conferred by this Act.

(6)   This section applies to deeds of appointment or discharge executed on or after the first day of January, eighteen hundred and eighty-two.

Part IV Powers of the Court

Appointment of new Trustees

41 Power of court to appoint new trustees

(1)   The court may, whenever it is expedient to appoint a new trustee or new trustees, and it is found inexpedient difficult or impracticable so to do without the assistance of the court, make an order appointing a new trustee or new trustees either in substitution for or in addition to any existing trustee or trustees, or although there is no existing trustee.

In particular and without prejudice to the generality of the foregoing provision, the court may make an order appointing a new trustee in substitution for a trustee who . . . [lacks capacity to exercise] [his functions as trustee], or is a bankrupt, or is a corporation which is in liquidation or has been dissolved.

(2)   The power conferred by this section may, in the case of a deed of arrangement within the meaning of the Deeds of Arrangement Act 1914, be exercised either by the High Court or by the court having jurisdiction in bankruptcy in the district in which the debtor resided or carried on business at the date of the execution of the deed.

(3)   An order under this section, and any consequential vesting order or conveyance, shall not operate further or otherwise as a discharge to any former or continuing trustee than an appointment of new trustees under any power for that purpose contained in any instrument would have operated.

(4)   Nothing in this section gives power to appoint an executor or administrator.

61 Power to relieve trustee from personal liability

If it appears to the court that a trustee, whether appointed by the court or otherwise, is or may be personally liable for any breach of trust, whether the transaction alleged to be a breach of trust occurred before or after the commencement of this Act, but has acted honestly and reasonably, and ought fairly to be excused for the breach of trust and for omitting to obtain the directions of the court in the matter in which he committed such breach, then the court may relieve him either wholly or partly from personal liability for the same.

62 Power to make beneficiary indemnify for breach of trust

(1)   Where a trustee commits a breach of trust at the instigation or request or with the consent in writing of a beneficiary, the court may, if it thinks fit, [. . .], make such order as to the court seems just, for impounding all or any part of the interest of the beneficiary in the trust estate by way of indemnity to the trustee or persons claiming through him.

(2)   This section applies to breaches of trust committed as well before as after the commencement of this Act.

69 Application of Act

(1)   This Act, except where otherwise expressly provided, applies to trusts including, so far as this Act applies thereto, executorships and administratorships constituted or created either before or after the commencement of this Act.

(2)   The powers conferred by this Act on trustees are in addition to the powers conferred by the instrument, if any, creating the trust, but those powers, unless otherwise stated, apply if and so far only as a contrary intention is not expressed in the instrument, if any, creating the trust, and have effect subject to the terms of that instrument.

TRUSTEE ACT 2000

2000 chapter 29

An Act to amend the law relating to trustees and persons having the investment powers of trustees; and for connected purposes.

Part I The Duty of Care

1 The duty of care

(1)   Whenever the duty under this subsection applies to a trustee, he must exercise such care and skill as is reasonable in the circumstances, having regard in particular—

(a)   to any special knowledge or experience that he has or holds himself out as having, and

(b)   if he acts as trustee in the course of a business or profession, to any special knowledge or experience that it is reasonable to expect of a person acting in the course of that kind of business or profession.

(2)   In this Act the duty under subsection (1) is called "the duty of care".

2 Application of duty of care

Schedule 1 makes provision about when the duty of care applies to a trustee.

Part II Investment

3 General power of investment

(1)   Subject to the provisions of this Part, a trustee may make any kind of investment that he could make if he were absolutely entitled to the assets of the trust.

(2)   In this Act the power under subsection (1) is called "the general power of investment".

(3)   The general power of investment does not permit a trustee to make investments in land other than in loans secured on land (but see also section 8).

(4)   A person invests in a loan secured on land if he has rights under any contract under which—

(a)   one person provides another with credit, and
(b)   the obligation of the borrower to repay is secured on land.

(5)   "Credit" includes any cash loan or other financial accommodation.

(6)   "Cash" includes money in any form.

4 Standard investment criteria

(1)   In exercising any power of investment, whether arising under this Part or otherwise, a trustee must have regard to the standard investment criteria.

(2)   A trustee must from time to time review the investments of the trust and consider whether, having regard to the standard investment criteria, they should be varied.

(3)   The standard investment criteria, in relation to a trust, are—

(a)   the suitability to the trust of investments of the same kind as any particular investment proposed to be made or retained and of that particular investment as an investment of that kind, and

(b)   the need for diversification of investments of the trust, in so far as is appropriate to the circumstances of the trust.

5 Advice

(1)   Before exercising any power of investment, whether arising under this Part or otherwise, a trustee must (unless the exception applies) obtain and consider proper advice about the way in which, having regard to the standard investment criteria, the power should be exercised.

(2)   When reviewing the investments of the trust, a trustee must (unless the exception applies) obtain and consider proper advice about whether, having regard to the standard investment criteria, the investments should be varied.

(3)   The exception is that a trustee need not obtain such advice if he reasonably concludes that in all the circumstances it is unnecessary or inappropriate to do so.

(4)   Proper advice is the advice of a person who is reasonably believed by the trustee to be qualified to give it by his ability in and practical experience of financial and other matters relating to the proposed investment.

6 Restriction or exclusion of this Part etc

(1)   The general power of investment is—

(a)   in addition to powers conferred on trustees otherwise than by this Act, but

(b)   subject to any restriction or exclusion imposed by the trust instrument or by any enactment or any provision of subordinate legislation.

(2)   For the purposes of this Act, an enactment or a provision of subordinate legislation is not to be regarded as being, or as being part of, a trust instrument.

(3)   In this Act "subordinate legislation" has the same meaning as in the Interpretation Act 1978.

7 Existing trusts

(1)   This Part applies in relation to trusts whether created before or after its commencement.

(2)   No provision relating to the powers of a trustee contained in a trust instrument made before 3rd August 1961 is to be treated (for the purposes of section 6(1)(b)) as restricting or excluding the general power of investment.

(3)   A provision contained in a trust instrument made before the commencement of this Part which—

(a)   has effect under section 3(2) of the Trustee Investments Act 1961 as a power to invest under that Act, or

(b)   confers power to invest under that Act,

is to be treated as conferring the general power of investment on a trustee.

Part III Acquisition of Land

8 Power to acquire freehold and leasehold land

(1)   A trustee may acquire freehold or leasehold land in the United Kingdom—

(a)   as an investment,
(b)   for occupation by a beneficiary, or
(c)   for any other reason.

(2)   "Freehold or leasehold land" means—

(a)   in relation to England and Wales, a legal estate in land,

(b)   in relation to Scotland—

    (i)   the estate or interest of the proprietor of the dominium utile or, in the case of land not held on feudal tenure, the estate or interest of the owner, or

    (ii)   a tenancy, and

(c)   in relation to Northern Ireland, a legal estate in land, including land held under a fee farm grant.

(3)   For the purpose of exercising his functions as a trustee, a trustee who acquires land under this section has all the powers of an absolute owner in relation to the land.

9 Restriction or exclusion of this Part etc

The powers conferred by this Part are—

(a)   in addition to powers conferred on trustees otherwise than by this Part, but

(b)   subject to any restriction or exclusion imposed by the trust instrument or by any enactment or any provision of subordinate legislation.

10 Existing trusts

(1)   This Part does not apply in relation to—

(a)   a trust of property which consists of or includes land which (despite section 2 of the Trusts of Land and Appointment of Trustees Act 1996) is settled land, or

(b)   a trust to which the Universities and College Estates Act 1925 applies.

(2)   Subject to subsection (1), this Part applies in relation to trusts whether created before or after its commencement.

Part IV Agents, nominees and custodians

Agents

11 Power to employ agents

(1)   Subject to the provisions of this Part, the trustees of a trust may authorise any person to exercise any or all of their delegable functions as their agent.

(2)   In the case of a trust other than a charitable trust, the trustees' delegable functions consist of any function other than—

(a)   any function relating to whether or in what way any assets of the trust should be distributed,

(b)   any power to decide whether any fees or other payment due to be made out of the trust funds should be made out of income or capital,

(c)   any power to appoint a person to be a trustee of the trust, or

(d)   any power conferred by any other enactment or the trust instrument which permits the trustees to delegate any of their functions or to appoint a person to act as a nominee or custodian.

(3)   In the case of a charitable trust, the trustees' delegable functions are—

    (a)   any function consisting of carrying out a decision that the trustees have taken;

    (b)   any function relating to the investment of assets subject to the trust (including, in the case of land held as an investment, managing the land and creating or disposing of an interest in the land);

    (c)   any function relating to the raising of funds for the trust otherwise than by means of profits of a trade which is an integral part of carrying out the trust's charitable purpose;

    (d)   any other function prescribed by an order made by the Secretary of State.

(4)   For the purposes of subsection (3)(c) a trade is an integral part of carrying out a trust's charitable purpose if, whether carried on in the United Kingdom or elsewhere, the profits are applied solely to the purposes of the trust and either—

    (a)   the trade is exercised in the course of the actual carrying out of a primary purpose of the trust, or

    (b)   the work in connection with the trade is mainly carried out by beneficiaries of the trust.

(5)   The power to make an order under subsection (3)(d) is exercisable by statutory instrument which shall be subject to annulment in pursuance of a resolution of either House of Parliament.

12 Persons who may act as agents

(1)   Subject to subsection (2), the persons whom the trustees may under section 11 authorise to exercise functions as their agent include one or more of their number.

(2)   The trustees may not authorise two (or more) persons to exercise the same function unless they are to exercise the function jointly.

(3)   The trustees may not under section 11 authorise a beneficiary to exercise any function as their agent (even if the beneficiary is also a trustee).

(4)   The trustees may under section 11 authorise a person to exercise functions as their agent even though he is also appointed to act as their nominee or custodian (whether under section 16, 17 or 18 or any other power).

13 Linked functions etc

(1)   Subject to subsections (2) and (5), a person who is authorised under section 11 to exercise a function is (whatever the terms of the agency) subject to any specific duties or restrictions attached to the function.

For example, a person who is authorised under section 11 to exercise the general power of investment is subject to the duties under section 4 in relation to that power.

(2)   A person who is authorised under section 11 to exercise a power which is subject to a requirement to obtain advice is not subject to the requirement if he is the kind of person from whom it would have been proper for the trustees, in compliance with the requirement, to obtain advice.

(3)   Subsections (4) and (5) apply to a trust to which section 11(1) of the Trusts of Land and Appointment of Trustees Act 1996 (duties to consult beneficiaries and give effect to their wishes) applies.

(4)   The trustees may not under section 11 authorise a person to exercise any of their functions on terms that prevent them from complying with section 11(1) of the 1996 Act.

(5)   A person who is authorised under section 11 to exercise any function relating to land subject to the trust is not subject to section 11(1) of the 1996 Act.

14 Terms of agency

(1)   Subject to subsection (2) and sections 15(2) and 29 to 32, the trustees may authorise a person to exercise functions as their agent on such terms as to remuneration and other matters as they may determine.

(2)   The trustees may not authorise a person to exercise functions as their agent on any of the terms mentioned in subsection (3) unless it is reasonably necessary for them to do so.

(3)   The terms are—

(a)   a term permitting the agent to appoint a substitute;

(b)   a term restricting the liability of the agent or his substitute to the trustees or any beneficiary;

(c)   a term permitting the agent to act in circumstances capable of giving rise to a conflict of interest.

15 Asset management: special restrictions

(1)   The trustees may not authorise a person to exercise any of their asset management functions as their agent except by an agreement which is in or evidenced in writing.

(2)   The trustees may not authorise a person to exercise any of their asset management functions as their agent unless—

(a)   they have prepared a statement that gives guidance as to how the functions should be exercised ("a policy statement"), and

(b)   the agreement under which the agent is to act includes a term to the effect that he will secure compliance with—

(i)   the policy statement, or

(ii)   if the policy statement is revised or replaced under section 22, the revised or replacement policy statement.

(3)   The trustees must formulate any guidance given in the policy statement with a view to ensuring that the functions will be exercised in the best interests of the trust.

(4)   The policy statement must be in or evidenced in writing.

(5)   The asset management functions of trustees are their functions relating to—

(a)   the investment of assets subject to the trust,

(b)   the acquisition of property which is to be subject to the trust, and

(c)   managing property which is subject to the trust and disposing of, or creating or disposing of an interest in, such property.

Nominees and custodians

16 Power to appoint nominees

(1)   Subject to the provisions of this Part, the trustees of a trust may—

(a)   appoint a person to act as their nominee in relation to such of the assets of the trust as they determine (other than settled land), and

(b)   take such steps as are necessary to secure that those assets are vested in a person so appointed.

(2)   An appointment under this section must be in or evidenced in writing.

(3)   This section does not apply to any trust having a custodian trustee or in relation to any assets vested in the official custodian for charities.

17 Power to appoint custodians

(1)   Subject to the provisions of this Part, the trustees of a trust may appoint a person to act as a custodian in relation to such of the assets of the trust as they may determine.

(2)   For the purposes of this Act a person is a custodian in relation to assets if he undertakes the safe custody of the assets or of any documents or records concerning the assets.

(3)   An appointment under this section must be in or evidenced in writing.

(4)   This section does not apply to any trust having a custodian trustee or in relation to any assets vested in the official custodian for charities.

18 Investment in bearer securities

(1)   If trustees retain or invest in securities payable to bearer, they must appoint a person to act as a custodian of the securities.

(2)   Subsection (1) does not apply if the trust instrument or any enactment or provision of subordinate legislation contains provision which (however expressed) permits the trustees to retain or invest in securities payable to bearer without appointing a person to act as a custodian.

(3)   An appointment under this section must be in or evidenced in writing.

(4)   This section does not apply to any trust having a custodian trustee or in relation to any securities vested in the official custodian for charities.

19 Persons who may be appointed as nominees or custodians

(1)   A person may not be appointed under section 16, 17 or 18 as a nominee or custodian unless one of the relevant conditions is satisfied.

(2)   The relevant conditions are that—

(a)   the person carries on a business which consists of or includes acting as a nominee or custodian;

(b)   the person is a body corporate which is controlled by the trustees;

(c)   the person is a body corporate recognised under section 9 of the Administration of Justice Act 1985.

(3)   The question whether a body corporate is controlled by trustees is to be determined in accordance with section 840 of the Income and Corporation Taxes Act 1988 [section 1124 of the Corporation Tax Act 2010].

(4)   The trustees of a charitable trust which is not an exempt charity must act in accordance with any guidance given by the [Charity Commission] concerning the selection of a person for appointment as a nominee or custodian under section 16, 17 or 18.

(5)   Subject to subsections (1) and (4), the persons whom the trustees may under section 16, 17 or 18 appoint as a nominee or custodian include—

(a)   one of their number, if that one is a trust corporation, or

(b)   two (or more) of their number, if they are to act as joint nominees or joint custodians.

(6)   The trustees may under section 16 appoint a person to act as their nominee even though he is also—

(a)   appointed to act as their custodian (whether under section 17 or 18 or any other power), or

(b)   authorised to exercise functions as their agent (whether under section 11 or any other power).

(7)   Likewise, the trustees may under section 17 or 18 appoint a person to act as their custodian even though he is also—

(a)   appointed to act as their nominee (whether under section 16 or any other power), or

(b)   authorised to exercise functions as their agent (whether under section 11 or any other power).

20 Terms of appointment of nominees and custodians

(1)   Subject to subsection (2) and sections 29 to 32, the trustees may under section 16, 17 or 18 appoint a person to act as a nominee or custodian on such terms as to remuneration and other matters as they may determine.

(2)   The trustees may not under section 16, 17 or 18 appoint a person to act as a nominee or custodian on any of the terms mentioned in subsection (3) unless it is reasonably necessary for them to do so.

(3)   The terms are—

(a)   a term permitting the nominee or custodian to appoint a substitute;

(b)   a term restricting the liability of the nominee or custodian or his substitute to the trustees or to any beneficiary;

(c)   a term permitting the nominee or custodian to act in circumstances capable of giving rise to a conflict of interest.

Review of and liability for agents, nominees and custodians etc

21 Application of sections 22 and 23

(1)   Sections 22 and 23 apply in a case where trustees have, under section 11, 16, 17 or 18—

(a)   authorised a person to exercise functions as their agent, or

(b)   appointed a person to act as a nominee or custodian.

(2)   Subject to subsection (3), sections 22 and 23 also apply in a case where trustees have, under any power conferred on them by the trust instrument or by any enactment or any provision of subordinate legislation—

(a)   authorised a person to exercise functions as their agent, or

(b)   appointed a person to act as a nominee or custodian.

(3)   If the application of section 22 or 23 is inconsistent with the terms of the trust instrument or the enactment or provision of subordinate legislation, the section in question does not apply.

22 Review of agents, nominees and custodians etc

(1)   While the agent, nominee or custodian continues to act for the trust, the trustees—

(a)   must keep under review the arrangements under which the agent, nominee or custodian acts and how those arrangements are being put into effect,

(b)   if circumstances make it appropriate to do so, must consider whether there is a need to exercise any power of intervention that they have, and

(c)   if they consider that there is a need to exercise such a power, must do so.

(2)   If the agent has been authorised to exercise asset management functions, the duty under subsection (1) includes, in particular—

(a)   a duty to consider whether there is any need to revise or replace the policy statement made for the purposes of section 15,

(b)   if they consider that there is a need to revise or replace the policy statement, a duty to do so, and

(c)   a duty to assess whether the policy statement (as it has effect for the time being) is being complied with.

(3)   Subsections (3) and (4) of section 15 apply to the revision or replacement of a policy statement under this section as they apply to the making of a policy statement under that section.

(4)   "Power of intervention" includes—

(a)   a power to give directions to the agent, nominee or custodian;

(b)   a power to revoke the authorisation or appointment.

23 Liability for agents, nominees and custodians etc

(1)   A trustee is not liable for any act or default of the agent, nominee or custodian unless he has failed to comply with the duty of care applicable to him, under paragraph 3 of Schedule 1—

    (a)   when entering into the arrangements under which the person acts as agent, nominee or custodian, or

    (b)   when carrying out his duties under section 22.

(2)   If a trustee has agreed a term under which the agent, nominee or custodian is permitted to appoint a substitute, the trustee is not liable for any act or default of the substitute unless he has failed to comply with the duty of care applicable to him, under paragraph 3 of Schedule 1—

    (a)   when agreeing that term, or
    (b)   when carrying out his duties under section 22 in so far as they relate to the use of the substitute.

Supplementary

24 Effect of trustees exceeding their powers

A failure by the trustees to act within the limits of the powers conferred by this Part—

(a)   in authorising a person to exercise a function of theirs as an agent, or
(b)   in appointing a person to act as a nominee or custodian,

does not invalidate the authorisation or appointment.

25 Sole trustees

(1)   Subject to subsection (2), this Part applies in relation to a trust having a sole trustee as it applies in relation to other trusts (and references in this Part to trustees—except in sections 12(1) and (3) and 19(5)—are to be read accordingly).

(2)   Section 18 does not impose a duty on a sole trustee if that trustee is a trust corporation.

26 Restriction or exclusion of this Part etc

The powers conferred by this Part are—

(a)   in addition to powers conferred on trustees otherwise than by this Act, but

(b)   subject to any restriction or exclusion imposed by the trust instrument or by any enactment or any provision of subordinate legislation.

27 Existing trusts

This Part applies in relation to trusts whether created before or after its commencement.

Part V Remuneration

28 Trustee's entitlement to payment under trust instrument

(1) Except to the extent (if any) to which the trust instrument makes inconsistent provision, subsections (2) to (4) apply to a trustee if—

  (a) there is a provision in the trust instrument entitling him to receive payment out of trust funds in respect of services provided by him to or on behalf of the trust, and

  (b) the trustee is a trust corporation or is acting in a professional capacity.

(2) The trustee is to be treated as entitled under the trust instrument to receive payment in respect of services even if they are services which are capable of being provided by a lay trustee.

(3) Subsection (2) applies to a trustee of a charitable trust who is not a trust corporation only—

  (a) if he is not a sole trustee, and

  (b) to the extent that a majority of the other trustees have agreed that it should apply to him.

(4) Any payments to which the trustee is entitled in respect of services are to be treated as remuneration for services (and not as a gift) for the purposes of—

  (a) section 15 of the Wills Act 1837 (gifts to an attesting witness to be void), and

  (b) section 34(3) of the Administration of Estates Act 1925 (order in which estate to be paid out).

(5) For the purposes of this Part, a trustee acts in a professional capacity if he acts in the course of a profession or business which consists of or includes the provision of services in connection with—

  (a) the management or administration of trusts generally or a particular kind of trust, or

  (b) any particular aspect of the management or administration of trusts generally or a particular kind of trust,

and the services he provides to or on behalf of the trust fall within that description.

(6) For the purposes of this Part, a person acts as a lay trustee if he—

  (a) is not a trust corporation, and
  (b) does not act in a professional capacity.

29 Remuneration of certain trustees

(1) Subject to subsection (5), a trustee who—

  (a) is a trust corporation, but
  (b) is not a trustee of a charitable trust,

is entitled to receive reasonable remuneration out of the trust funds for any services that the trust corporation provides to or on behalf of the trust.

(2)   Subject to subsection (5), a trustee who—

(a)   acts in a professional capacity, but

(b)   is not a trust corporation, a trustee of a charitable trust or a sole trustee,

is entitled to receive reasonable remuneration out of the trust funds for any services that he provides to or on behalf of the trust if each other trustee has agreed in writing that he may be remunerated for the services.

(3)   "Reasonable remuneration" means, in relation to the provision of services by a trustee, such remuneration as is reasonable in the circumstances for the provision of those services to or on behalf of that trust by that trustee and for the purposes of subsection (1) includes, in relation to the provision of services by a trustee who is an authorised institution under the Banking Act 1987 and provides the services in that capacity, the institution's reasonable charges for the provision of such services.

(4)   A trustee is entitled to remuneration under this section even if the services in question are capable of being provided by a lay trustee.

(5)   A trustee is not entitled to remuneration under this section if any provision about his entitlement to remuneration has been made—

(a)   by the trust instrument, or

(b)   by any enactment or any provision of subordinate legislation.

(6)   This section applies to a trustee who has been authorised under a power conferred by Part IV or the trust instrument—

(a)   to exercise functions as an agent of the trustees, or

(b)   to act as a nominee or custodian,

as it applies to any other trustee.

30 Remuneration of trustees of charitable trusts

(1)   The Secretary of State may by regulations make provision for the remuneration of trustees of charitable trusts who are trust corporations or act in a professional capacity.

(2)   The power under subsection (1) includes power to make provision for the remuneration of a trustee who has been authorised under a power conferred by Part IV or any other enactment or any provision of subordinate legislation, or by the trust instrument—

(a)   to exercise functions as an agent of the trustees, or

(b)   to act as a nominee or custodian.

(3)   Regulations under this section may—

(a)   make different provision for different cases;

(b)   contain such supplemental, incidental, consequential and transitional provision as the Secretary of State considers appropriate.

(4)   The power to make regulations under this section is exercisable by statutory instrument, but no such instrument shall be made unless a draft of it has been laid before Parliament and approved by a resolution of each House of Parliament.

31 Trustees' expenses

(1)   A trustee—

    (a)   is entitled to be reimbursed from the trust funds, or

    (b)   may pay out of the trust funds,

expenses properly incurred by him when acting on behalf of the trust.

(2)   This section applies to a trustee who has been authorised under a power conferred by Part IV or any other enactment or any provision of subordinate legislation, or by the trust instrument—

    (a)   to exercise functions as an agent of the trustees, or

    (b)   to act as a nominee or custodian,

as it applies to any other trustee.

32 Remuneration and expenses of agents, nominees and custodians

(1)   This section applies if, under a power conferred by Part IV or any other enactment or any provision of subordinate legislation, or by the trust instrument, a person other than a trustee has been—

    (a)   authorised to exercise functions as an agent of the trustees, or

    (b)   appointed to act as a nominee or custodian.

(2)   The trustees may remunerate the agent, nominee or custodian out of the trust funds for services if—

    (a)   he is engaged on terms entitling him to be remunerated for those services, and

    (b)   the amount does not exceed such remuneration as is reasonable in the circumstances for the provision of those services by him to or on behalf of that trust.

(3)   The trustees may reimburse the agent, nominee or custodian out of the trust funds for any expenses properly incurred by him in exercising functions as an agent, nominee or custodian.

33 Application

(1)   Subject to subsection (2), sections 28, 29, 31 and 32 apply in relation to services provided to or on behalf of, or (as the case may be) expenses incurred on or after their commencement on behalf of, trusts whenever created.

(2)   Nothing in section 28 or 29 is to be treated as affecting the operation of—

    (a)   section 15 of the Wills Act 1837, or

    (b)   section 34(3) of the Administration of Estates Act 1925,

in relation to any death occurring before the commencement of section 28 or (as the case may be) section 29.

SCHEDULE 1 Application of duty of care

Investment

1   The duty of care applies to a trustee—

(a)   when exercising the general power of investment or any other power of investment, however conferred;

(b)   when carrying out a duty to which he is subject under section 4 or 5 (duties relating to the exercise of a power of investment or to the review of investments).

Acquisition of land

2   The duty of care applies to a trustee—

(a)   when exercising the power under section 8 to acquire land;

(b)   when exercising any other power to acquire land, however conferred;

(c)   when exercising any power in relation to land acquired under a power mentioned in sub-paragraph (a) or (b).

Agents, nominees and custodians

3   (1)   The duty of care applies to a trustee—

(a)   when entering into arrangements under which a person is authorised under section 11 to exercise functions as an agent;

(b)   when entering into arrangements under which a person is appointed under section 16 to act as a nominee;

(c)   when entering into arrangements under which a person is appointed under section 17 or 18 to act as a custodian;

(d)   when entering into arrangements under which, under any other power, however conferred, a person is authorised to exercise functions as an agent or is appointed to act as a nominee or custodian;

(e)   when carrying out his duties under section 22 (review of agent, nominee or custodian, etc.).

(2)   For the purposes of sub-paragraph (1), entering into arrangements under which a person is authorised to exercise functions or is appointed to act as a nominee or custodian includes, in particular—

(a)   selecting the person who is to act,

(b)   determining any terms on which he is to act, and

(c)   if the person is being authorised to exercise asset management functions, the preparation of a policy statement under section 15.

Compounding of liabilities

4   The duty of care applies to a trustee—

    (a)   when exercising the power under section 15 of the Trustee Act 1925 to do any of the things referred to in that section;

    (b)   when exercising any corresponding power, however conferred.

Insurance

5   The duty of care applies to a trustee—

    (a)   when exercising the power under section 19 of the Trustee Act 1925 to insure property;

    (b)   when exercising any corresponding power, however conferred.

Reversionary interests, valuations and audit

6   The duty of care applies to a trustee—

    (a)   when exercising the power under section 22(1) or (3) of the Trustee Act 1925 to do any of the things referred to there;

    (b)   when exercising any corresponding power, however conferred.

Exclusion of duty of care

7   The duty of care does not apply if or in so far as it appears from the trust instrument that the duty is not meant to apply.

TRUSTS OF LAND AND APPOINTMENT OF TRUSTEES ACT 1996

1996 chapter 47

An Act to make new provision about trusts of land including provision phasing out the Settled Land Act 1925, abolishing the doctrine of conversion and otherwise amending the law about trusts for sale of land; to amend the law about the appointment and retirement of trustees of any trust; and for connected purposes.

Part I TRUSTS OF LAND

Introductory

1 Meaning of "trust of land"

(1)   In this Act—

    (a)   "trust of land" means (subject to subsection (3)) any trust of property which consists of or includes land, and

    (b)   "trustees of land" means trustees of a trust of land.

(2)   The reference in subsection (1)(a) to a trust—

(a)   is to any description of trust (whether express, implied, resulting or constructive), including a trust for sale and a bare trust, and

(b)   includes a trust created, or arising, before the commencement of this Act.

(3)   The reference to land in subsection (1)(a) does not include land which (despite section 2) is settled land or which is land to which the Universities and College Estates Act 1925 applies.

Settlements and trusts for sale as trusts of land

2 Trusts in place of settlements

(1)   No settlement created after the commencement of this Act is a settlement for the purposes of the Settled Land Act 1925; and no settlement shall be deemed to be made under that Act after that commencement.

(2)   Subsection (1) does not apply to a settlement created on the occasion of an alteration in any interest in, or of a person becoming entitled under, a settlement which—

(a)   is in existence at the commencement of this Act, or
(b)   derives from a settlement within paragraph (a) or this paragraph.

(3)   But a settlement created as mentioned in subsection (2) is not a settlement for the purposes of the Settled Land Act 1925 if provision to the effect that it is not is made in the instrument, or any of the instruments, by which it is created.

(4)   Where at any time after the commencement of this Act there is in the case of any settlement which is a settlement for the purposes of the Settled Land Act 1925 no relevant property which is, or is deemed to be, subject to the settlement, the settlement permanently ceases at that time to be a settlement for the purposes of that Act.

In this subsection "relevant property" means land and personal chattels to which section 67(1) of the Settled Land Act 1925 (heirlooms) applies.

(5)   No land held on charitable, ecclesiastical or public trusts shall be or be deemed to be settled land after the commencement of this Act, even if it was or was deemed to be settled land before that commencement.

(6)   Schedule 1 has effect to make provision consequential on this section (including provision to impose a trust in circumstances in which, apart from this section, there would be a settlement for the purposes of the Settled Land Act 1925 (and there would not otherwise be a trust)).

3 Abolition of doctrine of conversion

(1)   Where land is held by trustees subject to a trust for sale, the land is not to be regarded as personal property; and where personal property is subject to a trust for sale in order that the trustees may acquire land, the personal property is not to be regarded as land.

(2)   Subsection (1) does not apply to a trust created by a will if the testator died before the commencement of this Act.

(3)   Subject to that, subsection (1) applies to a trust whether it is created, or arises, before or after that commencement.

4 Express trusts for sale as trusts of land

(1)   In the case of every trust for sale of land created by a disposition there is to be implied, despite any provision to the contrary made by the disposition, a power for the trustees to postpone sale of the land; and the trustees are not liable in any way for postponing sale of the land, in the exercise of their discretion, for an indefinite period.

(2)   Subsection (1) applies to a trust whether it is created, or arises, before or after the commencement of this Act.

(3)   Subsection (1) does not affect any liability incurred by trustees before that commencement.

5 Implied trusts for sale as trusts of land

(1)   Schedule 2 has effect in relation to statutory provisions which impose a trust for sale of land in certain circumstances so that in those circumstances there is instead a trust of the land (without a duty to sell).

(2)   Section 1 of the Settled Land Act 1925 does not apply to land held on any trust arising by virtue of that Schedule (so that any such land is subject to a trust of land).

Functions of trustees of land

6 General powers of trustees

(1)   For the purpose of exercising their functions as trustees, the trustees of land have in relation to the land subject to the trust all the powers of an absolute owner.

(2)   Where in the case of any land subject to a trust of land each of the beneficiaries interested in the land is a person of full age and capacity who is absolutely entitled to the land, the powers conferred on the trustees by subsection (1) include the power to convey the land to the beneficiaries even though they have not required the trustees to do so; and where land is conveyed by virtue of this subsection—

        (a)   the beneficiaries shall do whatever is necessary to secure that it vests in them, and

        (b)   if they fail to do so, the court may make an order requiring them to do so.

(3)   The trustees of land have power to [acquire land under the power conferred by section 8 of the Trustee Act 2000.]

(4)   [...]

(5)   In exercising the powers conferred by this section trustees shall have regard to the rights of the beneficiaries.

(6)   The powers conferred by this section shall not be exercised in contravention of, or of any order made in pursuance of, any other enactment or any rule of law or equity.

(7)   The reference in subsection (6) to an order includes an order of any court or of the Charity Commission.

(8)   Where any enactment other than this section confers on trustees authority to act subject to any restriction, limitation or condition, trustees of land may not exercise the powers conferred by this section to do any act which they are prevented from doing under the other enactment by reason of the restriction, limitation or condition.

[(9)   The duty of care under section 1 of the Trustee Act 2000 applies to trustees of land when exercising the powers conferred by this section.]

7 Partition by trustees

(1)   The trustees of land may, where beneficiaries of full age are absolutely entitled in undivided shares to land subject to the trust, partition the land, or any part of it, and provide (by way of mortgage or otherwise) for the payment of any equality money.

(2)   The trustees shall give effect to any such partition by conveying the partitioned land in severalty (whether or not subject to any legal mortgage created for raising equality money), either absolutely or in trust, in accordance with the rights of those beneficiaries.

(3)   Before exercising their powers under subsection (2) the trustees shall obtain the consent of each of those beneficiaries.

(4)   Where a share in the land is affected by an incumbrance, the trustees may either give effect to it or provide for its discharge from the property allotted to that share as they think fit.

(5)   If a share in the land is absolutely vested in a minor, subsections (1) to (4) apply as if he were of full age, except that the trustees may act on his behalf and retain land or other property representing his share in trust for him.

[(6)   Subsection (1) is subject to section 21 (part unit: interests) and 22 (part unit: charging) of the Commonhold and Leasehold Reform Act 2002.]

8 Exclusion and restriction of powers

(1)   Sections 6 and 7 do not apply in the case of a trust of land created by a disposition in so far as provision to the effect that they do not apply is made by the disposition.

(2)   If the disposition creating such a trust makes provision requiring any consent to be obtained to the exercise of any power conferred by section 6 or 7, the power may not be exercised without that consent.

(3)   Subsection (1) does not apply in the case of charitable, ecclesiastical or public trusts.

(4)   Subsections (1) and (2) have effect subject to any enactment which prohibits or restricts the effect of provision of the description mentioned in them.

9 Delegation by trustees

(1)   The trustees of land may, by power of attorney, delegate to any beneficiary or beneficiaries of full age and beneficially entitled to an interest in possession in land subject to the trust any of their functions as trustees which relate to the land.

(2)   Where trustees purport to delegate to a person by a power of attorney under subsection (1) functions relating to any land and another person in good faith deals with him in relation to the

land, he shall be presumed in favour of that other person to have been a person to whom the functions could be delegated unless that other person has knowledge at the time of the transaction that he was not such a person.

And it shall be conclusively presumed in favour of any purchaser whose interest depends on the validity of that transaction that that other person dealt in good faith and did not have such knowledge if that other person makes a statutory declaration to that effect before or within three months after the completion of the purchase.

(3)   A power of attorney under subsection (1) shall be given by all the trustees jointly and (unless expressed to be irrevocable and to be given by way of security) may be revoked by any one or more of them; and such a power is revoked by the appointment as a trustee of a person other than those by whom it is given (though not by any of those persons dying or otherwise ceasing to be a trustee).

(4)   Where a beneficiary to whom functions are delegated by a power of attorney under subsection (1) ceases to be a person beneficially entitled to an interest in possession in land subject to the trust—

    (a)   if the functions are delegated to him alone, the power is revoked,

    (b)   if the functions are delegated to him and to other beneficiaries to be exercised by them jointly (but not separately), the power is revoked if each of the other beneficiaries ceases to be so entitled (but otherwise functions exercisable in accordance with the power are so exercisable by the remaining beneficiary or beneficiaries), and

    (c)   if the functions are delegated to him and to other beneficiaries to be exercised by them separately (or either separately or jointly), the power is revoked in so far as it relates to him.

(5)   A delegation under subsection (1) may be for any period or indefinite.

(6)   A power of attorney under subsection (1) cannot be [an enduring power of attorney or lasting power of attorney within the meaning of the Mental Capacity Act 2005].

(7)   Beneficiaries to whom functions have been delegated under subsection (1) are, in relation to the exercise of the functions, in the same position as trustees (with the same duties and liabilities); but such beneficiaries shall not be regarded as trustees for any other purposes (including, in particular, the purposes of any enactment permitting the delegation of functions by trustees or imposing requirements relating to the payment of capital money).

(8)   . . .

(9)   Neither this section nor the repeal by this Act of section 29 of the Law of Property Act 1925 (which is superseded by this section) affects the operation after the commencement of this Act of any delegation effected before that commencement.

Consents and consultation

10 Consents

(1)   If a disposition creating a trust of land requires the consent of more than two persons to the exercise by the trustees of any function relating to the land, the consent of any two of them to the exercise of the function is sufficient in favour of a purchaser.

(2)   Subsection (1) does not apply to the exercise of a function by trustees of land held on charitable, ecclesiastical or public trusts.

(3)   Where at any time a person whose consent is expressed by a disposition creating a trust of land to be required to the exercise by the trustees of any function relating to the land is not of full age—

(a)   his consent is not, in favour of a purchaser, required to the exercise of the function, but

(b)   the trustees shall obtain the consent of a parent who has parental responsibility for him (within the meaning of the Children Act 1989) or of a guardian of his.

11 Consultation with beneficiaries

(1)   The trustees of land shall in the exercise of any function relating to land subject to the trust—

(a)   so far as practicable, consult the beneficiaries of full age and beneficially entitled to an interest in possession in the land, and

(b)   so far as consistent with the general interest of the trust, give effect to the wishes of those beneficiaries, or (in case of dispute) of the majority (according to the value of their combined interests).

(2)   Subsection (1) does not apply—

(a)   in relation to a trust created by a disposition in so far as provision that it does not apply is made by the disposition,

(b)   in relation to a trust created or arising under a will made before the commencement of this Act, or

(c)   in relation to the exercise of the power mentioned in section 6(2).

(3)   Subsection (1) does not apply to a trust created before the commencement of this Act by a disposition, or a trust created after that commencement by reference to such a trust, unless provision to the effect that it is to apply is made by a deed executed—

(a)   in a case in which the trust was created by one person and he is of full capacity, by that person, or

(b)   in a case in which the trust was created by more than one person, by such of the persons who created the trust as are alive and of full capacity.

(4)   A deed executed for the purposes of subsection (3) is irrevocable.

Right of beneficiaries to occupy trust land

12 The right to occupy

(1)   A beneficiary who is beneficially entitled to an interest in possession in land subject to a trust of land is entitled by reason of his interest to occupy the land at any time if at that time—

    (a)   the purposes of the trust include making the land available for his occupation (or for the occupation of beneficiaries of a class of which he is a member or of beneficiaries in general), or

    (b)   the land is held by the trustees so as to be so available.

(2)   Subsection (1) does not confer on a beneficiary a right to occupy land if it is either unavailable or unsuitable for occupation by him.

(3)   This section is subject to section 13.

13 Exclusion and restriction of right to occupy

(1)   Where two or more beneficiaries are (or apart from this subsection would be) entitled under section 12 to occupy land, the trustees of land may exclude or restrict the entitlement of any one or more (but not all) of them.

(2)   Trustees may not under subsection (1)—

    (a)   unreasonably exclude any beneficiary's entitlement to occupy land, or
    (b)   restrict any such entitlement to an unreasonable extent.

(3)   The trustees of land may from time to time impose reasonable conditions on any beneficiary in relation to his occupation of land by reason of his entitlement under section 12.

(4)   The matters to which trustees are to have regard in exercising the powers conferred by this section include—

    (a)   the intentions of the person or persons (if any) who created the trust,

    (b)   the purposes for which the land is held, and

    (c)   the circumstances and wishes of each of the beneficiaries who is (or apart from any previous exercise by the trustees of those powers would be) entitled to occupy the land under section 12.

(5)   The conditions which may be imposed on a beneficiary under subsection (3) include, in particular, conditions requiring him—

    (a)   to pay any outgoings or expenses in respect of the land, or

    (b)   to assume any other obligation in relation to the land or to any activity which is or is proposed to be conducted there.

(6) Where the entitlement of any beneficiary to occupy land under section 12 has been excluded or restricted, the conditions which may be imposed on any other beneficiary under subsection (3) include, in particular, conditions requiring him to—

   (a) make payments by way of compensation to the beneficiary whose entitlement has been excluded or restricted, or

   (b) forgo any payment or other benefit to which he would otherwise be entitled under the trust so as to benefit that beneficiary.

(7) The powers conferred on trustees by this section may not be exercised—

   (a) so as prevent any person who is in occupation of land (whether or not by reason of an entitlement under section 12) from continuing to occupy the land, or

   (b) in a manner likely to result in any such person ceasing to occupy the land,

   unless he consents or the court has given approval.

(8) The matters to which the court is to have regard in determining whether to give approval under subsection (7) include the matters mentioned in subsection (4)(a) to (c).

Powers of court

14 Applications for order

(1) Any person who is a trustee of land or has an interest in property subject to a trust of land may make an application to the court for an order under this section.

(2) On an application for an order under this section the court may make any such order—

   (a) relating to the exercise by the trustees of any of their functions (including an order relieving them of any obligation to obtain the consent of, or to consult, any person in connection with the exercise of any of their functions), or

   (b) declaring the nature or extent of a person's interest in property subject to the trust,

   as the court thinks fit.

(3) The court may not under this section make any order as to the appointment or removal of trustees.

(4) The powers conferred on the court by this section are exercisable on an application whether it is made before or after the commencement of this Act.

15 Matters relevant in determining applications

(1) The matters to which the court is to have regard in determining an application for an order under section 14 include—

   (a) the intentions of the person or persons (if any) who created the trust,

   (b) the purposes for which the property subject to the trust is held,

   (c) the welfare of any minor who occupies or might reasonably be expected to occupy any land subject to the trust as his home, and

   (d) the interests of any secured creditor of any beneficiary.

(2)   In the case of an application relating to the exercise in relation to any land of the powers conferred on the trustees by section 13, the matters to which the court is to have regard also include the circumstances and wishes of each of the beneficiaries who is (or apart from any previous exercise by the trustees of those powers would be) entitled to occupy the land under section 12.

(3)   In the case of any other application, other than one relating to the exercise of the power mentioned in section 6(2), the matters to which the court is to have regard also include the circumstances and wishes of any beneficiaries of full age and entitled to an interest in possession in property subject to the trust or (in case of dispute) of the majority (according to the value of their combined interests).

(4)   This section does not apply to an application if section 335A of the Insolvency Act 1986 (which is inserted by Schedule 3 and relates to applications by a trustee of a bankrupt) applies to it.

Purchaser protection

16 Protection of purchasers

(1)   A purchaser of land which is or has been subject to a trust need not be concerned to see that any requirement imposed on the trustees by section 6(5), 7(3) or 11(1) has been complied with.

(2)   Where—

(a)   trustees of land who convey land which (immediately before it is conveyed) is subject to the trust contravene section 6(6) or (8), but

(b)   the purchaser of the land from the trustees has no actual notice of the contravention,

the contravention does not invalidate the conveyance.

(3)   Where the powers of trustees of land are limited by virtue of section 8—

(a)   the trustees shall take all reasonable steps to bring the limitation to the notice of any purchaser of the land from them, but

(b)   the limitation does not invalidate any conveyance by the trustees to a purchaser who has no actual notice of the limitation.

(4)   Where trustees of land convey land which (immediately before it is conveyed) is subject to the trust to persons believed by them to be beneficiaries absolutely entitled to the land under the trust and of full age and capacity—

(a)   the trustees shall execute a deed declaring that they are discharged from the trust in relation to that land, and

(b)   if they fail to do so, the court may make an order requiring them to do so.

(5)   A purchaser of land to which a deed under subsection (4) relates is entitled to assume that, as from the date of the deed, the land is not subject to the trust unless he has actual notice that the trustees were mistaken in their belief that the land was conveyed to beneficiaries absolutely entitled to the land under the trust and of full age and capacity.

(6)   Subsections (2) and (3) do not apply to land held on charitable, ecclesiastical or public trusts.

(7)   This section does not apply to registered land.

Supplementary

17 Application of provisions to trusts of proceeds of sale

(2) Section 14 applies in relation to a trust of proceeds of sale of land and trustees of such a trust as in relation to a trust of land and trustees of land.

(3) In this section "trust of proceeds of sale of land" means (subject to subsection (5)) any trust of property (other than a trust of land) which consists of or includes—

    (a) any proceeds of a disposition of land held in trust (including settled land), or

    (b) any property representing any such proceeds.

(4) The references in subsection (3) to a trust—

    (a) are to any description of trust (whether express, implied, resulting or constructive), including a trust for sale and a bare trust, and

    (b) include a trust created, or arising, before the commencement of this Act.

(5) A trust which (despite section 2) is a settlement for the purposes of the Settled Land Act 1925 cannot be a trust of proceeds of sale of land.

(6) In subsection (3)—

    (a) "disposition" includes any disposition made, or coming into operation, before the commencement of this Act, and

    (b) the reference to settled land includes personal chattels to which section 67(1) of the Settled Land Act 1925 (heirlooms) applies.

18 Application of Part to personal representatives

(1) The provisions of this Part relating to trustees, other than sections 10, 11 and 14, apply to personal representatives, but with appropriate modifications and without prejudice to the functions of personal representatives for the purposes of administration.

(2) The appropriate modifications include—

    (a) the substitution of references to persons interested in the due administration of the estate for references to beneficiaries, and

    (b) the substitution of references to the will for references to the disposition creating the trust.

(3) Section 3(1) does not apply to personal representatives if the death occurs before the commencement of this Act.

Part II Appointment and Retirement of Trustees

19 Appointment and retirement of trustee at instance of beneficiaries

(1) This section applies in the case of a trust where—

    (a) there is no person nominated for the purpose of appointing new trustees by the instrument, if any, creating the trust, and

(b)   the beneficiaries under the trust are of full age and capacity and (taken together) are absolutely entitled to the property subject to the trust.

(2)   The beneficiaries may give a direction or directions of either or both of the following descriptions—

(a)   a written direction to a trustee or trustees to retire from the trust, and

(b)   a written direction to the trustees or trustee for the time being (or, if there are none, to the personal representative of the last person who was a trustee) to appoint by writing to be a trustee or trustees the person or persons specified in the direction.

(3)   Where—

(a)   a trustee has been given a direction under subsection (2)(a),

(b)   reasonable arrangements have been made for the protection of any rights of his in connection with the trust,

(c)   after he has retired there will be either a trust corporation or at least two persons to act as trustees to perform the trust, and

(d)   either another person is to be appointed to be a new trustee on his retirement (whether in compliance with a direction under subsection (2)(b) or otherwise) or the continuing trustees by deed consent to his retirement,

he shall make a deed declaring his retirement and shall be deemed to have retired and be discharged from the trust.

(4)   Where a trustee retires under subsection (3) he and the continuing trustees (together with any new trustee) shall (subject to any arrangements for the protection of his rights) do anything necessary to vest the trust property in the continuing trustees (or the continuing and new trustees).

(5)   This section has effect subject to the restrictions imposed by the Trustee Act 1925 on the number of trustees.

20 Appointment of substitute for incapable trustee

(1)   This section applies where—

(a)   a trustee [lacks capacity (within the meaning of the Mental Capacity Act 2005) to exercise] his functions as trustee,

(b)   there is no person who is both entitled and willing and able to appoint a trustee in place of him under section 36(1) of the Trustee Act 1925, and

(c)   the beneficiaries under the trust are of full age and capacity and (taken together) are absolutely entitled to the property subject to the trust.

(2)   The beneficiaries may give to—

[(a)   a deputy appointed for the trustee by the Court of Protection,]

(b)   an attorney acting for him under the authority of [an enduring power of attorney or lasting power of attorney registered under the Mental Capacity Act 2005], or

(c)   a person authorised for the purpose by [the Court of Protection],

a written direction to appoint by writing the person or persons specified in the direction to be a trustee or trustees in place of the incapable trustee.

21 Supplementary

(1)   For the purposes of section 19 or 20 a direction is given by beneficiaries if—

(a)   a single direction is jointly given by all of them, or

(b)   (subject to subsection (2)) a direction is given by each of them (whether solely or jointly with one or more, but not all, of the others),

and none of them by writing withdraws the direction given by him before it has been complied with.

(2)   Where more than one direction is given each must specify for appointment or retirement the same person or persons.

(3)   Subsection (7) of section 36 of the Trustee Act 1925 (powers of trustees appointed under that section) applies to a trustee appointed under section 19 or 20 as if he were appointed under that section.

(4)   A direction under section 19 or 20 must not specify a person or persons for appointment if the appointment of that person or those persons would be in contravention of section 35(1) of the Trustee Act 1925 or section 24(1) of the Law of Property Act 1925 (requirements as to identity of trustees).

(5)   Sections 19 and 20 do not apply in relation to a trust created by a disposition in so far as provision that they do not apply is made by the disposition.

(6)   Sections 19 and 20 do not apply in relation to a trust created before the commencement of this Act by a disposition in so far as provision to the effect that they do not apply is made by a deed executed—

(a)   in a case in which the trust was created by one person and he is of full capacity, by that person, or

(b)   in a case in which the trust was created by more than one person, by such of the persons who created the trust as are alive and of full capacity.

(7)   A deed executed for the purposes of subsection (6) is irrevocable.

(8)   Where a deed is executed for the purposes of subsection (6)—

(a)   it does not affect anything done before its execution to comply with a direction under section 19 or 20, but

(b)   a direction under section 19 or 20 which has been given but not complied with before its execution shall cease to have effect.

Part III SUPPLEMENTARY

22 Meaning of "beneficiary"

(1)   In this Act "beneficiary", in relation to a trust, means any person who under the trust has an interest in property subject to the trust (including a person who has such an interest as a trustee or a personal representative).

(2)   In this Act references to a beneficiary who is beneficially entitled do not include a beneficiary who has an interest in property subject to the trust only by reason of being a trustee or personal representative.

(3)   For the purposes of this Act a person who is a beneficiary only by reason of being an annuitant is not to be regarded as entitled to an interest in possession in land subject to the trust.

23 Other interpretation provisions

(1)   In this Act "purchaser" has the same meaning as in Part I of the Law of Property Act 1925.

(2)   Subject to that, where an expression used in this Act is given a meaning by the Law of Property Act 1925 it has the same meaning as in that Act unless the context otherwise requires.

(3)   In this Act "the court" means—

(a)   the High Court, or
(b)   a county court.

SCHEDULE 1 Provisions Consequential On Section 2

Minors

1   (1)   Where after the commencement of this Act a person purports to convey a legal estate in land to a minor, or two or more minors, alone, the conveyance—

(a)   is not effective to pass the legal estate, but

(b)   operates as a declaration that the land is held in trust for the minor or minors (or if he purports to convey it to the minor or minors in trust for any persons, for those persons).

(2)   Where after the commencement of this Act a person purports to convey a legal estate in land to—

(a)   a minor or two or more minors, and

(b)   another person who is, or other persons who are, of full age,

the conveyance operates to vest the land in the other person or persons in trust for the minor or minors and the other person or persons (or if he purports to convey it to them in trust for any persons, for those persons).

(3)   Where immediately before the commencement of this Act a conveyance is operating (by virtue of section 27 of the Settled Land Act 1925) as an agreement to execute a settlement in favour of a minor or minors—

(a)   the agreement ceases to have effect on the commencement of this Act, and

(b)   the conveyance subsequently operates instead as a declaration that the land is held in trust for the minor or minors.

2   Where after the commencement of this Act a legal estate in land would, by reason of intestacy or in any other circumstances not dealt with in paragraph 1, vest in a person who is a minor if he were a person of full age, the land is held in trust for the minor.

Family charges

3   Where, by virtue of an instrument coming into operation after the commencement of this Act, land becomes charged voluntarily (or in consideration of marriage) [or the formation of civil partnership]) or by way of family arrangement, whether immediately or after an interval, with the payment of—

(a)   a rent charge for the life of a person or a shorter period, or

(b)   capital, annual or periodical sums for the benefit of a person,

the instrument operates as a declaration that the land is held in trust for giving effect to the charge.

Charitable, ecclesiastical and public trusts

4   (1)   This paragraph applies in the case of land held on charitable, ecclesiastical or public trusts (other than land to which the Universities and College Estates Act 1925 applies).

(2)   Where there is a conveyance of such land—

(a)   if neither section 37(1) nor section 39(1) of the Charities Act 1993 applies to the conveyance, it shall state that the land is held on such trusts, and

(b)   if neither section 37(2) nor section 39(2) of that Act has been complied with in relation to the conveyance and a purchaser has notice that the land is held on such trusts, he must see that any consents or orders necessary to authorise the transaction have been obtained.

(3)   Where any trustees or the majority of any set of trustees have power to transfer or create any legal estate in the land, the estate shall be transferred or created by them in the names and on behalf of the persons in whom it is vested.

Entailed interests

5   (1)   Where a person purports by an instrument coming into operation after the commencement of this Act to grant to another person an entailed interest in real or personal property, the instrument—

(a)   is not effective to grant an entailed interest, but

(b)   operates instead as a declaration that the property is held in trust absolutely for the person to whom an entailed interest in the property was purportedly granted.

(2)   Where a person purports by an instrument coming into operation after the commencement of this Act to declare himself a tenant in tail of real or personal property, the instrument is not effective to create an entailed interest.

Property held on settlement ceasing to exist

6   Where a settlement ceases to be a settlement for the purposes of the Settled Land Act 1925 because no relevant property (within the meaning of section 2(4)) is, or is deemed to be, subject to the settlement, any property which is or later becomes subject to the settlement is held in trust for the persons interested under the settlement.

WILLS ACT 1837

1837 chapter 26 7 Will 4 and 1 Vict

An Act for the amendment of the laws with respect to Wills.

[9 Signing and attestation of wills

No will shall be valid unless—

(a)   it is in writing, and signed by the testator, or by some other person in his presence and by his direction; and

(b)   it appears that the testator intended by his signature to give effect to the will; and

(c)   the signature is made or acknowledged by the testator in the presence of two or more witnesses present at the same time; and

(d)   each witness either—

    (i)   attests and signs the will; or

    (ii)   acknowledges his signature, in the presence of the testator (but not necessarily in the presence of any other witness),

but no form of attestation shall be necessary.]

15 Gifts to an attesting witness to be void

If any person shall attest the execution of any will to whom or to whose wife or husband any beneficial devise, legacy, estate, interest, gift, or appointment, of or affecting any real or personal estate (other than and except charges and directions for the payment of any debt or debts), shall be thereby given or made, such devise, legacy, estate, interest, gift, or appointment shall, so far only as concerns such person attesting the execution of such will, or the wife or husband of such person, or any person claiming under such person or wife or husband, be utterly null and void, and such person so attesting shall be admitted as a witness to prove the execution of such will, or to prove the validity or invalidity thereof, notwithstanding such devise, legacy, estate, interest, gift, or appointment mentioned in such will.

Part 5

The Law of Tort

CONSUMER PROTECTION ACT 1987

Part I Product Liability

1 Purpose and construction of Part I

(1) This Part shall have effect for the purpose of making such provision as is necessary in order to comply with the product liability Directive and shall be construed accordingly.

(2) In this Part, except in so far as the context otherwise requires—

. . .

"dependant" and "relative" have the same meanings as they have in, respectively, the Fatal Accidents Act 1976 and the Damages (Scotland) Act 1976;

"producer", in relation to a product, means—

(a) the person who manufactured it;

(b) in the case of a substance which has not been manufactured but has been won or abstracted, the person who won or abstracted it;

(c) in the case of a product which has not been manufactured, won or abstracted but essential characteristics of which are attributable to an industrial or other process having been carried out (for example, in relation to agricultural produce), the person who carried out that process;

"product" means any goods or electricity and (subject to subsection (3) below) includes a product which is comprised in another product, whether by virtue of being a component part or raw material or otherwise; and

"the product liability Directive" means the Directive of the Council of the European Communities, dated 25th July 1985, (No 85/374/EEC) on the approximation of the laws, regulations and administrative provisions of the member States concerning liability for defective products.

(3) For the purposes of this Part a person who supplies any product in which products are comprised, whether by virtue of being component parts or raw materials or otherwise, shall not be treated by reason only of his supply of that product as supplying any of the products so comprised.

2 Liability for defective products

(1) Subject to the following provisions of this Part, where any damage is caused wholly or partly by a defect in a product, every person to whom subsection (2) below applies shall be liable for the damage.

(2) This subsection applies to—

(a) the producer of the product;

(b)   any person who, by putting his name on the product or using a trade mark or other distinguishing mark in relation to the product, has held himself out to be the producer of the product;

(c)   any person who has imported the product into a member State from a place outside the member States in order, in the course of any business of his, to supply it to another.

(3)   Subject as aforesaid, where any damage is caused wholly or partly by a defect in a product, any person who supplied the product (whether to the person who suffered the damage, to the producer of any product in which the product in question is comprised or to any other person) shall be liable for the damage if—

(a)   the person who suffered the damage requests the supplier to identify one or more of the persons (whether still in existence or not) to whom subsection (2) above applies in relation to the product;

(b)   that request is made within a reasonable period after the damage occurs and at a time when it is not reasonably practicable for the person making the request to identify all those persons; and

(c)   the supplier fails, within a reasonable period after receiving the request, either to comply with the request or to identify the person who supplied the product to him.

(4)   . . .

(5)   Where two or more persons are liable by virtue of this Part for the same damage, their liability shall be joint and several.

(6)   This section shall be without prejudice to any liability arising otherwise than by virtue of this Part.

3 Meaning of "defect"

(1)   Subject to the following provisions of this section, there is a defect in a product for the purposes of this Part if the safety of the product is not such as persons generally are entitled to expect; and for those purposes "safety", in relation to a product, shall include safety with respect to products comprised in that product and safety in the context of risks of damage to property, as well as in the context of risks of death or personal injury.

(2)   In determining for the purposes of subsection (1) above what persons generally are entitled to expect in relation to a product all the circumstances shall be taken into account, including—

(a)   the manner in which, and purposes for which, the product has been marketed, its get-up, the use of any mark in relation to the product and any instructions for, or warnings with respect to, doing or refraining from doing anything with or in relation to the product;

(b)   what might reasonably be expected to be done with or in relation to the product; and

(c)   the time when the product was supplied by its producer to another;

and nothing in this section shall require a defect to be inferred from the fact alone that the safety of a product which is supplied after that time is greater than the safety of the product in question.

4 Defences

(1)   In any civil proceedings by virtue of this Part against any person ("the person proceeded against") in respect of a defect in a product it shall be a defence for him to show—

    (a)   that the defect is attributable to compliance with any requirement imposed by or under any enactment or with any Community obligation; or

    (b)   that the person proceeded against did not at any time supply the product to another; or

    (c)   that the following conditions are satisfied, that is to say—

        (i)   that the only supply of the product to another by the person proceeded against was otherwise than in the course of a business of that person's; and

        (ii)   that section 2(2) above does not apply to that person or applies to him by virtue only of things done otherwise than with a view to profit; or

    (d)   that the defect did not exist in the product at the relevant time; or

    (e)   that the state of scientific and technical knowledge at the relevant time was not such that a producer of products of the same description as the product in question might be expected to have discovered the defect if it had existed in his products while they were under his control; or

    (f)   that the defect—

        (i)   constituted a defect in a product ("the subsequent product") in which the product in question had been comprised; and

        (ii)   was wholly attributable to the design of the subsequent product or to compliance by the producer of the product in question with instructions given by the producer of the subsequent product.

(2)   In this section "the relevant time", in relation to electricity, means the time at which it was generated, being a time before it was transmitted or distributed, and in relation to any other product, means—

    (a)   if the person proceeded against is a person to whom subsection (2) of section 2 above applies in relation to the product, the time when he supplied the product to another;

    (b)   if that subsection does not apply to that person in relation to the product, the time when the product was last supplied by a person to whom that subsection does apply in relation to the product.

5 Damage giving rise to liability

(1)   Subject to the following provisions of this section, in this Part "damage" means death or personal injury or any loss of or damage to any property (including land).

(2)   A person shall not be liable under section 2 above in respect of any defect in a product for the loss of or any damage to the product itself or for the loss of or any damage to the whole or any part of any product which has been supplied with the product in question comprised in it.

(3)   A person shall not be liable under section 2 above for any loss of or damage to any property which, at the time it is lost or damaged, is not—

    (a)   of a description of property ordinarily intended for private use, occupation or consumption; and

    (b)   intended by the person suffering the loss or damage mainly for his own private use, occupation or consumption.

(4)   No damages shall be awarded to any person by virtue of this Part in respect of any loss of or damage to any property if the amount which would fall to be so awarded to that person, apart from this subsection and any liability for interest, does not exceed £275.

(5)   In determining for the purposes of this Part who has suffered any loss of or damage to property and when any such loss or damage occurred, the loss or damage shall be regarded as having occurred at the earliest time at which a person with an interest in the property had knowledge of the material facts about the loss or damage.

(6)   For the purposes of subsection (5) above the material facts about any loss of or damage to any property are such facts about the loss or damage as would lead a reasonable person with an interest in the property to consider the loss or damage sufficiently serious to justify his instituting proceedings for damages against a defendant who did not dispute liability and was able to satisfy a judgment.

(7)   For the purposes of subsection (5) above a person's knowledge includes knowledge which he might reasonably have been expected to acquire—

    (a)   from facts observable or ascertainable by him; or

    (b)   from facts ascertainable by him with the help of appropriate expert advice which it is reasonable for him to seek;

    but a person shall not be taken by virtue of this subsection to have knowledge of a fact ascertainable by him only with the help of expert advice unless he has failed to take all reasonable steps to obtain (and, where appropriate, to act on) that advice.

(8)   Subsections (5) to (7) above shall not extend to Scotland.

6 Application of certain enactments

(1)   Any damage for which a person is liable under section 2 above shall be deemed to have been caused—

    (a)   for the purposes of the Fatal Accidents Act 1976, by that person's wrongful act, neglect or default;

    (b)   for the purposes of section 3 of the Law Reform (Miscellaneous Provisions) (Scotland) Act 1940 (contribution among joint wrongdoers), by that person's wrongful act or negligent act or omission;

    (c)   for the purposes of section 1 of the Damages (Scotland) Act 1976 (rights of relatives of a deceased), by that person's act or omission; and

(d)   for the purposes of Part II of the Administration of Justice Act 1982 (damages for personal injuries, etc Scotland), by an act or omission giving rise to liability in that person to pay damages.

(2)   Where—

(a)   a person's death is caused wholly or partly by a defect in a product, or a person dies after suffering damage which has been so caused;

(b)   a request such as mentioned in paragraph (a) of subsection (3) of section 2 above is made to a supplier of the product by that person's personal representatives or, in the case of a person whose death is caused wholly or partly by the defect, by any dependant or relative of that person; and

(c)   the conditions specified in paragraphs (b) and (c) of that subsection are satisfied in relation to that request,

this Part shall have effect for the purposes of the Law Reform (Miscellaneous Provisions) Act 1934, the Fatal Accidents Act 1976 and the Damages (Scotland) Act 1976 as if liability of the supplier to that person under that subsection did not depend on that person having requested the supplier to identify certain persons or on the said conditions having been satisfied in relation to a request made by that person.

(3)   Section 1 of the Congenital Disabilities (Civil Liability) Act 1976 shall have effect for the purposes of this Part as if—

(a)   a person were answerable to a child in respect of an occurrence caused wholly or partly by a defect in a product if he is or has been liable under section 2 above in respect of any effect of the occurrence on a parent of the child, or would be so liable if the occurrence caused a parent of the child to suffer damage;

(b)   the provisions of this Part relating to liability under section 2 above applied in relation to liability by virtue of paragraph (a) above under the said section 1; and

(c)   subsection (6) of the said section 1 (exclusion of liability) were omitted.

(4)   Where any damage is caused partly by a defect in a product and partly by the fault of the person suffering the damage, the Law Reform (Contributory Negligence) Act 1945 and section 5 of the Fatal Accidents Act 1976 (contributory negligence) shall have effect as if the defect were the fault of every person liable by virtue of this Part for the damage caused by the defect.

(5)   In subsection (4) above "fault" has the same meaning as in the said Act of 1945.

(6)   Schedule 1 to this Act shall have effect for the purpose of amending the Limitation Act 1980 and the Prescription and Limitation (Scotland) Act 1973 in their application in relation to the bringing of actions by virtue of this Part.

(7)   It is hereby declared that liability by virtue of this Part is to be treated as liability in tort for the purposes of any enactment conferring jurisdiction on any court with respect to any matter.

(8)   Nothing in this Part shall prejudice the operation of section 12 of the Nuclear Installations Act 1965 (rights to compensation for certain breaches of duties confined to rights under that Act).

7 Prohibition on exclusions from liability

The liability of a person by virtue of this Part to a person who has suffered damage caused wholly or partly by a defect in a product, or to a dependant or relative of such a person, shall not be limited or excluded by any contract term, by any notice or by any other provision.

8 Power to modify Part I

(1) Her Majesty may by Order in Council make such modifications of this Part and of any other enactment (including an enactment contained in the following Parts of this Act, or in an Act passed after this Act) as appear to Her Majesty in Council to be necessary or expedient in consequence of any modification of the product liability Directive which is made at any time after the passing of this Act.

(2) An Order in Council under subsection (1) above shall not be submitted to Her Majesty in Council unless a draft of the Order has been laid before, and approved by a resolution of, each House of Parliament.

9 Application of Part I to Crown

(1) Subject to subsection (2) below, this Part shall bind the Crown.

(2) The Crown shall not, as regards the Crown's liability by virtue of this Part, be bound by this Part further than the Crown is made liable in tort or in reparation under the Crown Proceedings Act 1947, as that Act has effect from time to time.

Part II Consumer Safety

10 . . .

11 Safety regulations

(1) The Secretary of State may by regulations under this section ("safety regulations") make such provision as he considers appropriate . . . for the purpose of securing—

    (a) that goods to which this section applies are safe;

    (b) that goods to which this section applies which are unsafe, or would be unsafe in the hands of persons of a particular description, are not made available to persons generally or, as the case may be, to persons of that description; and

    (c) that appropriate information is, and inappropriate information is not, provided in relation to goods to which this section applies.

(2) Without prejudice to the generality of subsection (1) above, safety regulations may contain provision—

    (a) with respect to the composition or contents, design, construction, finish or packing of goods to which this section applies, with respect to standards for such goods and with respect to other matters relating to such goods;

(b) with respect to the giving, refusal, alteration or cancellation of approvals of such goods, of descriptions of such goods or of standards for such goods;

(c) with respect to the conditions that may be attached to any approval given under the regulations;

(d) for requiring such fees as may be determined by or under the regulations to be paid on the giving or alteration of any approval under the regulations and on the making of an application for such an approval or alteration;

(e) with respect to appeals against refusals, alterations and cancellations of approvals given under the regulations and against the conditions contained in such approvals;

(f) for requiring goods to which this section applies to be approved under the regulations or to conform to the requirements of the regulations or to descriptions or standards specified in or approved by or under the regulations;

(g) with respect to the testing or inspection of goods to which this section applies (including provision for determining the standards to be applied in carrying out any test or inspection);

(h) with respect to the ways of dealing with goods of which some or all do not satisfy a test required by or under the regulations or a standard connected with a procedure so required;

(i) for requiring a mark, warning or instruction or any other information relating to goods to be put on or to accompany the goods or to be used or provided in some other manner in relation to the goods, and for securing that inappropriate information is not given in relation to goods either by means of misleading marks or otherwise;

(j) for prohibiting persons from supplying, or from offering to supply, agreeing to supply, exposing for supply or possessing for supply, goods to which this section applies and component parts and raw materials for such goods;

(k) for requiring information to be given to any such person as may be determined by or under the regulations for the purpose of enabling that person to exercise any function conferred on him by the regulations.

(3) Without prejudice as aforesaid, safety regulations may contain provision—

(a) for requiring persons on whom functions are conferred by or under section 27 below to have regard, in exercising their functions so far as relating to any provision of safety regulations, to matters specified in a direction issued by the Secretary of State with respect to that provision;

(b) for securing that a person shall not be guilty of an offence under section 12 below unless it is shown that the goods in question do not conform to a particular standard;

(c) for securing that proceedings for such an offence are not brought in England and Wales except by or with the consent of the Secretary of State or the Director of Public Prosecutions;

(d) for securing that proceedings for such an offence are not brought in Northern Ireland except by or with the consent of the Secretary of State or the Director of Public Prosecutions for Northern Ireland;

(e) for enabling a magistrates' court in England and Wales or Northern Ireland to try an information or, in Northern Ireland, a complaint in respect of such an offence if the information was laid or the complaint made within twelve months from the time when the offence was committed;

(f) for enabling summary proceedings for such an offence to be brought in Scotland at any time within twelve months from the time when the offence was committed; and

(g) for determining the persons by whom, and the manner in which, anything required to be done by or under the regulations is to be done.

(4) Safety regulations shall not provide for any contravention of the regulations to be an offence.

(5) Where the Secretary of State proposes to make safety regulations it shall be his duty before he makes them—

(a) to consult such organisations as appear to him to be representative of interests substantially affected by the proposal;

(b) to consult such other persons as he considers appropriate; and

(c) in the case of proposed regulations relating to goods suitable for use at work, to consult [the Health and Safety Executive] in relation to the application of the proposed regulations to Great Britain;

but the preceding provisions of this subsection shall not to apply in the case of regulations which provide for the regulations to cease to have effect at the end of a period of not more than twelve months beginning with the day on which they come into force and which contain a statement that it appears to the Secretary of State that the need to protect the public requires that the regulations should be made without delay.

(6) The power to make safety regulations shall be exercisable by statutory instrument subject to annulment in pursuance of a resolution of either House of Parliament and shall include power—

(a) to make different provision for different cases; and

(b) to make such supplemental, consequential and transitional provision as the Secretary of State considers appropriate.

(7) This section applies to any goods other than—

(a) growing crops and things comprised in land by virtue of being attached to it;

(b) water, food, feeding stuff and fertiliser;

(c) gas which is, is to be or has been supplied by a person authorised to supply it by or under [section 7A of the Gas Act 1986 (licensing of gas suppliers and gas shippers) or paragraph 5 of Schedule 2A to that Act (supply to very large customers an exception to prohibition on unlicensed activities)] [or under Article 8(1)(c) of the Gas (Northern Ireland) Order 1996];

(d) controlled drugs and licensed medicinal products.

12 Offences against the safety regulations

(1) Where safety regulations prohibit a person from supplying or offering or agreeing to supply any goods or from exposing or possessing any goods for supply, that person shall be guilty of an offence if he contravenes the prohibition.

(2) Where safety regulations require a person who makes or processes any goods in the course of carrying on a business—

 (a) to carry out a particular test or use a particular procedure in connection with the making or processing of the goods with a view to ascertaining whether the goods satisfy any requirements of such regulations; or

 (b) to deal or not to deal in a particular way with a quantity of the goods of which the whole or part does not satisfy such a test or does not satisfy standards connected with such a procedure,

 that person shall be guilty of an offence if he does not comply with the requirement.

(3) If a person contravenes a provision of safety regulations which prohibits or requires the provision, by means of a mark or otherwise, of information of a particular kind in relation to goods, he shall be guilty of an offence.

(4) Where safety regulations require any person to give information to another for the purpose of enabling that other to exercise any function, that person shall be guilty of an offence if—

 (a) he fails without reasonable cause to comply with the requirement; or

 (b) in giving the information which is required of him—

 (i) he makes any statement which he knows is false in a material particular; or

 (ii) he recklessly makes any statement which is false in a material particular.

(5) A person guilty of an offence under this section shall be liable on summary conviction to imprisonment for a term not exceeding six months or to a fine not exceeding level 5 on the standard scale or to both.

13 Prohibition notices and notices to warn

(1) The Secretary of State may—

 (a) serve on any person a notice ("a prohibition notice") prohibiting that person, except with the consent of the Secretary of State, from supplying, or from offering to supply, agreeing to supply, exposing for supply or possessing for supply, any relevant goods which the Secretary of State considers are unsafe and which are described in the notice;

 (b) serve on any person a notice ("a notice to warn") requiring that person at his own expense to publish, in a form and manner and on occasions specified in the notice, a warning about any relevant goods which the Secretary of State considers are unsafe, which that person supplies or has supplied and which are described in the notice.

(2)   Schedule 2 to this Act shall have effect with respect to prohibition notices and notices to warn; and the Secretary of State may by regulations make provision specifying the manner in which information is to be given to any person under that Schedule.

(3)   A consent given by the Secretary of State for the purposes of a prohibition notice may impose such conditions on the doing of anything for which the consent is required as the Secretary of State considers appropriate. ·

(4)   A person who contravenes a prohibition notice or a notice to warn shall be guilty of an offence and liable on summary conviction to imprisonment for a term not exceeding six months or to a fine not exceeding level 5 on the standard scale or to both.

(5)   The power to make regulations under subsection (2) above shall be exercisable by statutory instrument subject to annulment in pursuance of a resolution of either House of Parliament and shall include power—

(a)   to make different provision for different cases; and

(b)   to make such supplemental, consequential and transitional provision as the Secretary of State considers appropriate.

(6)   In this section "relevant goods" means—

(a)   in relation to a prohibition notice, any goods to which section 11 above applies; and

(b)   in relation to a notice to warn, any goods to which that section applies or any growing crops or things comprised in land by virtue of being attached to it.

[(7)   A notice may not be given under this section in respect of any aspect of the safety of goods, or any risk or category of risk associated with goods, concerning which provision is contained in the General Product Safety Regulations 2005.]

14 Suspension notices

(1)   Where an enforcement authority has reasonable grounds for suspecting that any safety provision has been contravened in relation to any goods, the authority may serve a notice ("a suspension notice") prohibiting the person on whom it is served, for such period ending not more than six months after the date of the notice as is specified therein, from doing any of the following things without the consent of the authority, that is to say, supplying the goods, offering to supply them, agreeing to supply them or exposing them for supply.

(2)   A suspension notice served by an enforcement authority in respect of any goods shall—

(a)   describe the goods in a manner sufficient to identify them;

(b)   set out the grounds on which the authority suspects that a safety provision has been contravened in relation to the goods; and

(c)   state that, and the manner in which, the person on whom the notice is served may appeal against the notice under section 15 below.

(3)   A suspension notice served by an enforcement authority for the purpose of prohibiting a person for any period from doing the things mentioned in subsection (1) above in relation to any goods

may also require that person to keep the authority informed of the whereabouts throughout that period of any of those goods in which he has an interest.

(4) Where a suspension notice has been served on any person in respect of any goods, no further such notice shall be served on that person in respect of the same goods unless—

    (a) proceedings against that person for an offence in respect of a contravention in relation to the goods of a safety provision (not being an offence under this section); or

    (b) proceedings for the forfeiture of the goods under section 16 or 17 below,

are pending at the end of the period specified in the first-mentioned notice.

(5) A consent given by an enforcement authority for the purposes of subsection (1) above may impose such conditions on the doing of anything for which the consent is required as the authority considers appropriate.

(6) Any person who contravenes a suspension notice shall be guilty of an offence and liable on summary conviction to imprisonment for a term not exceeding six months or to a fine not exceeding level 5 on the standard scale or to both.

(7) Where an enforcement authority serves a suspension notice in respect of any goods, the authority shall be liable to pay compensation to any person having an interest in the goods in respect of any loss or damage caused by reason of the service of the notice if—

    (a) there has been no contravention in relation to the goods of any safety provision; and

    (b) the exercise of the power is not attributable to any neglect or default by that person.

(8) Any disputed question as to the right to or the amount of any compensation payable under this section shall be determined by arbitration or, in Scotland, by a single arbiter appointed, failing agreement between the parties, by the sheriff.

15 Appeals against suspension notices

(1) Any person having an interest in any goods in respect of which a suspension notice is for the time being in force may apply for an order setting aside the notice.

(2) An application under this section may be made—

    (a) to any magistrates' court in which proceedings have been brought in England and Wales or Northern Ireland—

        (i) for an offence in respect of a contravention in relation to the goods of any safety provision; or

        (ii) for the forfeiture of the goods under section 16 below;

    (b) where no such proceedings have been so brought, by way of complaint to a magistrates' court; or

    (c) in Scotland, by summary application to the sheriff.

(3) On an application under this section to a magistrates' court in England and Wales or Northern Ireland the court shall make an order setting aside the suspension notice only if the court is satisfied that there has been no contravention in relation to the goods of any safety provision.

(4)   On an application under this section to the sheriff he shall make an order setting aside the suspension notice only if he is satisfied that at the date of making the order—

(a)   proceedings for an offence in respect of a contravention in relation to the goods of any safety provision; or

(b)   proceedings for the forfeiture of the goods under section 17 below,

have not been brought or, having been brought, have been concluded.

(5)   Any person aggrieved by an order made under this section by a magistrates' court in England and Wales or Northern Ireland, or by a decision of such a court not to make such an order, may appeal against that order or decision—

(a)   in England and Wales, to the Crown Court;

(b)   in Northern Ireland, to the county court;

and an order so made may contain such provision as appears to the court to be appropriate for delaying the coming into force of the order pending the making and determination of any appeal (including any application under section 111 of the Magistrates' Courts Act 1980 or Article 146 of the Magistrates' Courts (Northern Ireland) Order 1981 (statement of case)).

16 Forfeiture: England and Wales and Northern Ireland

(1)   An enforcement authority in England and Wales or Northern Ireland may apply under this section for an order for the forfeiture of any goods on the grounds that there has been a contravention in relation to the goods of a safety provision.

(2)   An application under this section may be made—

(a)   where proceedings have been brought in a magistrates' court for an offence in respect of a contravention in relation to some or all of the goods of any safety provision, to that court;

(b)   where an application with respect to some or all of the goods has been made to a magistrates' court under section 15 above or section 33 below, to that court; and

(c)   where no application for the forfeiture of the goods has been made under paragraph (a) or (b) above, by way of complaint to a magistrates' court.

(3)   On an application under this section the court shall make an order for the forfeiture of any goods only if it is satisfied that there has been a contravention in relation to the goods of a safety provision.

(4)   For the avoidance of doubt it is declared that a court may infer for the purposes of this section that there has been a contravention in relation to any goods of a safety provision if it is satisfied that any such provision has been contravened in relation to goods which are representative of those goods (whether by reason of being of the same design or part of the same consignment or batch or otherwise).

(5)   Any person aggrieved by an order made under this section by a magistrates' court, or by a decision of such a court not to make such an order, may appeal against that order or decision—

(a)   in England and Wales, to the Crown Court;

(b)   in Northern Ireland, to the county court;

and an order so made may contain such provision as appears to the court to be appropriate for delaying the coming into force of the order pending the making and determination of any appeal (including any application under section 111 of the Magistrates' Courts Act 1980 or Article 146 of the Magistrates' Courts (Northern Ireland) Order 1981 (statement of case)).

(6)   Subject to subsection (7) below, where any goods are forfeited under this section they shall be destroyed in accordance with such directions as the court may give.

(7)   On making an order under this section a magistrates' court may, if it considers it appropriate to do so, direct that the goods to which the order relates shall (instead of being destroyed) be released, to such person as the court may specify, on condition that that person—

(a)   does not supply those goods to any person otherwise than as mentioned in section 46(7)(a) or (b) below; and

(b)   complies with any order to pay costs or expenses (including any order under section 35 below) which has been made against that person in the proceedings for the order for forfeiture.

17 Forfeiture: Scotland

(1)   In Scotland a sheriff may make an order for forfeiture of any goods in relation to which there has been a contravention of a safety provision—

(a)   on an application by the procurator-fiscal made in the manner specified in section 310 of the Criminal Procedure (Scotland) Act 1975; or

(b)   where a person is convicted of any offence in respect of any such contravention, in addition to any other penalty which the sheriff may impose.

(2)   The procurator-fiscal making an application under subsection (1)(a) above shall serve on any person appearing to him to be the owner of, or otherwise to have an interest in, the goods to which the application relates a copy of the application, together with a notice giving him the opportunity to appear at the hearing of the application to show cause why the goods should not be forfeited.

(3)   Service under subsection (2) above shall be carried out, and such service may be proved, in the manner specified for citation of an accused in summary proceedings under the Criminal Procedure (Scotland) Act 1975.

(4)   Any person upon whom notice is served under subsection (2) above and any other person claiming to be the owner of, or otherwise to have an interest in, goods to which an application under this section relates shall be entitled to appear at the hearing of the application to show cause why the goods should not be forfeited.

(5)   The sheriff shall not make an order following an application under subsection (1)(a) above—

(a)   if any person on whom notice is served under subsection (2) above does not appear, unless service of the notice on that person is proved; or

(b)   if no notice under subsection (2) above has been served, unless the court is satisfied that in the circumstances it was reasonable not to serve notice on any person.

(6)   The sheriff shall make an order under this section only if he is satisfied that there has been a contravention in relation to those goods of a safety provision.

(7)   For the avoidance of doubt it is declared that the sheriff may infer for the purposes of this section that there has been a contravention in relation to any goods of a safety provision if he is satisfied that any such provision has been contravened in relation to any goods which are representative of those goods (whether by reason of being of the same design or part of the same consignment or batch or otherwise).

(8)   Where an order for the forfeiture of any goods is made following an application by the procurator-fiscal under subsection (1)(a) above, any person who appeared, or was entitled to appear, to show cause why goods should not be forfeited may, within twenty-one days of the making of the order, appeal to the High Court by Bill of Suspension on the ground of an alleged miscarriage of justice; [and section 182(5)(a) to (e) of the Criminal Procedure (Scotland) Act 1995 shall apply to an appeal under this subsection as it applies to a stated case under Part X of that Act].

(9)   An order following an application under subsection (1)(a) above shall not take effect—

(a)   until the end of the period of twenty-one days beginning with the day after the day on which the order is made; or

(b)   if an appeal is made under subsection (8) above within that period, until the appeal is determined or abandoned.

(10)   An order under subsection (1)(b) above shall not take effect—

(a)   until the end of the period within which an appeal against the order could be brought under the Criminal Procedure (Scotland) Act 1975; or

(b)   if an appeal is made within that period, until the appeal is determined or abandoned.

(11)   Subject to subsection (12) below, goods forfeited under this section shall be destroyed in accordance with such directions as the sheriff may give.

(12)   If he thinks fit, the sheriff may direct that the goods be released, to such person as he may specify, on condition that that person does not supply those goods to any other person otherwise than as mentioned in section 46(7)(a) or (b) below.

18   Power to obtain information

(1)   If the Secretary of State considers that, for the purpose of deciding whether—

(a)   to make, vary or revoke any safety regulations; or

(b)   to serve, vary or revoke a prohibition notice; or

(c)   to serve or revoke a notice to warn,

he requires information which another person is likely to be able to furnish, the Secretary of State may serve on the other person a notice under this section.

(2)   A notice served on any person under this section may require that person—

(a)   to furnish to the Secretary of State, within a period specified in the notice, such information as is so specified;

(b)   to produce such records as are specified in the notice at a time and place so specified and to permit a person appointed by the Secretary of State for the purpose to take copies of the records at that time and place.

(3)   A person shall be guilty of an offence if he—

(a)   fails, without reasonable cause, to comply with a notice served on him under this section; or

(b)   in purporting to comply with a requirement which by virtue of paragraph (a) of subsection (2) above is contained in such a notice—

(i)   furnishes information which he knows is false in a material particular; or

(ii)   recklessly furnishes information which is false in a material particular.

(4)   A person guilty of an offence under subsection (3) above shall—

(a)   in the case of an offence under paragraph (a) of that subsection, be liable on summary conviction to a fine not exceeding level 5 on the standard scale; and

(b)   in the case of an offence under paragraph (b) of that subsection be liable—

(i)   on conviction on indictment, to a fine;

(ii)   on summary conviction, to a fine not exceeding the statutory maximum.

19 Interpretation of Part II

(1)   In this Part—

"controlled drug" means a controlled drug within the meaning of the Misuse of Drugs Act 1971;

"feeding stuff" and "fertiliser" have the same meanings as in Part IV of the Agriculture Act 1970;

"food" does not include anything containing tobacco but, subject to that, has the same meaning as in the [Food Safety Act 1990] or, in relation to Northern Ireland, the same meaning as in the [Food Safety (Northern Ireland) Order 1991];

"licensed medicinal product" means—

(a)   any medicinal product within the meaning of the Medicines Act 1968 in respect of which a product licence within the meaning of that Act is for the time being in force; . . .

(b)   any other article or substance in respect of which any such licence is for the time being in force in pursuance of an order under section 104 or 105 of that Act (application of Act to other articles and substances); [or

(c)   a veterinary medicinal product that has a marketing authorisation under the Veterinary Medicines Regulations 2006;]

"safe", in relation to any goods, means such that there is no risk, or no risk apart from one reduced to a minimum, that any of the following will (whether immediately or after a definite or indefinite period) cause the death of, or any personal injury to, any person whatsoever, that is to say—

(a)   the goods;

(b)   the keeping, use or consumption of the goods;

(c)   the assembly of any of the goods which are, or are to be, supplied unassembled;

(d)   any emission or leakage from the goods or, as a result of the keeping, use or consumption of the goods, from anything else; or

(e)   reliance on the accuracy of any measurement, calculation or other reading made by or by means of the goods,

and . . . "unsafe" shall be construed accordingly;

"tobacco" includes any tobacco product within the meaning of the Tobacco Products Duty Act 1979 and any article or substance containing tobacco and intended for oral or nasal use.

(2)   In the definition of "safe" in subsection (1) above, references to the keeping, use or consumption of any goods are references to—

(a)   the keeping, use or consumption of the goods by the persons by whom, and in all or any of the ways or circumstances in which, they might reasonably be expected to be kept, used or consumed; and

(b)   the keeping, use or consumption of the goods either alone or in conjunction with other goods in conjunction with which they might reasonably be expected to be kept, used or consumed.

Part V Miscellaneous and Supplemental

45 Interpretation

(1)   In this Act, except in so far as the context otherwise requires—

"aircraft" includes gliders, balloons and hovercraft;

"business" includes a trade or profession and the activities of a professional or trade association or of a local authority or other public authority;

"conditional sale agreement", "credit-sale agreement" and "hire-purchase agreement" have the same meanings as in the Consumer Credit Act 1974 but as if in the definitions in that Act "goods" had the same meaning as in this Act;

"contravention" includes a failure to comply and cognate expressions shall be construed accordingly;

"enforcement authority" means the Secretary of State, any other Minister of the Crown in charge of a Government department, any such department and any authority, council or other person on whom functions under this Act are conferred by or under section 27 above;

"gas" has the same meaning as in Part I of the Gas Act 1986;

"goods" includes substances, growing crops and things comprised in land by virtue of being attached to it and any ship, aircraft or vehicle;

"information" includes accounts, estimates and returns;

"magistrates' court", in relation to Northern Ireland, means a court of summary jurisdiction;

< . . . >

"modifications" includes additions, alterations and omissions, and cognate expressions shall be construed accordingly;

"motor vehicle" has the same meaning as in [the Road Traffic Act 1988];

"notice" means a notice in writing;

"notice to warn" means a notice under section 13(1)(b) above;

"officer", in relation to an enforcement authority, means a person authorised in writing to assist the authority in carrying out its functions under or for the purposes of the enforcement of any of the safety provisions or of any of the provisions made by or under Part III of this Act;

"personal injury" includes any disease and any other impairment of a person's physical or mental condition;

"premises" includes any place and any ship, aircraft or vehicle;

"prohibition notice" means a notice under section 13(1)(a) above;

"records" includes any books or documents and any records in non-documentary form;

"safety provision" means . . . any provision of safety regulations, a prohibition notice or a suspension notice;

"safety regulations" means regulations under section 11 above;

"ship" includes any boat and any other description of vessel used in navigation;

"subordinate legislation" has the same meaning as in the Interpretation Act 1978;

"substance" means any natural or artificial substance, whether in solid, liquid or gaseous form or in the form of a vapour, and includes substances that are comprised in or mixed with other goods;

"supply" and cognate expressions shall be construed in accordance with section 46 below;

"suspension notice" means a notice under section 14 above.

(2) Except in so far as the context otherwise requires, references in this Act to a contravention of a safety provision shall, in relation to any goods, include references to anything which would constitute such a contravention if the goods were supplied to any person.

(3) References in this Act to any goods in relation to which any safety provision has been or may have been contravened shall include references to any goods which it is not reasonably practicable to separate from any such goods.

(4)   . . .

(5)   In Scotland, any reference in this Act to things comprised in land by virtue of being attached to it is a reference to moveables which have become heritable by accession to heritable property.

50 Short title, commencement and transitional provision

(1)   This Act may be cited as the Consumer Protection Act 1987.

DEFAMATION ACT 1952

1952 chapter 66 15 and 16 Geo 6 and 1 Eliz 2

An Act to amend the law relating to libel and slander and other malicious falsehoods. [30th October 1952]

2 Slander affecting official, professional or business reputation

In an action for slander in respect of words calculated to disparage the plaintiff in any office, profession, calling, trade or business held or carried on by him at the time of the publication, it shall not be necessary to allege or prove special damage, whether or not the words are spoken of the plaintiff in the way of his office, profession, calling, trade or business.

3 Slander of title, etc

(1)   In an action for slander of title, slander of goods or other malicious falsehood, it shall not be necessary to allege or prove special damage—

   (a)   if the words upon which the action is founded are calculated to cause pecuniary damage to the plaintiff and are published in writing or other permanent form; or

   (b)   if the said words are calculated to cause pecuniary damage to the plaintiff in respect of any office, profession, calling, trade or business held or carried on by him at the time of the publication.

(2)   Section one of this Act shall apply for the purposes of this section as it applies for the purposes of the law of libel and slander.

5 Justification

In an action for libel or slander in respect of words containing two or more distinct charges against the plaintiff, a defence of justification shall not fail by reason only that the truth of every charge is not proved if the words not proved to be true do not materially injure the plaintiff's reputation having regard to the truth of the remaining charges.

6 Fair comment

In an action for libel or slander in respect of words consisting partly of allegations of fact and partly of expression of opinion, a defence of fair comment shall not fail by reason only that the truth of every allegation of fact is not proved if the expression of opinion is fair comment having regard to such of the facts alleged or referred to in the words complained of as are proved.

9 Extension of certain defences to broadcasting

(1) Section three of the Parliamentary Papers Act 1840 (which confers protection in respect of proceedings for printing extracts from or abstracts of parliamentary papers) shall have effect as if the reference to printing included a reference to broadcasting by means of wireless telegraphy.

10 Limitation on privilege at elections

A defamatory statement published by or on behalf of a candidate in any election to a local government authority [to the Scottish Parliament] or to Parliament shall not be deemed to be published on a privileged occasion on the ground that it is material to a question in issue in the election, whether or not the person by whom it is published is qualified to vote at the election.

11 Agreements for indemnity

An agreement for indemnifying any person against civil liability for libel in respect of the publication of any matter shall not be unlawful unless at the time of the publication that person knows that the matter is defamatory, and does not reasonably believe there is a good defence to any action brought upon it.

12 Evidence of other damages recovered by plaintiff

In any action for libel or slander the defendant may give evidence in mitigation of damages that the plaintiff has recovered damages, or has brought actions for damages, for libel or slander in respect of the publication of words to the same effect as the words on which the action is founded, or has received or agreed to receive compensation in respect of any such publication.

13 Consolidation of actions for slander etc

Section five of the Law of Libel Amendment Act 1888 (which provides for the consolidation, on the application of the defendants, of two or more actions for libel by the same plaintiff) shall apply to actions for slander and to actions for slander of title, slander of goods or other malicious falsehood as it applies to actions for libel; and references in that section to the same, or substantially the same, libel shall be construed accordingly.

16 Interpretation

(1) Any reference in this Act to words shall be construed as including a reference to pictures, visual images, gestures and other methods of signifying meaning.

17 Proceedings affected and saving

(1) This Act applies for the purposes of any proceedings begun after the commencement of this Act, whenever the cause of action arose, but does not affect any proceedings begun before the commencement of this Act.

(2) Nothing in this Act affects the law relating to criminal libel.

18 Short title, commencement extent and repeals

(1)   This Act may be cited as the Defamation Act 1952, and shall come into operation one month after the passing of this Act.

DEFAMATION ACT 1996

1996 chapter 31

An Act to amend the law of defamation and to amend the law of limitation with respect to actions for defamation or malicious falsehood. [4th July 1996]

Responsibility for publication

1 Responsibility for publication

(1)   In defamation proceedings a person has a defence if he shows that—

   (a)   he was not the author, editor or publisher of the statement complained of,

   (b)   he took reasonable care in relation to its publication, and

   (c)   he did not know, and had no reason to believe, that what he did caused or contributed to the publication of a defamatory statement.

(2)   For this purpose "author", "editor" and "publisher" have the following meanings, which are further explained in subsection (3)—

   "author" means the originator of the statement, but does not include a person who did not intend that his statement be published at all;

   "editor" means a person having editorial or equivalent responsibility for the content of the statement or the decision to publish it; and

   "publisher" means a commercial publisher, that is, a person whose business is issuing material to the public, or a section of the public, who issues material containing the statement in the course of that business.

(3)   A person shall not be considered the author, editor or publisher of a statement if he is only involved—

   (a)   in printing, producing, distributing or selling printed material containing the statement;

   (b)   in processing, making copies of, distributing, exhibiting or selling a film or sound recording (as defined in Part I of the Copyright, Designs and Patents Act 1988) containing the statement;

   (c)   in processing, making copies of, distributing or selling any electronic medium in or on which the statement is recorded, or in operating or providing any equipment, system or service by means of which the statement is retrieved, copied, distributed or made available in electronic form;

(d)   as the broadcaster of a live programme containing the statement in circumstances in which he has no effective control over the maker of the statement;

(e)   as the operator of or provider of access to a communications system by means of which the statement is transmitted, or made available, by a person over whom he has no effective control.

In a case not within paragraphs (a) to (e) the court may have regard to those provisions by way of analogy in deciding whether a person is to be considered the author, editor or publisher of a statement.

(4)   Employees or agents of an author, editor or publisher are in the same position as their employer or principal to the extent that they are responsible for the content of the statement or the decision to publish it.

(5)   In determining for the purposes of this section whether a person took reasonable care, or had reason to believe that what he did caused or contributed to the publication of a defamatory statement, regard shall be had to—

(a)   the extent of his responsibility for the content of the statement or the decision to publish it,

(b)   the nature or circumstances of the publication, and

(c)   the previous conduct or character of the author, editor or publisher.

(6)   This section does not apply to any cause of action which arose before the section came into force.

Offer to make amends

2 Offer to make amends

(1)   A person who has published a statement alleged to be defamatory of another may offer to make amends under this section.

(2)   The offer may be in relation to the statement generally or in relation to a specific defamatory meaning which the person making the offer accepts that the statement conveys ("a qualified offer").

(3)   An offer to make amends—

(a)   must be in writing,

(b)   must be expressed to be an offer to make amends under section 2 of the Defamation Act 1996, and

(c)   must state whether it is a qualified offer and, if so, set out the defamatory meaning in relation to which it is made.

(4)   An offer to make amends under this section is an offer—

(a)   to make a suitable correction of the statement complained of and a sufficient apology to the aggrieved party,

(b)   to publish the correction and apology in a manner that is reasonable and practicable in the circumstances, and

(c)   to pay to the aggrieved party such compensation (if any), and such costs, as may be agreed or determined to be payable.

The fact that the offer is accompanied by an offer to take specific steps does not affect the fact that an offer to make amends under this section is an offer to do all the things mentioned in paragraphs (a) to (c).

(5)   An offer to make amends under this section may not be made by a person after serving a defence in defamation proceedings brought against him by the aggrieved party in respect of the publication in question.

(6)   An offer to make amends under this section may be withdrawn before it is accepted; and a renewal of an offer which has been withdrawn shall be treated as a new offer.

3 Accepting an offer to make amends

(1)   If an offer to make amends under section 2 is accepted by the aggrieved party, the following provisions apply.

(2)   The party accepting the offer may not bring or continue defamation proceedings in respect of the publication concerned against the person making the offer, but he is entitled to enforce the offer to make amends, as follows.

(3)   If the parties agree on the steps to be taken in fulfilment of the offer, the aggrieved party may apply to the court for an order that the other party fulfil his offer by taking the steps agreed.

(4)   If the parties do not agree on the steps to be taken by way of correction, apology and publication, the party who made the offer may take such steps as he thinks appropriate, and may in particular—

(a)   make the correction and apology by a statement in open court in terms approved by the court, and

(b)   give an undertaking to the court as to the manner of their publication.

(5)   If the parties do not agree on the amount to be paid by way of compensation, it shall be determined by the court on the same principles as damages in defamation proceedings.

The court shall take account of any steps taken in fulfilment of the offer and (so far as not agreed between the parties) of the suitability of the correction, the sufficiency of the apology and whether the manner of their publication was reasonable in the circumstances, and may reduce or increase the amount of compensation accordingly.

(6)   If the parties do not agree on the amount to be paid by way of costs, it shall be determined by the court on the same principles as costs awarded in court proceedings.

(7)   The acceptance of an offer by one person to make amends does not affect any cause of action against another person in respect of the same publication, subject as follows.

(8)   In England and Wales or Northern Ireland, for the purposes of the Civil Liability (Contribution) Act 1978—

(a) the amount of compensation paid under the offer shall be treated as paid in bona fide settlement or compromise of the claim; and

(b) where another person is liable in respect of the same damage (whether jointly or otherwise), the person whose offer to make amends was accepted is not required to pay by virtue of any contribution under section 1 of that Act a greater amount than the amount of the compensation payable in pursuance of the offer.

(9) In Scotland—

(a) subsection (2) of section 3 of the Law Reform (Miscellaneous Provisions) (Scotland) Act 1940 (right of one joint wrongdoer as respects another to recover contribution towards damages) applies in relation to compensation paid under an offer to make amends as it applies in relation to damages in an action to which that section applies; and

(b) where another person is liable in respect of the same damage (whether jointly or otherwise), the person whose offer to make amends was accepted is not required to pay by virtue of any contribution under section 3(2) of that Act a greater amount than the amount of compensation payable in pursuance of the offer.

(10) Proceedings under this section shall be heard and determined without a jury.

4 Failure to accept offer to make amends

(1) If an offer to make amends under section 2, duly made and not withdrawn, is not accepted by the aggrieved party, the following provisions apply.

(2) The fact that the offer was made is a defence (subject to subsection (3)) to defamation proceedings in respect of the publication in question by that party against the person making the offer.

A qualified offer is only a defence in respect of the meaning to which the offer related.

(3) There is no such defence if the person by whom the offer was made knew or had reason to believe that the statement complained of—

(a) referred to the aggrieved party or was likely to be understood as referring to him, and

(b) was both false and defamatory of that party;

but it shall be presumed until the contrary is shown that he did not know and had no reason to believe that was the case.

(4) The person who made the offer need not rely on it by way of defence, but if he does he may not rely on any other defence.

If the offer was a qualified offer, this applies only in respect of the meaning to which the offer related.

(5) The offer may be relied on in mitigation of damages whether or not it was relied on as a defence.

The meaning of a statement

7 Ruling on the meaning of a statement

In defamation proceedings the court shall not be asked to rule whether a statement is arguably capable, as opposed to capable, of bearing a particular meaning or meanings attributed to it.

Summary disposal of claim

8 Summary disposal of claim

(1)   In defamation proceedings the court may dispose summarily of the plaintiff's claim in accordance with the following provisions.

(2)   The court may dismiss the plaintiff's claim if it appears to the court that it has no realistic prospect of success and there is no reason why it should be tried.

(3)   The court may give judgment for the plaintiff and grant him summary relief (see section 9) if it appears to the court that there is no defence to the claim which has a realistic prospect of success, and that there is no other reason why the claim should be tried.

Unless the plaintiff asks for summary relief, the court shall not act under this subsection unless it is satisfied that summary relief will adequately compensate him for the wrong he has suffered.

(4)   In considering whether a claim should be tried the court shall have regard to—

(a)   whether all the persons who are or might be defendants in respect of the publication complained of are before the court;

(b)   whether summary disposal of the claim against another defendant would be inappropriate;

(c)   the extent to which there is a conflict of evidence;

(d)   the seriousness of the alleged wrong (as regards the content of the statement and the extent of publication); and

(e)   whether it is justifiable in the circumstances to proceed to a full trial.

(5)   Proceedings under this section shall be heard and determined without a jury.

9 Meaning of summary relief

(1)   For the purposes of section 8 (summary disposal of claim) "summary relief" means such of the following as may be appropriate—

(a)   a declaration that the statement was false and defamatory of the plaintiff;

(b)   an order that the defendant publish or cause to be published a suitable correction and apology;

(c)   damages not exceeding £10,000 or such other amount as may be prescribed by order of the Lord Chancellor;

(d)   an order restraining the defendant from publishing or further publishing the matter complained of.

(2)   The content of any correction and apology, and the time, manner, form and place of publication, shall be for the parties to agree.

If they cannot agree on the content, the court may direct the defendant to publish or cause to be published a summary of the court's judgment agreed by the parties or settled by the court in accordance with rules of court.

If they cannot agree on the time, manner, form or place of publication, the court may direct the defendant to take such reasonable and practicable steps as the court considers appropriate.

[(2A) The Lord Chancellor must consult the Lord Chief Justice of England and Wales before making any order under subsection 1(c) in relation to England and Wales.

[(2B) The Lord Chancellor must consult the Lord Chief Justice of Northern Ireland before making any order under subsection 1(c) in relation to Northern Ireland.

[(2C) The Lord Chancellor may nominate a judicial office holder (as defined in section 109(4) of the Constitutional Reform Act 2005) to exercise his functions under this section.

[(2D) The Lord Chief Justice of Northern Ireland may nominate any of the following to exercise his functions under this section—

(a)   the holder of one of the offices listed in Schedule 1 to the Justice (Northern Ireland) Act 2002;

(b)   a Lord Justice of Appeal (as defined in section 88 of that Act).]

(3)   Any order under subsection (1)(c) shall be made by statutory instrument which shall be subject to annulment in pursuance of a resolution of either House of Parliament.

10 Summary disposal: rules of court

(1)   Provision may be made by rules of court as to the summary disposal of the plaintiff's claim in defamation proceedings.

(2)   Without prejudice to the generality of that power, provision may be made—

(a)   authorising a party to apply for summary disposal at any stage of the proceedings;

(b)   authorising the court at any stage of the proceedings—

(i)   to treat any application, pleading or other step in the proceedings as an application for summary disposal, or

(ii)   to make an order for summary disposal without any such application;

(c)   as to the time for serving pleadings or taking any other step in the proceedings in a case where there are proceedings for summary disposal;

(d)   requiring the parties to identify any question of law or construction which the court is to be asked to determine in the proceedings;

(e)   as to the nature of any hearing on the question of summary disposal, and in particular—

(i) authorising the court to order affidavits or witness statements to be prepared for use as evidence at the hearing, and

(ii) requiring the leave of the court for the calling of oral evidence, or the introduction of new evidence, at the hearing;

(f) authorising the court to require a defendant to elect, at or before the hearing, whether or not to make an offer to make amends under section 2.

Evidence concerning proceedings in Parliament

13 Evidence concerning proceedings in Parliament

(1) Where the conduct of a person in or in relation to proceedings in Parliament is in issue in defamation proceedings, he may waive for the purposes of those proceedings, so far as concerns him, the protection of any enactment or rule of law which prevents proceedings in Parliament being impeached or questioned in any court or place out of Parliament.

(2) Where a person waives that protection—

(a) any such enactment or rule of law shall not apply to prevent evidence being given, questions being asked or statements, submissions, comments or findings being made about his conduct, and

(b) none of those things shall be regarded as infringing the privilege of either House of Parliament.

(3) The waiver by one person of that protection does not affect its operation in relation to another person who has not waived it.

(4) Nothing in this section affects any enactment or rule of law so far as it protects a person (including a person who has waived the protection referred to above) from legal liability for words spoken or things done in the course of, or for the purposes of or incidental to, any proceedings in Parliament.

(5) Without prejudice to the generality of subsection (4), that subsection applies to—

(a) the giving of evidence before either House or a committee;

(b) the presentation or submission of a document to either House or a committee;

(c) the preparation of a document for the purposes of or incidental to the transacting of any such business;

(d) the formulation, making or publication of a document, including a report, by or pursuant to an order of either House or a committee; and

(e) any communication with the Parliamentary Commissioner for Standards or any person having functions in connection with the registration of members' interests.

In this subsection "a committee" means a committee of either House or a joint committee of both Houses of Parliament.

Statutory privilege

14 Reports of court proceedings absolutely privileged

(1)   A fair and accurate report of proceedings in public before a court to which this section applies, if published contemporaneously with the proceedings, is absolutely privileged.

(2)   A report of proceedings which by an order of the court, or as a consequence of any statutory provision, is required to be postponed shall be treated as published contemporaneously if it is published as soon as practicable after publication is permitted.

(3)   This section applies to—

    (a)   any court in the United Kingdom,

    (b)   the European Court of Justice or any court attached to that court,

    (c)   the European Court of Human Rights, and

    (d)   any international criminal tribunal established by the Security Council of the United Nations or by an international agreement to which the United Kingdom is a party.

In paragraph (a) "court" includes any tribunal or body exercising the judicial power of the State.

15 Reports, &c protected by qualified privilege

(1)   The publication of any report or other statement mentioned in Schedule 1 to this Act is privileged unless the publication is shown to be made with malice, subject as follows.

(2)   In defamation proceedings in respect of the publication of a report or other statement mentioned in Part II of that Schedule, there is no defence under this section if the plaintiff shows that the defendant—

    (a)   was requested by him to publish in a suitable manner a reasonable letter or statement by way of explanation or contradiction, and

    (b)   refused or neglected to do so.

For this purpose "in a suitable manner" means in the same manner as the publication complained of or in a manner that is adequate and reasonable in the circumstances.

(3)   This section does not apply to the publication to the public, or a section of the public, of matter which is not of public concern and the publication of which is not for the public benefit.

(4)   Nothing in this section shall be construed—

    (a)   as protecting the publication of matter the publication of which is prohibited by law, or

    (b)   as limiting or abridging any privilege subsisting apart from this section.

Supplementary provisions

17 Interpretation

(1)   In this Act—

"publication" and "publish", in relation to a statement, have the meaning they have for the purposes of the law of defamation generally, but "publisher" is specially defined for the purposes of section 1;

"statement" means words, pictures, visual images, gestures or any other method of signifying meaning; and

"statutory provision" means—

(a)   a provision contained in an Act or in subordinate legislation within the meaning of the Interpretation Act 1978

[(aa)   a provision contained in an Act of the Scottish Parliament or in an instrument made under such an Act,],or

(b)   a statutory provision within the meaning given by section 1(f) of the Interpretation Act (Northern Ireland) 1954.

20 Short title and saving

(1)   This Act may be cited as the Defamation Act 1996.

(2)   Nothing in this Act affects the law relating to criminal libel.

SCHEDULES

SCHEDULE 1 Qualified privilege (Section 15)

Part I Statements having qualified privilege without explanation or contradiction

1   A fair and accurate report of proceedings in public of a legislature anywhere in the world.

2   A fair and accurate report of proceedings in public before a court anywhere in the world.

3   A fair and accurate report of proceedings in public of a person appointed to hold a public inquiry by a government or legislature anywhere in the world.

4   A fair and accurate report of proceedings in public anywhere in the world of an international organisation or an international conference.

5   A fair and accurate copy of or extract from any register or other document required by law to be open to public inspection.

6   A notice or advertisement published by or on the authority of a court, or of a judge or officer of a court, anywhere in the world.

7   A fair and accurate copy of or extract from matter published by or on the authority of a government or legislature anywhere in the world.

8   A fair and accurate copy of or extract from matter published anywhere in the world by an international organisation or an international conference.

Part II Statements privileged subject to explanation or contradiction

9   (1)   A fair and accurate copy of or extract from a notice or other matter issued for the information of the public by or on behalf of—

        (a)   a legislature in any member State or the European Parliament;

        (b)   the government of any member State, or any authority performing governmental functions in any member State or part of a member State, or the European Commission;

        (c)   an international organisation or international conference.

    (2)   In this paragraph "governmental functions" includes police functions.

10   A fair and accurate copy of or extract from a document made available by a court in any member State or the European Court of Justice (or any court attached to that court), or by a judge or officer of any such court.

11   (1)   A fair and accurate report of proceedings at any public meeting or sitting in the United Kingdom of—

        (a)   a local authority [, local authority committee or in the case of a local authority which are operating executive arrangements the executive of that authority or a committee of that executive];

        (b)   a justice or justices of the peace acting otherwise than as a court exercising judicial authority;

        (c)   a commission, tribunal, committee or person appointed for the purposes of any inquiry by any statutory provision, by Her Majesty or by a Minister of the Crown [a member of the Scottish Executive]or a Northern Ireland Department;

        (d)   a person appointed by a local authority to hold a local inquiry in pursuance of any statutory provision;

        (e)   any other tribunal, board, committee or body constituted by or under, and exercising functions under, any statutory provision.

    [(1A)   In the case of a local authority which are operating executive arrangements, a fair and accurate record of any decision made by any member of the executive where that record is required to be made and available for public inspection by virtue of section 22 of the Local Government Act 2000 or of any provision in regulations made under that section.]

    (2) — [In sub-paragraphs (1)(a) and (1A)—

    "executive" and "executive arrangements" have the same meaning as in Part II of the Local Government Act 2000;]

"local authority" means—

(a) in relation to England and Wales, a principal council within the meaning of the M1 Local Government Act 1972, any body falling within any paragraph of section 100J(1) of that Act or an authority or body to which the M2 Public Bodies (Admission to Meetings) Act 1960 applies,

(b) in relation to Scotland, a council constituted under section 2 of the M3 Local Government etc (Scotland) Act 1994 or an authority or body to which the Public Bodies (Admission to Meetings) Act 1960 applies,

(c) in relation to Northern Ireland, any authority or body to which sections 23 to 27 of the M4 Local Government Act (Northern Ireland) 1972 apply; and

"local authority committee" means any committee of a local authority or of local authorities, and includes—

(a) any committee or sub-committee in relation to which sections 100A to 100D of the Local Government Act 1972 apply by virtue of section 100E of that Act (whether or not also by virtue of section 100J of that Act), and

(b) any committee or sub-committee in relation to which sections 50A to 50D of the Local Government (Scotland) Act 1973 apply by virtue of section 50E of that Act.

(3) A fair and accurate report of any corresponding proceedings in any of the Channel Islands or the Isle of Man or in another member State.

12 (1) A fair and accurate report of proceedings at any public meeting held in a member State.

(2) In this paragraph a "public meeting" means a meeting bona fide and lawfully held for a lawful purpose and for the furtherance or discussion of a matter of public concern, whether admission to the meeting is general or restricted.

13 (1) A fair and accurate report of proceedings at a general meeting of a UK public company.

(2) A fair and accurate copy of or extract from any document circulated to members of a UK public company—

(a) by or with the authority of the board of directors of the company,

(b) by the auditors of the company, or

(c) by any member of the company in pursuance of a right conferred by any statutory provision.

(3) A fair and accurate copy of or extract from any document circulated to members of a UK public company which relates to the appointment, resignation, retirement or dismissal of directors of the company.

(4) In this paragraph "UK public company" means—

(a) a public company within the meaning of section 1(3) of the Companies Act 1985 or Article 12(3) of the Companies (Northern Ireland) Order 1986, or

(b) a body corporate incorporated by or registered under any other statutory provision, or by Royal Charter, or formed in pursuance of letters patent.

(5)   A fair and accurate report of proceedings at any corresponding meeting of, or copy of or extract from any corresponding document circulated to members of, a public company formed under the law of any of the Channel Islands or the Isle of Man or of another member State.

14   A fair and accurate report of any finding or decision of any of the following descriptions of association, formed in the United Kingdom or another member State, or of any committee or governing body of such an association—

(a)   an association formed for the purpose of promoting or encouraging the exercise of or interest in any art, science, religion or learning, and empowered by its constitution to exercise control over or adjudicate on matters of interest or concern to the association, or the actions or conduct of any person subject to such control or adjudication;

(b)   an association formed for the purpose of promoting or safeguarding the interests of any trade, business, industry or profession, or of the persons carrying on or engaged in any trade, business, industry or profession, and empowered by its constitution to exercise control over or adjudicate upon matters connected with that trade, business, industry or profession, or the actions or conduct of those persons;

(c)   an association formed for the purpose of promoting or safeguarding the interests of a game, sport or pastime to the playing or exercise of which members of the public are invited or admitted, and empowered by its constitution to exercise control over or adjudicate upon persons connected with or taking part in the game, sport or pastime;

(d)   an association formed for the purpose of promoting charitable objects or other objects beneficial to the community and empowered by its constitution to exercise control over or to adjudicate on matters of interest or concern to the association, or the actions or conduct of any person subject to such control or adjudication.

15   (1)   A fair and accurate report of, or copy of or extract from, any adjudication, report, statement or notice issued by a body, officer or other person designated for the purposes of this paragraph—

(a)   for England and Wales or Northern Ireland, by order of the Lord Chancellor, and

(b)   for Scotland, by order of the Secretary of State.

(2)   An order under this paragraph shall be made by statutory instrument which shall be subject to annulment in pursuance of a resolution of either House of Parliament.

Part III Supplementary provisions

16   (1)   In this Schedule—

"court" includes any tribunal or body exercising the judicial power of the State;

"international conference" means a conference attended by representatives of two or more governments;

"international organisation" means an organisation of which two or more governments are members, and includes any committee or other subordinate body of such an organisation; and "legislature" includes a local legislature.

(2)   References in this Schedule to a member State include any European dependent territory of a member State.

(3)   In paragraphs 2 and 6 "court" includes—

(a)   the European Court of Justice (or any court attached to that court) and the Court of Auditors of the European Communities,

(b)   the European Court of Human Rights,

(c)   any international criminal tribunal established by the Security Council of the United Nations or by an international agreement to which the United Kingdom is a party, and

(d)   the International Court of Justice and any other judicial or arbitral tribunal deciding matters in dispute between States.

(4)   In paragraphs 1, 3 and 7 "legislature" includes the European Parliament.

17   (1)   Provision may be made by order identifying—

(a)   for the purposes of paragraph 11, the corresponding proceedings referred to in sub-paragraph (3);

(b)   for the purposes of paragraph 13, the corresponding meetings and documents referred to in sub-paragraph (5).

(2)   An order under this paragraph may be made—

(a)   for England and Wales or Northern Ireland, by the Lord Chancellor, and

(b)   for Scotland, by the Secretary of State.

(3)   An order under this paragraph shall be made by statutory instrument which shall be subject to annulment in pursuance of a resolution of either House of Parliament.

DEFAMATION ACT 2013

2013 chapter 26

An Act to amend the law of defamation

[25th April 2013]

BE IT ENACTED by the Queen's most Excellent Majesty, by and with the advice and consent of the Lords Spiritual and Temporal, and Commons, in this present Parliament assembled, and by the authority of the same, as follows:–

Requirement of serious harm

1 Serious harm

(1) A statement is not defamatory unless its publication has caused or is likely to cause serious harm to the reputation of the claimant.

(2) For the purposes of this section, harm to the reputation of a body that trades for profit is not "serious harm" unless it has caused or is likely to cause the body serious financial loss.

Defences

2 Truth

(1) It is a defence to an action for defamation for the defendant to show that the imputation conveyed by the statement complained of is substantially true.

(2) Subsection (3) applies in an action for defamation if the statement complained of conveys two or more distinct imputations.

(3) If one or more of the imputations is not shown to be substantially true, the defence under this section does not fail if, having regard to the imputations which are shown to be substantially true, the imputations which are not shown to be substantially true do not seriously harm the claimant's reputation.

(4) The common law defence of justification is abolished and, accordingly, section 5 of the Defamation Act 1952 (justification) is repealed.

3 Honest opinion

(1) It is a defence to an action for defamation for the defendant to show that the following conditions are met.

(2) The first condition is that the statement complained of was a statement of opinion.

(3) The second condition is that the statement complained of indicated, whether in general or specific terms, the basis of the opinion.

(4) The third condition is that an honest person could have held the opinion on the basis of—

   (a) any fact which existed at the time the statement complained of was published;

   (b) anything asserted to be a fact in a privileged statement published before the statement complained of.

(5) The defence is defeated if the claimant shows that the defendant did not hold the opinion.

(6) Subsection (5) does not apply in a case where the statement complained of was published by the defendant but made by another person ("the author"); and in such a case the defence is defeated if the claimant shows that the defendant knew or ought to have known that the author did not hold the opinion.

(7)   For the purposes of subsection (4)(b) a statement is a "privileged statement" if the person responsible for its publication would have one or more of the following defences if an action for defamation were brought in respect of it—

(a)   a defence under section 4 (publication on matter of public interest);

(b)   a defence under section 6 (peer-reviewed statement in scientific or academic journal);

(c)   a defence under section 14 of the Defamation Act 1996 (reports of court proceedings protected by absolute privilege);

(d)   a defence under section 15 of that Act (other reports protected by qualified privilege).

(8)   The common law defence of fair comment is abolished and, accordingly, section 6 of the Defamation Act 1952 (fair comment) is repealed.

4 Publication on matter of public interest

(1)   It is a defence to an action for defamation for the defendant to show that—

(a)   the statement complained of was, or formed part of, a statement on a matter of public interest; and

(b)   the defendant reasonably believed that publishing the statement complained of was in the public interest.

(2)   Subject to subsections (3) and (4), in determining whether the defendant has shown the matters mentioned in subsection (1), the court must have regard to all the circumstances of the case.

(3)   If the statement complained of was, or formed part of, an accurate and impartial account of a dispute to which the claimant was a party, the court must in determining whether it was reasonable for the defendant to believe that publishing the statement was in the public interest disregard any omission of the defendant to take steps to verify the truth of the imputation conveyed by it.

(4)   In determining whether it was reasonable for the defendant to believe that publishing the statement complained of was in the public interest, the court must make such allowance for editorial judgement as it considers appropriate.

(5)   For the avoidance of doubt, the defence under this section may be relied upon irrespective of whether the statement complained of is a statement of fact or a statement of opinion.

(6)   The common law defence known as the Reynolds defence is abolished.

5 Operators of websites

(1)   This section applies where an action for defamation is brought against the operator of a website in respect of a statement posted on the website.

(2)   It is a defence for the operator to show that it was not the operator who posted the statement on the website.

(3)   The defence is defeated if the claimant shows that—

(a)   it was not possible for the claimant to identify the person who posted the statement,

(b)   the claimant gave the operator a notice of complaint in relation to the statement, and

(c)   the operator failed to respond to the notice of complaint in accordance with any provision contained in regulations.

(4)   For the purposes of subsection (3)(a), it is possible for a claimant to "identify" a person only if the claimant has sufficient information to bring proceedings against the person.

(5)   Regulations may—

(a)   make provision as to the action required to be taken by an operator of a website in response to a notice of complaint (which may in particular include action relating to the identity or contact details of the person who posted the statement and action relating to its removal);

(b)   make provision specifying a time limit for the taking of any such action;

(c)   make provision conferring on the court a discretion to treat action taken after the expiry of a time limit as having been taken before the expiry;

(d)   make any other provision for the purposes of this section.

(6)   Subject to any provision made by virtue of subsection (7), a notice of complaint is a notice which—

(a)   specifies the complainant's name,

(b)   sets out the statement concerned and explains why it is defamatory of the complainant,

(c)   specifies where on the website the statement was posted, and

(d)   contains such other information as may be specified in regulations.

(7)   Regulations may make provision about the circumstances in which a notice which is not a notice of complaint is to be treated as a notice of complaint for the purposes of this section or any provision made under it.

(8)   Regulations under this section—

(a)   may make different provision for different circumstances;

(b)   are to be made by statutory instrument.

(9)   A statutory instrument containing regulations under this section may not be made unless a draft of the instrument has been laid before, and approved by a resolution of, each House of Parliament.

(10)   In this section "regulations" means regulations made by the Secretary of State.

(11)   The defence under this section is defeated if the claimant shows that the operator of the website has acted with malice in relation to the posting of the statement concerned.

(12)   The defence under this section is not defeated by reason only of the fact that the operator of the website moderates the statements posted on it by others.

6 Peer-reviewed statement in scientific or academic journal etc

(1) The publication of a statement in a scientific or academic journal (whether published in electronic form or otherwise) is privileged if the following conditions are met.

(2) The first condition is that the statement relates to a scientific or academic matter.

(3) The second condition is that before the statement was published in the journal an independent review of the statement's scientific or academic merit was carried out by—

    (a) the editor of the journal, and

    (b) one or more persons with expertise in the scientific or academic matter concerned.

(4) Where the publication of a statement in a scientific or academic journal is privileged by virtue of subsection (1), the publication in the same journal of any assessment of the statement's scientific or academic merit is also privileged if—

    (a) the assessment was written by one or more of the persons who carried out the independent review of the statement; and

    (b) the assessment was written in the course of that review.

(5) Where the publication of a statement or assessment is privileged by virtue of this section, the publication of a fair and accurate copy of, extract from or summary of the statement or assessment is also privileged.

(6) A publication is not privileged by virtue of this section if it is shown to be made with malice.

(7) Nothing in this section is to be construed—

    (a) as protecting the publication of matter the publication of which is prohibited by law;

    (b) as limiting any privilege subsisting apart from this section.

(8) The reference in subsection (3)(a) to "the editor of the journal" is to be read, in the case of a journal with more than one editor, as a reference to the editor or editors who were responsible for deciding to publish the statement concerned.

7 Reports etc protected by privilege

(1) For subsection (3) of section 14 of the Defamation Act 1996 (reports of court proceedings absolutely privileged) substitute—

    "(3) This section applies to—

        (a) any court in the United Kingdom;

        (b) any court established under the law of a country or territory outside the United Kingdom;

        (c) any international court or tribunal established by the Security Council of the United Nations or by an international agreement; and in paragraphs (a) and (b) "court" includes any tribunal or body exercising the judicial power of the State."

(2)   In subsection (3) of section 15 of that Act (qualified privilege) for "public concern" substitute "public interest".

(3)   Schedule 1 to that Act (qualified privilege) is amended as follows.

(4)   For paragraphs 9 and 10 substitute—

"9   (1)   A fair and accurate copy of, extract from or summary of a notice or other matter issued for the information of the public by or on behalf of—

(a)   a legislature or government anywhere in the world;

(b)   an authority anywhere in the world performing governmental functions;

(c)   an international organisation or international conference.

(2)   In this paragraph "governmental functions" includes police functions.

10   A fair and accurate copy of, extract from or summary of a document made available by a court anywhere in the world, or by a judge or officer of such a court."

(5)   After paragraph 11 insert—

"11A A fair and accurate report of proceedings at a press conference held anywhere in the world for the discussion of a matter of public interest."

(6)   In paragraph 12 (report of proceedings at public meetings)—

(a)   in sub-paragraph (1) for "in a member State" substitute "anywhere in the world";

(b)   in sub-paragraph (2) for "public concern" substitute "public interest".

(7)   In paragraph 13 (report of proceedings at meetings of public company)—

(a)   in sub-paragraph (1), for "UK public company" substitute "listed company";

(b)   for sub-paragraphs (2) to (5) substitute—

"(2)   A fair and accurate copy of, extract from or summary of any document circulated to members of a listed company—

(a)   by or with the authority of the board of directors of the company,

(b)   by the auditors of the company, or

(c)   by any member of the company in pursuance of a right conferred by any statutory provision.

(3)   A fair and accurate copy of, extract from or summary of any document circulated to members of a listed company which relates to the appointment, resignation, retirement or dismissal of directors of the company or its auditors.

(4)   In this paragraph "listed company" has the same meaning as in Part 12 of the Corporation Tax Act 2009 (see section 1005 of that Act)."

(8)   In paragraph 14 (report of finding or decision of certain kinds of associations) in the words before paragraph (a), for "in the United Kingdom or another member State" substitute "anywhere in the world".

(9) After paragraph 14 insert—

"14A A fair and accurate—

(a) report of proceedings of a scientific or academic conference held anywhere in the world, or

(b) copy of, extract from or summary of matter published by such a conference."

(10) For paragraph 15 (report of statements etc by a person designated by the Lord Chancellor for the purposes of the paragraph) substitute—

"15 (1) A fair and accurate report or summary of, copy of or extract from, any adjudication, report, statement or notice issued by a body, officer or other person designated for the purposes of this paragraph by order of the Lord Chancellor.

(2) An order under this paragraph shall be made by statutory instrument which shall be subject to annulment in pursuance of a resolution of either House of Parliament."

(11) For paragraphs 16 and 17 (general provision) substitute—

"16 In this Schedule—

"court" includes—

(a) any tribunal or body established under the law of any country or territory exercising the judicial power of the State;

(b) any international tribunal established by the Security Council of the United Nations or by an international agreement;

(c) any international tribunal deciding matters in dispute between States;

"international conference" means a conference attended by representatives of two or more governments;

"international organisation" means an organisation of which two or more governments are members, and includes any committee or other subordinate body of such an organisation;

"legislature" includes a local legislature; and

"member State" includes any European dependent territory of a member State."

Single publication rule

8 Single publication rule

(1) This section applies if a person—

(a) publishes a statement to the public ("the first publication"), and

(b) subsequently publishes (whether or not to the public) that statement or a statement which is substantially the same.

(2) In subsection (1) "publication to the public" includes publication to a section of the public.

(3)   For the purposes of section 4A of the Limitation Act 1980 (time limit for actions for defamation etc) any cause of action against the person for defamation in respect of the subsequent publication is to be treated as having accrued on the date of the first publication.

(4)   This section does not apply in relation to the subsequent publication if the manner of that publication is materially different from the manner of the first publication.

(5)   In determining whether the manner of a subsequent publication is materially different from the manner of the first publication, the matters to which the court may have regard include (amongst other matters)—

(a)   the level of prominence that a statement is given;

(b)   the extent of the subsequent publication.

(6)   Where this section applies—

(a)   it does not affect the court's discretion under section 32A of the Limitation Act 1980 (discretionary exclusion of time limit for actions for defamation etc), and

(b)   the reference in subsection (1)(a) of that section to the operation of section 4A of that Act is a reference to the operation of section 4A together with this section.

Jurisdiction

9 Action against a person not domiciled in the UK or a Member State etc

(1)   This section applies to an action for defamation against a person who is not domiciled—

(a)   in the United Kingdom;

(b)   in another Member State; or

(c)   in a state which is for the time being a contracting party to the Lugano Convention.

(2)   A court does not have jurisdiction to hear and determine an action to which this section applies unless the court is satisfied that, of all the places in which the statement complained of has been published, England and Wales is clearly the most appropriate place in which to bring an action in respect of the statement.

(3)   The references in subsection (2) to the statement complained of include references to any statement which conveys the same, or substantially the same, imputation as the statement complained of.

(4)   For the purposes of this section—

(a)   a person is domiciled in the United Kingdom or in another Member State if the person is domiciled there for the purposes of the Brussels Regulation;

(b)   a person is domiciled in a state which is a contracting party to the Lugano Convention if the person is domiciled in the state for the purposes of that Convention.

(5)   In this section—

"the Brussels Regulation" means Council Regulation (EC) No 44/2001 of 22nd December 2000 on jurisdiction and the recognition and enforcement of judgments in civil and commercial matters, as amended from time to time and as applied by the Agreement made on 19th October 2005 between the European Community and the Kingdom of Denmark on jurisdiction and the recognition and enforcement of judgments in civil and commercial matters (OJ No L299 16.11.2005 at p

62);

"the Lugano Convention" means the Convention on jurisdiction and the recognition and enforcement of judgments in civil and commercial matters, between the European Community and the Republic of Iceland, the Kingdom of Norway, the Swiss Confederation and the Kingdom of Denmark signed on behalf of the European Community on 30th October 2007.

10 Action against a person who was not the author, editor etc

(1) A court does not have jurisdiction to hear and determine an action for defamation brought against a person who was not the author, editor or publisher of the statement complained of unless the court is satisfied that it is not reasonably practicable for an action to be brought against the author, editor or publisher.

(2) In this section "author", "editor" and "publisher" have the same meaning as in section 1 of the Defamation Act 1996.

Trial by jury

11 Trial to be without a jury unless the court orders otherwise

(1) In section 69(1) of the Senior Courts Act 1981 (certain actions in the Queen's Bench Division to be tried with a jury unless the trial requires prolonged examination of documents etc) in paragraph (b) omit "libel, slander,".

(2) In section 66(3) of the County Courts Act 1984 (certain actions in the county court to be tried with a jury unless the trial requires prolonged examination of documents etc) in paragraph (b) omit "libel, slander,".

Summary of court judgment

12 Power of court to order a summary of its judgment to be published

(1) Where a court gives judgment for the claimant in an action for defamation the court may order the defendant to publish a summary of the judgment.

(2) The wording of any summary and the time, manner, form and place of its publication are to be for the parties to agree.

(3) If the parties cannot agree on the wording, the wording is to be settled by the court.

(4)   If the parties cannot agree on the time, manner, form or place of publication, the court may give such directions as to those matters as it considers reasonable and practicable in the circumstances.

(5)   This section does not apply where the court gives judgment for the claimant under section 8(3) of the Defamation Act 1996 (summary disposal of claims).

Removal, etc of statements

13 Order to remove statement or cease distribution etc

(1)   Where a court gives judgment for the claimant in an action for defamation the court may order—

(a)   the operator of a website on which the defamatory statement is posted to remove the statement, or

(b)   any person who was not the author, editor or publisher of the defamatory statement to stop distributing, selling or exhibiting material containing the statement.

(2)   In this section "author", "editor" and "publisher" have the same meaning as in section 1 of the Defamation Act 1996.

(3)   Subsection (1) does not affect the power of the court apart from that subsection.

Slander

14 Special damage

(1)   The Slander of Women Act 1891 is repealed.

(2)   The publication of a statement that conveys the imputation that a person has a contagious or infectious disease does not give rise to a cause of action for slander unless the publication causes the person special damage.

General provisions

15 Meaning of "publish" and "statement"

In this Act—

"publish" and "publication", in relation to a statement, have the meaning they have for the purposes of the law of defamation generally;

"statement" means words, pictures, visual images, gestures or any other method of signifying meaning.

16 Consequential amendments and savings etc

(1)   Section 8 of the Rehabilitation of Offenders Act 1974 (defamation actions) is amended in accordance with subsections (2) and (3).

(2)   In subsection (3) for "of justification or fair comment or" substitute "under section 2 or 3 of the Defamation Act 2013 which is available to him or any defence".

(3)   In subsection (5) for "the defence of justification" substitute "a defence under section 2 of the Defamation Act 2013".

(4)   Nothing in section 1 or 14 affects any cause of action accrued before the commencement of the section in question.

(5)   Nothing in sections 2 to 7 or 10 has effect in relation to an action for defamation if the cause of action accrued before the commencement of the section in question.

(6)   In determining whether section 8 applies, no account is to be taken of any publication made before the commencement of the section.

(7)   Nothing in section 9 or 11 has effect in relation to an action for defamation begun before the commencement of the section in question.

(8)   In determining for the purposes of subsection (7)(a) of section 3 whether a person would have a defence under section 4 to any action for

17 Short title, extent and commencement

(1)   This Act may be cited as the Defamation Act 2013.

(2)   Subject to subsection (3), this Act extends to England and Wales only.

(3)   The following provisions also extend to Scotland—

(a)   section 6;
(b)   section 7(9);
(c)   section 15;
(d)   section 16(5) (in so far as it relates to sections 6 and 7(9));
(e)   this section.

(4)   Subject to subsections (5) and (6), the provisions of this Act come into force on such day as the Secretary of State may by order made by statutory instrument appoint.

(5)   Sections 6 and 7(9) come into force in so far as they extend to Scotland on such day as the Scottish Ministers may by order appoint.

(6)   Section 15, subsections (4) to (8) of section 16 and this section come into force on the day on which this Act is passed.

LAW REFORM (CONTRIBUTORY NEGLIGENCE) ACT 1945

1 Apportionment of liability in case of contributory negligence

(1)   Where any person suffers damage as the result partly of his own fault and partly of the fault of any other person or persons, a claim in respect of that damage shall not be defeated by reason of the fault of the person suffering the damage, but the damages recoverable in respect thereof

shall be reduced to such extent as the court thinks just and equitable having regard to the claimant's share in the responsibility for the damage:

Provided that—

(a)   this subsection shall not operate to defeat any defence arising under a contract;

(b)   where any contract or enactment providing for the limitation of liability is applicable to the claim, the amount of damages recoverable by the claimant by virtue of this subsection shall not exceed the maximum limit so applicable.

(2)   Where damages are recoverable by any person by virtue of the foregoing subsection subject to such reduction as is therein mentioned, the court shall find and record the total damages which would have been recoverable if the claimant had not been at fault.

(3), (4)   . . .

(5)   Where, in any case to which subsection (1) of this section applies, one of the persons at fault avoids liability to any other such person or his personal representative by pleading the Limitation Act 1939, or any other enactment limiting the time within which proceedings may be taken, he shall not be entitled to recover any damages . . . from that other person or representative by virtue of the said subsection.

(6)   Where any case to which subsection (1) of this section applies is tried with a jury, the jury shall determine the total damages which would have been recoverable if the claimant had not been at fault and the extent to which those damages are to be reduced.

(7)   . . .

4 Interpretation

The following expressions have the meanings hereby respectively assigned to them, that is to say—

"court" means, in relation to any claim, the court or arbitrator by or before whom the claim falls to be determined;

"damage" includes loss of life and personal injury;

. . .

"fault" means negligence, breach of statutory duty or other act or omission which gives rise to a liability in tort or would, apart from this Act, give rise to the defence of contributory negligence.

7 Short title and extent

This Act may be cited as the Law Reform (Contributory Negligence) Act 1945.

OCCUPIERS LIABILITY ACT 1957

1957 CHAPTER 31

An Act to amend the law of England and Wales as to the liability of occupiers and others for injury or damage resulting to persons or goods lawfully on any land or other property from dangers due to the state of the property or to things done or omitted to be done there, to make provision as to the operation in relation to the Crown of laws made by the Parliament of Northern Ireland for similar purposes or otherwise amending the law of tort, and for purposes connected therewith

[6 June 1957]

BE IT ENACTED by the Queen's most Excellent Majesty, by and with the advice and consent of the Lords Spiritual and Temporal, and Commons, in this present Parliament assembled, and by the authority of the same, as follows:–

Liability in tort

1 Preliminary

(1)   The rules enacted by the two next following sections shall have effect, in place of the rules of the common law, to regulate the duty which an occupier of premises owes to his visitors in respect of dangers due to the state of the premises or to things done or omitted to be done on them.

(2)   The rules so enacted shall regulate the nature of the duty imposed by law in consequence of a person's occupation or control of premises and of any invitation or permission he gives (or is to be treated as giving) to another to enter or use the premises, but they shall not alter the rules of the common law as to the persons on whom a duty is so imposed or to whom it is owed; and accordingly for the purpose of the rules so enacted the persons who are to be treated as an occupier and as his visitors are the same (subject to subsection (4) of this section) as the persons who would at common law be treated as an occupier and as his invitees or licensees.

(3)   The rules so enacted in relation to an occupier of premises and his visitors shall also apply, in like manner and to the like extent as the principles applicable at common law to an occupier of premises and his invitees or licensees would apply, to regulate—

(a)   the obligations of a person occupying or having control over any fixed or moveable structure, including any vessel, vehicle or aircraft; and

(b)   the obligations of a person occupying or having control over any premises or structure in respect of damage to property, including the property of persons who are not themselves his visitors.

[(4)   A person entering any premises in exercise of rights conferred by virtue of—

(a)   section 2(1) of the Countryside and Rights of Way Act 2000, or

(b)   an access agreement or order under the National Parks and Access to the Countryside Act 1949,

is not, for the purposes of this Act, a visitor of the occupier of the premises.]

2 Extent of occupier's ordinary duty

(1)   An occupier of premises owes the same duty, the "common duty of care", to all his visitors, except in so far as he is free to and does extend, restrict, modify or exclude his duty to any visitor or visitors by agreement or otherwise.

(2)   The common duty of care is a duty to take such care as in all the circumstances of the case is reasonable to see that the visitor will be reasonably safe in using the premises for the purposes for which he is invited or permitted by the occupier to be there.

(3)   The circumstances relevant for the present purpose include the degree of care, and of want of care, which would ordinarily be looked for in such a visitor, so that (for example) in proper cases—

(a)   an occupier must be prepared for children to be less careful than adults; and

(b)   an occupier may expect that a person, in the exercise of his calling, will appreciate and guard against any special risks ordinarily incident to it, so far as the occupier leaves him free to do so.

(4)   In determining whether the occupier of premises has discharged the common duty of care to a visitor, regard is to be had to all the circumstances, so that (for example)—

(a)   where damage is caused to a visitor by a danger of which he had been warned by the occupier, the warning is not to be treated without more as absolving the occupier from liability, unless in all the circumstances it was enough to enable the visitor to be reasonably safe; and

(b)   where damage is caused to a visitor by a danger due to the faulty execution of any work of construction, maintenance or repair by an independent contractor employed by the occupier, the occupier is not to be treated without more as answerable for the danger if in all the circumstances he had acted reasonably in entrusting the work to an independent contractor and had taken such steps (if any) as he reasonably ought in order to satisfy himself that the contractor was competent and that the work had been properly done.

(5)   The common duty of care does not impose on an occupier any obligation to a visitor in respect of risks willingly accepted as his by the visitor (the question whether a risk was so accepted to be decided on the same principles as in other cases in which one person owes a duty of care to another).

(6)   For the purposes of this section, persons who enter premises for any purpose in the exercise of a right conferred by law are to be treated as permitted by the occupier to be there for that purpose, whether they in fact have his permission or not.

3 Effect of contract on occupier's liability to third party

(1) Where an occupier of premises is bound by contract to permit persons who are strangers to the contract to enter or use the premises, the duty of care which he owes to them as his visitors cannot be restricted or excluded by that contract, but (subject to any provision of the contract to the contrary) shall include the duty to perform his obligations under the contract, whether undertaken for their protection or not, in so far as those obligations go beyond the obligations otherwise involved in that duty.

(2) A contract shall not by virtue of this section have the effect, unless it expressly so provides, of making an occupier who has taken all reasonable care answerable to strangers to the contract for dangers due to the faulty execution of any work of construction, maintenance or repair or other like operation by persons other than himself, his servants and persons acting under his direction and control.

(3) In this section "stranger to the contract" means a person not for the time being entitled to the benefit of the contract as a party to it or as the successor by assignment or otherwise of a party to it or as the successor by assignment or otherwise of a party to it, and accordingly includes a party to the contract who has ceased to be so entitled.

(4) Where by the terms or conditions governing any tenancy (including a statutory tenancy which does not in law amount to a tenancy) either the landlord or the tenant is bound, though not by contract, to permit persons to enter or use premises of which he is the occupier, this section shall apply as if the tenancy were a contract between the landlord and the tenant.

(5) This section, in so far as it prevents the common duty of care from being restricted or excluded, applies to contracts entered into and tenancies created before the commencement of this Act, as well as to those entered into or created after its commencement; but, in so far as it enlarges the duty owed by an occupier beyond the common duty of care, it shall have effect only in relation to obligations which are undertaken after that commencement or which are renewed by agreement (whether express or implied) after that commencement.

4 . . .

Liability in contract

5 Implied term in contracts

(1) Where persons enter or use, or bring or send goods to, any premises in exercise of a right conferred by contract with a person occupying or having control of the premises, the duty he owes them in respect of dangers due to the state of the premises or to things done or omitted to be done on them, in so far as the duty depends on a term to be implied in the contract by reason of its conferring that right, shall be the common duty of care.

(2) The foregoing subsection shall apply to fixed and moveable structures as it applies to premises.

(3) This section does not affect the obligations imposed on a person by or by virtue of any contract for the hire of, or for the carriage for reward of persons or goods in, any vehicle, vessel, aircraft or other means of transport, or by or by virtue of any contract of bailment.

(4)   This section does not apply to contracts entered into before the commencement of this Act.

General

6 Application to Crown

This Act shall bind the Crown, but as regards the Crown's liability in tort shall not bind the Crown further than the Crown is made liable in tort by the Crown Proceedings Act 1947, and that Act and in particular section two of it shall apply in relation to duties under sections two to four of this Act as statutory duties.

8 Short title etc

(1)   This Act may be cited as the Occupiers' Liability Act 1957.

OCCUPIERS LIABILITY ACT 1984

1984 CHAPTER 3

An Act to amend the law of England and Wales as to the liability of persons as occupiers of premises for injury suffered by persons other than their visitors; and to amend the Unfair Contract Terms Act 1977, as it applies to England and Wales, in relation to persons obtaining access to premises for recreational or educational purposes

[13th March 1984]

BE IT ENACTED by the Queen's most Excellent Majesty, by and with the advice and consent of the Lords Spiritual and Temporal, and Commons, in this present Parliament assembled, and by the authority of the same, as follows:-

1 Duty of occupier to persons other than his visitors

(1)   The rules enacted by this section shall have effect, in place of the rules of the common law, to determine—

    (a)   whether any duty is owed by a person as occupier of premises to persons other than his visitors in respect of any risk of their suffering injury on the premises by reason of any danger due to the state of the premises or to things done or omitted to be done on them; and

    (b)   if so, what that duty is.

(2)   For the purposes of this section, the persons who are to be treated respectively as an occupier of any premises (which, for those purposes, include any fixed or movable structure) and as his visitors are—

    (a)   any person who owes in relation to the premises the duty referred to in section 2 of the Occupiers' Liability Act 1957 (the common duty of care), and

(b)   those who are his visitors for the purposes of that duty.

(3)   An occupier of premises owes a duty to another (not being his visitor) in respect of any such risk as is referred to in subsection (1) above if—

(a)   he is aware of the danger or has reasonable grounds to believe that it exists;

(b)   he knows or has reasonable grounds to believe that the other is in the vicinity of the danger concerned or that he may come into the vicinity of the danger (in either case, whether the other has lawful authority for being in that vicinity or not); and

(c)   the risk is one against which, in all the circumstances of the case, he may reasonably be expected to offer the other some protection.

(4)   Where, by virtue of this section, an occupier of premises owes a duty to another in respect of such a risk, the duty is to take such care as is reasonable in all the circumstances of the case to see that he does not suffer injury on the premises by reason of the danger concerned.

(5)   Any duty owed by virtue of this section in respect of a risk may, in an appropriate case, be discharged by taking such steps as are reasonable in all the circumstances of the case to give warning of the danger concerned or to discourage persons from incurring the risk.

(6)   No duty is owed by virtue of this section to any person in respect of risks willingly accepted as his by that person (the question whether a risk was so accepted to be decided on the same principles as in other cases in which one person owes a duty of care to another).

[(6A)   At any time when the right conferred by section 2(1) of the Countryside and Rights of Way Act 2000 is exercisable in relation to land which is access land for the purposes of Part I of that Act, an occupier of the land owes (subject to subsection (6C) below) no duty by virtue of this section to any person in respect of—

(a)   a risk resulting from the existence of any natural feature of the landscape, or any river, stream, ditch or pond whether or not a natural feature, or

(b)   a risk of that person suffering injury when passing over, under or through any wall, fence or gate, except by proper use of the gate or of a stile.

[(6AA)   Where the land is coastal margin for the purposes of Part 1 of that Act (including any land treated as coastal margin by virtue of section 16 of that Act), subsection (6A) has effect as if for paragraphs (a) and (b) of that subsection there were substituted "a risk resulting from the existence of any physical feature (whether of the landscape or otherwise).".]

(6B)   For the purposes of subsection (6A) above, any plant, shrub or tree, of whatever origin, is to be regarded as a natural feature of the landscape.

(6C)   Subsection (6A) does not prevent an occupier from owing a duty by virtue of this section in respect of any risk where the danger concerned is due to anything done by the occupier—

(a)   with the intention of creating that risk, or

(b)   being reckless as to whether that risk is created.]

(7)   No duty is owed by virtue of this section to persons using the highway, and this section does not affect any duty owed to such persons.

(8)   Where a person owes a duty by virtue of this section, he does not, by reason of any breach of the duty, incur any liability in respect of any loss of or damage to property.

(9)   In this section—

"highway" means any part of a highway other than a ferry or waterway;

"injury" means anything resulting in death or personal injury, including any disease and any impairment of physical or mental condition; and

"movable structure" includes any vessel, vehicle or aircraft.

[1A Special considerations relating to access land]

[In determining whether any, and if so what, duty is owed by virtue of section 1 by an occupier of land at any time when the right conferred by section 2(1) of the Countryside and Rights of Way Act 2000 is exercisable in relation to the land, regard is to be had, in particular, to—

   (a)   the fact that the existence of that right ought not to place an undue burden (whether financial or otherwise) on the occupier,

   (b)   the importance of maintaining the character of the countryside, including features of historic, traditional or archaeological interest, and

   (c)   any relevant guidance given under section 20 of that Act.]

3 Application to Crown

Section 1 of this Act shall bind the Crown, but as regards the Crown's liability in tort shall not bind the Crown further than the Crown is made liable in tort by the Crown Proceedings Act 1947.

4 Short title, commencement and extent

(1)   This Act may be cited as the Occupiers' Liability Act 1984.

UNFAIR CONTRACT TERMS ACT 1977

1977 CHAPTER 50

An Act to impose further limits on the extent to which under the law of England and Wales and Northern Ireland civil liability for breach of contract, or for negligence or other breach of duty, can be avoided by means of contract terms and otherwise, and under the law of Scotland civil liability can be avoided by means of contract terms

[26th October 1977]

BE IT ENACTED by the Queen's most Excellent Majesty, by and with the advice and consent of the Lords Spiritual and Temporal, and Commons, in this present Parliament assembled, and by the authority of the same, as follows:–

Part I Amendment of Law for England and Wales and Northern Ireland

Introductory

1 Scope of Part I

(1)　For the purposes of this Part of this Act, "negligence" means the breach—

(a)　of any obligation, arising from the express or implied terms of a contract, to take reasonable care or exercise reasonable skill in the performance of the contract;

(b)　of any common law duty to take reasonable care or exercise reasonable skill (but not any stricter duty);

(c)　of the common duty of care imposed by the Occupiers' Liability Act 1957 or the Occupiers' Liability Act (Northern Ireland) 1957.

(2)　This Part of this Act is subject to Part III; and in relation to contracts, the operation of sections 2 to 4 and 7 is subject to the exceptions made by Schedule 1.

(3)　In the case of both contract and tort, sections 2 to 7 apply (except where the contrary is stated in section 6(4)) only to business liability, that is liability for breach of obligations or duties arising—

(a)　from things done or to be done by a person in the course of a business (whether his own business or another's); or

(b)　from the occupation of premises used for business purposes of the occupier;

and references to liability are to be read accordingly [but liability of an occupier of premises for breach of an obligation or duty towards a person obtaining access to the premises for recreational or educational purposes, being liability for loss or damage suffered by reason of the dangerous state of the premises, is not a business liability of the occupier unless granting that person such access for the purposes concerned falls within the business purposes of the occupier].

(4)　In relation to any breach of duty or obligation, it is immaterial for any purpose of this Part of this Act whether the breach was inadvertent or intentional, or whether liability for it arises directly or vicariously.

Avoidance of liability for negligence, breach of contract, etc

2 Negligence liability

(1)　A person cannot by reference to any contract term or to a notice given to persons generally or to particular persons exclude or restrict his liability for death or personal injury resulting from negligence.

(2)　In the case of other loss or damage, a person cannot so exclude or restrict his liability for negligence except in so far as the term or notice satisfies the requirement of reasonableness.

(3)   Where a contract term or notice purports to exclude or restrict liability for negligence a person's agreement to or awareness of it is not of itself to be taken as indicating his voluntary acceptance of any risk.

3 Liability arising in contract

(1)   This section applies as between contracting parties where one of them deals as consumer or on the other's written standard terms of business.

(2)   As against that party, the other cannot by reference to any contract term—

    (a)   when himself in breach of contract, exclude or restrict any liability of his in respect of the breach; or

    (b)   claim to be entitled—

        (i)   to render a contractual performance substantially different from that which was reasonably expected of him, or

        (ii)   in respect of the whole or any part of his contractual obligation, to render no performance at all,

except in so far as (in any of the cases mentioned above in this subsection) the contract term satisfies the requirement of reasonableness.

4 Unreasonable indemnity clauses

(1)   A person dealing as consumer cannot by reference to any contract term be made to indemnify another person (whether a party to the contract or not) in respect of liability that may be incurred by the other for negligence or breach of contract, except in so far as the contract term satisfies the requirement of reasonableness.

(2)   This section applies whether the liability in question—

    (a)   is directly that of the person to be indemnified or is incurred by him vicariously;

    (b)   is to the person dealing as consumer or to someone else.

Liability arising from sale or supply of goods.

5 "Guarantee" of consumer goods

(1)   In the case of goods of a type ordinarily supplied for private use or consumption, where loss or damage—

    (a)   arises from the goods proving defective while in consumer use; and

    (b)   results from the negligence of a person concerned in the manufacture or distribution of the goods,

liability for the loss or damage cannot be excluded or restricted by reference to any contract term or notice contained in or operating by reference to a guarantee of the goods.

(2)   For these purposes—

(a)   goods are to be regarded as "in consumer use" when a person is using them, or has them in his possession for use, otherwise than exclusively for the purposes of a business; and

(b)   anything in writing is a guarantee if it contains or purports to contain some promise or assurance (however worded or presented) that defects will be made good by complete or partial replacement, or by repair, monetary compensation or otherwise.

(3)   This section does not apply as between the parties to a contract under or in pursuance of which possession or ownership of the goods passed.

6 Sale and hire-purchase

(1)   Liability for breach of the obligations arising from—

(a)   [section 12 of the Sale of Goods Act 1979] (seller's implied undertakings as to title, etc);

(b)   section 8 of the Supply of Goods (Implied Terms) Act 1973 (the corresponding thing in relation to hire-purchase),

cannot be excluded or restricted by reference to any contract term.

(2)   As against a person dealing as consumer, liability for breach of the obligations arising from—

(a)   [section 13, 14 or 15 of the 1979 Act] (seller's implied undertakings as to conformity of goods with description or sample, or as to their quality or fitness for a particular purpose);

(b)   section 9, 10 or 11 of the 1973 Act (the corresponding things in relation to hire-purchase),

cannot be excluded or restricted by reference to any contract term.

(3)   As against a person dealing otherwise than as consumer, the liability specified in subsection (2) above can be excluded or restricted by reference to a contract term, but only in so far as the term satisfies the requirement of reasonableness.

(4)   The liabilities referred to in this section are not only the business liabilities defined by section 1(3), but include those arising under any contract of sale of goods or hire-purchase agreement.

7 Miscellaneous contracts under which goods pass

(1)   Where the possession or ownership of goods passes under or in pursuance of a contract not governed by the law of sale of goods or hire-purchase, subsections (2) to (4) below apply as regards the effect (if any) to be given to contract terms excluding or restricting liability for breach of obligation arising by implication of law from the nature of the contract.

(2)   As against a person dealing as consumer, liability in respect of the goods' correspondence with description or sample, or their quality or fitness for any particular purpose, cannot be excluded or restricted by reference to any such term.

(3)   As against a person dealing otherwise than as consumer, that liability can be excluded or restricted by reference to such a term, but only in so far as the term satisfies the requirement of reasonableness.

[(3A) Liability for breach of the obligations arising under section 2 of the Supply of Goods and Services Act 1982 (implied terms about title etc in certain contracts for the transfer of the property in goods) cannot be excluded or restricted by references to any such term.]

(4) Liability in respect of—

(a) the right to transfer ownership of the goods, or give possession; or

(b) the assurance of quiet possession to a person taking goods in pursuance of the contract,

cannot [[in a case to which subsection (3A) above does not apply)]] be excluded or restricted by reference to any such term except in so far as the term satisfies the requirement of reasonableness.

(5) . . .

Other provisions about contracts

8 Misrepresentation

. . .

9 Effect of breach

(1) Where for reliance upon it a contract term has to satisfy the requirement of reasonableness, it may be found to do so and be given effect accordingly notwithstanding that the contract has been terminated either by breach or by a party electing to treat it as repudiated.

(2) Where on a breach the contract is nevertheless affirmed by a party entitled to treat it as repudiated, this does not of itself exclude the requirement of reasonableness in relation to any contract term.

10 Evasion by means of secondary contract

A person is not bound by any contract term prejudicing or taking away rights of his which arise under, or in connection with the performance of, another contract, so far as those rights extend to the enforcement of another's liability which this Part of this Act prevents that other from excluding or restricting.

Explanatory provisions

11 The "reasonableness" test

(1) In relation to a contract term, the requirement of reasonableness for the purposes of this Part of this Act, section 3 of the Misrepresentation Act 1967 and section 3 of the Misrepresentation Act (Northern Ireland) 1967 is that the term shall have been a fair and reasonable one to be included having regard to the circumstances which were, or ought reasonably to have been, known to or in the contemplation of the parties when the contract was made.

(2) In determining for the purposes of section 6 or 7 above whether a contract term satisfies the requirement of reasonableness, regard shall be had in particular to the matters specified in Schedule 2 to this Act; but this subsection does not prevent the court or arbitrator from holding, in accordance with any rule of law, that a term which purports to exclude or restrict any relevant liability is not a term of the contract.

(3)   In relation to a notice (not being a notice having contractual effect), the requirement of reasonableness under this Act is that it should be fair and reasonable to allow reliance on it, having regard to all the circumstances obtaining when the liability arose or (but for the notice) would have arisen.

(4)   Where by reference to a contract term or notice a person seeks to restrict liability to a specified sum of money, and the question arises (under this or any other Act) whether the term or notice satisfies the requirement of reasonableness, regard shall be had in particular (but without prejudice to subsection (2) above in the case of contract terms) to—

(a)   the resources which he could expect to be available to him for the purpose of meeting the liability should it arise; and

(b)   how far it was open to him to cover himself by insurance.

(5)   It is for those claiming that a contract term or notice satisfies the requirement of reasonableness to show that it does.

12 "Dealing as consumer"

(1)   A party to a contract "deals as consumer" in relation to another party if—

(a)   he neither makes the contract in the course of a business nor holds himself out as doing so; and

(b)   the other party does make the contract in the course of a business; and

(c)   in the case of a contract governed by the law of sale of goods or hire-purchase, or by section 7 of this Act, the goods passing under or in pursuance of the contract are of a type ordinarily supplied for private use or consumption.

[(1A) But if the first party mentioned in subsection (1) is an individual paragraph (c) of that subsection must be ignored.]

[(2)   But the buyer is not in any circumstances to be regarded as dealing as consumer—

(a)   if he is an individual and the goods are second hand goods sold at public auction at which individuals have the opportunity of attending the sale in person;

(b)   if he is not an individual and the goods are sold by auction or by competitive tender.]

(3)   Subject to this, it is for those claiming that a party does not deal as consumer to show that he does not.

13 Varieties of exemption clause

(1)   To the extent that this Part of this Act prevents the exclusion or restriction of any liability it also prevents—

(a)   making the liability or its enforcement subject to restrictive or onerous conditions;

(b)   excluding or restricting any right or remedy in respect of the liability, or subjecting a person to any prejudice in consequence of his pursuing any such right or remedy;

(c)   excluding or restricting rules of evidence or procedure;

and (to that extent) sections 2 and 5 to 7 also prevent excluding or restricting liability by reference to terms and notices which exclude or restrict the relevant obligation or duty.

(2)   But an agreement in writing to submit present or future differences to arbitration is not to be treated under this Part of this Act as excluding or restricting any liability.

14 Interpretation of Part I

In this Part of this Act—

"business" includes a profession and the activities of any government department or local or public authority;

"goods" has the same meaning as in [the Sale of Goods Act 1979]:

"hire-purchase agreement" has the same meaning as in the Consumer Credit Act 1974;

"negligence" has the meaning given by section 1(1);

"notice" includes an announcement, whether or not in writing, and any other communication or pretended communication; and

"personal injury" includes any disease and any impairment of physical or mental condition.

32 Citation and extent

(1)   This Act may be cited as the Unfair Contract Terms Act 1977.